W9-CCV-580

THE TOWNSEND LECTURES

The Department of Classics at Cornell University is fortunate to have at its disposal the Prescott W. Townsend Fund—established by Mr. Townsend's widow, Daphne Townsend, in 1982. Since 1985, income from the fund has been used to support the annual visit of a distinguished scholar in the field of classics. Each visiting scholar delivers a series of lectures, which, revised for book publication, are published by Cornell University Press in Cornell Studies in Classical Philology.

During the semester of their residence, Townsend lecturers effectively become members of the Cornell Department of Classics and teach a course to Cornell students as well as deliver the lectures.

The Townsend Lectures bring to Cornell University, and to Cornell University Press, scholars of international reputation who are in the forefront of current classical research and whose work represents the kind of close reading of texts which has become associated with current literary discourse, or reflects broad interdisciplinary concerns, or both.

CORNELL STUDIES IN CLASSICAL PHILOLOGY

EDITED BY

Frederick M. Ahl, Kevin Clinton, John E. Coleman,
Gregson Davis, Judith R. Ginsburg, G. M. Kirkwood,
Gordon M. Messing, Phillip Mitsis, Alan Nussbaum,
Pietro Pucci, Jeffrey S. Rusten, Danuta Shanzer

VOLUME LIV

Animal Minds and Human Morals:
The Origins of the Western Debate
by Richard Sorabji

ALSO IN THE TOWNSEND LECTURES

Culture and National Identity in Republican Rome
by Erich S. Gruen

Horace and the Dialectic of Freedom:
Readings in "Epistles 1"
by W. R. Johnson

Artifices of Eternity: Horace's Fourth Book of Odes
by Michael C. J. Putnam

Socrates, Ironist and Moral Philosopher
by Gregory Vlastos

Animal Minds and Human Morals

The Origins of the Western Debate

Richard Sorabji

Cornell University Press

Ithaca, New York

© 1993 by Richard Sorabji

All rights reserved. Except for brief quotations in a review, this book,
or parts thereof, must not be reproduced in any form without
permission in writing from the publisher. For information
address Cornell University Press, Sage House,
512 East State Street, Ithaca, New York 14850.

First published 1993 Cornell University Press.

Library of Congress Cataloging-in-Publication Data

Sorabji, Richard.
  Animal minds and human morals : the origins of the Western debate / Richard
Sorabji.
    p. cm. — (Cornell studies in classical philology ; v. 54. The Townsend lectures)
  Includes bibliographical references (p.   ) and indexes.
  ISBN 0-8014-2948-x
    1. Philosophy of mind—History. 2. Animal intelligence—Philosophy—History.
3. Animal welfare—Philosophy—History. 4. Animal rights—History. 5. Philosophy,
Ancient. 6. Philosophy, Medieval. I. Title. II. Series: Cornell studies in classical
philology ; v. 54. III. Series: Cornell studies in classical philology. Townsend lectures.
B187 .M55S67 1993
179'.3—dc20   93–25811

Photoset in North Wales by
Derek Doyle & Associates, Mold Clwyd.
Printed in Great Britain

Contents

You can't import hares to Ithaca.
                  Aristotle *History of Animals* 8.28, 606a3

To Norman Kretzmann
and David Furley

Introduction

I was led from an early age to reflect on the roles we conventionally assign to animals by a family story concerning my aunt, Cornelia Sorabji. One of her first legal briefs, as a young woman in India in the 1890s, was to defend an elephant, which had been deprived by the local rajah of the sugar-palm grove bequeathed to it. The rajah sent a carriage and outriders with drawn swords, to bring her to the palace for the hearing. As she climbed the palace steps, she saw a fierce dog at the top, which she patted. The bench consisted of the rajah himself, swinging on a swing equipped with a musical box playing 'Champagne Charlie is my name'. As Cornelia approached, the rajah declared, 'Your case is won.' Being a young woman, she was indignant. She wanted to plead the case. 'Plead, you shall,' said the rajah, 'but the case is won.' He continued swinging until she stopped, and repeated, 'The case is won.' As she returned down the steps, she asked the Prime Minister what was going on. 'His Highness long ago decided,' the Prime Minister replied, 'that he would never understand the complexities of the law. He therefore hit upon a simple stratagem. If the dog liked the defence counsel, the case was won; if not, not.'[1]

The present enquiry arose from my wish to chart an extensive, but virtually unnoticed, ancient debate in the philosophy of mind about the analysis of a large number of mental capacities. How does perception differ from belief, for example? This is still a central question in the philosophy of mind. But the ancient debate seemed to be driven by an Aristotelian and Stoic view of the nature of mankind, that only mankind has reason or belief. It was this that made it necessary to re-analyse so many of the mental capacities that we seem to share with animals. (For ease of reading, despite my sympathies, I shall not call them 'other' animals, nor substitute 'humankind' for mankind.) The re-analysis proved fruitful in inspiring new psychological distinctions in the philosophy of mind.[2]

---

[1] Cornelia Sorabji, *India Calling*, Nisbet and Co., London 1934, 94-9.
[2] In Chapter One, I compare the similar fruitfulness of ancient Scepticism. Greek Scepticism, however, was not as fruitful as Indian in inspiring mysticism; nor was it the source of ancient idealism (Myles Burnyeat, 'Idealism in Greek Philosophy: what Descartes saw and Berkeley missed', *Phil. Rev.* 91, 1982, 3-40), which I have argued arose from problems about Creation (*Time, Creation and the Continuum*, London and Ithaca NY 1983, ch. 18). Nor did it lead to the idea of one's body as part of the external

1

Meanwhile, however, voices were raised on the other side, to say that animals do have reason, especially among some of Aristotle's immediate successors, and in the Platonist and Pythagorean tradition. The issue was quite central for the Stoics, for whom human rationality was so important, and for the Neoplatonists, when the justification of animal sacrifice was challenged by one of their number, Porphyry. There is no exact analogue in the modern literature to the Aristotelian and Stoic denial of reason. But we, too, have lived through a period when endless ingenuity was spent on maintaining the behaviourist view that all animal behaviour can be accounted for in terms of stimulus and response. Now, at last, an open-minded effort is being made to discover what cognitive states we should, and what we shouldn't, ascribe to various species of animal.

I was not at first concerned with any of the moral issues. I was only interested in charting the debate in the philosophy of mind, until I noticed how bad were the arguments designed to show that animals were very different from us. It all sounded rather grand, when Aristotle said that we have reason and they don't. But under pressure, the Stoics retreated to the position that at least they don't have syntax. The moral conclusion was meant to be 'They don't have syntax, so we can eat them.' My embarrassment increased when I noticed that the modern debate, among the followers of Chomsky and critics of the language abilities of chimpanzees, had reached exactly the same point. It has become crucial whether animals have syntax. This, of course, is a question of great scientific interest, but of no moral relevance whatsoever. Aristotle, I believe, was driven almost entirely by scientific interest in reaching his decision that animals lack reason. But in the next generation the Stoics and Epicureans had a moral concern, because they both had theories of justice which denied justice to animals, on the grounds that animals lack reason. The Stoics further saw animals as providentially designed for us.

The most comprehensive treatment of the subject in antiquity is that of Porphyry's treatise *On Abstinence from Animal Food*. This is not only a thoroughgoing attack on the killing of animals. It is also a mine of information on the earlier philosophical and anthropological literature and a key to the ideals of a major Neoplatonist.

Unfortunately, the Stoic view of animals, with its stress on their irrationality, became embedded in Western, Latin-speaking Christianity above all through Augustine. Western Chistianity concentrated on one half, the anti-animal half, of the much more evenly balanced ancient debate. Although there were other strands in Western

---

world (Burnyeat, op. cit.), which was instead encouraged by Epictetus' insistence (*Diss.* 1.1.23-4; 4.1.72-80) on distinguishing what is under one's control from what is not.

Christianity, I think this accounts for the relative complacency of our Western Christian tradition about the killing of animals. The ancient philosophers were less complacent. In the eighteenth century the tide began to turn, and in the last fifteen years it has accelerated, with a widespread rethinking of our treatment of animals. But I do not believe that the right defence of animals has yet been found. The modern philosophical defences seem to me to be too one-dimensional. What is clear, however, is that we should treat animals very much better than we do. My own diet has changed as a result of reflecting on the ancient texts, at least when I am choosing for myself, although I still enjoy whatever food I am served by others. I do not mention that as a particularly compelling position, and I have no wish to tell anyone else what to do. I explain in the concluding chapter why I think decisions must be complex, and suggest an alternative approach.

What is true is that recent developments in animal ethology and in practical ethics are only the latest chaper in a debate that began in antiquity.[3] Much of the story has not been told, although aspects are taken up in two valuable German books, one on vegetarianism, and one on the nature of humans and animals.[4] I have confined myself largely to philosophical texts, especially those in the philosophy of mind, and those on the philosophy of ethics and religion although the non-philosophical literature deserves treatment. To give a clearer picture, I have focused on issues I took to be central, and omitted some I took to be minor. The story could be still further enriched by attention to non-philosophical texts.

Acknowledgments

The material for this book was delivered as the Townsend Lectures in the Classics Department at Cornell University in October to November 1991, and prepared for press with the help of funds from the Townsend Bequest. I should like to thank my hosts in the Cornell Classics Department for this opportunity, and also the Ancient and Medieval Philosophy specialists at Cornell, Phil Mitsis, Joe de Filippo and Danuta Shanzer in Classics, Gail Fine, Terry Irwin and Norman Kretzmann in Philosophy, for their many helpful discussions. In addition, the Townsend Bequest arranged for excellent written comments to be sent to me, one set from my fellow-guest at Cornell, Dale Jamieson, who is an expert on animal rights, and one from a very perceptive Classical scholar now identified as Brad Inwood. Paul Vander Waerdt gave me a most valuable set of detailed comments on

---

[3] I hope to take up other aspects of ancient practical ethics in a later book on whether ancient philosophy can tell us how to live.

[4] Johannes Haussleiter, *Der Vegetarismus in der Antike*, Berlin 1855; Urs Dierauer, *Tier und Mensch im Denken der Antike*, Amsterdam 1977.

Chapters Nine to Twelve. I have great pleasure in dedicating the book to my friends Norman Kretzmann and David Furley.

Earlier versions were presented as the Simon Lectures in spring 1990 in the Philosophy Department at Toronto, where I should particularly like to thank my host in Trinity College, Doug Hutchinson, for his valuable discussion and hospitality, and as the Gray Lectures in the Classics Faculty at Cambridge University in spring 1991, where I enjoyed discussion with many old friends.

Finally, I am extremely grateful to Gertrud Watson for typing the book and to Elaine Miller for the labour of compiling the index locorum with the expert help of Dirk Baltzly.

Part I

Mind

CHAPTER ONE

The crisis: the denial of reason to animals

The philosophical treatment of animals in Ancient Greece began as early as Pythagoras in the sixth century BC, or even Hesiod in the eighth. But, as mentioned in the Introduction, a large part of the story has not been told. In particular, I want to show what a crisis was provoked when Aristotle denied reason to animals. It was a crisis both for the philosophy of mind and for theories of morality, and the issues raised then are still being debated today. I shall take philosophy of mind first.

The crisis

If animals are to be denied reason (*logos*), and with it belief (*doxa*), then their perceptual content must be compensatingly expanded, to enable them to find their way around in the world. On the other hand, it must not be expanded in such a way that perception becomes tantamount to belief. The distinction between these was as much debated then as it is now. It is not only perception that will need to be distinguished from belief, but the possession of concepts, memory, intention, emotion and speech, if these too can be found in animals that lack belief. The project will require a wholesale re-analysis of all these mental capacities. And the concept of reason may itself be subject to shifting. It is well known that ancient scepticism provided one motive for drawing distinctions between different capacities of mind. What I would add is that concern with man and his place in nature above the animals provided another.

The moral question of how we should treat animals is another issue which has become very prominent in the last few years. In antiquity, it had primitive social and religious roots, to which I shall turn in Chapter Thirteen. But in moral philosophy, as in the philosophy of mind, the question of animal rationality came to play a central role. For one thing, the Stoic school connected moral responsibility with the giving of rational assent and this led to further re-analysis, this time of the concepts of voluntary action and impulse. For another thing, the Stoics and Epicureans both had theories of justice which disqualified

irrational animals from consideration. According to the Stoics, justice
depends on a process (*oikeiôsis*) of extending fellow feeling, a process
which can naturally reach only as far as beings who are rational like
ourselves. The Epicureans came to the same conclusion from another
direction, since for Epicurus, as for Hobbes who read him, justice
extends only to those who are capable of making contracts, and hence,
at least according to his followers, only to rational animals.

The Aristotelian and Stoic denial of rationality to animals proved all
too congenial to Jews and Christians. It was opposed chiefly in the
Pythagorean and Platonist traditions, by the Cynics and by those
free-thinking Aristotelians who did not go along with their master. The
Christians were not the first to take an anti-animal view,[1] but they
exploited the anti-animal views they found in the Stoics. And I believe
it accounts for some of our own complacency about animals that we are
heirs of a Western Christian tradition which selected just one side
from a much more wide-ranging Greek debate. Even now, I believe, we
have not found the right rationale for a better treatment of animals,
and that will be the theme of the final chapter of this book.

The Presocratics

The preconditions for the crisis were not firmly laid down until Plato,
for many of the earlier Presocratic philosophers, if we can believe later
reports, did not even make the requisite distinctions. Parmenides,
Anaxagoras, Empedocles, Democritus and even the poet Homer are
accused by Aristotle and subsequent writers of not distinguishing
intellect or intelligence (*nous, phronêsis*) from perception (*aisthêsis*), or
other aspects of soul (*psukhê*).[2] One piece of evidence used by Aristotle
is that Anaxagoras ascribes intellect (*nous*) to all animals, great and
small, high and low. Instead of taking this at face value, Aristotle
treats it as evidence that Anaxagoras does not mean the kind of
intellect that corresponds to intelligence, but merely means soul. He
would similarly discount Empedocles' claim that all things, including
presumably the four elements earth, air, fire and water, have
intelligence and thought (*phronêsis, nôma*), and the claim of Diogenes
of Apollonia that the other animals besides man have thought.[3] Nor

---

[1] Here I agree with Catherine Osborne, 'Topography in the *Timaeus*', *Proceedings of
the Cambridge Philological Society* 1989, against John Passmore, *Man's Responsibility
for Nature*, London 1974, 13-14.

[2] Aristotle *Metaph.* 4.5, 1009b12-31; *DA* 1.2, 404b1-6; 405a8-16; 3.3, 427a19-29;
Theophrastus *Sens.* 23; Aëtius 4,5.12 (*Dox. Gr.* 392,4-7).

[3] Empedocles frr. 103 DK (from Simplicius); 110,10 (from Hippolytus and Sextus);
Diogenes of Apollonia fr. 4 DK (from Diogenes Laertius). See Catherine Osborne for the
convincing suggestion that the four elements are implied to have loves and hates when it
is said by Empedocles that they are moved by love and hate, 'Empedocles recycled',
Classical Quarterly 37, 1987, at 46-7.

can we make much of Cleidemus' distinction between the organs of hearing (*akoai*) on which the air falls and the mind (*nous*) to which they have to pass (*diapempein*) their message before they can discern (*krinein*). The mind here need not be distinct from the rest of the soul.[4]

Admittedly, Aristotle is probably exaggerating. For there is at least one Presocratic philosopher who seems to have anticipated his own viewpoint, even though his claims had to await reinforcement by Aristotle. Alcmaeon (late sixth century BC) says that man differs from the other animals, because he alone has understanding (*xunienai*), whereas the other animals perceive (*aisthanesthai*), but do not understand.[5] It is also probably Alcmaeon, judging from the correct identification of the brain rather than the heart as the seat of perception, whom Plato describes as saying that understanding (*epistêmê*) comes from a stabilisation of memory and belief (*doxa*), while memory and belief come from the hearing, sight and smell provided by the brain.[6] Not only does this statement distinguish understanding from perception; it also anticipates Aristotle's own developmental theory of the higher functions,[7] and even improves on it by identifying the brain as the seat of perception. There were others too in the fifth century BC who sought to distinguish men from animals. Anaxagoras says that we master animals through our unique experience, memory, expertise (*sophia*) and technical knowledge (*tekhnê*)[8] while Protagoras, at least in Plato's representation of him, agrees that technology is possessed by man alone.[9]

Plato

Plato's most important contribution lay in his dramatic narrowing of the content of perception, and his corresponding expansion of the content of belief. This innovation in the *Theaetetus* has been well described by others.[10] Plato there argues that the soul uses the senses merely as channels to perceive sense qualities like whiteness, but cannot use them for distinguishing and comparing qualities, or for hitting on something's *being* the case or *being* white (*ousia*), or the truth (*alêtheia*). For that requires reasoning (*sullogismos*) and belief

[4] Theophrastus *de Sensibus* 38.
[5] Alcmaeon fr. 1a DK, from Theophrastus *Sens.* 25.
[6] Plato *Phaedo* 96B.
[7] Aristotle *An. Post.* 2.19.
[8] Anaxagoras fr. 21B (= Plutarch *de Fort.* 98F)
[9] Plato *Protagoras* 321D; 322A.
[10] John Cooper, 'Plato on sense-perception and knowledge: *Theaetetus* 184-6', *Phronesis* 15, 1970, 123-46; Myles Burnyeat, 'Plato on the grammar of perceiving', *Classical Quarterly* 26, 1976, 29-51. Michael Frede, 'Observations on perception in Plato's later dialogues', in his *Essays in Ancient Philosophy*, Minneapolis 1987.

(*doxazein*).[11] Reasoning is in turn described as the silent debate of the soul with itself, and belief as the silent conclusion of this debate, or as silent affirmation and negation in the debate, or the silent answer to a question[12] – to a question posed in the inner debate.

So far the narrowing of perception produces no crisis for animals. For in many works, we shall see, Plato is willing to grant them a reasoning part of the soul. And even where he denies this (and he does waver on the subject to the end), he is still not obliged to deny them belief (*doxa*), since he is perfectly ready to associate belief with the lower, non-reasoning parts of the soul.

Plato's extension to animals of a rational part of the soul is suggested by his repeated supposition that animals are reincarnated humans. Reversing Darwin, he made humans precede animals.[13] Why do foxes have elongated heads? To accommodate the movements of the rational part of the soul distorted in a previous human incarnation. The rational part is not said to be missing, but merely unused, and not even this is said of those reincarnated as birds.[14] Indeed, in two playful passages, it is envisaged that cranes may be intelligent (*phronimos*), and may give names and class men below themselves,[15] and the recognitional capacity (*sunesis*) of dogs is said to show a love of learning (*philomathes*) which is the same as philosophy (*philosophon*).[16]

But even if reason (*logismos, logos, logistikon*) is sometimes denied to animals[17] (and on this Plato's last work, the *Laws*, seems to waver),[18] it remains clear that the non-rational parts of the soul must also entertain beliefs. This is crucial to Plato's analysis of virtue and vice in the *Republic*, where self-control involves the rational and non-rational parts of the soul sharing the same beliefs (*homodoxein*), and licentiousness involves beliefs (*doxai*) acting as bodyguards of lust.[19] Again, the beliefs (*doxazein*) produced by illusion are explicitly said not to belong to the rational part of the soul.[20] The point is crucial too to Plato's growing awareness in the *Phaedrus* of the different

[11] Plato *Theaetetus* 184D-187B, at 186D; 187A.

[12] Plato *Theaetetus* 189E-190A, *Sophist* 263E ff; *Philebus* 38C-E.

[13] Plato *Timaeus* 42B-D; 91D-92C; *Phaedo* 81D-82B; *Republic* 620A-D; *Phaedrus* 249B.

[14] Plato *Timaeus* 91D-92C. Angela Hobbs has offered me the further powerful evidence that it is the *rational* souls who are warned by God of their possible future incarnation as animals at *Timaeus* 42B-D.

[15] Plato *Statesman* 263D.

[16] Plato *Republic* 376B.

[17] Plato *Symposium* 207A-C; *Republic* 441A-B; *Laws* 963E. Cf. the etymology in *Cratylus* 399C: only man (*anthrôpos*) reflects on what he sees (*anathrei ha opôpe*).

[18] Plato *Laws* 961D seems to grant intellect (*nous*) to animals, despite the passage just cited (963E), which appears to deny them reason (*logos*).

[19] Plato *Republic* 442B-D; 574D.

[20] Ibid. 603A.

reasons for giving in to temptation. The lowest part of the soul can think it right (*axioun*) that it should be indulged.[21] Again, in the *Timaeus*, it is plants, not animals, which are distinguished as lacking belief (*doxa*).[22] And the non-rational parts of the soul contain two unwise counsellors (*sumbouloi*), anger which is hard to dissuade (*dusparamuthêtos*) and expectation (*elpis*) which is easily led astray.[23] In the *Laws* too, we find fear and confidence described as beliefs (*doxai*) which are contrasted with reasoning (*logismos*).[24] On one interpretation (the commonest), Plato is explicitly talking about animals when he says in the *Republic* that a precarious form of true belief can be found in the nature of a beast and a slave.[25]

There may seem to be two exceptions to what I have said, both of them connected with Plato's *Theaetetus*. In one passage, to be further discussed below, Plato makes Socrates argue that perception is not knowledge, because it cannot grasp that anything '*is*' thus or so, and hence cannot grasp truth. For that you need reasoning and belief. In the course of this argument, he says:

> So both humans and beasts (*thêria*) can perceive some things straight away on being born, namely all those impressions (*pathêmata*) which reach the soul by way of the body. But reflections (*analogismata*) about these as regards being (*ousia*) and utility come to those beings which (*hois an*) acquire them only with difficulty over time through much trouble and education (*paideia*).[26]

Here the crisis almost breaks out. 'Those beings which' does not quite say that no beasts can aspire to reflections about things being (*ousia*) thus and so, and hence does not quite confine beasts to mere sense impressions (*pathêmeta*). An attentive reader might well wonder whether Plato's Socrates is likely to count beasts as capable of education (*paideia*). But in the absence of an explicit statement here, or of any further statement elsewhere to reinforce such doubts, the remark is not enough to precipitate the crisis.

It might be thought that a further doubt is raised in the *Theaetetus*. For Socrates is made to present belief (*doxa*) as a stage in silent inner thinking (*dianoeisthai*).[27] As the thinking involves the soul asking itself questions and giving itself answers, it may seem to be that

---

[21] Plato *Phaedrus* 255E-256A.

[22] Plato *Timaeus* 77A-C.

[23] Ibid. 69D. For pleasure and pain as unwise counsellors, see *Laws* 644C.

[24] Plato *Laws* 644C-D; 645A.

[25] Plato *Republic* 430B. But William Fortenbaugh argues that the reference is to a bestial human, *Aristotle on Emotion*, London 1975, 55, n. 1.

[26] Plato *Theaetetus* 186B-C. I am very grateful to Myles Burnyeat, author of an incomparable book on the *Theaetetus*, for pressing this passage on me, and to Willie Charlton for the main part of my response.

[27] Plato *Theaetetus* 189E-190A; similarly *Sophist* 263E-264A; *Philebus* 38C-E.

special kind of dialectical thinking practised only by philosophers. In that case, belief would not be available to beasts – or even to most humans. But to this there are two answers. First, the *Theaetetus* later recognises beliefs which require no more than fitting a present perception to a memory imprint, and the *Philebus* gives a similar account.[28] Secondly, the *Philebus* passage shows that the inner questioning that leads up to belief need involve no more than questions about whether the thing perceived is a man or an effigy set up by the shepherds.[29]

Aristotle's denial of reason and belief

The crisis came when Aristotle reverted to a position closer to Alcmaeon's, denying animals reason (*logos*), reasoning (*logismos*), thought (*dianoia*, *nous*), intellect (*nous*) and belief (*doxa*).[30] He must then compensate them by giving them a rich enough perceptual content to deal with the world. Typically, an animal that follows a scent does not merely perceive the scent in isolation, but perceives it as belonging to something, or at least as lying in a certain direction, and otherwise would not go in the right direction for it. But this already involves *connecting* the scent with a subject or a direction. I shall talk of this connecting as *predicating* the scent of a subject on direction, though I shall not mean anything extra by the word, and I shall describe the animal as perceiving *that* the scent comes from that direction, or perceiving it *as* coming from there. I shall not mean perceiving *that* to involve more than perceiving *as*, nor either of them to involve more than making the *connexion* to which I have referred. The point that matters to me is that Plato's simple perceiving of a scent, without connecting it with anything, will no longer be adequate to describe what animals do, once they are denied reason. Perceptual content must be expanded to allow for this kind of connexion or predication. And this is all the more true of the animal that watches to see if it has been noticed by its quarry, or seeks to extricate the cheese from the mousetrap. I shall explain more fully in Chapter Two just how much, or how little, this connecting involves.

In denying animals reason, Aristotle intends to deny them the capacity for true or false thought and belief. An impression may persist, partly because of Aristotle's well-known gradualism in biology, that he does not really deny this to animals after all. But I think it is

---

[28] Plato *Theaetetus* 193B-195E. Plato does not deny that this provides a good account of some cases of belief, but only that it provides an account of all cases of false belief.

[29] I thank Myles Burnyeat again.

[30] See Aristotle *DA* 1.2, 404b4-6; 2.3, 414b18-19 with 32-3 and 415a7-8; 3.3, 428a19-24; 3.10, 433a12; 3.11, 434a5-11; *PA* 1.1, 641b7; *EE* 2.8, 1224a27; *Pol.* 7.13, 1332b5; *NE* 1.7, 1098a3-4; *Metaph.* 1.1, 980b28; *Mem.* 450a16.

necessary to distinguish his formal theoretical statements on animals from the casual everyday descriptions which we all find it hard to avoid applying to them, whatever our theory. Thus admittedly in the *History of Animals* Books 8 and 9 (whose authenticity has recently been defended), we find animals credited with technical knowledge (*tekhnikos*) and thought (*dianoia, nous*).[31] But this must be seen in the context of the programmatic warnings at the beginning of each of these books in 8.1 and 9.1, and it is punctuated by further warnings: it is only *as if* the dolphins calculate (*hôsper analogisamenoi*) how big a breath they need before diving.[32] It would be unnecessary, as well as tedious, for Aristotle to repeat these caveats every time.

Of the formal theoretical statements, the one at the opening of the *Metaphysics* (1.1) admittedly grants animals intelligence (*phronêsis*; another word for this is *sunesis*: understanding), and this ascription has been much emphasised.[33] But Aristotle himself points out that *phronêsis* is different in wild animals and in men.[34] It is simply intelligence, or as he says, foresight. It could not be the human capacity, discussed in the *Nicomachean Ethics*, to see what moral virtue calls for in a particular situation in the light of a philosophical understanding of what matters in life. The *Metaphysics* passage which grants animals *phronêsis* treats it as a more striking concession that some animals can learn. It adds that animals have little experience (*empeiria*) – I shall consider what that means later – and no reasoning (*logismos*), technical knowledge (*tekhnê*), or scientific understanding (*epistêmê*) at all.

Even Aristotle's gradualism in biology is carefully qualified so that it allows for a sharp intellectual distinction between animal and man. This gradualism is most fully expressed in *Parts of Animals* 4.5, 681a12-28 and *History of Animals* 8.1. But the first only discusses the border between plants and animals, while in the second where he does consider the border between animals and man, he carefully applies his gradualism to temperaments, not to intellect. Thus when he says that most animals have traces (*ikhnê*) of human characteristics, this is illustrated by their actually sharing with us certain temperaments, but when it comes to *intellectual* capacities, only by their having

[31] *Tekhnikos, HA* 9, 615a19; 616a4; 620b10; 622b23; *dianoia* 612b20; 616b20; 22; 27, 30; *nous* 610b22; cf. *noeros PA* 2.2, 648a3-4. Authenticity: see Balme s.v. 'Aristotle' in bibliography.

[32] *HA* 9, 631a27.

[33] Aristotle *Metaph.* 1.1, 980b1-981a3. The ascription of *phronêsis* is discussed by W. Fortenbaugh, 'Aristotle: animals, emotion and moral virtue', *Arethusa* 4, 1971, 137-65; by G.E.R. Lloyd, *Science, Folklore and Ideology*, Cambridge 1983, 18-35; by Jean-Louis Labarrière, 'De la phronèsis animale', in P. Pellegrin et al. eds, *Actes du colloque d'Oléron sur Biologie, Logique et Métaphysique chez Aristote*, in preparation; and by Eve Cole, 'Theophrastus and Aristotle on animal intelligence' in W. Fortenbaugh and Dimitri Gutas, eds, *Rutgers University Studies in Classical Humanities*, vol. 5, 44-62.

[34] Aristotle *NE* 6.7, 1141a22-8.

likenesses (*homoiotêtes*) of the kind of understanding that has to do
with thought (*hê peri tên dianoian sunesis*). Again, whereas some
differences from animals are only a matter of degree, others are more
distant – a matter of mere analogy. The latter is again illustrated by
the *intellectual* capacities: as technical knowledge (*tekhnê*), expertise
(*sophia*) and understanding (*sunesis*) are to man, so some other similar
capacity (and he calls it other: *hetera*) stands to certain animals. This
schema (as A is to B so some other C is to D) is what Aristotle
standardly means by an analogy, and it implies that animals only have
something other than *tekhnê*, *sophia* or *sunesis*. There is a continuity of
temperament, but not of intellect, only an analogy:[35]

> For even in most of the other animals there are traces (*ikhnê*) of
> psychological traits which are more clearly differentiated among men.
> Tameness and wildness, docility and stubbornness, boldness and
> cowardice, fear, confidence, anger, mischief and analogues (*homoiotêtes*)
> of intellectual understanding (*hê peri tên dianoian sunesis*) are present
> in many of them, as was said in the case of their physical parts. Some
> differ from men, and man from many animals, in degree, since some
> traits of this kind exist more in man, some more in the other animals.
> But other traits differ by being analogous (*tôi analogon*). For as technical
> skill (*tekhnê*), expertise (*sophia*) and understanding (*sunesis*) are to man,
> so there is some different (*hetera*) natural capacity of the kind in some of
> the animals.

The statement at the opening of *History of Animals* 9.1 is similarly
qualified.[36] The capacities which animals are said to have are to do
with emotions (*dunamis tis peri hekaston tôn tês psukhês pathêmatôn*).
Most of these are not intellectual, although intelligence (*phronêsis*)
does get mentioned as one. And then it is added that some animals can
learn or teach, because they can distinguish (*diaisthanesthai*) not only
sounds, but also signs (*sêmeia*). There is nothing new here. Most of it is
said in the *Metaphysics* passage, and the ability to use signs is attested
in *On the Soul* 2.8, 420b32 and *Politics* 1.2, 1253a10-14.

The formal denials of various intellectual capacities have already
been noted. Animals lack reason (*logos*),[37] reasoning (*logismos*),[38]
thought (*dianoia*),[39] intellect (*nous*),[40] and belief (*doxa*).[41] Some
confusion may arise from the fact that perceptual appearance
(*phantasia*), which at least many animals enjoy, is sometimes called a

---

[35] Aristotle *HA* 8.1, 588a18-31. I read this differently from Jean Louis Labarrière,
op. cit.
[36] *HA* 9.1, 608a11-21.
[37] *DA* 3.3, 428a24; *EE* 2.8, 1224a27; *Pol.* 7.13, 1332b5; *NE* 1.7, 1098a3-4.
[38] *DA* 3.10, 433a12.
[39] *PA* 1.1, 641b7.
[40] *DA* 1.2, 404b4-6.
[41] *DA* 3.3, 428a19-24; *Mem.* 450a16.

sort of thinking (*noêsis, noein*), but I shall deal with that below in Chapter Three. The denials are not peripheral, but central to Aristotle's concerns. His account in the *Nicomachean Ethics* of the happiest life for a human depends on finding something unique to humans (*idion*, not *koinon*) – reason (*logos*) – or, if humans are to be distinguished from God, then practical reason.[42] The structure of much of the rest of the treatise *On the Soul* is governed by his distinguishing in *On the Soul* 2.3 between the soul of plant, animal and human, and, in parallel with that, between the capacities to use food, to perceive and to think,[43] although Aristotle does admittedly hedge at this point on whether it is only mankind that thinks.[44] The distinction of human and animal capacities at the very opening of the *Metaphysics* leads up in 1.2 to a defence of philosophy as the activity that brings humans closest to God. Finally, the denial to animals of another rational activity, speech (*logos*) in *Politics* 1.2, is supposed to account for their inability to form a civic society.[45]

It may be argued that Aristotle took a different view very early in his career, if it is right – and I doubt that it is – to resuscitate as a genuine excerpt from Aristotle a certain passage in Iamblichus' patchwork, the *Exhortation to Philosophy* (*Protrepticus*). It was rescuscitated by I. Düring, who is followed by Jonathan Barnes. But it had been dropped from the list of fragments of Aristotle's *Protrepticus* by Werner Jaeger and assigned by him to Porphyry and by D.J. Allan to Posidonius.[46] The passage allows that animals have some small glints (*aithugmata*) of intelligence (*phronêsis*) and (contrary to the mature Aristotle) reason (*logos*). It denies only that they have the philosophical understanding (*sophia theôrêtikê*) to which the reader is being exhorted. By way of compensation for this lack, it says that many animals have greater accuracy in their senses (*aisthêseis*) and strength

---

[42] Alternatively, if humans are not to be distinguished from God for present purposes, their happiness will consist in the same type of activity, a possibility that Aristotle considers in *Nicomachean Ethics* 10.7-8.

[43] *DA* 2.3, 414b18-19; 32-3; 415a7-8.

[44] Ibid. 414b18-19.

[45] *Pol.* 1.2, 1253a8-18.

[46] The passage is Iamblichus' *Protrepticus* 36, 7-13 (Pistelli). The whole treatise is translated into English by Thomas M. Johnson, 1907, repr. Grand Rapids, Michigan, 1988. The ascription of this passage to Aristotle was due to I. Bywater, 'On a lost dialogue of Aristotle', *Journal of Philology* 2, 1869, 55-69. Werner Jaeger's denial in *Aristotle: Fundamentals of his Development* 2, 1948, 62, translated from the German of *Aristoteles*, 1923, was followed by Richard Walzer and W.D. Ross in their editions of Aristotle's *Protrepticus*, but repudiated by I. Düring in his edition, who is followed by Jonathan Barnes, revised edition of the Oxford translation of Aristotle, in two volumes, p. 2407. I thank Eric Lewis and Jill Kraye for drawing my attention respectively to Barnes and Allan. Edelstein and Kidd do not recognise the passage as a fragment of Posidonius, nor does Andrew Smith as a fragment of Porphyry, in their editions of those authors, and Jaeger never carried out his intention of defending the ascription to Porphyry, which, however, I find plausible.

in their impulses (*hormai*). To the case made by others against Aristotelian authorship, I would add that the passage sounds post-Aristotelian, because sensation and impulse were the two hallmarks of animals in Stoic theory. Admittedly, Düring allows for this by postulating a Stoicising Neo-Pythagorean writer as having filtered the Aristotle. But the word *aithugmata* (glints) is used elsewhere by Porphyry in his *Letter to Anebo*, as reported by Iamblichus,[47] and is not otherwise attested for Aristotle. That makes Porphyry an attractive candidate. Posidonius, on the other hand, seems to me extremely unlikely, since, like other Stoics, he denied reason both to animals and to children.[48]

The closest Aristotle comes to allowing reasoning to animals is perhaps in his discussion of practical syllogisms, (*syllogizesthai* literally means reasoning) in the *de Motu Animalium*, chapter 7. There after detailing some syllogisms which are clearly confined to humans, since they involve such premises (*protaseis*) as 'a house is a good thing', 'I need a cloak', and 'I am a human', he gives an example in which appetite says 'I must drink', perception 'This is drink', and drinking follows at once.[49] Immediately after this, Aristotle says that this is the way in which animals (*zôia*) are impelled (*hormân*) to move and act. Does he mean by a combination of appetite and perception, or does he mean by entertaining syllogistic premises, which would suggest reasoning? Certainly, the premises in the immediately preceding example are ones which individually an irrational animal could grasp, since 'I must drink' and 'This is drink' can be apprehended without reason. If, moreover, drawing the conclusion and drinking is simply a causal process, there seems to be nothing to stop an animal engaging in practical syllogism, or reasoning. There are a number of 'ifs' here, and perhaps that is why Aristotle does not notice how close he has come to allowing reasoning to animals. Certainly, he does not seem to notice. I shall return to the question in Chapter Seven.

[47] Iamblichus *Myst.* 3.20 (148,2); 3.21 (151,1).

[48] ap. Galenum *PHP* (animals) 5.6.38, 334,7-8; (children) 5.5.2,316,23-5 (= frr. 33 and 169 in Edelstein and Kidd's *Posidonius*).

[49] Aristotle *de Motu Animalium* 7, 701a33-4. I am grateful to Gary Matthews for pressing on me a text which I had earlier been inclined to dismiss.

CHAPTER TWO

Perceptual content expanded

Aristotle's expansion

To compensate for the denial of reason and belief to animals, perceptual content must be expanded. And this Aristotle carries out in what may well be conscious opposition to Plato's *Theaetetus*. In *On the Soul* 2.6 and 3.1, he starts by recognising Plato's objects of perception, colours and flavours, for example, each of which is called proper (*idion*) in the sense that it can be perceived by only one of the five senses. But he goes beyond that when he adds the common qualities (*koina*) perceptible by more than one sense: movement, rest, shape, extension number, unity.[1] Plato had overlooked these when he said that you cannot perceive through one sense what you perceive through another.[2] Moreover, the properties which Plato calls common (*koina*), such as likeness and difference, and which he (Plato) assigns to the province of reason,[3] are most consciously treated by Aristotle as yet further objects of perception:

> with what do we further perceive that (white and sweet) differ? It must be by perception for they are perceptibles.[4]

This already involves perceiving *that* something is the case – that the qualities differ. I shall refer to perceiving *that* something is the case as perceiving a proposition, although I shall still intend no more than I intended earlier by my talk of predication. I do not mean to commit myself on whether such propositions need consist of concepts, although that is something that I shall discuss in the next chapter. Propositions here are what is introduced by a 'that'-clause and such propositions are also involved, on one view, in Aristotle's remaining class of perceptual objects, the coincidental (*kata sumbebêkos*) sense objects. At least they are if this class is to be illustrated by the examples of perceiving *that*

---

[1] *DA* 2.6, 418a17-18; 3.1,425a16; *Sens.* 442b5.
[2] Plato *Theaetetus* 184E-185A.
[3] Ibid. 184D-187B.
[4] *DA* 3.2, 426b12-427a14; cf. 3.7, 431a20-431b1; *Som.* 455a17-18.

the white thing is the son of Diares or the son of Cleon.[5] I am not myself quite convinced of this. But there is none the less a great deal of propositional perceiving that Aristotle recognises. One can perceive *that* the white thing is this or something else, whether the white thing is a man or not, that the approaching thing is a man and is white, what the coloured or sounding thing is, or where, that the beacon is lit, that something is pleasant, that we are perceiving, walking, thinking, living, existing, in dreams that we are sleeping, whether this is bread, whether it is baked, 'this is sweet' and 'this is drink'. And the lion perceives that the ox is near and rejoices because or that he will get a meal.[6]

It would be wrong to suppose that this propositional perception really involves an inference of reason[7] merely on the ground that some of the perceived objects are said to be coincidental (*kata sumbebêkos*) sense-objects. 'Coincidental' does not imply that they are perceived only indirectly by way of inference. I have argued elsewhere that the reason why colour is said to be essential to sight is that sight is *defined* as the perception of brightness and colour.[8] By contrast the son of Diares is called a coincidental sense-object, because he is not definitionally related to colours seen, and hence not to sight.

Propositions are involved again in Aristotle's idea of perceptual appearance. *Phantasia*, discussed in *On the Soul* 3.3, covers both what I might call perceptual and post-perceptual appearance. Examples of post-perceptual appearance would be imagination, dreams and memory, all due to prior perception, and such appearances are often non-propositional.[9] But an example of perceptual appearance given by Aristotle is the propositional appearance *that* the sun is quite small, only a foot across. This appearance, too, is due to (*hupo*) the perceiving.[10] The word *phantasia* is used in connexion with perception, propositional or otherwise, just so long as we want to talk of things appearing. Plato and Aristotle in their discussions explicitly connect *phantasia* with the verb 'to appear' (*phainesthai*).[11] To mark the

---

[5] *DA* 2.6, 418a21-3; 3.1, 425a25-7, as interpreted by Stanford Cashdollar, 'Aristotle's account of incidental perception', *Phronesis* 18, 1973, 156-75.

[6] *DA* 2.6, 418a16; 3.3, 428b21-2; 3.6, 430b29-30; *NE* 3.3, 1113a1; 7.3, 1147a25-30; 7.6, 1149a35; *Mot.* 701a32-3, cited by Cashdollar. Also *NE* 3.10, 1118a20-3; 9.9, 1170a29-b1; *DA* 3.2, 425b12; 3.7, 431b5; *Insom.* 1, 458b14-15; 3, 462a3.

[7] This view is rejected by David Hamlyn, *Aristotle's de Anima, books II and III*, Oxford 1968; Stanford Cashdollar op. cit., who ascribes it to J.I. Beare, W.D. Ross, Irving Block and Charles Kahn.

[8] Richard Sorabji, 'Aristotle on demarcating the five senses', *Philosophical Review* 80, 1971, 55-79, repr. in J. Barnes, M. Schofield, R. Sorabji, eds., *Articles on Aristotle*, vol. 4, London 1979.

[9] *DA* 3.8, 432a11-13.

[10] *DA* 3.3, 428b26.

[11] Plato *Sophist* 264A-B; Aristotle *DA* 3.3, 428a13-14. For Plato on *phantasia*, see M.W. Bundy, *The Theory of Imagination in Classical and Medieval Thought*, University

connexion of phantasia with appearing, and to bring out the continuity between different texts, I shall use the translation 'appearance', although readers should be aware that some translators will render the same word as 'imagination', or as 'impression'. A perceptual appearance is more likely than a post-perceptual appearance to be an appearance *that* something is the case, or, as we would sometimes prefer to say, an appearance *as of* something's being the case. The latter is not propositional in the sense of involving a *that*-clause, but it is predicational: something is *predicated* of something. There is not merely an appearance of whiteness, but of whiteness as belonging to something or as being located somewhere. I shall call this, too, propositional, meaning no more than that it is predicational. Aristotle grants perceptual appearance to animals, even though he seems uncertain whether it belongs to all animals,[12] as the Stoics would maintain.

It cannot detract from the clear example of propositional appearance that the sun is only one foot across that Aristotle later goes on to contrast appearance with affirming or denying (*phasis*, *apophasis*) something as true or false, on the grounds that, unlike truth and falsity, it does not involve a combining of concepts (*sumplokê noêmatôn*).[13] Aristotle has so often described appearance as liable to be false,[14] that in this passage he must be talking about a different type of appearance, namely contemplating mental images (*phantasmata*) in what I have called post-perceptual appearance. This interpretation is, if anything, confirmed by another passage which might at first sight seem to be dissociating perception from predication.[15] Here Aristotle has in mind a contrast between simply perceiving something and finding it pleasant or unpleasant (*hêdesthai*, *lupeisthai*). What he says is that the first is like simply saying (*phanai monon*), the second (and I take it he means finding it pleasant or unpleasant)[16] is like saying it or gainsaying it *of* something (*kataphanai*, *apophanai*). There is no suggestion here that sense perception has to *confine* itself to simple saying. On the contrary, it is stated that finding the thing pleasant or unpleasant is itself an exercise of the perceptual faculty (*energein têi aisthêtikêi mesotêtei*). Moreover when the contrast is repeated two or three lines later, the talk of simple perceiving is replaced by talk of having a mental image (*phantasma*), which understandably involves

---

of Illinois Studies in Language and Literature, Urbana 1927, ch. 2 and *passim*.

[12] Contrast *DA* 415a11; 428a10; 22; 24 with the more generous 433b28; 434a1-5. On some readings, the only exception allowed at 428a11 is the grub (*skôlêx*), not the ant and bee.

[13] Aristotle *DA* 3.8, 432a10-12, cited by Terence Irwin, *Aristotle's First Principles*, Oxford 1988, § 168.

[14] Aristotle *DA* 3.3, 428a12; 18; b2; 17; 29.

[15] Aristotle *DA* 3.7, 431a8-12.

[16] Not the subsequent pursuit or avoidance.

no predication.[17] That appearance does none the less in some cases involve a combination (*sunthesis*) of terms is recognised by Aristotle's follower Alexander.[18]

The propositional (or predicational) content of perception and perceptual appearance helps to answer another problem. It has been thought that Aristotle oscillates wildly on the mental capacities he allows to animals.[19] Having distinguished animals from men as lacking reason in *On the Soul*, for example, he none the less allows the lion in the *Nicomachean Ethics* to entertain a proposition about the ox he is going to eat: that it is near. It can now be seen that this suggested oscillation is apparent rather than real. Perception was all along treated in *On the Soul* as admitting a propositional content; that was not the prerogative of reason.

Aristotle's expansion of perceptual content has a further significance, because from perceptions memory is derived and from memories experience (*empeiria*).[20] So the greater the content of animal perception, the greater the content of their memory and experience.

The Stoics on perceptual content in animals

We have seen how generous a content Aristotle gives to sense perception. And I have said that the denial of reason and belief to animals necessitated an expansion of their perceptual content. Ought we then not to find the same expansion in the Stoics, who also denied to animals reason and belief, although they slightly redefined reason?[21] They certainly allowed a generous content to perceptual appearances in humans. But as regards animals, the orthodox interpretation of the Stoics creates a problem, since it drastically restricts the perceptual content of animals to the same miserable confines as we found in Plato's *Theaetetus*. On this interpretation, which has attracted the ablest scholars,[22] perceptual appearance (*phantasia*) has propositional

[17] Aristotle *DA* 3.7, 431a14-16.

[18] Alexander *DA* 67,20-2.

[19] William W. Fortenbaugh, 'Aristotle: animals, emotion and moral virtue', *Arethusa* 4, 1971, 137-65.

[20] Aristotle *An Post.* 2.19, 100a5-6; *Metaph.* 1.1, 980b29-30.

[21] Reason is a collection of conceptions, Galen *PHP* 5.3, p. 304, de Lacy with English translation (= *SVF* 2.841) and as such can by the Middle Platonists be distinguished from the intellect as being its tool, 'Albinus' *Didaskalikos*, ch. 4, ed. in Hermann's *Plato*, by P. Louis as *Epitomé* in Budé and as Alcinoos *Enseignement* by John Whittaker in the most recent Budé (English translations by George Burges, 1854; Jeremiah Reedy 1991).

[22] Michael Frede, 'Stoics and sceptics on clear and distinct impressions', in Myles Burnyeat, ed., *The Skeptical Tradition*, Berkeley, California 1983, repr. in his *Essays in Ancient Philosophy*, Minneapolis 1987; Brad Inwood, *Ethics and Human Action in Early Stoicism*, Oxford 1985, 73-4, A.A. Long and D.N. Sedley, *The Hellenistic Philosophers* vol. 1, Cambridge 1987, 240; Jean-Louis Labarrière, '*Phantasia* et *logos* chez les animaux', in J. Brunschwig and M. Nussbaum, eds., *Passions and Perceptions*, Proceedings of the Fifth International Symposium on Hellenistic Philosophy, Cambridge

content only in humans, not in animals. How then are animals to do what they do in the world, since they have also been robbed of reason? Were the Stoics unaware of what animals are capable of doing? This seems unlikely. The Stoic Chrysippus produced an example, which greatly impressed King James I of England,[23] of a hunting dog which performs the analogue of a syllogism at the crossroads where its quarry might have gone in any of three directions. The dog sniffs the first two, perceives no scent and takes the third *without* sniffing. Of course, Chrysippus did not propose to admit that the dog was actually reasoning or forming *doxai* (beliefs). It was only doing something analogous. But how could there be any analogy, if its sense perception allowed it only to grasp a scent? If its behaviour is to be explicable, it must apprehend the absence of a scent and apprehend it as pertaining to one direction rather than another, all of which involves predication, even negative predication. I think the answer is that the Stoics did after all allow propositional, that is, predicational, content to perceptual appearance (*phantasia*) in the case of animals.

It may seem that there is an insuperable objection. How can an animal's perceptual appearance (*phantasia*) be propositional, even in the weak sense of involving predication, if it does not have concepts? Conceptions (*ennoiai*) and preconceptions (*prolêpseis*) for the Stoics are acquired only at a late stage, not only after perception, but after memory and experience (*empeiria*) has been acquired.[24] The absence of concepts from animals and infants has been given as one reason for denying that in Stoic theory their perceptual appearances have propositional content, at least in some sense of 'propositional'.[25]

The answer, as regards my sense of the word, will be given in the next chapter. We shall see that it is not obvious to many contemporary analytic philosophers that perceiving-that and perceiving-as involve the use of concepts. It need not have been obvious to the Stoics either. At the very least, they may have thought that animals without concepts can have the perceptual appearance of something *as* white. If this is conceded, it may still be objected that an appearance as of white falls short of an appearance *that* something is white, that the latter does involve the deployment of concepts and that it alone would be

---

1993. I am very grateful to all these authors and to Myles Burnyeat's and Doug Hutchinson's friendly and helpful discussion.

[23] The King responded that his hound could summon others, but was told that was by royal prerogative: see William J. Costello, *The Scholastic Curriculum at Early Seventeenth Century Cambridge*, Harvard Mass. 1958, 24-6. Information kindly sent me by Arthur Madigan.

[24] Aëtius 4.11.1-4 (*Dox. Gr.* 400; *SVF* 2.83).

[25] Michael Frede, op. cit.; A.A. Long and D.N. Sedley, op. cit., 240. The sense of 'propositional' here presumably relates to the Stoics' usage rather than to mine, but my interest is in seeing whether the lack of concepts would debar animals from having the appearance, propositional in my sense, *that* something is the case.

counted by the Stoics as corresponding to a proposition (*lekton*). But I am not aware that either the Stoics, or we ourselves, make such a neat distinction between *as* and *that*.

Let me turn now to a consideration on the other side. I think the Stoic texts show that a perceptual appearance which is propositional in the sense explained does not depend on being verbalised by its owner. For the texts repeatedly insist on using the modal idea that such propositional appearances are *verbalisable*, not that they are *verbalised*. If they are in fact verbalised, this is due to an independent operation of the mind. For example, the Stoics say not that perceptual appearance sets out in words what appears, but that it comes first (*proêgeitai*), and that subsequently (*eita*) thought (*dianoia*) sets out in words (*ekpherei logôi*) how one is affected by the perceptual appearance.[26] Similarly, perceptual appearance is something in accordance with which we are able to say (*eipein ekhomen*) – whether or not we do say – that there is a white subject acting on us.[27] Again, a true or false perceptual appearance is one of which it is *possible* (*esti*) to make, not one which itself makes, a true or false assertion (*katêgoria*). An example is the false assertion that the oar under water is bent.[28] Similarly, a rational perceptual appearance (*logikê phantasia*) is that in accordance with which it is *possible* (*esti*) to present in words (*parastêsai logôi*) what appears (*to phantasthen*).[29] There are further related points: for example, things perceived (*aisthêta*) are true not directly (*ex eutheias*), but by reference to parallel (*parakeimena*) things thought (*noêta*).[30]

This is already enough to show that perceptual appearances *that* something is the case, or *as of* something being the case, do not depend on people putting into words the proposition which appears to them. Nor presumably do they depend on people conceiving it as a thought, if the thought is merely '*parallel*' to the perception. It may be objected that this last testimony is isolated and that propositional appearances may therefore still depend on being *conceptualised*, even if they do not depend on being *verbalised*. But the Stoics do not draw attention to the possibility of conceptualisation without verbalisation – on one interpretation they even exclude it.[31]

[26] Diogenes Laertius *Lives* 7.49.
[27] Aëtius 4.12.1 (*Dox. Gr.* 401; *SVF* 2.54).
[28] Sextus *M* 7.244.
[29] Ibid. 8.70 (*SVF* 2.187).
[30] Ibid. 8.10 (*SVF* 2.195).
[31] So A.A. Long, 'Language and Thought in Stoicism', in his (ed.) *Problems in Stoicism*, London 1971, 75-113 at 82-4, cited with approval by Brad Inwood op. cit., 43, although some of the evidence depends on treating a *lekton* as said rather than sayable. On the other side, Michael Frede has pointed out to me that if the Stoics accepted an original giver of names, that person must have relied on non-verbalised concepts, when he imposed the first names. But though the first names were natural (onomatopoeic) for the Stoics, I have noticed no reference to a name-giver.

The suggestion that propositional appearances do not depend on being conceptualised is quite compatible with the claim that adult humans *do as a matter of fact* always conceive their perceptual appearances as thoughts. And there are texts which imply this, for we are repeatedly told that rational appearances, i.e. those of adult rational beings, are thoughts (*noêseis*), and that a *phantasma* falling on a rational soul is a thought (*ennoêma*).[32] But what convinces me less is the view[33] that an adult human's perceptual appearance depends for its existence on the conceptualisation which it is given. The conceptualisation may be invariable, but, like the verbalisation, I think it may be a logically independent operation.

Whatever may be true of adult humans, what are we to think of animals and infants? I have been saying that propositional appearances are defined as verbalisable and conceptualisable, not as verbalised and conceptualised. But must they be verbalisable and conceptualisable *by their owners*, or is it enough that they should be in principle verbalisable and conceptualisable *by us*? The texts do not say directly, but the weaker requirement, that propositional appearances need only be verbalisable and conceptualisable *by us*, would allow animals and infants to have perceptual appearances of a propositional sort.

What exactly goes on in a dog when it has the appearance of a scent as lying in a certain direction, the Stoics do not say. But it would be compatible with their view that the dog's *phantasia* should consist of a three-dimensional picture in which a warm glow, corresponding to the scent, lies in a certain corner, corresponding to the direction.[34] The dog would not have to bring together two items corresponding to our concepts of scent and direction, but the scent and the direction would both be represented in such a picture, and we would have to predicate the scent of the direction in order accurately to express the dog's *phantasia*.

Whatever the mechanism, the suggestion is that a dog's *phantasia* can be propositional. I think that the Stoics' own account of propositions fits perfectly well with what I have said, although I do not wish to suggest that they speak of propositions only in the very weak sense that I have offered of what is introduced by a 'that'-clause. The Stoic words for a proposition are *axiôma* and *lekton*, although *lekton* is a wider term, because it includes not only *axiômata*, but also questions, oaths and commands.[35] It may be thought that the Stoics were

---

[32] Aëtius 4.11.1-4 (*Dox. Gr.* 400; *SVF* 2.83); Diogenes Laertius *Lives* 7.51; 7.61; Stobaeus 1, p. 136,21, Wachsmuth (both in *SVF* 1.65); ps-Galen *Def. Med.* XIX 381, Kühn (*SVF* 2.89).

[33] Michael Frede, op. cit., 153-4; A.A. Long and D.N. Sedley, op. cit., 240.

[34] I thank Gisela Striker for this clarification of my interpretation.

[35] Diogenes Laertius *Lives* 7.66-7.

beginning to articulate the intentional character of propositions.[36] They saw, in other words, that it is perfectly possible to entertain the proposition that I shall inherit a fortune without my inheriting a fortune ever coming to be the case. The Stoics say that a *lekton* has neither full being nor non-being, but has an intermediate status: it merely subsists (*huphistasthai*) and is a something (*ti*) rather than a being (*on*).[37] Its lack of being is connected with its inability to act or be acted on.[38] What interests me for the present is that an *axiôma* is defined as assertible (*apophanton*), rather than asserted,[39] and a *lekton* is literally a sayable, rather than a thing said. Admittedly, the *-ton* ending could in principle imply something actually said, rather than merely sayable. But we know that not all *lekta* are *actually* said, because the effects of causes are all *lekta*, albeit 'incomplete ones', that is, they are predicates like being cut, or being burned, and many such effects have presumably never been put into words.[40] I assume that *lekta* are also conceptualisable. But I would hesitate to say that, as in some modern accounts of propositions, concepts would be actual *components* in a *lekton*. For the Stoics as materialists think of mental entities like concepts (*ennoiai, prolêpseis*) as being corporeal, and hence as having full being, whereas the *lekton* is one of the incorporeals, which lacks full being.[41]

So far it sounds as if a Stoic proposition could be entertained by an animal, since it may only have to be sayable or conceptualisable in principle, not actually said or conceived. But there is a severe difficulty which must be confronted first. A *lekton* is defined as corresponding only to a *rational* appearance,[42] and rational appearances are apparently confined to rational animals.[43] It may then seem to follow that what appears to a non-rational animal cannot have corresponding to it a *lekton*. But in fact this conclusion does not follow. For the *lekton* is being defined in the passage in question by reference to a sufficient, not a necessary, condition: what subsists in accordance with a rational perceptual appearance will certainly be a *lekton*, but there may be other *lekta* too. Indeed, we know there are. The ones that would interest us would subsist in accordance with *non-rational* perceptual appearances. But we know there must be *lekta* which correspond to no

---

[36] Victor Caston has made this suggestion in connexion with the Stoic concept of an *ennoêma* (literally, what is in thought), which, unlike a proposition, suffers from complete non-being: *Aristotle on Intentionality*, Ph.D. diss., Austin Texas 1992, p. 15.

[37] Diogenes Laertius *Lives* 7.63; Sextus M 8.70 (*SVF* 2.187); 10.218 (*SVF* 2.331); Plutarch *adv. Colot.* 1116B-C; *CN* 1074D (*SVF* 2.335).

[38] Plutarch *CN* 1073E; Proclus *in Tim.* (Diehl) 3.95.10-14.

[39] Diogenes Laertius *Lives* 7.65 (*SVF* 2.193); Aulus Gellius *Attic Nights* 16.8.1 (*SVF* 2.194).

[40] Sextus M 9.211. The point is well made by Long and Sedley op. cit. 201-2.

[41] Sextus M 10.218 (*SVF* 2.331).

[42] Sextus M 8.70; Diogenes Laertius *Lives* 7.63.

[43] Diogenes Laertius *Lives* 7.51.

appearances at all: the effects of causes which have never been noticed and so have never appeared to anyone.

There are three other apparent obstacles to my suggestion that Stoic animals can enjoy the appearance *that* something is the case, despite their lack of words and concepts. I shall address them in turn, before passing on to my positive evidence. The second problem is that rational perceptual appearances (*logikai phantasiai*) are said to be those of rational animals and are thoughts (*noêseis*), while non-rational appearances are those of non-rational animals.[44] It may then seem that the appearances enjoyed by non-rational animals are not conceptualisable at all, and *a fortiori* not conceptualisable as propositions. But the conclusion does not follow. For rational appearances might still be only a subclass of those that are conceptualisable, namely, those that are conceptualisable *by their owners*.

A third reason for doubt has been drawn from the text, if it represents Stoic theory at all,[45] which tells us that 'this is white' can be perceived (*percipere*) only in a way by the senses; it has to be grasped (*comprehendere*) by the mind (*animus*). But so far from casting doubt on the propositional character of appearance in animals, this may even confirm it. For if the senses can 'in a way' perceive 'this is white', that may be precisely because they present a non-verbalised appearance as of something's being white. There is another much more emphatic text that has been cited, which says that sense perception attends to or grasps (*epiballein, lambanein*) only colour, flavour and sound, whereas 'this is white', or 'this is sweet' is something that does not fall under it.[46] But this is the theory of Plato's *Theaetetus*, and there is nothing I know of in the passge to connect it to the Stoics. Further, no conclusion can be drawn from the text which tells us that the five senses are reporters (*nuntii*) of what they sense, the mind passes judgement (*judicat*) on what they report (*nuntiare*) and deliberation and reflection (*deliberatio, consideratio*) gather (*colligere*) from the reports what each thing is.[47] For this leaves it open how much the senses can be said to report.

Fourthly, a number of inferences have been drawn from Seneca's statement that perceptual appearances (*visus speciesque*) enjoyed by animals are turbid and jumbled (*turbidas et confusas*). But this does not tell us that they are inarticulate or unconnected with *lekta* (sayables).[48]

Let me turn from the obstacles to the positive evidence. One of the

[44] Ibid.

[45] Cicero *Acad.* 2.21, cited by Michael Frede, op. cit. and Jean-Louis Labarrière in J. Brunschwig and M. Nussbaum, eds., *Passions and Perceptions*, Proceedings of the Fifth International Symposium on Hellenistic Philosophy, Cambridge 1993.

[46] Sextus *M* 7.345, cited by Michae Frede, op. cit.

[47] Calcidius *in Tim.* 220, Waszink (*SVF* 2.879).

[48] Brad Inwood, op. cit., 73-4; Jean Louis Labarrière in *Passions and Perceptions* Proceedings of the Fifth International Symposium on Hellenistic Philosophy, 1993, citing Seneca *On Anger* 1.3.7.

most important considerations is Chrysippus' hunting dog. When it comes to its three-way crossroads, it is said, 'virtually' (*dunamei*) to go through a syllogism about its quarry: 'The animal went either this way, or that way, or the other way. But not this way, or that way. So that way.'[49] Chrysippus is not here conceding that the dog really reasons. But he presumably allows that it has perceptual appearances, even negative ones corresponding to the absence of a scent. And he seems quite happy to think that he, Chrysippus, can conceptualise and verbalise those appearances and do so in propositional form. The dog is not simply perceiving an unlocated scent.

So much for Chrysippus' dog. But what about Hierocles' frog? When this frog comes to a ditch, it blows itself up into a puffball, raises its little feet above its head for a soft landing, and, says Hierocles, is conscious (*sunaisthanetai*) of how far the drop is.[50] The Stoics Chrysippus, Seneca and Hierocles all talk about the self-preservation of animals depending on their awareness of their own persons.[51] Here it would not be enough to secure preservation that an animal's own body should appear to it without further characterisation. Admittedly neither Hierocles nor the others use the verb 'to appear' (*phainesthai*). But he repeatedly says that animals grasp (*antilambanesthai, katalambanein*) or are conscious ((*sun*)*aisthanesthai*) that their parts serve such and such a purpose, or that this is a strong point, that a weak point, in themselves or others. At least in many cases, then (I am not saying in all), the perceptual content of animal perception can be expressed in propositional (that is, in predicational) form.

Another striking piece of evidence is the method Seneca chooses for downgrading the mental capacities of animals by a process of redefinition. He denies that animals are capable of anger, because they are not rational,[52] whereas anger involves rational assent to the appearance of injustice (*species iniuriae*).[53] They merely seem to be angry because they have an appearance, albeit a muddled and confused one,[54] and an involuntary reaction (*impetus*), which is not, however, a rational one. Here in downgrading their capacities, Seneca none the less concedes that animals entertain at least a muddled appearance. And that muddled appearance is presumably a propositional one – the appearance that injustice has occurred.

The same view of animals is put in the mouth of a non-Stoic

---

[49] Sextus *PH* 1.69; Plutarch *De Sollertia Animalium* 969A-B; Philo *De Animalibus* 45; Porphyry *Abst.* 3.6; Aelian *Nat. An.* 6.59; Basil *Hexaemeron* 9.4.

[50] Hierocles, *Berliner Klassikertexte* 4, Berlin 1906, H. von Arnim, 1.39-5.7. The new edition by A.A. Long has only just come into my hands: *Corpus dei papiri filosofici greci e latini (CPF)*, vol. 1, Florence 1992, pp. 268-451. The relevant text is at pp. 300-26.

[51] Chrysippus ap. Diogenem Laertium *Lives* 7.85; Seneca *Ep.* 121,7-10.

[52] Seneca *On Anger* 1.3.4.

[53] Ibid. 2.3-4.

[54] Ibid. 1.3.7.

character, but with the standard Stoic example of a syllogistic premise (if it is day, it is light), by Plutarch. Only man has the idea of one thing *following* (*akolouthon*) from another.

> Even wild animals (*thêria*) have knowledge of the existence of things (*huparxeôs gnôsis*) but nature gave awareness and recognition of following (*akolouthou theôria kai krisis*) to man alone. Wolves, dogs and birds surely perceive (*aisthanesthai*) that it is day and light. But that if it is day, it is light, nothing other than man understands.[55]

This passage, though not explicitly mentioning the Stoics, is closely related to one which is standardly taken to refer to them. The Stoics hold that inference from signs is peculiar to man. Such inference involves syllogistic premises of an 'if ... then' variety, like those discussed in the Plutarch passage. In reserving it for man, the Stoics concede that non-rational animals receive perceptual appearances. What then do they deny? Not, it turns out, that these appearances are propositional, although that would have clinched the case, but only that these animals have appearances arising from inference and combination (*metabatikê, sunthetikê*), appearances which explain (*dioper*) our having the concepts of following (*akolouthia*: the same word as in the Plutarch text) and of signs:

> They say that man differs from the irrational animals not in uttered discourse (*logos*), for crows, parrots and jays utter articulate sounds, but in inner discourse, nor in just simple appearance (*phantasia*), for they too have appearances, but in inferential and combinatory (*metabatikê, sunthetikê*) appearance. And that is why man, having a concept of following (*akolouthia*), immediately grasps through following the idea of a sign (*sêmeion*). For a sign is itself of the form 'if this, then that'. So the existence of signs follows from the nature and constitution of man.[56]

Sextus exploits the animal's inability to grasp 'if-then' again, when he attacks the Stoic definition of a sign as corresponding to the 'if'-clause in a sound conditional statement (*sunêmmenon*).

> Yet why do we talk about humans when some of the (Stoics) transfer understanding of signs even to irrational animals. For the dog follows signs when it tracks the wild animal by its footprints, yet it does not for all that derive the appearance of a proposition (*axiôma*), 'if this is a footprint, there is a wild animal here'. And the horse leaps forward and gets ready (*orouei*) to run when the goad is applied or the whip brandished, but it does not dialectically judge a conditional (*sunêmmenon*), 'if the whip is brandished, I must run'.[57]

[55] Plutarch *On the E at Delphi* 386F-387A. I thank Brad Inwood for the reference.
[56] Sextus *M* 8.275-6.
[57] Ibid. 8.270-1.

Finally, Sextus Empiricus argues against the Stoics and other dogmatists that the perceptual appearances of other animals are not inferior to our own.[58] If he had known of a Stoic theory that they are not even propositional, he would have had to combat this first.

My interpretation implies an opposite answer to the interesting question that has been raised in recent literature, whether we should compare the Stoics with Donald Davidson or Daniel Dennett.[59] Davidson would be the orthodox choice, because he denies propositional attitudes to animals.[60] But I would prefer Dennett, if a selection is to be made, because Dennett allows the ascription of propositional attitudes to animals, provided their behaviour can be analysed *by us* in intentional terms.[61]

The Epicureans

The upshot would be that both Aristotle and the Stoics compensated animals for the loss of *doxa*, belief, by expanding the content of perception. Finally, the Epicureans also gave to perception a limited predicational content. The predicational content is limited, because although all perceptions and perceptual appearances are said to be true, they are true only of the films of atoms that impinge on the sense organs.[62] They are not true (or false) of the physical objects which transmit those films, although they may be true of how those objects *appear*.[63] Such truth about the *appearance* of the objects may mean that perception gives animals a sufficient guide to cope with the world.

The Epicureans, however, focused less on the need to expand perceptual content, because they had such varying views on the other resources available to animals. One Epicurean allows a mind to animals, while another, who denies this, none the less allows them analogues of belief. The most generous statement is that of Lucretius, who ascribes a mind (*mens, animus*) to horse, lion and deer.[64] He also

[58] Sextus *PH* 1.62-4.

[59] Christopher Gill, 'Is there a concept of person in Greek Philosophy?' in Stephen Everson, ed., *Psychology*, Cambridge 1991, at 173; 185-6; 190.

[60] Donald Davidson, 'Rational animals', *Dialectica* 36, 1982, 318-27, repr. in E. Lepore and B.P. McLaughlin, eds., *Actions and Events: Perspectives on the Philosophy of Donald Davidson*, Oxford 1985, 473-80.

[61] Daniel Dennett, 'Conditions of personhood', in A. Rorty, ed., *The Identities of Persons*, Berkeley and Los Angeles 1976, at 181-7.

[62] Sextus M 7.205; 7.208-10; 8.63; Epicurus *Letter to Herodotus* in Diogenes Laertius *Lives* 10.50-1.

[63] Vision, for example, sees a tower as small and round, or as large and square. Sextus *M* 7.208-9; Lucretius 4.353-63.

[64] Lucretius 2.265; 268; 270; 3.299. For the disagreement on mind, see H. Diels, ed., Philodemus *Über die Götter* 1, p. 63; Julia Annas, 'Epicurus on agency', in J. Brunschwig, M. Nussbaum, eds., *Passions and Perceptions*, Cambridge 1993.

insists that animals can dream,[65] a process in which the mind (*mens, animus, mens animi*) or thought (the corresponding word in Epicurus is *dianoia*) selects for close attention some of the many configurations of atoms that impinge on us.[66] Other Epicureans do deny to animals reason and reasoning (*logos, logismos, epilogismos*),[67] and Philodemus adds that animals lack thinking (*nôesis*),[68] except insofar as perceptual consciousness, or consciousness of one's own impulses can be called thinking.[69] He suggests that they lack belief (*doxa*) and false belief (*pseudodoxia*).[70] But it is he who maintains that animals can have something analogous to expectation (*prosdokia*),[71] and at one point, instead of speaking of analogues of belief, he even ascribes them analogous *beliefs*.[72]

[65] Lucretius 4.984-1010.

[66] Epicurus *Letter to Herodotus* in Diogenes Laertius *Lives* 10.51; Lucretius 4.728-31; 747-8; 750-61; 767; 803-15; 975-7.

[67] Hermarchus ap. Porphyrium *Abstinence* 1.12 (*logos*); Polystratus *On Irrational Contempt* col. 6 Indelli (*logismos*); col. 7 (*logismos* at least such as ours); Philodemus *On the Gods* col. 13, line 2 Diels (*epilogismos*); 15.28 (*logismos*).

[68] Philodemus *On the Gods* 12.17; 13.39.

[69] Ibid. 13.16; 13.39-40.

[70] Ibid. 13.6-7 (*doxa*); 14.34 (*pseudodoxia*).

[71] Ibid. 13.17-18.

[72] Ibid. 14.6-8.

CHAPTER THREE

Concepts and perceptual appearance without reason or belief

How can the lion perceive that the ox is near, if it does not have the concept of an ox? And how can it perceive that the ox is near without believing that the ox is near, which it is not supposed to be able to do? These are the two questions which I shall address in this chapter.

Aristotle on concepts

On the first, the concepts, Aristotle might find two answers. First, some animals may perhaps have concepts. Secondly, Aristotle might take comfort from certain modern discussions which purport to show that one can perceive something as near, without having the corresponding concepts.[1] As it happens, this connects with our other question, because it is said that belief differs precisely in this regard: one cannot believe something to be near without having the corresponding concepts.

A suggested example of perceiving-as without concepts is provided by the person who perceives a mountainside as having a certain very complicated contour, without having the concept of a contour as complicated as that. It is not a simple S-bend, for example. The plausibility of this claim will depend partly on what it is to have a concept: on various accounts of that, no concept would be needed.[2] But there is a more formal argument for perceptual predication without

---

[1] See Gareth Evans, *The Varieties of Reference*, Oxford 1982; Christopher Peacocke, 'Analogue Content', *Proceedings of the Aristotelian Society*, supp. vol. 60, 1986, 1-17; id. 'Perceptual Content', in J. Almog, J. Perry, H. Wettstein, eds., *Themes from Kaplan*, Oxford 1989; Timothy Crane, 'The Waterfall illusion', *Analysis* 48, 1988, 142-7; Alan Millar, 'What's in a look?', *Proceedings of the Aristotelian Society* 86, 1985-6, 83-97.

[2] Peter Geach, *Mental Acts*, London 1957, makes a recognitional capacity amount to possession of a concept, but our observer may not have a concept in that sense, since he may not even be able to recognise the contour again. Still more is required for concept possession by Christopher Peacocke, 'What are concepts?', *Midwest Studies in Philosophy* 1989, and in Terence Irwin's account of Aristotle, *Aristotle's First Principles*, Oxford 1988, §169, on which see below. On these accounts, *a fortiori* no concept will be needed.

concepts, which can be expressed in terms of another example of Aristotle's. The argument is that if you can rationally wonder with regard to the perceived length of a footrule and the perceived diameter of the sun whether these two lengths are really the same, you must be conceptualising them differently – even if you are conceptualising each as 'that length'. For after all no one can rationally wonder whether A is A, where A is one and the same concept, but only whether A is B. None the less, even though you are conceptualising the two lengths differently, you may be perceiving them in exactly the *same* way, so it is claimed. At any rate you are not conscious of a difference, and *inter alia* you may be perceiving them as the same length. All this implies that your *perceiving* them does not involve conceptualising.[3]

The modern argument would add a further claim. The perception of two lengths as matching and the belief that they match will not have strictly identical contents in these cases. For concepts will enter into the very content of the belief. Does this make the modern position after all alien to Aristotle's?[4] Not necessarily. For one thing, the contents, even if not identical, must be very closely related, if the belief is to be an endorsement of the perception. For another thing, questions of difference of content are well within Aristotle's repertoire. Plato had laid it down that different faculties like knowledge and belief must have different objects,[5] and Aristotle followed this line of thought when he said that, in giving an account of psychological faculties, we must first give an account of their objects.[6] But Plato's insistence on different objects is hard to accommodate in those dialogues where he treats knowledge as simply a kind of belief which meets certain extra conditions.[7] Similarly, Aristotle might have found it hard to see how perceiving the ox as near can have a different content from believing that the ox is near, if the belief can be an endorsement of the perception. The modern insistence that the content is different, but very closely related, would constitute an addition to Aristotle's views, but not a departure in a totally different direction.

Aristotle's other defence for his description of the lion perceiving the ox as near would be to argue that some animals do have concepts. He does discuss the issue of whether perception involves concepts, in a passage, *An. Post.* 2.19, which may again be a development of Alcmaeon.[8] The passage is sometimes suspected of 'vacillating' between our acquisition of universal concepts and our acquisition of

---

[3] Example adapted from Christopher Peacocke (1986 and forthcoming). For a related argument see Timothy Crane op. cit.

[4] I thank Mark Sainsbury for raising the question.

[5] Plato *Republic* 477C-D.

[6] Aristotle *DA* 2.4, 415a20-2; 2.6, 418a7-8; cf. 1.1, 402b14-16.

[7] Plato *Meno* 97C-98A; *Theaetetus* 201C-210B.

[8] Assuming it is Alcmaeon who is in question at Plato *Phaedo* 95B.

universal truths.[9] In fact there is no conflict: to acquire one is to
acquire the other as the preceding discussion in *An. Post.* 2.8-11 shows.
To acquire the universal truth that lunar eclipse is some kind of lunar
loss of light, or that it is a lunar loss of light due to the earth's
screening of the sun, is to acquire an (increasingly scientific) concept of
lunar eclipse. The discussion at *An. Post.* 2.19 clearly shows that sense
perception must chronologically precede (so that it does not
presuppose) the formation of universal concepts. On this both Stoics
and Epicureans would agree. Perceptual appearance for them precedes,
and cannot presuppose, the formation of conceptions (*ennoiai*) and preconceptions (*prolêpseis*).[10]

Aristotle does not go back on this when he says that perception
involves receiving *forms*.[11] The forms are perceptible, not intelligible,
forms, and I have argued elsewhere that they are particulars,
particular colour patches, for example.[12] They are not universal
concepts. When Aristotle twice says that perception is of the universal,
of man, not of the man Callias,[13] he is not withdrawing his repeated
claim that what we perceive is particular.[14] He will not want like Plato
to allow that a baby's first perceptions already presuppose universal
concepts, or he will have lost his alternative to Plato's view that a baby
is born with access to universal concepts inherited from a previous
life.[15] His alternative is that universal concepts can be acquired by a
gradual transition starting from sense perception. So when he says
that universal perception is of the universal, his point is that, if we
take perception in general rather than a particular act of perceiving,
we will cite as its object things like man, rather than things like
Callias. And this is meant further to ease the transition from memories
of individual men perceived to the first universal in the soul, e.g. man.
It may seem confusing when Aristotle adds[16] that this first universal is
present in the soul upon the stabilisation there of a *single*
undifferentiated thing (*stantos tôn adiaphorôn henos*), because we

---

[9] Jonathan Barnes, *Aristotle's Posterior Analytics*, Oxford 1975, 249; 260, citing F.
Solmsen, *Die Entwicklung der Aristotelischen Logik und Rhetorik*, Berlin 1929, 95-101.
The correct view is given by Deborah Modrak, *Aristotle: the Power of Perception*,
Chicago, 1987, 162; 164.

[10] See for the Stoics e.g. Cicero *Acad.* 2.30-1; Aëtius 4.11,1-4 (*Dox. Gr.* 400; *SVF* 2.83),
and for the Epicureans e.g. Diogenes Laertius *Lives* 10.31, and Philodemus *On the Gods*
col. 12, line 10 (Diels): animals lack *hupolêpseis*. I doubt Diels' view in his edition (p. 63)
that in Polystratus *On Irrational Contempt*, col. 1, the words 'each of these' refer to
concepts possessed by animals.

[11] Aristotle *DA* 2.12, 424a18-19; a23; b2-3; 3.2, 427a8-9; 3.12, 434a30.

[12] Richard Sorabji, 'Intentionality and physiological processes: Aristotle's theory of
sense perception', in M. Nussbaum and A. Rorty, eds., *Essays on Aristotle's de Anima*,
Oxford 1992.

[13] Aristotle *An. Post* 1.31, 87b28-30; 2.19, 100a16-18.

[14] Aristotle *DA* 2.5, 417b22-3; *An. Post* 1.18, 81b6; 1.31, 87b28-39; 2.19, 100a17.

[15] Plato *Phaedo* 75B-C.

[16] Aristotle *An. Post* 2.19, 100a15-16.

have been told that the universal is not stabilised until *many* perceptions have lingered (*monê*) in the soul in the form of memories.[17] But the easiest (not the only) interpretation is that the single undifferentiated thing is not a single perception, but a concept like that of man which is not differentiated into further sub-species. The passage runs as follows:

> We must then have some capacity, but not such as to be superior to these in accuracy. And it evidently belongs to all animals. For they have an innate discriminative capacity which is called perception. But when perception is present, in some animals the sense image (*aisthêma*) comes to remain (*monê*), and in some not. Where it does not at all, or does not for certain things, there and for those things there is no awareness (*gnôsis*) outside perception. But there is [such awareness] in those animals which can keep it (*ekhein*) in their minds (*psukhê*) after perception. And when many such [sense images] have come [to remain], there comes then to be a certain distinction, so that reason (*logos*) develops out of their remaining in the case of some animals, and in the case of others not. Thus out of perception arises memory, so we say, and out of memory often repeated of the same thing, experience (*empeiria*). For memories which are many in number are a single case of experience. And from experience, or from the whole universal come to rest (*êremêsan*) in the mind, the one beside the many which is one and the same in all of them, comes the origin of technical skill (*tekhnê*) and scientific understanding (*epistême*), skill if it is concerned with coming into being, understanding if with being. Thus dispositions are neither present as determinate entities, nor developed out of cognitively superior dispositions, but out of perception. As when a rout occurs in a battle, if one man makes a stand, so does another and then another, until it has got back to the start of the rout. The mind is such as to be capable of this effect.
>
> But let us say again what was said before, but with insufficient clarity. When one undifferentiated [species] has made a stand, a first universal is in the mind. [This happens] because, whereas one perceives a particular, perception is of the universal, e.g. of man, not of the man Callias. Again a stand is made among these [undifferentiated species], until the undivided [species] and the universal [genera] are standing, e.g. an animal of this kind until animal.[18]

Although perception does not presuppose universal concepts, Aristotle does not deny that once one has such concepts, one may bring them to bear in perception. Could Aristotle's lion then bring to bear the concept of an ox? The evidence is conflicting. In one text, Aristotle denies that animals (*thêria*) have any universal apprehension

---

[17] Ibid. 2.19, 99b36-100a6.
[18] Ibid. 2.19, 99b32-100b3.

(*katholou hupolêpsis*).[19] But on the other hand, he says that animals have a little experience (*empeiria*: compare our 'empirical'). 'Little' need not mean 'none', as the commentator Alexander, followed by Asclepius, half suspects.[20] And, on the only natural interpretation, in the passage just translated, experience is equated with the possession of a rudimentary universal in the phrase, 'experience, or the universal stabilised in the soul'.[21] Rather cleverly, Aristotle makes the transition to the experienced man's universal smooth, by saying here that experience is no more than a collection of particular memories of the same thing.[22] In other words, many memories of oxen *are* the experiential concept of an ox, a theory not unknown in modern science.[23] When Aristotle says 'experience, or ...', the 'or' is most unlikely to be introducing a new, unexplained alternative to experience,[24] because Aristotle's whole purpose is to show how smoothly we can progress from lower levels of cognition to higher ones, even if at the still higher level of scientific concepts, we just have to be capable of spotting the truth (*nous*).

Admittedly, the man of experience is described as knowing the particular (*kath'hekaston*) not the universal (*katholou*),[25] and as not yet having the single universal (*mia katholou*) involved in technical understanding (*tekhnê*).[26] But what counts as universal and what as particular is relative to context, and it turns out that he is not denied low-level universals after all. He knows that fowl is good for health, but not the explanatory, technical universal that light meat is good for health. He can operate with the low-level universal 'this remedy', 'this illness'. But he lacks the explanatory, technical universal that this remedy helps all phlegmatic, or bilious, or feverish people, when they have this illness.

---

[19] Aristotle *NE* 7.3, 1147b5, cited by Christopher Gill, 'Is there a concept of person in Greek Philosophy?', in Stephen Everson, ed., *Aristotle's Philosophy of Mind*, Cambridge 1991, at 179-80, but in citing *Metaph.* 1.1, he does not advert to its contrary implication. The passage is also stressed by Terry Irwin, *Aristotle's First Principles*, §169. Robert Bolton suggests to me the passage could be discounted, if it is only denying to animals universal maxims of the kind Aristotle is discussing ('chicken is good for health').

[20] Aristotle *Metaph.* 1.1, 980b26-7, with Alexander in *Metaph.* 4,15; Asclepius in *Metaph.* 7,24.

[21] Aristotle *An. Post* 2.19, 100a6-8.   [22] Ibid. 2.19, 100a5-6.

[23] E.E. Smith and D.L. Medin, *Categories and Concepts*, Cambridge Mass. 1981, ch. 7, 'The exemplar view'. I owe the reference to Alvin Goldman.

[24] It has been suggested to me that the 'or', instead of glossing 'experience', might introduce an alternative to experience, meaning 'or better'. But that would be a very abrupt introduction of an unexplained alternative. It has also been suggested to me that if 'or' introduces an alternative, that alternative might be explained, if it is the technological skill (*tekhnê*) which is introduced by Aristotle below. But the end of Aristotle's sentence says that what has been referred to is not technological skill itself but merely that from which comes the origin (*arkhê*) of technological skill. It would be hard to reinterpret the end of the sentence as meaning that experience provides the origin of technological skill, and technological skill the origin of scientific understanding (*epistêmê*).

[25] Aristotle *NE* 6.7, 1141b14-21.   [26] Aristotle *Metaph.* 1.1, 981a5-7.

On the suggestion I am making, for the lion to have a rudimentary concept of an ox is no more than for it to have many memories of individual oxen. But I must acknowledge another interpretation which makes Aristotle's requirements for concept possession very much steeper. To possess a concept F, you must recognise some feature as a *reason* you could give for calling something F, so that you would not be misled by a merely concomitant feature.[27] I call this a steep requirement, because I am not sure that all humans could meet the demand for freedom from error and ability to speak and give reasons, and I am not sure that there always are further reasons for calling something, say, a pain.

The Stoics were less accommodating than Aristotle. They did not allow his view that experience already involved the possession of rudimentary concepts. For them concepts are acquired only after experience.[28] Moreover, some Stoics denied animals the ability to learn by experience (*experisci, experimentum, usus*), in contexts where others might have allowed it.[29] This is not altogether surprising. For although they agree with Aristotle that experience is a multiplicity (*plêthos*) of similar appearances from many memories,[30] and treat memory as a storing of appearances,[31] some of them deny memory to animals, as we shall see in Chapter Four, on the grounds that memory involves reason.

Perceptual appearance without belief in Aristotle

So much for animal concepts. We must now confront the other question. If the lion can perceive that the ox is near, how does this differ from believing (*doxazein*) that the ox is near, which the lion is not supposed to be able to do? One modern answer would be precisely that believing involves concepts.[32] Aristotle, however, makes at least four attempts to distinguish belief from perception.

First he introduces the idea that perception is a kind of discriminating (*krinein, kritikê*). It has been argued by Theo Ebert that *krinein* does not in the Greek of Aristotle's time mean an ordinary judgement,[33] even though, as we shall see in Chapter Four, it does

[27] See Terence Irwin's very interesting interpretation in *Aristotle's First Principles*, Oxford 1988, §169.

[28] Aëtius, 4.11.1-4 (*Dox. Gr.* 400; *SVF* 2.83).

[29] Seneca *Ep.* 121,19-23; Hierocles 1.51-3.52 (von Arnim and Schubart).

[30] Aëtius, 4.11.1-4 (*Dox. Gr.* 400; *SVF* 2.83).

[31] Sextus *M* 7.372 (*SVF* 2.56).

[32] Gareth Evans, *The Varieties of Reference*, Oxford 1982, 227; Christopher Peacocke, 'Analogue content', *Proceedings of the Aristotelian Society*, supp. vol. 60, 1986, p. 14, n. 11.

[33] Theo Ebert, 'Aristotle on what is done in perceiving', *Zeitschrift für philosophische Forschung* 37, 1983, 181-98. It is already used for giving a legal judgement as well as for discriminating.

later on in Hellenistic texts. If so, there should be no danger of confusing it with *doxa* (belief). But it can cover a wide range of activities short of belief from the perception of colour to the perception of propositions. It can cover, for example, the kind of activity in which a bird engages in selecting some feathers for its nest while discarding others.

Aristotle's second device for making perception fall short of belief commits him to disagreeing with Plato. For Plato had defined perceptual appearance (*phantasia*) and illusion as kinds of belief (*doxa*).[34] Aristotle denies that perceptual appearance is belief,[35] and he produces a brilliant argument for his denial: we can have the perceptual appearance that the sun is quite small, only a foot across, but we may believe that it is very large.[36] This argument enables Aristotle to treat perception and perceptual appearance as only a half-way house on the way to *doxa*. His argument has been much repeated in the modern literature against the view that perception is some function of belief,[37] and indeed it conclusively proves that the perceptual appearance that p cannot be the belief *that p*. The opposition would need to show that it was some *other* belief.

Aristotle further attempts the harder task of saying how appearance differs from belief (*doxa*). This had never been attempted before, and it is not surprising if his attempt is not altogether persuasive. He has two arguments separated by a 'furthermore',[38] and it is wrong to strike out one as if it were a repetition of the other.[39] First, belief involves being convinced (*pistis, pisteuein*), which animals cannot be. Perhaps Aristotle would have defended this denial by saying that animals cannot be unconvinced either. Aristotle's other claim is that belief involves being persuaded (*pepeisthai, peithô*), which in turn implies possessing reason (*logos*). This has been called a 'rhetorical' criterion for belief, on the grounds that persuasion involves dialogue with *others*,[40] or,

[34] Plato *Sophist* 263E-264D; *Republic* 603A.

[35] *DA* 3.3, 428a18-24; b3-10. Also appearance is not, and is not thought to be, any kind of reasoning (*dianoia*) or apprehension (*hupolêpsis*), 3.3, 427b14-15; 27-8, where these capacities *include* belief (*doxa*), 3.3, 427b8-13; 24-6.

[36] Aristotle *DA* 3.3, 428b3-10; the example is repeated at *Insom.* 1, 458b29; 2, 460b18. In this last passage, Aristotle contrasts what appears (*phainetai*) with what we say (*phamen*) and give as our verdict (if *krinein* here has its legal sense).

[37] It is recognised as a difficulty by D.M. Armstrong, *A Materialist Theory of the Mind*, London 1968 (relevant section reprinted in Jonathan Dancy, *Perceptual Knowledge*, Oxford 1988), and it is urged as a difficulty against theories such as those of D.M. Armstrong and George Pitcher (*A Theory of Perception*, Princeton 1971) by F. Jackson, *Perception*, Cambridge 1977; J. Fodor, *The Modularity of Mind*, Cambridge Mass. 1983; Timothy Crane, 'The waterfall illusion', *Analysis* 48, 1988, 142-7; id., *The Content and Causation of Thought*, ch. 4, Ph.D. Diss., Cambridge 1989.

[38] Aristotle *DA* 3.3, 428a18-24. The Loeb and Oxford translations obscure the meaning.

[39] Biehl, Torstrik, W.D. Ross.

[40] Jean-Louis Labarrière, 'Imagination humaine et imagination animale chez Aristote', *Phronesis* 29, 1984, 17-49, at 31-4.

according to another commentator, *communication*.[41] But I think that what Aristotle actually has in mind is Plato's definition of belief in the *Theaetetus* and *Sophist* as the outcome of a silent conversation (*logos*) within the soul.[42] Plato says explicitly that others are not involved,and I assume that correspondingly Aristotle would allow his persuasion to be self-persuasion.[43] Otherwise all conclusions drawn from rational self-persuasion would have to be downgraded from beliefs to mere appearances, and this can hardly be Aristotle's intention.[44] The denial that what animals have is belief is not a mere piece of verbal legislation. In the absence of conviction and self-persuasion, Aristotle would think we were wrong to describe their state as belief.

This verdict would hardly be true of the English word 'belief'. The nervous examinee who believes that 1066 is the date of the Battle of Hastings may, through nervousness, not be convinced, and need not have been persuaded. Plato's treatment of *doxa* in the *Theaetetus*, as described in Chapter One, is more plausible, because he allows that, while some beliefs are the result of persuading oneself in an internal debate, others, like the belief that Socrates is coming down the road, are due to memory and perception, with persuasion playing no obvious role.

The conviction and persuasion required by Aristotle do not look quite the same as the assent (*sunkatathesis*) to appearance that was later made a prerequisite for belief by the Stoics. But the Aristotelian Alexander substitutes that Stoic notion for Aristotle's persuasion.[45] And still later, the Neoplatonist Simplicius provides a rationale. Conviction just is assent (*sunkatathesis*) to something as true; it is the goal aimed at by persuasion. Persuasion is assent in process of being produced by reasoning (*logos*), while conviction is that assent already in existence.[46]

Aristotle's denial of belief and reason to animals in the *de Anima* passage is emphatic:

> It remains then to see if [appearance (*phantasia*)] is belief (*doxa*), for belief comes both true and false. But belief involves conviction (*pistis*),

[41] Christopher Gill, 'Is there a concept of person in Greek Philosophy?', in Stephen Everson, ed., *Ancient Philosophy of Mind*, Cambridge 1991, at 180. This is also the interpretation of William Fortenbaugh, *Aristotle on Emotion*, London 1975, p. 69n.

[42] Plato *Theaetetus* 189E-190A; Sophist 263E ff.

[43] If self-persuasion is envisaged, this will actually enhance the comparison made by Gill op. cit., 191 with Donald Davidson's view that belief involves the capacity for belief about beliefs.

[44] Fortenbaugh has suggested to me that belief might involve only the *possibility* of being persuaded, and given this weaker requirement, the persuasion envisaged could still plausibly be taken to be persuasion by *others*. But I do not find this a very natural reading. For Aristotle says belief *always* involves being convinced, and it is the *conviction* which implies being persuaded and presumably such persuasion is not a mere possibility, but has actually taken place.

[45] Alexander *de Anima* 67,16-20.

[46] Simplicius(?) *in DA* 3 211,22-7.

since in believing one cannot fail to be convinced (*pisteuein*) by what one believes, whereas conviction is found in no beasts (*thêria*), appearance in many. Furthermore, all belief involves conviction, conviction involves having been persuaded (*pepeisthai*) and persuasion (*peithô*) involves reason (*logos*). Yet whereas appearance is found in some beasts, reason is not.[47]

After this denial, it would be strange if Aristotle went back and allowed belief to animals after all. Such a contradiction has been detected in a later passage,[48] where he offers to explain why belief is believed (*dokei*) to be absent from something – probably from animals.[49] But there is no reason to think he is not *endorsing* the explanandum: their lack of belief. The chief problem resides in the ambiguity of the pronouns or articles ('they lack that one and this implies that'). But I think he means that animals are thought to lack belief because they lack a certain kind of appearance (*phantasia*) which implies belief, namely the kind of ability to manipulate images which has just been described as involved in practical reasoning. Animals do, however, we are explicitly told,[50] possess another kind of appearance. In other words, it is not one kind of *belief*, but one kind of *appearance*, which animals are here being granted. The interpretation to the contrary is encouraged by unnecessary tinkering with the manuscripts and the deletion of their reading 'this implies that', although even that deletion does not justify saddling Aristotle with a contradiction on whether animals have belief.

Perceptual appearance and thinking

Even if Aristotle never concedes belief to animals, it has been suggested that he concedes thinking (*noêsis*), by equating certain kinds of appearance (*phantasia*) with thinking. It is true that in *On the Motion of Animals* thinking and appearance are bracketed together as helping to explain the voluntary movements of animals,[51] and treated as if they were much the same thing. A similar role for thinking along with deliberate choice (*proairesis*) is suggested early in *On the Soul*.[52] But this time we are warned that the suggestion is only a preliminary one by its being called an appearance (*phainetai*), and by our

---

[47] Aristotle *DA* 3.3, 428a18-24.

[48] Ibid. 3.11, 434a10-11, as interpreted by D.W. Hamlyn, *Aristotle's De Anima, books II and III*, Clarendon Aristotle Series, Oxford 1968, 153.

[49] On another interpretation, from appearance (*phantasia*).

[50] Aristotle *DA* 3.11, 434a5-7.

[51] Aristotle *Mot.* 7, 701a34-6; 701b18-19. In humans, by contrast, thinking is distinguished from appearance: 8, 702a18-20.

[52] *DA* 1.3, 406b24-5.

knowledge that deliberate choice is elsewhere denied to animals.[53] The correction of the preliminary statement comes in *On the Soul* Book 3, although, curiously enough, that is where the equation of appearance and thinking has chiefly been detected. In the most discussed passage, Aristotle says, 'if someone were to classify appearance as a sort of thinking (*hôs noêsin tina*)'.[54] But it has been acknowledged that he immediately goes on to say, 'in the other animals neither thinking (*noêsis*) nor reasoning (*logismos*) is found, but appearance (*phantasia*)'.[55] It has also been acknowledged that the 'as' (*hôs*) in 'classify as' may constitute a qualification. So does the 'a sort of (*tina*) thinking' and the 'if someone were to classify'. I cannot therefore see that any weight can be rested on this passage. Nor can much be gained from the passage which says that appearance (*phantasia*) is believed (*dokei*) to be one of two kinds of thinking (*noein*),[56] since this is clearly reporting the views of others. Moreover, the passage and its surroundings distinguish appearance from at least two kinds of thinking. First it is not reasoning (*dianoia, dianoeisthai*)[57] or (equivalently) apprehension (*hupolêpsis*), capacities which are explained as presupposing reason, as admitting correctness and incorrectness, and, when correct, as covering scientific understanding (*epistêmê*), belief (*doxa*) and practical understanding (*phronêsis*).[58] Appearance is not even thought (*dokei*) to be that kind of apprehension (*hupolêpsis*).[59] But equally appearance is also said to be different from another kind of thinking, the intuitive understanding (*nous*) which is always correct,[60] and which differs from reasoning (*dianoia*) in involving no steps of reasoning. According to Aristotle's official account, human thinking requires appearance, but is not the same thing. It requires it, because it requires a certain type of appearance, namely a mental image (*phantasma*) on which to operate.[61]

Why then is Aristotle at all attracted, as he sometimes is, by the popular equation of appearance with thinking? We need to distinguish thinking *that* something is the case from other kinds of thinking. In *On*

[53] This, I think, is why animals do not engage in action (*praxis*) in the full sense, *NE* 6.2, 1139a20. Further, they cannot exercise deliberate choice, because they cannot deliberate, *HA* 1.1, 488b24-6.

[54] *DA* 3.10, 433a9-10, cited by Jean-Louis Labarrière, 'Imagination humaine et imagination animal chez Aristote', *Phronesis* 29, 1984, 17-49, at 20-1; cf. 26-30.

[55] *DA* 3.10, 433a11-12.

[56] Ibid. 3.3, 427b27-8.

[57] Ibid. 427b14-15.

[58] Ibid. 427b8-14; 24-6.

[59] Ibid. 427b27-28.

[60] Ibid. 428a1-5; 16-18.

[61] My understanding of *phantasma* as mental image (*Aristotle on Memory*, London 1972) I take to be confirmed by the very pictorial account of it throughout *On Memory* and *On Dreams*. This interpretation has been defended by Pamela Huby, 'Aristotle, *De Insomniis* 462a18', *Classical Quarterly* 25, 1975, 151-2.

the Soul and *On Memory*, Aristotle discusses the idle contemplation of pleasant or frightening things and the contemplation of mental images (*phantasmata*) which we have placed before our eyes (*pro ommatôn*). Such contemplation can be desribed as thinking (*noein, noêsis, noêma, nous, dianoeisthai*).[62] But it is unlike thinking *that* something is the case, and is therefore unlike belief. Indeed, Aristotle contrasts it with belief.[63] He can therefore safely attribute it to animals, and he can equate it, when speaking in the popular way, with one kind of appearance, a kind which I have called post-perceptual appearance, although he classifies it differently.[64] It is of such appearance that he says no combination of concepts and no affirmation or negation, is involved.[65] Such contemplation of pleasant or frightening things is, presumably, as capable as sense perception of prompting animal behaviour. Aristotle tells us that it stirs our bodies, although in the human case it does not necessarily lead to action.[66] To grant that animals may engage in thinking in this sense is not yet to accord them anything like belief.

The idea that appearance that something is the case can amount to thinking it the case was introduced only after Aristotle by the Stoics. We are repeatedly told by them that rational appearances (*logikai phantasiai*), i.e. those of rational beings as opposed to animals, actually are thoughts (*noêseis*), and that a *phantasma* falling on a rational soul already is a thought (*ennoêma*).[67] In Chapter Two, I took the Stoics to mean that humans frame their appearances in terms of concepts. On the other hand, for animals, appearances are not thus conceptualised, merely conceptualisable by us. Moreover, the Stoics would still agree with Aristotle's view that appearance falls short of belief and other mental states.

Perceptual appearance without belief in the Stoics

Why does it fall short? The answer lies in the concept of assent (*sunkatathesis, adsensio*) which was introduced by Zeno of Citium, the man who founded the Stoa around 300 BC. Appearances are received by the senses, but distinct from these is the assent of the soul (*anima*),

---

[62] Aristotle *Mem.* 1, 449b30-450a7; 450b20-451a2; *On the Soul* 3.3, 427b21-4; 3.9, 432b29-433a1.

[63] Aristotle *DA* 3.3, 427b21-4.

[64] Aristotle calls it perceptual (*DA* 3.11, 434a5), not to imply that perception is currently going on (which is how I have used the term), but to contrast it with *deliberative* appearance: the manipulation of mental images in deliberation.

[65] Aristotle *DA* 3.8, 432a11-13.

[66] Ibid. 3.9, 432b29-433a1; *Mot.* 11, 703b7-8.

[67] Aëtius 4.11.1-4 (*Dox. Gr.* 400; *SVF* 2.83); Diogenes Laertius *Lives* 7.51; 7.61; Stobaeus 1, p. 136,21, Wachsmuth (both in *SVF* 1.65); ps-Galen *Def. Med.* XIX 381, Kühn (*SVF* 2.89). Aristotle's follower Alexander of Aphrodisias disagrees, *Fate* 186,3-12.

mind (*animus*), or (in humans) reason (*logos, logikê dunamis*).[68] And something much more important to the Stoics than belief depends on this assent, namely perception (*aisthêsis, sensus*). Perception is not the same as appearance, but requires, or rather actually is, an assent to appearance.[69] One source, Cicero's spokesman for Antiochus, who tried to harmonise Platonism and Stoicism, draws a conclusion for animals. They must either be granted assent, or denied perception.[70] For the Stoics the second course would be easy, for animals could be granted appearance (*phantasia*), while being denied the assent necessary for perception (*aisthêsis*).

The Stoics are indeed said to hold that animals lack assent.[71] They assent neither to factual appearances, nor to evaluative ones about what is to be done. Why should the Stoics have supposed this? One rationale would be the thought that animals cannot withhold assent and so should not be said to give it either. This rationale would moreover explain the rival reports we have that the Stoics made animals assent to their appearances, but assent invariably and automatically.[72] It is usual to sweep one set of reports or the other under the carpet and make the most of the other. But in fact they are both intelligible, because from a non-Stoic point of view they come to the same thing. Animals are, as Clement says, carried away with (*sunapopheresthai*) their appearances. We can see why some people should express this by saying that they always assent, while others should say that, since they cannot withhold assent, this does not amount to assent after all.

From the Stoic point of view, however, the two statements do not come to the same thing. For they hope[73] the idea that reason can withhold assent gives them a way of showing that our actions can be 'up to us', in spite of their belief in determinism – the belief that whatever happens has all along been inevitable or necessary. Speaking from an indeterminist perspective,[74] I agree that there is a very large difference between those who are capable of reflecting on their appearances and those who are not. And I think the capacity so to reflect is indeed relevant to moral responsibility: if you fail to

---

[68] Cicero *Acad.* 1.40-1; 2.145; Calcidius *in Tim.* 220; Clement *Stromateis* 2.20,110-111, Stählin, 487, Potter (= *SVF* 2.714); Origen *On First Principles* 3.1.3; Alexander *Quaest.* 3.13; *Fate* 183,21-184,5.

[69] Porphyry *On the Soul* on the Stoics ap. Stobaeum *Ecl.* 1.349,23, Wachsmuth (= *SVF* 2.74); Lucullus, representative of Antiochus, ap. Ciceronem *Acad.* 2.37; Aëtius 4.8.12 (*Dox. Gr.* 396,3-4; *SVF* 2.72).

[70] loc. cit.

[71] Clement of Alexandria *Stromateis* 2.20,110-111, Stählin, 487, Potter (= *SVF* 2.714); Origen *On First Principles* 3.1.3; cf. Seneca *Ep.* 113,18-19.

[72] Alexander *Quaest.* 3.13, 107,6-12; *Fate* 183,21-184,5; Nemesius *On the Nature of Man*, 35, Matt., 291,1-6 (= *SVF* 2.991).

[73] Origen *On First Principles* 3.1.2-4.

[74] Richard Sorabji, *Necessity, Cause and Blame*, London and Ithaca NY 1980.

interrogate appearances when you can, you may very well be to blame. But if I believed in determinism, I would see those capable of reflection and those incapable as on the same footing. No amount of reflection, in my view, would make them liable to praise and blame, if their actions had been inevitable all along. Some of the ancient reporters may have shared this attitude, and if so, it is not surprising if they saw no important difference between saying that animals cannot withhold assent and saying that they give it.

The Stoics might ask their opponents: with what could animals give assent? Humans are standardly said to do so by means of reason, although one text makes even this obscure.[75] Animals, too, are said by the Stoics to have a command centre (*hêgemonikon*). But instead of consisting of reason, it consists merely of their life, sensation and impulse.[76] If it is this with which the opponents suppose animals can assent, it becomes all too clear that the so-called assent is merely an impulse following the appearance. This is a far cry from assent based on the reflective interrogation of appearance which is the Stoic ideal for humans.

This debased kind of animal assent receives further endorsement and elaboration among the late Neoplatonists. According to (pseudo?)-Philoponus, the horse's habituation (*ethismos*) to the whip is a kind of assent, although a kind that involves no use of reason. Habituation contrasts with being persuaded, which is a rational kind of assent.[77]

Since for the Stoics animals lack assent, at least in the proper sense, they will also lack belief (*doxa*). For belief involves assent,[78] and the fullest Stoic analysis of belief describes it as assent to the unwarranted, or weak and changeable supposition (*hupolêpsis*),[79] where supposition is also the outcome of assent.[80] Thus appearance falls short both of perception and of belief, but the animal's lack of belief will not seem such a shortcoming to the Stoics as it does to Aristotle. For whereas Aristotle presents belief as an asset secured by

[75] Iamblichus *On the Soul* ap. Stobaeum *Ecl.* 1.368,12-20 (= *SVF* 2.826), lists assent as a function distinct from reason in the human mind, although Clement, Origen and Alexander, in the references given above, imply that in humans it is reason that gives assent.
[76] Arius Didymus *Epitome of Physics* (*Dox. Gr.* p. 471, SVF 2.821); Philo *de Animalibus* 29; Cicero *ND* 2.29.
[77] (Pseudo?)-Philoponus *in DA 3* 488,36-489,6; 497,2-14; 500,29. I am indebted to Peter Lautner, work in preparation.
[78] Plutarch *Col.* 1122A-F, reporting the Platonist Academy's response to the Stoics. Cicero *Acad.* 2.108.
[79] Stobaeus *Ecl.* 2.111,18-112,8 W. (= *SVF* 3.548); cf. Cicero *Acad.* 1.41-2; Plutarch *Sto. Rep.* 1056E-F; Sextus M 7.151. See Carlos Levy, 'Le concept de doxa des Stoïciens à Philon d'Alexandrie', in Jacques Brunschwig and Martha Nussbaum, eds., *Passions and Perceptions*, Cambridge, 1993.
[80] Plutarch *Sto. Rep.* 1056A.

human rationality, the Stoics view it as a defective state of mind which the wise man will avoid, as involving either unwarrantedness or weakness.

The Stoic denial of belief to animals is in one respect analogous to a denial that is more familiar to contemporary readers, that of Donald Davidson.[81] Each denial is based on making belief involve a complex attitude. For the Stoics, every belief is an assent to (the content of) an appearance; for Davidson, beliefs give rise to beliefs about beliefs. His idea is that any one belief presupposes a stock of beliefs, and this makes the believer subject to surprise (why not simply, to a switch of belief? The top flight of British diplomats is trained to eschew surprise as an unnecessary disturbance),[82] when his beliefs conflict. Surprise itself involves beliefs about one's beliefs departing from the truth acceptable to others, and that he suspects (although he candidly grants he is not sure how to complete the argument) is possible only for beings who have linguistic communication. Controversially, he takes animals to lack surprise, linguistic communication, and beliefs about beliefs.[83] On noticing each other's noticing the evidence is at present anecdotal. But it is amazing how simple a little situation can make the noticing of noticing a tempting explanation of behaviour. Whiten and Byrne narrate the anecdote of a chimpanzee going to a banana box to get a banana and lifting the lid. When he saw an intruding chimpanzee watching, he slammed down the lid, went to sit elsewhere and looked away, as if there were nothing of interest in the region of the banana box. Already we are tempted to say the deceiving chimpanzee expected the intruder to notice that he himself was not noticing anything of interest. The story continues, admittedly at a more conjectural level. The intruding chimpanzee pretended to go away, but looked back through a chink in the fence, expecting perhaps the deceiver to think that its expectation had been fulfilled.[84]

The Stoic idea that animals cannot withhold assent is startling, when we think of Chrysippus' hound hesitating at the crossroads, or think of animals learning or resisting temptation. How can the blind man's guide dog learn to withhold assent from the command to cross a busy road? Or how can a mouse learn not to go for the cheese in the

[81] Donald Davidson, 'Rational animals', *Dialectica* 36, 1982, 318-27, repr. in E. Lepore and B.P. McLaughlin, eds., *Actions and Events: Perspectives on the Philosophy of Donald Davidson*, Oxford 1985, 473-80.

[82] Surprise might rather be considered an inefficient reaction.

[83] On linguistic communication in animals, see Chapter Seven below. For surprise reactions in monkeys cheated of their expected food, see O.L. Tinklepaugh, 'An experimental study of representative factors in monkeys', *Journal of Comparative Psychology* 8, 1928, 197-236. For belief about the beliefs of others in dogs, see Konrad Lorenz on dogs that deceive in *Man Meets Dog* ch. 18.

[84] Andrew Whiten and Richard W. Byrne, 'The manipulation of attention in primate tactical deception' in Byrne and Whiten, eds., *Machiavellian Intelligence: Social Expertise and the Evolution of Intellect in Monkeys, Apes and Humans*, Oxford 1988.

mousetrap after its first narrow escape, if it cannot withhold assent from the pleasant appearance? Is it that the appearance changes, so as no longer to be pleasant? Or would the Stoics fall back on the idea, which we shall find in some of them in a later chapter, that animals do not learn by experience? The same questions can be asked of the gorillas who are said to learn to withhold assent after a time from the warning calls of a fellow gorilla who has cried 'wolf' too often. Perhaps the appearance of danger has changed. But how rapidly can appearance change? In the double sheepdog trials in which each dog is required to pen its sheep unaided, it looks as if the dog who finishes first struggles to withhold assent from the appearance that it should help the other dog. Perhaps the Stoics would say the appearance that it should help fluctuates as the dog alternately sits and stands. Such fluctuation is postulated by them in cases of human temptation.[85] One way or another, the Stoics will have to re-analyse these and other cases.

Appearance without belief in the Sceptics

Aristotle and the Stoics provide the two main answers to the question how there can be perceptual appearance without reason and belief. But the views of other schools and of other members of these schools are related in interesting ways to theirs, and I will conclude the chapter by looking at these other views.

The Sceptics of Plato's Academy, who were the Stoics' fiercest critics, took the Stoic view on assent even further. It is not only animals, according to Arcesilaus, the man who committed Plato's Academy for a while to scepticism, but humans who can dispense with assent, although, unlike animals, they consciously withhold it. This is what the sceptic does: he suspends judgement (*epekhei*). The appearance (*phantasia*) that something is good leads directly to the impulse (*hormê*) to act, without the need for assent (*sunkatathesis*) or opinion (*doxa*) to intervene.[86] The other branch of Scepticism, the followers of Pyrrho, spoke in a similar way. They claimed to give assent only to involuntary appearances, for example to the proposition that honey *appears* (*phainetai*) sweet, but not to the proposition that it *is* sweet so far as concerns *logos*, or is such as it appears to be.[87] The latter is given the label *dogma*, a word akin to *doxa* (belief), and the Pyrrhonists claim by contrast to live *adoxastôs* (without beliefs).[88] It is disputed,

---

[85] Plutarch *On Moral Virtue* 446F-447A (= *SVF* 3.459); Stobaeus *Ecl.* 2.88 (= *SVF* 3.378).

[86] Plutarch *Col.* 1122A-F, cf. *Sto. Rep.* 1055F ff.

[87] Sextus *PH* 1.13 and 19-24; Timon ap. Diogenem Laertium *Lives* 9.105.

[88] Sextus *PH* 1.15; 1.23; 1.226; 1.231; 2.102; 2.246; 2.254; 2.258; 3.2; 3.235; Timon's account of Pyrrho in Aristocles ap. Eusebium PE 14.18,2-4.

both among themselves and among modern scholars interpreting them,[89] how much a Pyrrhonist eschews: philosophical doctrines only, or all beliefs.

The Pyrrhonist's denial that he gives assent is unlike the Stoic denial that animals give assent. It is not based on the suggestion that in general humans cannot give and withhold assent, but on the contrary represents a special claim by the sceptic to be withholding it. And I am inclined to take the academic sceptic the same way.[90] If this is a disclaimer of all belief, it is, I think, still harder to maintain than the corresponding disclaimer about animals, in face of the sceptic's everyday behaviour. Although the lack of assent in animals may be differently grounded – assent is not in their repertoire – the result was alleged by Pyrrho to be the same: *ataraxia*, or freedom from disturbance. He pointed to the example of a pig that went on eating on board a ship in a storm.[91]

Independent views in Aristotle's school

So far I have explained how perceptual appearance could be distinguished from belief by Aristotle, the Stoics and the Sceptics. However, Aristotle's own school did not always agree with him. Its free-thinking character is one of its most striking characteristics. Just as Aristotle had been ready to criticise some of the central ideas of his teacher Plato, so his successors questioned or rejected some central ideas of his. If this is an exception to the usual deference of schools to their founder, it has been suggested that it is an exception that proves the rule, since the Aristotelian school nearly disappeared for two hundred years after its third free-thinking head Strato.[92] The second head Theophrastus is recorded by Porphyry as saying that animals engage in reasonings (*logismoi*).[93] This claim, which is not qualified with an 'as if', appears to be Theophrastus', not Porphyry's.[94]

[89] Michael Frede, 'Des Skeptikers Meinungen', *Neue Hefte für Philosophie* 15-16, 1979, 102-29, repr. as 'The Skeptic's beliefs', in his *Essays in Ancient Philosophy*, Minneapolis 1987, ch. 10; Myles Burnyeat, 'Can the sceptic live his scepticism?', in M. Schofield, M.F. Burnyeat, J. Barnes, eds., *Doubt and Dogmatism*, Oxford 1980; J. Barnes, 'The beliefs of a Pyrrhonist', *Proceedings of the Cambridge Philological Society* n.s. 28, 1982, 1-29; Tad Brennan, 'Does the sceptic have beliefs?', forthcoming *Bulletin of the Institute of Classical Studies* new series vol. 1, 1993.

[90] But on another interpretation of Plutarch *Col.* 1122C, it is not the Academic sceptic alone, but all men, to whom assent and belief are denied: Gisela Striker, 'Sceptical strategies' in *Doubt and Dogmatism* 54-83, at 68-9.

[91] Diogenes Laertius *Lives* 9.68.

[92] David Sedley, elaborating in conversation his 'Philosophical allegiance', in J. Barnes and M.T. Griffin, *Philosophia Togata*, Oxford 1989.

[93] Porphyry *On Abstinence from Animal Food*, 3.25.

[94] The divergence from Aristotle would still remain striking, even on the totally unsubstantiated hypothesis that Theophrastus' work was a dialogue. The fragments show no more than that it was polished in style as if for publication. See W. Fortenbaugh,

Admittedly, Theophrastus still uses the conventional label for animals: irrational (*aloga*).[95] The word on its own need not signify anything: Plutarch even has a treatise called *That Irrational Creatures Use Reason*. But once Theophrastus rests explanatory weight on the label. The lynx, being irrational (*alogos*), would not have enough knowledge (*sophia*) to hide its urine, to prevent humans using it for making rings. Even the rational (*logikoi*) acquire such knowledge only by prolonged study.[96] But I think that Theophrastus could here feel it unnecessary to enter his qualification that animals are after all capable of some reasonings, because they obviously fall so far short of the reasoning that would be required for the kind of grudging behaviour (*phthonos*) he describes here. The ascription of reasonings to animals fits with Theophrastus' remarks in his treatise *On the Senses* that the other animals are merely inferior in thinking (*dianoia*), whereas plants are entirely deprived of thought (*pantelôs aphêirêsthai to phronein*).[97]

Theophrastus' successor, Strato, in turn, takes the view, subsequently endorsed by a number of Platonists, that perception involves thinking (*noein, nous, dianoia*), which (therefore) belongs to all animals.[98] His evidence is that words can fall on our sight or hearing without our taking them in, until we subsequently turn our minds to them. Only then, presumably, are we conscious of them. Another pupil of Aristotle's, Eudemus of Rhodes, though still using the label 'irrational', appears from Aelian's *de Natura Animalium* to have collected many examples of cleverness in animals, along with emotion, the ability to count and even a sense of injustice.[99] It is the last which is most significant: the lions who punish bears, and protect the saviour-woodcutter, or the foal that punishes its unnatural human father and desecrates his grave. For this appears to contradict Aristotle's denial of a sense of justice in the *Politics*.[100] Compared with the ferment of independent thought which Aristotle generated in his

---

Quellen zur Ethik Theophrasts, Amsterdam 1984, 127.

[95] ap. Porphyrium *Abstinence* 2.22; ap. Photium *Bibliotheca* 278, 528a40-b27.

[96] ap. Photium, loc. cit. I thank Pamela Huby and Robert Sharples for discussion of the passage.

[97] Theophrastus *de Sensibus* 44-5, English translation by G.M. Stratton.

[98] Strato ap. Plutarchum *Soll.* 961A; Sextum M 7.350; Porphyrium *Abstinence* 3.21; Epiphanium *Against Heresies* 3.2.9 (in *Dox. Gr.* 592,16-18). Aenesidemus as a sceptic is more likely to have exploited for sceptical purposes the view that perception involves thinking than actually to have endorsed it, as Sextus suggests he did. But other Platonists did hold that perception implies *nous*: Plutarch *Soll.* 961A-B = Porphyry *Abstinence* 3.21; Proclus, *Platonic Theology* 3.6, Saffrey and Westerink 23,25-24,6. The last distinguishes *nous* (intellect) sharply from *logos* (reason).

[99] Wehrli collects only some of the citations from Aelian in the Eudemus volume (frr. 126-32) in the series *Die Schule des Aristoteles*, and he doubts their authenticity, but with no very good reason. See Anthony Preus 'Animal and human souls in the Peripatetic School', *Skepsis* 1, 1990, 67-99.

[100] Aristotle *Pol.* 1.2, 1253a8-18. Aelian *Nat. Anim.* 3.21; 4.8; 4.45.

immediate successors, there is something almost disappointing about the orthodox Aristotelianism of Alexander of Aphrodisias 500 years later, although one must admire that as the greatest elaboration and defence of Aristotle's position. Just before Alexander, in the second century AD, there was one more unorthodox statement from the Aristotelian, Aristocles of Messene, who argued that human perception involves belief (*doxa*). But his ground is one that Aristotle would have found inadequate, that perceiving involves cognising (*gnôrizein*) something.[101]

Epicureans

One last school sharply separated perception and perceptual appearance from belief and that was the Epicureans. Perceptions and perceptual appearances are all true, true of the films of atoms that impinge on the sense organs. Falsehood comes in with our beliefs in which we discriminate (*krinein*) among these appearances and add to them or subtract from them.[102] Correspondingly, animals have perception and perceptual appearance, but, at least on Philodemus' view, they do not have belief.[103] It may bring out the distinction between perceptual appearance and belief still further that the Epicureans give a causal account of the truth of the former, not unlike certain modern accounts of what it is for primitive perceptual states to have informational content. A perceptual appearance is true if it comes from an existing thing and is like (*hopoios*), or in accordance with (*kata*), it.[104]

The Platonists

What, finally, of the Platonists? With them we need to distinguish the question whether perception is or includes belief and reason as part of itself from the question whether it is invariably *accompanied* by belief and reason. Plato's sharp distinction in the *Theaetetus* of perception from belief and reason is compatible with his earlier claim in the *Phaedo* that perception is always, even in a newborn baby, *accompanied* by the recollection of Forms (and hence, as he would later say, by reason).[105]

Plato's insistence on accompaniment by reason is interestingly

---

[101] Aristocles ap. Eusebium *PE* 14.18,23-4.

[102] Sextus M 7.205; 7.208-10; 8.63; Epicurus *Letter to Herodotus* in Diogenes Laertius *Lives* 10.50-1.

[103] Philodemus *On the Gods*, col. 13.6-7; 14.34, Diels (*doxa, pseudodoxia*).

[104] Sextus *M* 7.205; 8.63. Cf. F. Dretske, *Knowledge and the Flow of Information*, Cambridge Mass. 1981; Tyler Burge, 'Individualism and psychology', *Philosophical Review* 95, 1986, 3-45.

[105] Plato *Phaedo* 75B-C.

developed in the *Didaskalikos*, a Middle Platonist treatise of the
second century AD which draws both on Plato's *Theaetetus* and on the
Stoics.[106] According to it, there are three things we can perceive:
whiteness, that which is white, and that which has not only whiteness,
but the full collection of properties – fire or honey for example.
Perception (*aisthêsis*) discriminates (*krinei*), the first two, not without
belief-type reason (*doxastikos logos*), while belief-type reason
discriminates the third with the aid of perception.[107] The type of
reason in question consists of a collection of acquired, as opposed to
innate, beliefs, and it will be seen in Chapter Six that the beliefs may
be being thought of as concepts (*ennoiai*). If even a newborn baby
perceives with the aid of concepts in the manner of Plato's *Phaedo*, it
cannot be with these concepts, just because these concepts are not
innate, like those of Plato's *Phaedo*, but acquired. The implications of
this seem to be acknowledged, when the discussion refers to one's first
perception of a thing before any belief-type reason has been formed.

The Middle Platonist theory is still reflected among the late
Neoplatonists, Damascius, Olympiodorus and Priscian of Lydia.
Talking of the *human* soul or perceptual faculty, they agree that it
contains *logoi*,[108] and I would understand these *logoi* as concepts,
although they are also made to play extra roles.[109] Priscian gives us an
active role in relation to these concepts. They are projected
(*proballesthai*) outwards, so that they fit (*epharmozein*) with the forms
(*eidê*) or appearances (*emphaseis*) derived in perception from the
outside world.[110] The empirically acquired concepts postulated by
Aristotle were accepted by the Neoplatonists alongside the non-
empirical concepts of Plato, although they were in various ways
downgraded (details in Chapter Six) most harshly by Olympiodorus.[111]
Priscian, by contrast, is prepared to entertain the idea of *doxastikos
logos*, the collection of acquired belief or concepts, and Hermeias of
Alexandria has a similar idea when he speaks of humans assembling
in their minds (*sunathroizein en têi dianoiâi*) the universal horse after
seeing individual horses.[112] Priscian adds that *doxastikos logos* unites
with sense perception in apprehending body.

None of this, however, throws light on whether *animal* sense

---

[106] Pseudo-Albinus, *Didaskalikos*, ch. 4, in Hermann's Plato, vol. 6, translated into
English by George Burges, in the Bohn Classical Library Plato, vol. 6, 1854, by Jeremiah
Reedy 1991, into French by P. Louis as *Épitomé* in the Budé series, and in a new Budé
edition by John Whittaker as Alcinoos, *Enseignement* 1991.

[107] *Didaskalikos*, ch. 4, p. 155,37-156,9, Hermann.

[108] Damascius *in Phaedonem* Part 1,274, Part 2,15, Westerink; Priscian of Lydia
Metaphrasis of Theophrastus' de Anima, CAG suppl. vol. l, part 2, p. 7, lines 11-16.
Olympiodorus *in Phaedonem* Lecture 11.7; 12.1, lines 9-25, Westerink.

[109] They can be norms or standards, and they can also be actively creative.

[110] Priscian loc. cit.

[111] Olympiodorus *Commentary on Plato's Phaedo*, Lecture 12.1, lines 9-25, Westerink.

[112] Priscian op. cit. 19,10-13; Hermeias *in Phdr.* 171,10, Couvreur.

perception involves concepts. For according to Priscian, there are animals who have no capacities advanced enough for this,[113] while the Hermeias passage explicitly denies that animals can assemble universals. These doubts about animals are shared, as we shall see in Chapter Thirteen, by other late Neoplatonists who deny reason to animals: Iamblichus, Proclus, Sallustius and Simplicius or Priscian, whichever is the author of *in DA 3*.

Simplicius or Priscian quotes Iamblichus with approval for saying that humans have perception in a different sense from animals. Human perception has a rational form (*logoeidês*), whereas animal perception is directed to body and to that which is external (*to exô*). It can recognise (*gnôsis*) that the seen thing is a man, but it cannot recognise that this first recognition (*gnôsis*; elsewhere *krisis*) is true. For that would involve its being directed inwards towards its own *gnôsis*. Such reversion (*epistrophê*) toward itself is possible for reason, and for the senses insofar as they can imitate (*apomimeisthai*) reason, but not for the senses of irrational beings which cannot get away from body.[114] This verdict, unlike Davidson's in the discussion cited above,[115] still allows animal perception to be propositional (that the seen thing is a man). But it is more in the spirit of Davidson, when it takes it that judgments of truth are judgments about judgments, and not, for example, judgments about propositions.

---

[113] Priscian op. cit. 25,5-8.

[114] Simplicius (?) *in DA 3* 173,1-7; 187,35-9; 210,15-211,13; 290,4-8. The passages are very well explained by Peter Lautner, to whom I am indebted, in 'Rival theories of self-awareness in late Neoplatonism', *Bulletin of the Institute of Classical Studies* n.s. 1, 1993, forthcoming.

[115] Donald Davidson, 'Rational animals', loc. cit.

CHAPTER FOUR

Memory, preparation and emotion without rational belief

The lion may or may not have the concept of an ox. But in either case, it can, according to Aristotle and the Stoics, perceive that the ox is near, without believing that the ox is near, or otherwise using reason. Can it remember that the ox was near? Can it plan that the ox should be near? Can it rejoice that the ox is near, and can the ox fear that the lion is near? Can animals have such memories, intentions, and emotions, if they are denied beliefs about nearness, as they are by Aristotle and the Stoics?

For memory, preparation and emotion, the Stoics mounted a whole programme to show how these are replaced in animals by counterfeit versions which do not require belief. They saw this as essential to their case, because all these capacities had been cited as proofs of animal reason.[1] Aristotle's strategy was different. He did not seek to downgrade animal capacities, but rather to argue that even human memory is not a function of reason. He also provides the materials for showing that emotion need not involve belief. This is the opposite of Donald Davidson's view that *all* propositional attitudes depend ultimately on beliefs.[2]

We shall see in Chapter Nine that the two different approaches are also applied to voluntary action. Whereas Aristotle divorces even human voluntary action from reason, the Stoics downgrade animal behaviour, to make it all non-voluntary.

Memory in Aristotle

Aristotle is quite peculiarly insistent that memory belongs to the

[1] Plutarch *Sollertia* 966B; 961A-F, repeated Porphyry *Abstinence* 3.21-2; cf. 3.1. Proclus later agrees that intellect (*nous*), though not reason (*logos*), is implied by animal perception, appearance and memory. *Platonic Theology* 3.128, citing the classification of these as intellectual in Plato's *Philebus*.

[2] Donald Davidson, 'Rational animals', *Dialectica* 36, 1982, 318-27, repr. in E. Lepore and B.P. McLaughlin, eds., *Actions and Events: Perspectives on the Philosophy of Donald Davidson*, Oxford 1985, 473-80. See p. 475.

perceptual, not the rational, part of the soul, and he adds the same for appearance (*phantasia*). He regards it as one of the two or three main tasks of his chapter on memory (*mnêmê*) to establish this,[3] and he has to argue it in face of the fact that humans can remember objects of thought.[4] By contrast, in the chapter on deliberately reminding oneself, he distinguishes this activity from memory as being as it were a sort of reasoning (*sullogismos*).[5] His eagerness to classify states of mind on one side or the other of the perception/reason frontier struck me as unnecessary, when I first encountered it. It recurs in his treatment of sleep and dreams.[6] But the reason becomes obvious in the treatise *On Memory and Reminding Oneself* from the use to which Aristotle puts his view. He infers from it that animals can have memory, but cannot deliberately remind themselves.[7] This has further significance because, if animals can have memory, they can also have a little experience,[8] since experience is defined as consisting of many memories.[9]

Memory, being independent of intellect, will be independent also of belief. We should not think that Aristotle has after all violated this independence when he remarks that memory involves *saying* in one's soul that one has encountered the thing before.[10] For such metaphorical references to saying are common enough to be discounted.[11] What Aristotle does think, however, is that remembering involves making a connexion between two things. He defines it as the having of a mental image (*phantasma*), which is regarded not as a thing in its own right, but as being *of*, indeed a copy (*eikôn*) of, the thing imaged.[12] Animals are evidently considered capable of making such a connexion between image and thing imaged.

Memory in the Stoics

As regards memory, we have already noticed Proclus' concession that

---

[3] Aristotle *Mem.* 1, 449b4-5; 449b28-450a25; 451a14.

[4] Ibid. 450a12-13; 24-5.

[5] Ibid. 2, 453a8-14. The translation of *anamimnêskesthai* as 'reminding oneself', rather than 'recollecting', brings out that this for Aristotle is no mere synonym of 'remembering', but stands for a deliberate act of causing oneself to be reminded by an association of ideas. Elsewhere, the translation 'being reminded' explains Plato's insistence at *Phaedo* 73C-74A, *Phaedrus* 249D, on an association of ideas, and does justice to the passive form of the verb.

[6] Aristotle *Som.* 453b13; *Insom.* 458b1-2; 459a21-2.

[7] Aristotle *Mem.* 1, 450a15-18; 453a7-9; cf. *Metaph.* 1.1, 980a28-9; *An. Post.* 2.19, 99b36-100a3; *HA* 1.1, 488b24-6.

[8] Aristotle *Metaph.* 1.1, 980b26-7.

[9] Aristotle *An. Post.* 2.19, 100a5-6; *Metaph.* 1.1, 980b29-30.

[10] Aristotle *Mem.* 1, 449b22-3.

[11] A list is given by Stanford Cashdollar, 'Aristotle's account of incidental perception', *Phronesis* 18, 1973, 156-75.

[12] Aristotle *Mem.* 1, 450b11-451a2, 451a14-17.

animal memory implies intellect,[13] while the Epicureans characteristically display a division of opinion.[14] But the Stoics make memory involve reflection (*consideratio deliberatio*),[15] and Cicero's spokesman for the eclectic Antiochus, who may represent Stoic thought, reinforces this by adding that memory involves *assent*.[16] If memory requires rational reflection and full-blooded assent, animals will, on their view, not be capable of it. How can this be made plausible?

The Stoic response is supplied by Seneca, and it consists of redefining what animals can do. They lack genuine memory; what they have is only perceptual recognition:

> The dumb animal grasps what is present by its senses. It is reminded (*reminiscitur*) of the past when it encounters something that alerts its senses. Thus the horse is reminded of the road when it is brought to where it starts. But in its stable it has no memory of it, however often it has been trodden. As for the third time, the future, that does not concern dumb animals.[17]

Preparation, intention and attention

There is at least one difficulty about this view. Without memory, how can animals search for something previously encountered, but now absent? For such forward-looking activities as search, the Stoics have a similar strategy of downgrading animal accomplishments. Plutarch challenges the Stoic view of animals:

> But suppose it true that perception does not need intellect (*nous*) for its work. Still, when perception has finished engendering in the animal the distinction between what is foreign to it and what properly belongs (*oikeion*), what is it that then remembers and fears the painful and longs for the beneficial, contriving (*mêkhanesthai*), if that is not present, to secure its presence among them, preparing (*paraskeuazesthai*) lairs and refuges, and again traps for prey and escape routes from attackers?[18]

But, Plutarch complains, the Stoics downgrade this preparing in animals to a mere as-if preparing:

> As for those who foolishly say of animals that they do not feel pleasure, nor anger, nor fear, nor do they make preparations (*paraskeuazesthai*), nor remember, but the bee only 'as-if' (*hôsanei*) remembers, and the

---

[13] Proclus *Platonic Theology* 3.128.

[14] One Epicurean text, that of Diogenes of Oenoanda, recovered in stone from a Turkish hillside, subordinates memory to thought (*dianoia*), because in memory thought receives likenesses of what was formerly perceived: new fr. 5.3.3-14, Smith. On the other hand, Epicurus' successor Hermarchus treats at least some memory as irrational (*alogos*) and contrasts it with reasoning (*epilogismos*): Hermarchus ap. Porphyrium *Abstinence* 1.10.

[15] Calcidius *in Timaeum* 220.

[16] Cicero *Acad.* 2.38.

[17] Seneca *Ep.* 124,16.

[18] Plutarch *Sollertia* 961C; repeated by Porphyry *Abstinence* 3.22.

swallow 'as-if' makes preparations, and the lion is 'as-if' angry, and the deer 'as-if' afraid: – I do not know how they will treat someone who says that they do not see nor hear either, but 'as-if' see and 'as-if' hear, and do not give voice (*phônein*), but 'as-if' give voice, and in general do not live, but 'as-if' live. For these last statements, I believe, are no more contrary to plain evidence than their own.[19]

I think we may be able to guess how the Stoics defended their downgrading of animal 'preparations'. For Plutarch gives us a list of Stoic definitions of human preparation and kindred 'impulses' in the intervening lines. A fuller report of the same definitions is provided in Arius Didymus' epitome of Stoic ethics, which is preserved in fragmentary form by Stobaeus.

It is the practical impulses (*praktikai hormai*) that are being defined, and it is commonly taken that these are rational impulses (*logikai hormai*) found only in rational beings, because practical action (*prattein*) is itself defined as rational, and as therefore beyond the scope of animals. Animals can be activated (*energein*), but cannot act (*prattein*),[20] evidently because there is no possibility of reason withholding assent. None the less, it is a striking fact about the first four definitions that with very little modification they could be applied to animals. And there is good reason to suppose that the Stoics would have wanted to make this application. For in the preceding lines, Arius Didymus distinguishes between the impulses of rational beings and of irrational beings as two species of impulse. The difference is that whereas rational impulse is a movement of the rational mind (*dianoia*) towards something involved in practical action (*prattein*), impulse in general is rather a movement of the soul (*psukhê*) towards something. If reference to practical action (*prattein*) is replaced by reference to activation (*energein*), the ensuing definitions of the first four human impulses will become applicable, *mutatis mutandis*, to animals, although Stobaeus does not record the animal versions, and Arius Didymus may himself have left them out of his epitome. The relevant part of Stobaeus' text needs interpretation, but can be translated as follows:

> They say that there are several species of practical impulse, among them the following: intention (*prothesis*), attention (*epibolê*), preparation (*paraskeuê*), taking in hand (*enkheirêsis*), ... They say that intention is an indication of going on to complete something (*sêmeiôsis epiteleseôs*), attention is one impulse preceding another (*hormê pro hormês*), preparation is one action preceding another (*praxis pro praxeôs*), taking

---

[19] Plutarch *Sollertia* 961E-F; repeated by Porphyry loc. cit.
[20] Alexander *de Fato* 205,38; Simplicius *in Cat.* 306,26 (reading *prattein* for *plattein*); cf. 318,18-19.

in hand is an impulse to do with something already in hand (*hormê epi tinos en khersin êdê ontos*) ...[21]

These definitions are so minimalistic, that animals should be capable of satisfying them, provided it is understood that no rational mind (*dianoia*) is involved in the movement. That in turn means that the swallow's 'as-if' preparation of its nest will consist of successive activations. If an animal has 'as-if' intention, attention and taking in hand, these will be respectively a non-rational indication of going on to complete something, a non-rational impulse preceding another and a non-rational impulse to do with something already in hand.

Foresight

Other Stoic texts suggest that in conceding 'as-if' preparation to animals, the Stoics are not conceding foresight. After denying to the horse memory, other than recognitional, Seneca adds, we have seen, that the future does not concern (*pertinere ad*) dumb animals (*muta*) either − that is, it does not concern any animals at all.[22] Cicero explains more fully. Beasts (*beluae*) have little sense (*sentire*) of past or future. Humans are different: because of their reason, they can recognise causes and effects, antecedents and sequels and similarities. That way they can join the future to the past, survey the whole course of their lives and make preparations (*praeparare*).[23] A similar thought is found in the second century BC in the historian Polybius in his account of social development. Because humans, unlike animals, can foresee (*prooran*) the future and reason (*sullogizesthai*) that a similar misfortune can befall each of them, they feel indignant at ingratitude and form a moral sense.[24] The Jewish philosopher Philo sides with the Stoics against his own nephew when he denies that animals do anything with foresight.[25]

The extent of animal foresight was none the less a matter of disagreement. Aristotle had allowed animals certain forward-looking capacities, provided they did not involve reason. On the one hand, he allows the lion, in a passage discussed in Chapter Two, to rejoice at, or because of, the future tense proposition that he *will* make a meal of the ox whom he perceives.[26] In the *Nicomachean Ethics*, he comments that people call animals intelligent, because they evidently have (*ekhonta*

---

[21] Stobaeus *Ecl.* 2.7 (Wachsmuth vol. 2, pp. 86-7). There is an admirable discussion in Brad Inwood, *Ethics and Human Action in Early Stoicism*, Oxford 1985, appendix 2.
[22] Seneca *Ep.* 124,16.
[23] Cicero *Off.* 1.11.
[24] Polybius *Universal History* 6.5.10-6.6.9.
[25] Philo *On Animals*, contrast 30, 34, 43, 65 with 97.
[26] *NE* 3.10, 1118a20-3.

phainetai) foresight (*dunamis pronoêtikê*).[27] He also grants to animals, if I was right in my discussion of appearance in Chapter Three, an ability to contemplate pleasant things even when they are not perceptually present, and so to go in search of them. Again, in the *History of Animals* he describes how cranes fly up high in order (*pros*) to get an extensive view, come down to rest if they see bad weather, keep watch when on the ground and signal, if they see anything.[28] On the other hand, he denies that animals can deliberate,[29] or manipulate mental images in the way that deliberation requires.[30] Nor do they have hope (*elpis*), or expectation for the future (*prosdokia tou mellontos*).[31] Theophrastus, or Plutarch commenting on him, develops one part of Aristotle's view, by allowing that the octopus, though not the chameleon, changes its colour from forethought (*pronoia*).[32] And Plutarch insists on the ability of animals to expect, intend, prepare and hope.[33] Sextus, for his own dialectical purposes, uses the argument that birds understand and foretell the future.[34]

The Epicureans, as usual, lack an agreed position. According to Philodemus in the first century BC, animals experience impulse (*hormê*) and that is directed to the future, although it is often dull (*narkôdês*).[35] So they must possess something at least analogous to foresight (*proorasis*) and expectation (*prosdokia*).[36] There is a passage in Polystratus, the third head of the school, which has been taken to bear on memory, but I think it is concerned only with foresight. It does not deny animals memory, but denies only that they remember in such a way as to secure benefits or avoid repeated harm, because they cannot recognise consequences or signs.[37]

Aristotle on emotion

It is not only cognition, but also emotion, that must be made independent of belief, if it is to be ascribed to animals who lack belief. The two problems are connected, because Aristotle defines anger, pity and fear as involving cognition in the *Topics* and *Rhetoric*.[38] In the

[27] Ibid. 6.7, 1141a22-8.
[28] *History of Animals* 9.10, 614b18; 26.
[29] *HA* 1.1, 488b24-6.
[30] *DA* 3.11, 434a5-12.
[31] *PA* 3.6, 669a19-21.
[32] Plutarch *Sollertia* 978E-F.
[33] Ibid. 960F; 961C; 966B.
[34] Sextus *PH* 1.77.
[35] Philodemus *On the Gods* col. 13, lines 4-5, 16-21.
[36] Ibid. 13.16-21.
[37] Polystratus *On Irrational Contempt* 3-4, Diels. I am taking this differently from Julia Annas, 'Epicurus on agency', in J. Brunschwig and M. Nussbaum, eds., *Passions and Perceptions*, Cambridge 1993, much as I have learnt from her paper.
[38] *Top.* 6.13, 151a16-17; 8.1, 156a32-3; *Rhet.* 2.2, 1378a31-3; 2.5, 1382a21-5;

Topics, he seems to be responding to Plato's *Philebus*, where Plato says that pleasure often goes with (*meta*) a false belief (*doxa*). Aristotle remarks that anger needs to be defined as distress, not with, but on account of (*dia*) an apprehension (*hupolêpsis*) of having been slighted.[39] The word *hupolêpsis*, according to Aristotle, covers belief (*doxa*), along with scientific understanding (*epistêmê*) and practical insight (*phronêsis*).[40]

The cognitive aspect of emotion becomes clearer, when we look at further details of the definitions. Anger is said to be a desire, coupled with distress, for revenge on account of the appearance (*phainomenos*) of an inappropriate slight. Fear is distress or agitation resulting from the appearance (*phantasia*) of future harm which appears (*phainesthai*) close. Because it is accompanied by an expectation (*prosdokia*) of harm, frightened people think (*oiesthai, nomizein*) that something is going to happen to them. Pity is distress at the appearance (*phainomenos*) of undeserved harm, that appears (*phainesthai*) close, befalling someone else, when one could expect (*prosdokan*) such a thing to befall oneself or people close to one. Hence one must be able to think (*oiesthai*) one could suffer in that way.

It has been held that the *cognitive* aspect of emotion creates a serious difficulty for Aristotle. Does it not conflict with his ascription of emotions to animals, which is particularly common in his biological works?[41] Worse, the emotions of anger and pity even involve an *evaluative* cognition. For the harm is evaluated as inappropriate or undeserved according to the *Rhetoric*, and though Aristotle's pupil Eudemus ascribes to animals a sense of injustice,[42] Aristotle expressly denies this in the *Politics*.[43] It will not protect Aristotle from the charge of inconsistency, I think, to say that he uses different explanatory frameworks in different places. For he is not an antirealist who believes that explanations are merely helpful devices which need not correspond to the real nature of things. Fortunately, I believe a different answer to the charge of confusion is available.

First, pity is not ascribed to animals, while anger is defined in terms of an evaluation only in the legal context of the *Rhetoric*, where we are dealing with humans, not in the *Topics*, nor yet in the biological

---

1382b29-1383a8; 2.8, 1385b13-28.

[39] Aristotle *Top.* 6.13, 151a16-17; Plato *Philebus* 37E10. The point is made by William W. Fortenbaugh, 'Aristotle's *Rhetoric* on emotions', *Archiv für Geschichte der Philosophie* 52, 1970, 40-70, repr. in Jonathan Barnes, Malcolm Schofield, Richard Sorabji, eds., *Articles on Aristotle* 4, London 1979.

[40] Aristotle *DA* 3.3, 427b25.

[41] William W. Fortenbaugh, 'Aristotle: animals, emotion and moral virtue', *Arethusa* 4, 1971, 137-65.

[42] Eudemus ap. Aelianum, *On the Nature of Animals* 3.21; 4.8; 4.45.

[43] Aristotle *Pol.* 1.2, 1253a8-18, cited by William W. Fortenbaugh, *Aristotle on Emotion*, London 1975, 35-6.

context of *On the Soul*.[44] Secondly, as regards the cognitive aspect of emotion, Aristotle has left himself free to ascribe appearance (*phantasia*) to animals and it is noteworthy how often 'appearance' is the term he uses in defining emotions. Had he had animals clearly in mind, which he does not in the *Rhetoric*, he would have been free to describe the relevant cognition as an appearance throughout.

Such a move is even recommended, though not out of any interest in animals, by the Aristotelian Aspasius, who commented on Aristotle's *Ethics* in the first half of the second century AD. Aspasius attacks another Aristotelian, Andronicus, who almost two centuries earlier had borrowed the term from Aristotle's *Topics* and defined the emotions as involving an apprehension (*hupolêpsis*) of good or harm. Aspasius is conscious of Stoic theory, and assumes that apprehension is connected with assent (*sunkatathesis*). These are not needed for emotion, he says. You can have an emotion merely because of the perceptual appearance (*phainesthai kata tên aisthêsin*) that something is pleasant or distressing, even *before* there has been assent and apprehension. This is particularly clear with the basic appetites (*epithumiai*). And you can be moved by the pleasure of a witty saying, without apprehending either before *or after* that any good is present.[45]

One of the Stoics, the independently minded Posidonius, offered a different reason for defining emotions in terms of appearance, not belief. People do not get frightened when merely persuaded by reason (*logos*) that some harm is imminent, but only when they get an appearance (*phantasia*) of it. For our irrational (*alogon*) part could not be stirred by reason, without the aid of something like a picture (*anazôgraphêsis*).[46]

There are, however, still two obstacles to Aristotle's defining animal emotion as involving no more than the *appearance* of good or harm. The first question is whether mere appearance would be enough, for Aristotle allows that *post*-perceptual appearance, the mere *imagining* of terrible things for example, does not provoke fear in humans. But even in humans it can stir the heart or other organs. It is just that the intellect (*nous*) or reasoning (*logistikon*) part of the soul gives no corresponding command.[47]

The second obstacle is more formidable. In the *Politics*, Aristotle suggests that animals lack any sense, not only of justice and injustice, but also of good and bad, harm and benefit.

---

[44] *DA* 1.1, 403a25-b9.

[45] Aspasius *in NE* 44,33-45,10. Cf. on lust responding directly to music without intervention of assent or will, Diogenes of Babylon ap. Philodemum *de Musica*; Augustine *contra Julianum* 5.5.23.

[46] Posidonius ap. Galenum *Platonis et Hippocratis Placita* (*PHP*), book 5, p. 330, with translation, Philip de Lacy in *Corpus Medicorum Graecorum* 5.4.1,2. (= Mueller, Teubner edition p. 455; Kühn, Galen vol. 5, pp. 473-4). Compare Plotinus 6.7.33.23 for love requiring imagery (Jo Sen, work in progress), but contrast Aristotle *DA* 3.3, 427b21-4.

[47] Aristotle *DA* 3.3, 427b21-4; 3.9, 432b29-433a1; *Mot.* 11, 703b7-8.

Voice (*phônê*) is a sign (*sêmeion*) of painful and pleasant, which is why it belongs to the other animals as well. For their nature reaches as far as having a sense (*aisthêsis*) of the painful and pleasant and signalling (*sêmainein*) these to each other. But speech (*logos*) is for revealing (*dêloun*) benefit and harm (*to sumpheron kai to blaberon*), and hence too justice and injustice (*to dikaion kai to adikon*). For it is a unique property (*idion*) of man as against the other animals that he alone has a sense (*aisthêsis*) of good and bad (*agathon kai kakon*), just and unjust and so on. And it is sharing in these that makes a household and a city state.[48]

Harm and benefit are not identical to injustice and justice, but are rather the subjects of dispute, when justice is in question. Aristotle has here gone beyond what he needs in saying that animals have no sense of harm and benefit, good and bad. But if he sticks to it, he will, needlessly, debar himself from allowing animals anger and fear after all. I do not think, however, that he does stick to it, for he says here that animals can feel pleasure and pain. But feeling pleasure and pain (*hêdesthai, lupeisthai*) are defined in *On the Soul* as a sensory exercise directed towards good and bad as such.[49]

After Aristotle there was widespread disagreement. The Epicurean Philodemus endorses or leaves unchallenged the claim that anger requires an apprehension (*hupolêpsis*) of having been harmed.[50] Yet he thinks that animals suffer real agitation (*tarakhê*) and have analogues of our emotions,[51] even though he denies belief to them.[52] This turns out to be possible only because they can have analogues of belief.[53]

The Stoics on emotion

The Stoics pursued the opposite strategy to Aristotle's with regard to emotion, just as they did with memory and intention. Their strategy was to downgrade animal capabilities. They had to, because they held that genuine emotions involved judgments. The word *krisis* is no longer confined, as with Aristotle, to mere discrimination. It appears in the texts alongside *doxa* as meaning judgment, although it is not explicitly said like *doxa* be confined to false, unwarranted, or hesitant judgment. Animals, as incapable of judgment, cannot have genuine

[48] Aristotle *Pol.* 1.2, 1253a10-18. I am grateful to Steve White for insisting on the difficulty.

[49] Aristotle *DA* 3.7, 431a10-12. The passage is discussed also in Chapter Two above. With the suggestion in *Pol.* 1.2 that animals may lack a sense of benefit or harm (*sumpheron, blaberon*) compare the ambiguous passage in Plato *Tht.* 186C, which may have been denying them reflections on utility (*ôpheleia*).

[50] Philodemus *On Anger*, col. 47, lines 19-32; 49,27-50,8.

[51] Philodemus *On the Gods* 11.4-15.4, Diels, esp. 11.19-20; 11,28-34; 13.30-1; 13.34-5; 14.7-8; 14.21-8; 14.29-30.

[52] Ibid. 13.6-7 (*doxa*); 14.34 (*pseudodoxia*).

[53] Ibid. 13.17-18 (analogue of *prosdokia*: belief about the future). 14.6-8 may even contemplate allowing beliefs analogous to ours.

emotion. That was the view of the Stoics[54] other than Posidonius.[55]

The founder of Stoicism, Zeno of Citium, said that emotions were physical contractions, dilations and so on, that followed on certain judgments.[56] Chrysippus took a more intellectualist view. Emotions just were certain judgments about the presence of good or harm.[57] One motive for developing such a view may have been the hope of showing that rational philosophising could be sufficient to free you from emotions by changing your judgments. It would not be sufficient on Zeno's view, presumably, because the contractions and dilations might outlast the judgments.[58] Chrysippus himself was forced to admit a chronological mismatch in the opposite direction. The beliefs about good and harm may outlast the emotion when you get used to them. He thus had to modify his definition and say that an emotion was certain fresh (*prosphatos*) judgments about good and harm. One source even ascribes this addition to Zeno before him.[59] 'Fresh' is not a purely chronological notion, since the judgment can be refreshed by dwelling on it.

Some Stoics found Chrysippus' account too intellectualist. At least, Diogenes of Babylon is accused by the Epicurean Philodemus of allowing music to affect the emotions by non-rational means.[60] A later Stoic, Posidonius, reintroduces Plato's two non-rational parts of the soul, which the other Stoics had rejected,[61] and makes them into sources of emotion. Although Plato had included beliefs within the rational parts of the soul, as I have argued in Chapter One, Posidonius offers numerous counter-examples against the identification of

[54] Cicero *Tusc.* 4.31; Augustine *City* 8.17; Plutarch *Sollertia* 961D, excerpted by Porphyry *Abstinence* 3.22; Galen *PHP* Book 4, p. 260; Book 5, pp. 294; 334, de Lacy.

[55] Last two passages in Galen. Galen's testimony on Posidonius is discounted by Janine Fillion-Lahilles, *Le De ira de Sénèque et la philosophie stoïcienne des passions*, Paris 1984, 124, 156-9.

[56] Galen *PHP* Book 4, pp. 240, 248; Book 5, p. 334, de Lacy.

[57] Galen *PHP* Book 4, pp. 238, 246, 262; Book 5, p. 292, de Lacy; Plutarch *Sollertia* 961D, excerpted by Porphyry *Abstinence* 3.22.

[58] I am drawing here on the perceptive attempt by Martha Nussbaum to make sense of Chrysippus' view – a view which is certainly shared by some contemporary psychologists. See Martha Nussbaum, 'The Stoics on the extirpation of the passions', *Apeiron* 20, 1987, 129-77 and Keith Oatley, P.N. Johnson-Laird, 'Towards a cognitive theory of emotions', *Cognition and Emotion* 1, 1987, 29-50. Nussbaum further elaborates her view in *The Therapy of Desire: Theory and Practice in Hellenistic Ethics*, forthcoming.

[59] Galen *PHP* Book 4, pp. 238, 282-90; Book 5, p. 332, de Lacy. A small part is quoted in *SVF* 3.481. The 'fresh' definition is ascribed to Zeno by Cicero *Tusculan Disputations* 3,74-5 (= *SVF* 1.212).

[60] Martha Nussbaum, 'Poetry and the passions: two Stoic views', in J. Brunschwig and M. Nussbaum, eds., *Passions and Perceptions*, Proceedings of the Fifth International Symposium on Hellenistic Philosophy, Cambridge 1993, commenting on Diogenes *de Musica*, as paraphrased by his Epicurean critic Philodemus, *de Musica* Book 4. But why should not effect (emotion) be unlike cause (music)?

[61] Galen *PHP* Books 4 and 5.

emotion with judgment, and these are recorded by Galen.[62]

Those attracted to Plato, like Posidonius and Galen, along with the genuine Platonists Plutarch and Porphyry, seized on the unfortunate consequence of Chrysippus', and even of Zeno's, view that animals can no longer be assigned emotions.[63] Conversely, Plutarch reports the argument that, since animals obviously do have emotions, they must have reason.[64] Once again if the Stoics were to answer the problem, they would have to redefine the mental capacities of animals, just as they had done for memory and preparation.

Such a redefinition was very cleverly worked out by Seneca, who had also redefined animal memory as mere perceptual recognition. In his treatise *On Anger*, he denies that dumb animals (*muta animalia*) have emotions.[65] The reason in the case of anger is that there are four stages in the emotion: first the initial appearance (*species*) of injustice, secondly an involuntary agitation of the mind (*agitatio animi*) in response to the appearance, thirdly the voluntary and rational assent of the mind to the appearance and fourthly an uncontrollable surge which carries us away. It is wrong to suppose that anger occurs at the second stage; it requires all four stages.[66] The reason why animals do not experience anger is that they are not rational, which means, evidently, that they cannot reach stage three. It is allowed that they have appearances (*species*) – presumably the appearance of injustice – even though muddled and confused ones (*turbidae, confusae*), and that they experience the agitation (*agitatio*). But this does not amount to anger. It merely accounts for the popular misconception that they can be angry.[67]

As there is voice admittedly, but unintelligible, disorderly and incapable of words, as there is a tongue, but tied, not free for varied movements, so the command centre (*principale*) itself is too coarse and inexact. So it receives sensations and appearances (*species*) of things to summon it to strive (*impetus*), but they are muddled and confused (*turbidae, confusae*).
...

So that first agitation of the mind (*agitatio animi*) inflicted by the appearance of injustice (*species iniuriae*) is no more anger than is the appearance of injustice itself. It is the subsequent striving (*impetus*) which not only receives the appearance of injustice but approves it (*adprobavit*) that is anger, the incitement of a mind (*concitatio animi*) proceeding to vengeance by will and judgment (*voluntas, iudicium*). It is

[62] Galen *PHP* Book 4, pp. 264-80; Book 5, p. 332, de Lacy.
[63] Galen, drawing on Posidonius, *PHP* Book 4, p. 260; Book 5, pp. 294, 334; Plutarch *Sollertia* 961D, excerpted by Porphyry *Abstinence* 3.22.
[64] Plutarch *Sollertia* 966B.
[65] Seneca *On Anger* 1.3 (6-8).
[66] Ibid. 2.3-4.
[67] Ibid. 1.3.3-8.

never doubted that fear involves flight, and anger striving. See then if you think anything can be pursued or avoided without the assent of the mind (*adsensus animi*). ...

So that you may know how passions begin, grow, or burst out, the first movement is not voluntary (*voluntarius*), like a preparation for passion and a sort of threat. The second is accompanied by a not intractable act of the will (*voluntas*) to the effect that I ought to be revenged, because I have been harmed, or that he ought to be punished, because he has committed a crime. The third movement is out of control. It wants revenge not only if that is appropriate, but at all costs, and has overcome reason (*ratio*).[68]

Seneca's analysis of anger is interesting not only for its treatment of animals. Like Sartre in modern times,[69] he seeks to represent emotion as voluntary, which was the official Stoic view,[70] and he connects voluntariness with assent of the rational will (*voluntas*). There are other texts which tell us that the Stoics made the emotions involve some kind of assent. Grief and pleasure involve not only a contraction or dilation, but a belief that these contractions and dilations are right.[71] But it is Seneca who adds that in anger the assent of the rational will is what makes the emotion voluntary.

While the Stoic downgrading of psychological capacities in animals is of high interest for the reflection it provokes on these capacities, I find it entirely implausible. If animals enjoy only 'as-if' preparation we lose explanation of animal behaviour. Moreover, it is uneconomical to suppose that human anger always involves the extra act of assent. And while it would be difficult to know what the horse in its stable is remembering, this could at least be the subject of investigation.

Thinking and universals without rationality

Perceptual appearance, concept-possession, memory, preparation, and emotion were not the only animal capacities to be divorced from rationality. The memorist doctors had a programme of their own to show that all we would ordinarily regard as thinking could be conducted without reason, on the basis of memory alone. I shall return to this in Chapter Six. meanwhile we shall see in Chapter Five that some thinkers allowed animals access to universals without rationality, although others did so only insofar as they conceded rationality to animals.

---

[68] Ibid. 1.3.7; 2.3.5; 2.4.1.
[69] Jean-Paul Sartre, *Esquisse d'une théorie des émotions*, Paris 1939, tr. by P. Mairet as *Sketch for a Theory of the Emotions*, London 1962.
[70] Cicero *Academica* 1.39; in our power *Tusc.* 4.14.
[71] Ps-Andronicus *On Emotions* 1 (*SVF* 3.391) Cicero *Tusc.* 3.61; 72; 74-5.

CHAPTER FIVE

Forms, universals and abstraction in animals

Can animals grasp Platonic Forms, or universals, or perform abstractions? Aristotle, I argued in Chapter Three, in one mood allows animals some access to universal concepts, despite their supposed lack of rationality. He does so by maintaining that experience (*empeiria*), the most rudimentary universal in the soul, is no more than a collection of particular memories of the same thing. The rudimentary concept of an ox is a collection of memories of oxen. Whether or not Aristotle's lion perceives the ox as an ox, it certainly perceives it as a meal (1118a23).

Plato, by contrast, believes that we have concepts of Forms inherited from our previous lives. Diogenes Laertius, drawing on an account by Alcimus, quotes Plato as saying that animals, too, grasp the Form (*tês ideas*) and for this purpose have a natural intellect (*nous phusikos*). Thus they have an innate awareness of likeness (*emphutos tês homoiotêtos theôria*). Otherwise they could not remember likenesses, or what their food is like, or recognise their kin.[1] The closest to this in the extant dialogues of Plato is the rather different statement in the *Phaedrus* that the soul of an animal can pass at a future incarnation into a man, provided it has in the past seen, and therefore could recollect, the Forms.[2]

The late Neoplatonists took a more restrictive view. Under the influence of Iamblichus, as we shall see in Chapter Thirteen, they began to deny reason to animals. One of them, Hermeias of Alexandria, claims that only humans and the rational soul can, while animals cannot, assemble in their minds (*sunathroizein en têi dianoiāi*) the universal horse, after seeing individual horses.[3]

Not all Platonists were so restrictive. At an earlier date around AD 200, the eclectic Platonist and doctor Galen claims that animals can recognise the form (*eidos*) which is common (*koinon*) to all roads, or men, or donkey-drivers, or camels, and equally the form which is unique (*idion*) to this road, or to Dion the donkey-driver. Even the donkey can do this, thought to be the stupidest (*anoêtotatos*) of animals

---

[1] Diogenes Laertius *Lives of Eminent Philosophers* 3.15.
[2] Plato *Phaedrus* 249B-C.   [3] Hermeias *in Phdr.* 171,10, Couvreur.

– though Galen's opponents who deny the difference between being numerically one and the same, and being one and the same in form (*eidos*) may be stupider.[4]

A late Neoplatonist text by Simplicius (or, on one view, by Priscian) has a different rationale for ascribing universals to animals. Aristotle's apparent denial of appearances (*phantasiai*) to the ant, bee and grub means that they have imprinted (*tupoi*) appearances only of food taken generally (*koinoteron*). Or bees may have the appearance of food in this grove, but not from this flower.[5] This text appeals to *phantasia*, instead of to intellect or reason, and makes it explicit that phantasia can be directed to universals, although the universals sound like the confused ones which Aristotle ascribes to children who call all men 'father' indifferently.[6]

The subject was continued after the end of antiquity in medieval Islam, and Avempace (Ibn Bajja, died AD 1138) goes still further in the course of an attack on Galen. The imaginative faculty, which is involved in animal desire, does not seek one and the same water or food, but seeks the universal (water, food). Thus cranes, pigeons, the pintailed sand grouse, and all gregarious animals do perceive the universal in a way, though Galen's domestic donkey cannot manage that.[7] Elsewhere Avempace's account is more nuanced. What the animal perceives is *intermediate* between the universal intelligible form and the material individual form.[8] This sounds like a good description of the object of human imagination, when someone is thinking not of the universal house (as in 'a house is a shelter'), nor of the particular house where, say, he or she was born, but of a house which is single (and to that extent like the particular house), but with regard to which there is no answer to the question how many rooms it has (so that to that extent it is like the universal).

Avempace does not tell us how *phantasia* can be directed to a universal. The materials for an answer might be found in Aristotle, although he does not himself say that *phantasia* is so directed. If the most rudimentary universal in the soul is a collection of memories, and memory is[9] the having of an image (*phantasma*), then a collection of *phantasiai*, even if not a single one, could result in a universal. There

---

[4] Galen *de Methodo Medendi*, Kühn vol. 10, pp. 132-4; 138-9.

[5] Simplicius (?) *in DA 3*, 209, 17-25, commenting on *DA* 3.3, 428a10-11.

[6] Aristotle *Phys.* 1.1, 184b11. The same phenomenon is reported for the calls of baby vervet monkeys by Dorothy Cheney and Robert Seyfarth, *How Monkeys See the World*, Chicago 1990.

[7] Ibn Bajja, *Means of Recognising the Agent Intellect*, p. 108 (Fakhry), tr. by Thérèse-Anne Druart, 'Avempace et l'intellect agent', *Bulletin de Philosophie Médiévale* 22, 1980, 73-7, at 76. I am most grateful to her for the information on this controversy.

[8] Ibn Bajja *Regimen of the Solitary* articles 12-13, tr. into Spanish by Palacios as *El Régimen del Solitario*, pp. 108-15.

[9] Aristotle *Mem.* 1, 451a15-17.

is a further point. Once one has acquired a universal concept through a collection of *phantasmata*, it ought to be possible to use a single *phantasma*, or image, to represent that universal. Aristotle describes how this can be done, not indeed by animals, but by the human intellect. In thinking of the (universal) triangle, we put a particular triangular image before our mind's eye, but ignore those features of the image which are irrelevant, such as its exact height, rather in the way that Berkeley was later to describe.[10] Even animals have the option of treating their imagery in more than one way, either as a thing in its own right, like the canvas of a picture, or as a copy of something else, like a pictorial representation.[11] But Avempace would be going beyond Aristotle, if he allowed that an animal, lacking intellect, could regard its imagery as representing a universal.

Avempace was writing later than Avicenna (Ibn Sina, *c.* 980-1037), whose theory was distinctively different. Animals have not only imagination, but also an estimative faculty. It is this estimative faculty, not reason, not instinct, and not the Stoics' self-consciousness, which enables the sheep to realise that this wolf is dangerous and malicious.[12] The estimative faculty is capable of a certain amount of abstraction, for malice is realised only sometimes in matter, and can be abstracted from matter. But the abstraction is not complete, because the malice is apprehended as tied to a particular perceptible form and set of material accidents.[13] It is only with intellectual abstraction that we get a universal form 'suitable for being predicated of everything', and abstracted not only from matter, but from the material accidents of quantity, quality, place and posture.[14]

Averroes (*c.* AD 1126-1198) denies that animals are capable of any abstraction.[15] But Thomas Aquinas takes up Avicenna's idea that to apprehend the danger of the wolf, the sheep needs a natural estimative faculty. Man, he says, however, apprehends danger not by this natural, instinctive power, but by a cogitative power called the particular reason, which compares individual notions, just as the intellectual reason, which is distinct from it, compares universal notions.[16] John Locke turns this around. Animals are perfectly capable of reasoning in particular ideas, and so can be said to have reason. But on the other hand, they cannot perform any abstraction at all, and so have no general ideas.[17]

[10] Ibid. 1, 449b30-450a7.
[11] Ibid. 1, 450b12-451a2.
[12] Avicenna Latinus, *de Anima*, ed. S. van Riet, 86,99-3; 89,48-52.
[13] Ibid. 118,6-119,25.
[14] Ibid. 120,26-41.
[15] Averroes, *Short Commentary on Aristotle's de Anima*, tr. by Gomez Gonzalez into Spanish, Madrid 1987, pp. 190-1.
[16] Thomas Aquinas *Summa Theologiae* 1, 2.78, a. 4, *respondeo*.
[17] John Locke, *Essay Concerning Human Understanding* 2.11.10-11.

CHAPTER SIX

The shifting concept of reason

It was not only other psychological concepts (perception, appearance, belief, memory, practical impulse, foresight, emotion, experience, concept-acquisition) that shifted under pressure from the concept of reason. The concept of reason itself shifted, though not necessarily under similar pressures.

Plato

The concept of reason is made prominent in Plato's *Republic*, where he argues that there is in us a part with which we reason. He calls it a part of the soul. The idea that we have a soul was in Greece very seldom denied (an exception is the Aristotelian Dicaearchus, who represents one of his interlocutors, Pherecrates, as saying that the soul is not anything at all).[1] It was seldom denied because it was taken uncontroversially to mean that there is something that animates us. Whether that something is the atoms of Epicurus, the breath (*pneuma*) of the Stoics, or the life-manifesting capacities of Aristotle was the controversial issue. Particularly controversial nowadays is Plato's idea that the soul is an incorporeal self capable of surviving after death. It is because we have restricted our concept of the soul to something like Plato's concept that we find the very idea that we have a soul controversial.

The claim that the soul has parts is new in Plato's *Republic*, because earlier in the *Phaedo* he had assigned non-rational functions to the *body*. It had not then occurred to him to postulate non-rational parts of the *soul*. In the *Republic*, he produces a very gripping logical argument for the claim that there must be different parts within us. I will present it in a version adapted to bring out its plausibility.

Sometimes we appear to be in opposite states at the same time. A thirsty man in a desert, coming across contaminated water, may at the same time want to drink this water and want not to drink it. And these are opposite states, at least by the criterion later offered by Aristotle,

---

[1] Cicero *Tusculan Disputations* 1.21 and 1.24.

that they exhibit the maximum difference, while being in the same range, having as they do an intermediate between them[2] – the intermediate of indifference to the water. Admittedly, my second finger can be simultaneously large and small: large in relation to the little finger and small in relation to the middle one. But the thirsty man appears to be in opposite states in relation to the very *same* thing, this water, and so is a different case. Now the only way in which the paper on which these words are printed can be in opposite states, black and white, at the same time is if the black and the white are in different *parts* of the paper. And there is no obvious reason – what would it be? – why opposite desires should have a different logic from other opposites. If not, there must be a sense of 'parts' in which the opposite desires are in different *parts* of the man.

This does not yet make persuasive Plato's further claims, that the parts in question are parts of the *soul*, that there are precisely three such parts, that one should be called the rational part and the others should be called the spirited and appetitive parts. It does not on its own disprove the earlier *Phaedo* idea that there are two parts, soul and body. But these further claims are ones which he now maintains, and for most of which he goes on to argue. According to his terminology, the part with which the soul reasons (*logizetai*) is the rational (*logistikon*) part. It is this which forbids one, for example, to drink contaminated water. It does so by using a process of reasoning (*logismos*)[3] and the capacity of reason (*logos*).[4] It can also counteract illusion by measuring, counting and weighing.[5]

The three-part division of the soul is most prominent in the *Republic*, *Phaedrus* and *Timaeus*. In other dialogues, the division of the soul is either missing, or only implicit. And in Plato's last dialogue, the *Laws*, what most scholars find implicit is a division of the soul into only two parts, rational and irrational.[6] Such a division is adopted by Aristotle in his own ethical writings, but subsequently criticised by him.[7]

In one later dialogue, the *Theaetetus*, Plato introduces something new. Perception had not been assigned a clear position in the divided

[2] Aristotle *Cat.* 6a17-18, *Metaph.* 5.10, 1018a27-8; 10.4, 1055a27-9; 1055b1-2. Where there is no intermediate, as with odd and even, at least there are things which, unlike numbers, possess neither contrary, *Cat.* 10, 12a6 ff. and *Metaph.* 10.4, 1055b24-5, if the latter is treating odd and even as illustrating contraries rather than privations.

[3] *Republic* 439C-D.

[4] Ibid. 440B.

[5] Ibid. 602D-603B.

[6] Documentation in William Fortenbaugh, *Aristotle on Emotion*, London 1975, 23.

[7] Paul Vander Waerdt, 'Aristotle's criticism of soul division', *American Journal of Philology* 108, 1987, 627-43, sees the criticism of bipartition at Aristotle *DA* 3.9, 432a26 as directed against his former self, rather than against Plato, against the other bipartitions which he lists in his note 6, or against those (presumably members of Plato's Academy) mentioned by Aristotle at *Top.* 126a6-14.

soul, as Aristotle complains.[8] But it is now sharply distinguished from reasoning (*sullogismos*),[9] and hence by implication divorced – although that is not mentioned – from the rational part of the soul.

Reason and the rational part of the soul are not presented by Plato as infallible, except[10] in the philosopher. In his last work, the *Laws*, he introduces a further caveat. You can have people who are superlatively rational (*panu logistikoi*), whose beliefs accord with reason (*doxa kata logon*) and who have excellent reasons (*kaloi logoi*) in their souls, and who yet are unwise (*amathia*), because they do not love what seems excellent to them.[11]

So far I have presented the rational part of the soul as if it were a computer, confined to reasoning. But it has desires as well. According to the *Republic*, it *loves*, and enjoys the *pleasures*, of learning and wisdom and is *intent* on knowing the truth. It is *willing* to follow reasoning.[12] The pleasures of learning were already ascribed to the rational soul in the *Phaedo*, before Plato thought of adding on non-rational parts.[13] It is thanks to its desires, presumably, that the rational part does not merely report what it thinks, but prevents (*kôluein*) or restrains (*katekhein*) certain actions.[14] In the *Laws* passage mentioned above, however, Plato seems to be moving away from the idea that the person whose reason is in good order will have the right desires.

Aristotle

Aristotle introduces a whole series of changes into the concept of reason. In a well-known passage,[15] he complains that various earlier divisions of the soul (and I think he includes Plato's)[16] do not carve

[8] Aristotle *DA* 3.9, 432a30-1. See F. Solmsen, 'Antecedents of Aristotle's psychology and the scale of beings', *American Journal of Philogoy* 76, 1955; William Fortenbaugh, 'On the antecedents of Aristotle's bipartite psychology', *Greek, Roman and Byzantine Studies* 11, 1970 and for a different interpretation, Paul Vander Waerdt, *AJP* 1987, 631-2; 636-7.

[9] *Theaetetus* 186D.

[10] *Republic* 477E.

[11] *Laws* 689A-C; this is pointed out by C.F. Goodey, 'Mental disabilities and human values in Plato's late dialogues', *Archiv für Geschichte der Philosophie*, forthcoming.

[12] Plato *Republic* 580D-581B; 583A; 604D.

[13] Plato *Phaedo* 114E.

[14] Plato *Republic* 439C-D; 606C.

[15] Aristotle *DA* 3.9, 432a22-b7. For the different interpretation of Terry Irwin and Michael Frede, see below.

[16] This orthodox view has been powerfully challenged in a penetrating article by Paul Vander Waerdt, 'Aristotle's criticism of soul-division', *American Journal of Philology* 108, 1987, 627-43. None the less, while he has rightly identified targets other than Plato in the lines following 432a24-6, I am not persuaded that Plato is not among those attacked in the immediately following lines. For Plato's location of certain desires in the reasoning part of the soul, see above. As for perception, he does not firmly locate it (F. Solmsen, 'Antecedents of Aristotle's psychology and scale of beings', *American Journal of*

things at the joints. Although he finds certain earlier divisions adequate[17] when he is doing ethics, politics, or rhetoric, here where he is doing natural science, he feels it necessary to move instead in the direction first adumbrated in the *Theaetetus*. Neither desire nor sense perception should be incorporated into reason, but should be recognised as distinct capacities. But secondly – and this is less commonly noticed[18] – all beliefs (*doxai*) should be incorporated into reason. The argument is that belief involves a rational process of being persuaded, whether by others or by oneself.[19] That Aristotle is talking of being persuaded rather than merely feeling convinced is crucial for the conclusion, because persuasion involves reasons. Once that is noted, the comparison recently made with Donald Davidson's view becomes more apt.[20] Davidson offers a reason for supposing that belief involves the capacity for beliefs about beliefs. Aristotle's insistence that belief involves persuasion would deliver this result by another means. For if it is self-persuasion that is in question, this at least involves beliefs about one's beliefs.

Aristotle's intention, in bringing in persuasion, is to upgrade belief by connecting it with the giving to oneself or others of reasons. But the actual effect may be to downgrade reason by connecting it with all beliefs, whether reflective or not. Ideally, he should have identified a lower class of unreflective beliefs. But the only category he has left over is that of *appearances*.

Aristotle introduces a third revision into some passages. Reason (*logos*) is to be contrasted with the intellectual intuition (*nous*) which grasps scientific definitions (like that of lunar eclipse), ethical values and ethical decisions.[21] Aristotle's talk of *nous* here echoes Plato's choice of the word *noêsis* for the supreme intellectual intuition of the Forms, of what Goodness is, for example.[22] Aristotle compares it with vision, thereby making the excellent point that certain things just have

---

Philology, 1955, 148-64), except that the sensations of plants are, not surprisingly, associated with the bottom part of the soul, *Timaeus* 77B, and in the *Theaetetus* Plato finally comes to treat perception as non-rational, 186C-D.

17 Aristotle *NE* 1.13, 1102a25-7.

18 The point is recognised by William Fortenbaugh, *Aristotle on Emotion*, London 1975, 39-40; 42.

19 Aristotle *DA* 3.3, 428a22-4, tr. in Chapter Three, where I argue for the relevance of self-persuasion. I must renew my warning that the Loeb and Oxford translations make the passage unintelligible.

20 Christopher Gill, 'Is there a concept of person in Greek Philosophy?' in Stephen Everson, ed., *Ancient Philosophy of Mind*, Cambridge 1991, at 191, would have a still stronger case, if he abandoned on p. 180 the erroneous substitution of conviction for persuasion, which he quotes from the Oxford translation.

21 Aristotle *NE* 6.8, 1142a25-6; 6.11, 1143a35-b5; 7.8, 1151a17-18, analysed in Richard Sorabji, 'Aristotle on the role of intellect in virtue', *Proceedings of the Aristotelian Society* 74, 1973-4, 107-29, repr. in A Rorty, ed., *Essays on Aristotle's Ethics*, Berkeley and Los Angeles 1980, ch. 12.

22 Plato *Republic* 511D-E.

to be *spotted*.[23] He is not claiming that we have some infallible method for spotting; it is merely that 'spotting' is a success-verb, applicable only to cases where we are right.[24] On this usage, reason (*logos*), does not cover all thinking, because it excludes intellectual spotting. But *nous*[25] and *logos* are not always so sharply differentiated. *Nous* can be that with which the soul reasons,[26] or alternatively can fall under *logos*.[27]

Aristotle's fourth revision introduces one of several distinctions within the concept of reason, distinctions which will be necessary if reason is to be presented as man's defining characteristic. Because exercises of reason (unlike spotting) can be incorrect, as well as correct, we find Aristotle distinguishing off *right* reason (*orthos logos*), a term which he says is common in others,[28] but to which he gives a new emphasis. When Aristotle makes reason the distinguishing mark of men, he is referring to reason, right *or wrong*, as later authors emphasise.[29]

Fifthly, Aristotle differentiates theoretical and practical reason,[30] introducing these terms (*theôrêtikos* vs. *praktikos logos*) into the language for the first time. And it is only practical reason that is unique to man, for theoretical reason is shared with God.

Sixthly, Aristotle distinguishes within the rational part of the soul between a part that reasons for itself and a part that listens (*epipeithês, katêkoös, peitharkhikos, peithesthai, aisthanesthai,*

---

[23] Aristotle *NE* 6.11, 1143a35-b5; 6.13, 1144b8-13. I think we need not shun (Jonathan Barnes, *Aristotle's Posterior Analytics*, Oxford 1975, 257) the translation 'intuition', for this translation need not imply any method, as the talk of 'spotting' perhaps makes clearer.

[24] Aristotle *DA* 3.3, 428a17.

[25] *Nous* is once defined as that with which the soul reasons (*dianoeisthai*) and apprehends (*hupolambanein*), *DA* 3.4, 429a22-3, terms which cover true belief (*doxa*), scientific understanding (*epistêmê*) and practical understanding (*phronêsis*), *DA* 3.3, 427b8-13; 24-6. Indeed, one of the terms (*dianoia*) had been contrasted by Plato with *noêsis* as corresponding to the inferior reasoning of mathematics, *Republic* 511D-E.

[26] *Logos* can cover all the functions of *nous* just listed, and even the special function of intellectual spotting. For this spotting is an exercise of practical understanding (*phronêsis*), *NE* 6.8, 1142a26-30; 6.11, 1143a32-b14; 6.12, 1144a28-31; 6.13, 1144b1-17, which is itself described as being or involving reason (*logos*), *NE* 6.5, 1140b5; 20; 6.13, 1144b27-8. Further, spotting is introduced as falling under that part of the soul that has reason (*logos*), and under the particular part that is ratiocinative (*logistikon*), *NE* 6.2, 1139a6; 11-15.

[27] When thought inspires action, the term *nous* (intellect) can be interchanged with the term *logos* (reason), *DA* 3.10, 433b6; 8, or with Plato's term, *to logistikon* (the reasoning part of the soul), which gives orders. See *DA* 3.9, 432b27 *to logistikon kai ho kaloumenos nous* (the reasoning part and what is called intellect); 433a2: *nous epitattei* (intellect gives orders).

[28] *NE* 2.2, 1103b32; 6.13, 1144b23; cf. *DA* 3.3, 427b13. The reference is not to Plato *Phaedo* 73A; 94A.

[29] See Galen *PHP* Book 4, p. 254, de Lacy; Plutarch *Sollertia* 962C, copied by Porphyry *Abstinence* 3.2 (but 3.19 seems to ignore the distinction).

[30] *Pol.* 7.14, 1333a25; *NE* 1.7, 1098a3.

akouein, akoustikos) to reason.[31] It is this distinction that enables
Aristotle to treat all humans as having or sharing in reason, even
natural slaves who are said not to reason for themselves.[32] He is conscious that it is an innovation to describe this part as having reason
(*logos*), rather than being irrational (*alogos*). For in Plato it was an
irrational part of the soul, the spirited part, that listened (*katêkoös,
hupêkoös*) to, or allied with (*summakhos*), reason.[33] Indeed, Plato
specially argued that this part was distinct from the rational.[34] And
yet the need for such a concept is already present both in the *Republic*,
where the reason of ordinary citizens is to take its cue from the
philosopher kings, and in the *Laws*.[35]

In the seventh place, Aristotle's disagreement with Plato is still
more extensive, because Plato says that some people, in his opinion,
never acquire reason (*logistikon, logismos*) and others acquire it only
late. Children do not have it at all.[36] It is only one part of Aristotle's
reply that those who can listen to the reason of others at least
participate in reason, and even in a sense have it. Another part of his
reply concerns children. Unlike natural slaves, they can be said to have
the power of deliberation (*to bouleutikon*). The qualification is that the
power is incomplete (*ateles*).[37] Reason, then, may be complete or
incomplete.

In separating desire from reason, as I believe Aristotle does in *DA*
3.9, he is rejecting the view taken by himself in earlier works and by
some members of Plato's Academy, that the rational part of the soul
(*logistikon*) incorporates a rational desire (*boulêsis*). The result, if I am
right, is to produce a further innovation. It makes reason a neutral
instrument that can be used well or badly, rather than one whose
natural tendency is in the direction of wisdom. The latter conception of
reason has been ascribed to the ancients in general.[38] But I rather

---

[31] Aristotle *NE* 1.7, 1098a3-5; 1.13, 1102b30-1103a3; *EE* 2.1, 1219b27-31.

[32] Aristotle *Pol.* 1.5, 1254b21-4; 1.13, 1260b3-8. See Chapter Eleven for Aristotle's
wavering between the description having (*ekhein*) reason and merely sharing in it
(*metekhein, koinônein*).

[33] Plato *Republic* 440B-D; *Timaeus* 70A.

[34] Plato *Republic* 440E-441A.

[35] For the *Laws*, see William Fortenbaugh *Aristotle on Emotion*, London 1975, 23-5;
29-31.

[36] Plato *Republic* 441A-B.

[37] Aristotle *Politics* 1.13, 1260a12-14.

[38] Michael Frede, 'The Stoic doctrine of the affections of the soul', in M. Schofield and
G. Striker, eds, *The Norms of Nature*, Cambridge 1986, 93-110, at 100-1. I should
acknowledge the rival interpretation of *DA* 3.9 put to me by Michael Frede, and
expounded by Terry Irwin, *Aristotle's First Principles*, Oxford 1988, p. 595, n. 2,
according to which *DA* 3.9, 432a22-b7, does not *endorse* the claim that desire is an
entirely distinct capacity from reason. On the other side, Paul Vander Waerdt agrees,
loc. cit., that at 3.9 Aristotle is rejecting the inclusion of rational desire (*boulêsis*) within
reason (*logistikon*), whether in the manner of his own earlier scheme which had involved
a bipartition of the soul (*Rhet.* 1.10, 1368b27-1369a4; *NE* 5.11, 1138b11), or in the

doubt if the mature Aristotle would agree: the tendency to wisdom belongs not to reason (*logos*), but to right reason (*orthos logos*). And a sign of this, as I am reminded by Paul Vander Waerdt, is that Aristotle discusses the rational faculty of *deinotês* (cleverness) in *Nicomachean Ethics* 6.13, and explicitly constrasts it with *phronêsis* (practical wisdom), as having no tendency in the direction of good rather than evil, unlike *phronêsis* which was originally introduced as involving *right* reason.

Even in Plato and the Stoics, the reason of ordinary humans is notoriously fallible. *Boulêsis*, for the Stoics, that is desire that accords with right reason, is found only in that very rare being, the wise person.[39] But what the Stoics do concede is that it is natural, even if rare, for human reason to be attracted to the genuinely good.[40] And Plato much of the time treats reason as having the right desires. I have to say 'much of the time', because of the caveat noted above, that in the *Laws* Plato allows reason might be in superlative order, and yet one might still fail to love what is good.[41] This acknowledgment in the *Laws* does anticipate Aristotle's neutral concept of reason.

I recently saw a very helpful checklist of criteria for the modern concept of reason.[42] Its twenty or more entries looked completely higgledy-piggledy, until one saw how they derived in various ways from the ancient distinctions. The list referred to reasoning and to believing on the basis of reasons. It concentrated under some headings on practical reason, and it distinguished right reason. All these ideas stem from Aristotle. At first sight it might look like an anomaly that the list referred to concept formation. But we should remember that Aristotle makes it a function of intellect (*nous*) to form scientific concepts like lunar eclipse, and that, although this function of intellect is sometimes contrasted with reasoning, it can also be treated as an exercise of reason. We shall now see that after Aristotle the Stoics connect reason with concepts still more tightly.

The Stoics

According to the Stoic Chrysippus in the third century BC, reason just is a certain collection of conceptions. It includes deliberately cultivated conceptions and naturally acquired preconceptions (*ennoiôn te tinôn*

manner of the tripartition which he quotes from Plato's Academy at *Top.* 126a13.

[39] Cicero *Tusc.* 4.12

[40] See A. Bonhoeffer, *Epictet und die Stoa*, Stuttgart 1890, 223-9; 235; Brad Inwood, *Ethics and Human Action in Early Stoicism*, Oxford 1985, 227-8, on the Stoic idea that rational desire (*orexis*), at least in its natural form, is directed to what is genuinely good.

[41] Plato *Laws* 689A-C.

[42] Robert Solomon, 'Existentialism, emotions and the cultural limits of rationality', paper delivered at the East-West Colloquium on Culture and Rationality, Mount Abu, India, Jan. 7-10, 1991, subsequently published in a fuller version in *Philosophy*

kai prolêpseôn athroisma).[43] We shall see that this innovation was to prove influential.

A further innovation among the Stoics was massively to expand the province of reason. It began to become apparent in Chapters Three and Four how perception and, in humans, perceptual appearance, along with memory and the emotions were all made functions of reason. The concept of rational assent was repeatedly called into play, partly in order to represent us as responsible for our emotions, actions and perceptual judgments. Non-rational animals were left with little but appearances (*phantasiai*).

The Stoic expansion of reason shows itself in the fact that, except for Posidonius, they dropped the two non-rational parts of the soul that we find in Plato's *Republic, Phaedrus* and *Timaeus*. In considering Plato's thirsty man tempted by contaminated water, we are no longer to think of his desire for the water as produced by a non-rational part. All that is acting is reason itself, only reason is oscillating between drinking and not drinking with a rapidity which makes the word 'fluttering' (*ptoia*) appropriate for the oscillation.[44]

The Middle Platonists

In one of the Middle Platonists, we find an attempt to accommodate both Plato's rationalistic theory of concept acquisition and Aristotle's empiricist account. In order to do so, it seems to have drawn on the Stoic idea of reason as comprising two types of concept, the deliberately cultivated *ennoiai* and the naturally acquired *prolêpseis*. But the Stoic distinction gets transmuted.

The text in question, the *Didaskalikos*, is of disputed authorship, but comes from the second century AD. Corresponding to the Stoics' two kinds of concept, the Middle Platonist text distinguishes two types of reason, the higher scientific reason (*epistêmonikos logos*) and the lower belief-type reason (*doxastikos logos*).[45] Moreover, scientific reason is said, like the Stoics' reason, to consist (*sunestêke*) of conceptions (*ennoiai*). But these conceptions, which are called natural (*phusikai*), are remembered (*mnême*) in the Platonic fashion from a previous life:

> It was then [in the previous life] called intuition (*noêsis*), but now a natural conception (*phusikê ennoia*), and a natural conception is also called by him [Plato] simple scientific understanding (*epistême*

East and West 42, 1992, 597-621.

[43] Galen *PHP* 5.3.1, p. 304, de Lacy (= *SVF* 2.841); cf. Aëtius 4.11.3-4 in *Dox. Gr.* 400,17-26 (= *SVF* 1.149; 2.83).

[44] Stobaeus *Eclogae* 2.88 ff (*SVF* 3.378); Plutarch *On Moral Virtue* 446F-447A (*SVF* 3.459).

[45] Albinus/Alcinous (?) *Didaskalikos*, ch. 4, ed. Hermann *Plato* Teubner edition vol. 6 (English translations by George Burges, in the Bohn Classical Library *Plato*, vol. 6,

haplê), or a fledgling of the soul, or sometimes memory (*mnêmê*). And natural scientific reason (*epistêmonikos logos*) consists (*sunestêke*) of these instances of simple scientific understanding (*haplai epistêmai*), and arises in us naturally.[46]

The natural conceptions of which the higher type of reason, *epistêmonikos*, consists seem to correspond to the Stoics' naturally acquired preconceptions. And just as these natural conceptions, which make up scientific reason, are called instances of scientific understanding (*epistêmai*), so the constituents of belief-type reason appear to be called belief (*doxa*).[47] Are these beliefs also conceptions, as Larry Schrenk has conjectured? Certainly, the Stoics would have said that thoughts (*dianoêseis*) are stirred-up conceptions (*ennoiai*).[48] If so, the Middle Platonist belief-type conceptions will correspond to the Stoics' deliberately cultivated ones (*ennoiai*), though again with Platonic transmutations.

The transmutations in this case are considerable, because the *Didaskalikos* draws on the account in Plato's *Theaetetus* of belief (*doxa*) as something empirically acquired. It is produced by our fitting a perception to a memory imprinted in the wax tablet of our minds.[49] If these beliefs, which constitute belief-type reason, are also conceptions, then the *Didaskalikos* will be accommodating Aristotle's empiricist account of concept acquisition, alongside (or rather at a level below) Plato's account of concepts as recollected from a previous life. Even if they are not conceptions, the text will be giving an empiricist account of our acquisition of the lower type of reason.

We can also now understand another feature of the *Didaskalikos*' account of reason. It draws a sharper distinction than Aristotle's between (natural) reason (*logos*) and intellect (*nous*), and it bases this distinction on the idea that natural reason is a tool (*organon*), indeed probably intellect's tool. This makes sense, given that natural reason is conceived in the Stoic manner as being a set of conceptions. A set of conceptions could very well serve as the tool of intellect.

Meanwhile the recognition of a lower type of reason based on empirical experience should make it easier to grant reason to animals. As it happens, the *Didaskalikos* does grant the transmigration of

---

London 1854 and by Jeremiah Reedy 1991; Budé editions by P. Louis 'Epitomé', and by John Whittaker 'Alcinoos', *Enseignement*, 1991). My account is indebted to Larry Schrenk, 'Faculties of judgement in the *Didaskalikos*', *Mnemosyne*, 44, 1991, 347-63.

[46] *Didaskalikos* ch. 4, 155, 27-31 in the original edition of Hermann, where the lines are not numbered. The new Budé edition by John Whittaker assigns line numbers 31 to 36. The line numbers below follow Hermann.

[47] At any rate, the lower type of reason is described not only as being of belief type (*doxastikos*), but also as being belief (*doxa*) 154,24-5.

[48] Larry Schrenk, op. cit.

[49] *Didaskalikos* 154,35-155,12, drawing on Plato *Theaetetus* 193B-195E.

human souls into animals.[50] But it also rather surprisingly speaks of irrational souls whose faculties include appearance (*phantasia*), not reasoning (*logismos*), and it describes these as having a different substance (*ousia*), and being mortal.[51] If these are animal souls, they lack reason after all.

Neoplatonists

The Neoplatonists pick up the Middle Platonist idea that there is a lower belief-type reason (*doxastikos logos*). This is explicitly referred to by the late Neoplatonist Priscian.[52] And Hermeias of Alexandria speaks of the empirically acquired concepts which constitute this kind of reason, when he says that humans assemble in their minds (*sunathroizein en têi dianoiāi*) the universal horse after seeing individual horses.[53] Empirically acquired concepts are also accepted by Porphyry, Syrianus, Proclus, Ammonius, Philoponus, Simplicius and Olympiodorus,[54] although Olympiodorus is disparaging about them, Simplicius sometimes doubtful,[55] and there was a debate about whether they were precise enough for the purposes of mathematics.[56] One answer was that they needed to be corrected by the precise concepts which we have inherited, in Platonic fashion, in our intellects from a previous life. We have both kinds of concepts, the Aristotelian and the Platonic.

The Neoplatonists also pick up and adapt the distinction sometimes drawn by Aristotle between intuitive intellect (*nous*) and reason (*logos*). We find intellect (*nous*), indeed two or three kinds of intellect in late Neoplatonism, placed higher in the ontological hierarchy than reason (*logos, logikê ousia, logikê zôê, logikê energeia, logikê psukhê*).[57]

---

[50] *Didaskalikos* 178,29.

[51] Ibid. 178,21-5.

[52] Priscian *Metaphrasis of Theophrastus' de Anima, CAG* supp. vol. 1, part 2, 19,10-13.

[53] Hermeias *in Phdr.* 171,10, Couvreur.

[54] Porphyry, *Commentary on Ptolemy's Harmonics* 13,15-14,28; Syrianus *in Metaph.* 12,29-13,3; 91,20-34; 95,29 ff; Proclus *Commentary on Euclid's Elements 1* 51,4-13; cf. 12,2-15,5; 48,1-57,8; Ammonius *in Isag.* 41,19-20; 42,10-21; Philoponus *in Phys.* 11,24-13,3; *in DA* 57,28-58,6; Simplicius *in Cat.* 84,23-8; Simplicius (?) *in DA 3* 233,7-17; 277,1-6; 277,30-278,6. For Olympiodorus see next note. Most of these references are supplied by Ian Mueller, 'Aristotle's doctrine of abstraction in the commentators', in Richard Sorabji, ed., *Aristotle Transformed: The Ancient Commentators and Their Influence*, London and Ithaca NY 1990, ch. 20. I have also benefited from discussion with Frans de Haas.

[55] Olympiodorus *Commentary on Plato's Phaedo* 12.1, lines 9-25, Westerink, but see also 12.2; Simplicius *in Phys.* 1075, 2-20.

[56] Mueller shows that according to Syrianus and Simplicius, Pythagorean mathematics confines itself to non-empirical concepts, and even ordinary mathematics may require both kinds, while according to Proclus, ordinary mathematics also does without the empirical ones.

[57] Simplicius *in DA* 40,20-2; 102,11-12; and Simplicius, if he is the author of *in DA 3*, 217,28-32; 218,29-32; 220,21-6; 28-34; 221,24-8. For references to Simplicius and Philoponus, see H.J. Blumenthal, 'Simplicius and others on Aristotle's discussions of

Reason is thought of as a function of the soul (*psukhê*), rather than of the intellect.[58] Unlike the intellect, it makes transitions (*diexodikai meta-baseis*), progresses (*proienai*) and unfolds (*anelixis*), whereas the gaze of intellect is unchanging and simple.[59] Reason (*logos*) and reasoning (*logismos, logizesthai*) are connected with a kind of thinking (*dianoia*) which Plato classed below philosophical understanding in his *Republic*,[60] and indeed the Neoplatonist distinction is more commonly put as that between *dianoia* and *nous*. *Dianoia*, like the thinking of *logos*, is an activity of soul, as opposed to intellect.[61] It makes transitions, takes one thing after another progressively, and consequently is spread out in time.[62] In contrast, the thought in which the intellect engages is not spread out, but timeless.[63] It involves no division or complexity, but comprehends its object within a single focus.[64]

Despite, or rather because of, the superiority of intellect (*nous*), Proclus grants intellect to many animals as something implied by their perception, appearance and memory, even though he denies them reason.[65] His rationale is that the higher faculty, intellect, should be more comprehensive than the lower and his interest is in honouring intellect, not animals.

The basic Neoplatonist distinction between reason and intellect was passed on to the Latin Middle Ages by Boethius,[66] and was still being discussed and modified in the thirteenth century by Thomas Aquinas.[67]

---

reason', in *Gonimos, Neoplatonic and Byzantine Studies Presented to Leendert G. Westerink at 75*, a volume of Arethusa, Buffalo NY 1988, 103-19.

[58] Simplicius (?) *in DA* 217,28-32; 218,29-32; 221,24-8.

[59] Simplicius *in DA* 42,20-2; 100,20-1; 102,11-12; Simplicius (?) *in DA* 226,36-7.

[60] Plotinus e.g. 5.3.3 (35-6) and John Rist, 'Integration and the undescended soul in Plotinus', *American Journal of Philology* 88, 1967, at 416; Simplicius (?) in DA 226,36-7; Philoponus *in DA* 260,18; cf. Plato *Republic* 511D.

[61] Plotinus 3.7.11 (36-45).

[62] Plotinus e.g. 3.6.11 (36-40); 5.3.17 (23-5); 6.9.5 (7-12); Simplicius (?) *in DA* 226,36-7; Philoponus *in DA* 260,23-5.

[63] Plotinus 4.4.1.

[64] Philoponus *in DA* 267,11-16; Philoponus (?) *in DA 3* 550,7-8; for Plotinus see Richard Sorabji, *Time, Creation and the Continuum*, London and Ithaca NY 1983, 152-3, with replies by A.C. Lloyd, 'Non-propositional thought in Plotinus', *Phronesis* 31, 1986, 258-65; Steven Strange, 'Plotinus on the articulation of being', in preparation, presented to the Society for Ancient Greek Philosophy, December 1989. For a modern endorsement of the distinction of intellect, see Stephen Clark, 'Reason as *daimôn*' in Christopher Gill, ed., *The Person and the Human Mind*, Oxford 1990.

[65] Proclus *Platonic Theology* 3.128.

[66] Boethius *Consolation of Philosophy* 4, prose 6 (cf. *On the Trinity* 2, lines 16-17): reasoning (*ratiocinatio*) is related to intellectual understanding (*intellectus*) as time to eternity, as involving movement from one stage to another.

[67] Thomas Aquinas *Summa Theologiae* 1, q. 79, a. 8 agrees that there are two different exercises (*actus*). For reasoning (*ratiocinatio*) involves moving towards understanding (*intelligere*). But these two exercises are exercises of one and the same power, just as are motion and rest. So reason (*ratio*) is not after all a distinct power from intellectual understanding (*intellectus*).

The memorists

Michael Frede has drawn attention to a group of empiricist doctors, the memorists, who took a very different view of reason. Their point was partly a verbal one: they restricted the name of reason to certain syllogistic operations favoured by Aristotelian logicians, which they themselves regarded as useless. They did, however, have a substantial point: reason was unnecessary, not only to animals (whom they were not discussing), but even to humans. The work could be done by memory, and memory was not itself, as it was for the Stoics, a function of reason. Memory, not reason, was what enabled us to think, infer, reflect, believe, assume, examine, generalise and know.[68]

Fascinating as it is to find this line of thought so early, I am not convinced by Frede's further suggestion that the Epicureans took a similar line. For to humans the Epicureans allow reason (*logos*),[69] while to animals they deny not only reason,[70] but also, in the case of one author, thinking (*noêsis*) and belief (*doxa, pseudodoxia*).[71] In another author, memory is subordinated to thought (*dianoia*), because in memory thought receives likenesses of what was formerly perceived.[72] In yet another, memory is said to be in abeyance during dreams,[73] even while thought (*dianoia*) or equivalently the mind (*mens, animus, mens animi*) is at work.[74] The Epicureans do not seem to have an agreed position on the analysis of mental capacities, but these various positions do all agree in being incompatible with memorism.

Surprisingly, it is not the empiricist Epicureans, but the Platonists, who have given the largest role to memory in the texts we have so far surveyed. In the *Didaskalikos*, both scientific and belief-type reason are dependent on memory.

If anyone may be compared with the memorists, it is Hume in the eighteenth century, who says that all that animals need and all that men need most of the time is an association of ideas based on custom. This enables them to know what to expect in the world and to learn from experience. They do not need reasoning, in any stronger sense.[75]

---

[68] Michael Frede, 'An empiricist view of knowledge: memorism', in Stephen Everson, ed., *A Philosophical Introduction to Ancient Epistemology*, Cambridge 1990, 224-50.

[69] Hermarchus ap. Porphyrium *Abstinence* 1.12; Epicurus ap. Ciceronem *ND* 1.48.

[70] Ibid.

[71] Philodemus *On the Gods* 12.17; 13.39 (*noêsis*); 13.6-7 (*doxa*) 14.34 (*pseudodoxia*).

[72] Diogenes of Oenoanda, new fr. 5.3.3-14, Smith. Admittedly, some memory at least is treated by Hermarchus as irrational (*alogos*) and contrasted with reasoning (*epilogismos*), ap. Porphyrium *Abstinence* 1.10.

[73] Lucretius 4.765.

[74] Epicurus *Letter to Herodotus* 51, in Diogenes Laertius *Lives* 10.51; Lucretius 4.728-31; 747-8; 750-61; 767; 803-15; 975-7.

[75] David Hume, *Enquiry Concerning Human Understanding* 82-5; *A Treatise of Human Nature* 1.3.16.

Leibniz had made an explicit comparison between the empiricist doctors of antiquity and animals. Neither have knowledge of cause and effect. They merely expect good or harm from the same thing in similar circumstances, and this requires only memory. But man, according to Leibniz, is different. He has reason, and so goes beyond the universals of induction and experience. Man is capable of producing deductive syllogisms, knowing universal necessary truths and in general of acquiring scientific understanding of the kind described by Aristotle.[76] After distinguishing the Rationalist doctors of antiquity from the Empiricist doctors and the so-called Methodists, Leibniz continues:

I have shown that it is enough for animals to be mere empiricists in order to be able to do all that they do, and that memory is enough for the connexions they need to make, when they have a fresh experience like their former ones and expect a sequel like the former sequels. Humans also very often make similar connexions which are successful. But as the connexions lack any necessity, they very often also fail, since the same causes are not in play. It is therefore man's advantage not to be merely empiricist and possessed of memory which serves for inductive inference, but to be rationalist as well and capable of constructing demonstrative syllogisms and recognising necessary truths which yield absolutely universal and unchangeable propositions. That is what makes man capable of demonstrative sciences, of which one finds no trace in animals.

[76] Leibniz, 'Extrait du Dictionnaire de M. Bayle, article "Rorarius", p. 2599 sqq. de l'édition de l'an 1702, avec mes remarques', in Gerhardt, ed., *Philosophische Schriften* 4, 524-54, at 525-6. The same account of reasoning, without reference to the ancient empiricist doctors, has been pointed out to me by Don Rutherford in the contemporary *New Essays Conerning Human Understanding*, written 1704-5, published 1765, Academy edition series 6, vol. 6, preface pp. 50-1; book 2, ch. 11, §11, p. 143; 2.33.18, p. 271; 4.17.3, pp. 475-6, tr. by Peter Remnant and Jonathan Bennett, Cambridge 1981.

CHAPTER SEVEN

Speech, skills, inference and other proofs of reason

The argumentative Greeks did not just lie down and accept the denial of reason to animals on the mere say-so of Aristotle and the Stoics. And indeed it is hard to deny that the chimpanzee who put two sticks together to extend his reach for a banana[1] was exercising reason in *some* sense, although we have in the last chapter found that term to be too blunt an instrument to be very informative on its own. Aristotle's own successors, Theophrastus and Strato, disagreed with him,[2] and so did the Pythagoreans and Platonists, up until Iamblichus.[3]

The case for animal reason was based on many capacities, including those studied in Chapters Three and Four above: perception,[4] memory, preparation and emotion.[5] One of the most important passages from Plutarch was partially translated in Chapter Four. Other capacities cited as proofs of animal reason were animal speech,[6] skills,[7] virtues,[8]

---

[1] Wolfgang Koehler, *The Mentality of Apes*, London 1925, 127.

[2] See Chapter Three.

[3] The Platonists Plutarch and Porphyry supply two of the most important texts. On Celsus, a pro-animal Platonist attacked by Origen, see Chapter Fourteen. Eve Cole has allowed me to see a valuable unpublished paper 'Plotinus on the souls of beasts', in which she cites Plotinus' ascription of rationality to animals at 3.2.7 (34-6); 6.7.9 (13-14); 3.3.4 (41-4), as representing one strand, though only one strand, in his thought. For the disagreement of some Platonists, see Chapter Thirteen on Iamblichus and later Neoplatonists, and on Heraclides Ponticus.

[4] Plutarch *Sollertia* 961A-B, repeated Porphyry *Abstinence* 3.21; Sextus M 7.350; Epiphanius *Against Heresies* 3.2.9 (*Dox. Gr.* 592,16-18; Porphyry *Abstinence* 3.1.4. On Proclus *Platonic Theology* 3.6, see next note.

[5] Plutarch *Sollertia* 966B; 961A-F, the latter repeated by Porphyry *Abstinence* 3.21-2; cf. 3.1.4. Proclus distinguishes intellect (*nous*) from reason (*logos*), and holds that only the former is implied by perception, appearance and memory, *Platonic Theology* 3.6, Saffrey and Westerink 23,25-24,6.

[6] Philo *de Animalibus* 12-15; Plutarch *Sollertia* 973A; Sextus PH 1.73 ff.; Porphyry *Abstinence* 3.3-6.

[7] Philo *de Animalibus* 16-66; Sextus *PH* 1.65-72; Plutarch *Sollertia* 960E-961F; 966B-985C.

[8] Philo *de Animalibus* 62; 64; Plutarch *Sollertia* 962A-963B; 966B; *Gryllos* 986F-992E;

vices,[9] and even the liability to madness.[10] Animal skills were carefully divided up into those learnt from humans and those derived from nature or self-taught. Examples of the latter were collected under the headings of pursuit and avoidance, preparations for the future, knowledge of how to use their own bodily parts, the creation of useful things and the ability to heal their wounds.[11]

The most important passages are in Philo of Alexandria, Plutarch, Sextus Empiricus and Porphyry.[12] To take two examples, Plutarch has a discussion, later repeated by Porphyry, which starts from pursuit and avoidance. He introduces a functional argument, that perception, perceptual appearance, toil, pain and distress could not serve their purpose of promoting pursuit and avoidance, without such obviously rational activities as reasoning (*logizesthai*), discriminating (*krinein*), remembering (*mnêmoneuein*), attending (*prosekhein*), expectation (*prosdokia*), intent (*prothesis*), preparation (*paraskeuê*), hope (*elpizein*), fear (*dedoikenai*), appetite (*epithumein*) and grief (*askhallein*). Strato says that even perceiving requires thought because it requires attention. Be that as it may, reason is implied by memory, fear, craving (*pothoun*), devising (*mêkhanesthai*) and preparation, and by animal emotions (*pathê*) which include fear, anger (*thumos*), envy (*phthonos*), jealousy (*zêlotopia*), regret (*metanoia*) and pleasure (*hêdonê*).[13] Plutarch then appends virtue, vice and madness, and concludes with a list from 'the philosophers', which adds in care (*epimeleia*) for young, gratitude (*kharis*), resentment (*mnêsikakia*), and the ability to find what they need.[14]

The sceptic Sextus Empiricus wants to argue that the appearances enjoyed by a dog are no less trustworthy than ours. He ascribes (internal) reason to a dog on the basis of its choice and avoidance, its knowledge of skills (*tekhnai*), its apprehension of virtues, its understanding (*sunetos*), its inferences and its ability to deal with wounds. The first three marks are said to be ones in which reason is anchored (*saluei*). The complete set provides the perfection (*teleiotês*) of reason.

Since perception, memory, preparation and emotion have already been discussed above, I will concentrate in this chapter on some of the

---

Sextus *PH* 1.67-8; Porphyry *Abstinence* 3.11-13; 3.22-3.

[9] Philo *de Animalibus* 66-70; Plutarch *Sollertia* 962B-963A; Porphyry *Abstinence* 3.13; 22-3. Cf. Seneca *de Ira* 1.3.7: animals lack reason, and so lack virtue and vice.

[10] Plutarch *Sollertia* 963C-F; repeated Porphyry *Abstinence* 3.24.

[11] Philo *de Animalibus* 16-66; Sextus *PH* 1.65-72; Plutarch *Sollertia* 960E-F, repeated Porphyry *Abstinence* 3.21; Plutarch *Sollertia* 966B; Porphyry *Abstinence* 3.9-10.

[12] Philo *de Animalibus*, Plutarch *Sollertia*; *That Irrational Animals Have Reason*: cf. *On the Eating of Flesh*; Sextus *PH* 1.63 ff.; Porphyry *On Abstinence from Animal Food* Book 3.

[13] Plutarch *Sollertia* 960E-961E; repeated Porphyry *Abstinence* 3.21-2.

[14] Plutarch *Sollertia* 962A-963F; (repeated Porphyry *Abstinence* 3.23-4) and 966B, illustrated up to 985C.

other proofs of animal reason, starting with speech, and moving on to skills and inference.

Speech

The power of speech in animals is vividly illustrated by the ancient story of Apsethos who taught his caged parrots to say 'Apsethos is a god', and then released them all over Libya. The ruse was spotted by a wily Greek who recaptured some parrots and taught them to say, 'Apsethos shut us up and compelled us to say "Apsethos is a god".' This palinode led the Libyans to burn Apsethos.[15]

In evaluating the difference between humans and animals, the possession of language, spoken or otherwise, has become a central issue. This is illustrated for example in the modern experiments with teaching chimpanzees non-spoken sign language or other symbols. It was already said by Descartes in a letter to Henry More that lack of speech was the true difference between animals and man.[16]

The questions whether animals have speech and whether they have reason were closely connected in Greek thought. This was partly because the same word *logos* could be used equally for speech or reason. Moreover, Plato defined thought (*dianoia, dianoeisthai*) as silent, inner speech (*logos, dialogos, dialegesthai*).[17] There is foreshadowed in Aristotle, and more fully expressed in the Hellenistic period which followed Aristotle's death, a standard distinction between spoken (*prophorikos*) and internal (*endiathetos*) *logos*.[18] It is as if there were a single thing that could be manifested in inner reasoning or in speech. Some philosophers ascribe both kinds of *logos* to animals, citing birds for the clearest examples of speech.[19] But other unnamed philosophers grant animals external *logos*, not internal,[20] while Galen and some Pythagoreans allow them internal without external.[21]

What were the arguments on whether animals have speech? Socrates is said already to have denied to them articulation (*arthroun*).[22] Aristotle allowed that some of them make meaningful sounds (*phônê, sêmantikos psophos, sêmainein*).[23] But they do not have

[15] Nicely told by Catherine Osborne, *Rethinking Early Greek Philosophy*, London 1987, pp. 70-2 and 233, quoting Hippolytus *Refutation* 6, chs 7-8; Maximus of Tyre 29.4; Aelian *Varia Historia* 14.30; Scholion to Dio Chrysostom *Orat.* 1.14..

[16] Descartes Letter to Henry More, 5 February 1649, Letter 537, in Adam, Tannéry (AT), eds., vol. 5, pp. 275-9.

[17] Plato *Theaetetus* 189E-190A; *Sophist* 263E ff.

[18] Aristotle *An. Post.* 1.10, 76b24-5;

[19] Sextus *PH* 1.65 ff; 1.73 ff; Porphyry *Abstinence* 3.2 ff; 3.7 ff; Philo, ascribing a view to his nephew, *de Animalibus* 12 ff; 16 ff; Plutarch *Sollertia* 973A.

[20] Sextus *M* 8.275.

[21] Galen *Protreptic* ch. 1; Pythagoreans ap. Aëtium 5.20 (*Dox. Gr.* 432a15 ff).

[22] Xenophon *Mem.* 1.4.12.

[23] Aristotle *DA* 2.8, 420b9-421a6; *Pol.* 1.2,1253a10-14. Some animals recognise

words (*onomata*), because words involve a convention (*sunthêkê*).[24] It might be said of some birds that they have articulate utterance (*dialektos*),[25] in other words segmentation (*diarthrôsis*) of utterance by the tongue. But even this is qualified by an 'as it were' (*hôsper*)[26] – it is not clear why, because Aristotle does think that birds use their tongue for segmentation.[27] More important is the fact that Aristotle denies animals speech (*logos*). This has tremendous consequences.[28] For speech does more than signify (*sêmainein*) what is pleasant or painful, which animals can manage. Rather it can convey (*dêloun*) what is advantageous or harmful, and hence what is just or unjust, and this is crucial for the formation of the households and cities in which men live.

The Stoics returned to the question of animal utterance. According to Diogenes of Babylon, animals have a voice (*phônê*), but it is merely air struck by an *impulse* (*hormê*), whereas the human voice is sent out by the mind (*dianoia*) and is articulated (*enarthros*).[29] That animal utterance is not articulated was conceded even by Philo's nephew.[30] But other persons unnamed allowed, and the Platonist Plutarch insisted, that crows, parrots, jays and starlings do produce articulate utterance.[31] There was therefore another line for the Stoics to fall back on. Chrysippus denied that ravens, crows and children could be said to speak, and Varro offers the justification that they lack syntax. The Latin word for speaking (*loqui*), he erroneously says, is connected with *locus*, a place, and implies being able to put words in the right place.[32] Modern discussions have reached exactly the same point. It was suggested that chimpanzees, though unable to speak, could learn sign language.[33] Back came the answer that the chimpanzees at best operated with single terms: they did not string them together syntactically.[34] This reply fitted with Chomsky's view that the syntactic abilities of man are a unique property of the human species.[35] Evidence of very rudimentary chimpanzee syntax has now been

---

significant differences (*sêmeiôn diaphorai*) as well as differences in sounds: *HA* 9.1, 608a20, repeated by Porphyry *Abstinence* 3.15.

[24] Aristotle *Int.* 2, 16a26-9.

[25] Aristotle *HA* 4.9, 536a21; b2-3; b11-12.

[26] Ibid. 535a28-30.

[27] Ibid. 536a21.

[28] Aristotle *Pol.* 1.2, 1253a9-18.

[29] Diogenes Laertius *Lives* 7.55 (*SVF* 3 Diog. 17).

[30] Philo *de Animalibus* 44, which assumes the tongue is what segments sound.

[31] Sextus *M* 8.275; Plutarch *Sollertia* 973A.

[32] Varro *de lingua Latina* 6.56 (*SVF* 2.143).

[33] R.A. Gardner and B.T. Gardner, 'Teaching sign language to a chimpanzee', *Science* 165, 1969, 664-72.

[34] One of many objections raised by H.S. Terrace, e.g. in 'Animal cognition: thinking without language', *Philosophical Transactions of the Royal Society of London* B 308, 1985, 113-28.

[35] Noam Chomsky, *Cartesian Linguistics*, New York 1966; and *Language and Mind*, New York 1968.

adduced.[36] A parallel controversy is found in Gassendi's reply to Descartes' *Second Meditation*. Gassendi cites animal cries in answer to Descartes' claim that animals cannot speak, and dismisses Descartes' objection that they cannot weave (*contexere*) the cries together.[37]

By far the best treatment of animal speech is that of Porphyry in his treatise *On Abstinence from Animal Food*. He makes among others four points.[38] First, animals must at least understand speech, because they obey our calls. And this implies that they have the same appearance (*phantasia*) in their minds as the speaker who calls them.[39] At least this is so on the Aristotelian theory according to which sounds are meaningful (*sêmantikos*) through being accompanied by an appearance, and speech is a symbol of such things in the mind.[40] Porphyry is right to remind us that speaking is only one part of a larger process and has understanding as its counterpart. Contemporary investigations of chimpanzees and children take the same point into account.[41]

But there is more. Animals understand not only what the individual speaker means. They actually understand *Greek*,[42] unless the point is merely that parrots and other birds *imitate* Greek. The point that they understand it seems to me a very good one. There was a recent report that the British cavalry was buying Polish horses, and the worry was whether the horses would learn English. At first, I took this to be a joke. But, of course, it is absolutely serious. If those horses do not learn English, the British cavalry will not enjoy its customary success on the occasion of the next cavalry charge.

It may be protested that at any rate animals do not themselves speak, because we do not understand them. But Porphyry replies that hunters and herdsmen do appear to understand animal communication,[43] and the same was alleged two centuries earlier for the Pythagorean Apollonius of Tyana.[44] Moreover, as Sextus had also pointed out, we do

[36] Patricia M. Greenfield and Sue Savage-Rumbaugh, 'Imitation, grammatical development and the invention of protogrammar by an ape', in N.A. Krasnegor, D. Rumbaugh, R.L. Schiefelbusch, M. Studdert-Kennedy, eds., *Biological and Behavioural Determinants of Language-Development*, Hillsdale NJ 1991, 429-45.

[37] Translated by E.S. Haldane and G.R.T. Ross, *The Philosophical Works of Descartes* vol. 2, Cambridge 1911, p. 146.

[38] Porphyry *Abstinence* 3.3-6.

[39] Ibid. 3.5.2.

[40] Aristotle *DA* 2.8,430b22; *Int.* 1, 16a3-4.

[41] Chimpanzee understanding of commands to select photographs is demonstrated on videos which Duane Rumbaugh was kind enough to show me at the Language Research Center in Atlanta. With children, the abilities to understand, to repeat and to produce meaningful utterance have been shown to develop at different rates: E. Sue Savage-Rumbaugh, James L. Pate, Janet Lawson, S. Tom Smith, Steven Rosenbaum, 'Can a chimpanzee make a statement?' *Journal of Experimental Psychology*, General, 112, 1983, 457-92, with replies 493-512, at 475.

[42] Porphyry *Abstinence* 3.4.4.

[43] Ibid. 3.5.

[44] Ibid. 3.3.

not understand foreigners, but we do not conclude that they cannot speak.[45] Even though I shall express some reservations below about animal speech, the point about foreigners seems to me an important one. It imposes a constraint on modern discussions of the related subject whether animals have *beliefs*. There are those who say that we cannot know what beliefs animals have, because we cannot know exactly how they conceptualise things. Does Aristotle's lion believe that the *ox* is near, or that his *meal* is near? From this sort of doubt conclusions have been drawn about whether animals have beliefs or concepts at all. On one view, 'a little bit they do, and a little bit they don't'.[46] On another view, they certainly do not, for in ascribing genuine beliefs we certainly cannot substitute the descriptions 'the ox' and 'his meal' indifferently. Yet with animals, it is said, there is no basis for differentiation, because there is no such thing as a description the lion would accept. Humans (including foreigners) are held to be different, ultimately on the grounds they have language.[47] But putting humans on one side,[48] we need not look for a description the lion would accept, but, as with infants who cannot yet accept our descriptions, need only narrow down the appropriate description of a belief by careful observation and sometimes interaction, remembering that the descriptions appropriate even to adult human beliefs are typically vague and indeterminate. To ascribe an absolutely precise thought would often be to distort. A good example is supplied by Cheney and Seyfarth[49] of narrowing down the information conveyed in the (non-automatic) alarm calls of monkeys, by comparing what the monkeys take as the appropriate types of response to different inter-related calls in various types of environment and individual circumstances.

The fourth and last point to be extracted is best put in Porphyry's own charming words:

[45] Ibid. and Sextus *PH* 1.74.

[46] Stephen P. Stich, 'Do animals have beliefs?', *Australasian Journal of Philosophy* 57, 1979.

[47] Donald Davidson, 'Rational animals', *Dialectica* 36, 1982, 318-27, repr. in E. Lepore and B.P. McLaughlin, eds., *Actions and Events: Perspectives on the Philosophy of Donald Davidson*, Oxford 1985, 473-480.

[48] The argument on humans is that there is such a thing as a description a human would accept, because a human has a large stock of beliefs. But one cannot have a large stock of beliefs without being subject to surprise, which implies belief about belief. (I questioned the need for surprise in humans, and the absence of surprise and of belief about belief in animals, in Chapter Three above). It also requires the idea of intersubjective truth acceptable to others, and hence linguistic communication, which animals lack. Davidson candidly acknowledges that he is not sure how to complete the argument for the need for linguistic communication, and that he has not argued for animals lacking it.

[49] Dorothy L. Cheney and Robert M. Seyfarth, *How Monkeys See the World*, Chicago 1990, esp. ch. 5, 166-73. Between 1983 and 1987 Daniel Dennett became more pessimistic about these studies, as shown by ch. 7, and appendix, of his *The Intentional*

At any rate in Carthage we reared a partridge that came flying tamely to us. As time went by, and familiarity made it very tame, we saw it not only greeting us, attending to us and playing with us, but even uttering in response to our utterances, and, as far as it could, answering us. And this it did not in the way that partridges usually call each other, but differently, and not when one was silent. It was only when one uttered that it uttered in reply.[50]

It is not clear exactly what Porphyry's partridge did. But Konrad Lorenz explains in *King Solomon's Ring* why the communication system of his ravens, though very efficient, was not normally at all like human speech.[51] Unlike the communication of some animals,[52] it operated automatically and responses could not be inhibited, however inappropriate. When the ravens saw Lorenz carrying a black dangling object, even though they knew him, and even though the object was a bathing costume and not a raven, they could not inhibit the automatic warning call and attack. There was, however, the exceptional case of his pet raven Roah. This bird saw Lorenz in a place which might naturally elicit among ravens the innate danger call 'krackrackrack' and the innate danger signal of flying overhead with wobbling tail. He executed the normal overhead wobbling movements, and looked back to see if Lorenz was following him to safety. But instead of uttering the innate warning call, which he always used with fellow ravens, he substituted his own name, the name Roah by which Lorenz called him, with human intonation. Why?

Paul Grice has said that for a speaker to mean something is for the speaker to intend to produce an effect in the hearer.[53] And so far Roah did surely intend to produce an effect, at the very least that Lorenz should follow him out of danger. But Grice makes some extra requirements. We can ignore his wish that the intended effect should always be a mental state rather than an action, for this is desiderated only for reasons of neatness, a neatness which is not in the end achieved.[54] Grice's important point is that the speaker should intend to

---

Stance, Cambridge Mass. 1987. But the subject is continuing.

[50] Porphyry *Abstinence* 3.4. For the partridge repeating words and joining them together, cf. the first-century AD poet Statius, *Silvae* 2.4.20.

[51] Konrad Lorenz, *King Solomon's Ring*, London 1952, chs 8 and 11.

[52] This is not the case with all species, see e.g. Carolyn A. Ristau, ed., *Cognitive Ethology: The Minds of Other Animals*, Hillsdale NJ 1991, ch. 6, 'Truth and deception in animal communication', by Dorothy L. Cheney and Robert M. Seyfarth, and ch. 8, 'Do animals have the option of withholding signals when communication is inappropriate?' by Peter Marler, Stephen Karakashian and Marcel Gyger.

[53] Paul Grice, 'Meaning', *Philosophical Review* 66, 1957, 377-88.

[54] Paul Grice, 'Utterer's meaning and intentions', *Philosophical Review* 78, 1969, 147-77: in the hope of finding a common factor among the diverse intended effects, Grice suggests it is always intended that the receiver believes that the utterer believes or wants something. But it turns out that even this does not achieve uniformity, and I think that animal ethologists need not feel constrained by this particular requirement when

produce the effect not by merely automatic means. For example, if the raven cawed so loud that Lorenz would be startled into running a mile, the effect would be automatically produced. Rather, in order to mean something, the speaker must intend to produce the effect by means of the recognition of that intention. Such an intention has not been found even in monkeys.[55] But it may be thought that Roah achieved it. For why else should he have substituted his own name for Lorenz?

Unfortunately, we here run into a problem that is common in animal ethology. Would the articulated version of Roah's strategy read 'If I use Raven-talk, Lorenz won't recognise my intention'? Or would it merely read 'If I use Raven-talk, he won't run away'? But against the second, it may be said that Roah would not have heard 'Roah', or any other human sound, work as an automatic trigger of flight. So he could only expect it to work through the recognition of his intention.

If, then, the bird Roah meant something (the utterer's meaning), this is not yet to say that the sound 'Roah' meant something (the sound's meaning). For this, according to Grice, ravens would need it to be part of their *repertoire* so to use the sound.[56] Curiously enough, Cheney and Seyfarth suggest an opposite result for their vervet monkeys. The monkeys may not themselves mean anything by Grice's criterion of intending their intention to be recognised, yet their alarm calls have meanings.[57] They have meanings in the weaker sense that they convey information.

Cheney and Seyfarth have now developed their ideas in a very original way. They suggest that awareness of what goes on in other minds, as opposed to awareness of others' probable behaviour, may be a distinguishing ability unique to humans. This is a very interesting distinguishing criterion which I have not seen proposed by philosophers either in antiquity or since.[58] But I take Roah's solitary act of meaning to go against it, and I wonder if such acts may not be more common in the case of chimpanzees. They are regularly spoken of as 'indicating' things to each other or to their trainers, for example which button to press, and there are very interesting studies of 'indicating' in chimpanzees.[59] Can none of these cases of indicating be shown to involve Gricean meaning?[60]

looking for cases of animal meaning: Dorothy L. Cheney and Robert M. Seyfarth, *How Monkeys See the World*, Chicago 1990, ch. 5.

[55] Dorothy L. Cheney and Robert M. Seyfarth, op. cit., p. 144.

[56] Paul Grice, 'Utterer's meaning, sentence meaning and word meaning', *Foundations of Language* 4, 1968, 1-18.

[57] Cheney and Seyfarth, ch. 8.

[58] Cheney and Seyfarth, talk at Wolfson College, Oxford, 18 June 1992. The criterion of knowledge of God was proposed in antiquity: see below.

[59] E. Sue Savage-Rumbaugh et al., 'Can a chimpanzee make a statement?', op. cit., 1983.

[60] The relevance of Grice's initial account of utterer's meaning is that it calls for an awareness of other minds even in the case where the utterer only wants to elicit a

A graphic ascription of utterer's meaning to Pompey's cornered elephants is quoted from Pliny in Chapter Ten below.

Skills

If we turn now from speech to animal skills, we find that a whole battery of counter-arguments was deployed to show that their skills were merely natural, or as we would say, instinctual, and therefore not due to reason. Animal skills, it was objected, are stereotyped. Thomas Aquinas even repeats this in relation to Chrysippus' hunting dog.[61] This first reply hardly takes account of the skills learnt from man, e.g. the often cited case of circus animals, and is refuted by modern research on animals in the wild.[62] A second reply was that plants also manage to do the right things, and this is obviously due to nature.[63] A third reply, the most controverted of all, was that animals do not learn,[64] and *inter alia* do not learn from experience.[65] Porphyry takes the lead in answering this. The nightingale does learn its song, as Aristotle had already pointed out,[66] and animals learn from their tamers.[67] In any case, learning is inessential to rationality, since God does not learn.[68]

Some Stoics took a middle way which still denied rationality to animals, but without ascribing their skills to *unconscious* instinct. There was a certain *consciousness* of their own persons, liabilities and powers which nature had implanted in them, but which none the less fell short of rationality.[69] The fragmentary text of Hierocles is

---

behavioural response. A request is as significant as a statement from this point of view, for the response is to be elicited through the recognition of the intention. Chimpanzees take less readily than children to pointing to indicate meaning. But they do whimper, touch, or direct another's arm. They can learn to point, glance, look at, gesture, hold out the hand, or pick up (Savage-Rumbaugh et al., 468; 478; 479; 483).

[61] Nemesius *Nature of Man* 2.19; Origen *Against Celsus* 4.87. The arguments are well analysed by Urs Dierauer, *Tier und Mensch im Denken der Antike*, Amsterdam 1977. Similarly Thomas Aquinas of Chrysippus' dog, *Summa Theologiae* Ia, IIae, q. 13, a. 2, reply to objection 2.

[62] On the different uses by individual herons, but only some individuals, of different kinds of fishing bait, some bait adapted by the breaking of twigs, see Donald R. Griffin, reporting H. Higuchi, in 'Progress toward a cognitive ethology', in C.A. Ristau, ed., *Cognitive Ethology, The Minds of Animals*, Hillsdale, NJ 1991.

[63] Philo *de Animalibus* 79; 94-5.

[64] Philo *de Animalibus* 78; 81; Plutarch *Gryllos* 992A; Porphyry *Abstinence* 3.6; 3.10.

[65] Seneca *Ep.* 121,19-23; Hierocles 1.51-3.52 (von Arnim and Schubart, *Berlin Klassikertexte* 4, Berlin 1906), now re-edited by A.A. Long, *Corpus dei papiri filosofici greci e latini (CPF)*, vol. 1, Florence 1992, 268-451. The corresponding portion of text is on pp. 300-16.

[66] Porphyry, *Abstinence* 3.6, relying on Aristotle *HA* 4.9, 536b14-19.

[67] Plutarch *Sollertia* 961D; *Gryllos* 992A; Porphyry *Abstinence* 3.6; 3.10; cf. 3.15.

[68] Porphyry *Abstinence* 3.10.

[69] Chrysippus, according to Diogenes Laertius *Lives* 7.85; Seneca *Ep.* 121,7-10; Hierocles op. cit. 1.39-5.7.

particularly interesting, as Brad Inwood has brought out.[70] It describes the animal's knowledge of how to use its own bodily parts for attack or defence. It shows how knowledge of one's own liabilities is bound up with knowledge of others; the chicken knows that the bull is not dangerous to it, but the weasel or hawk is. Hierocles even ascribes a continuous self-consciousness to animals that is uninterrupted by sleep, as shown by sleeping humans pulling up their bedclothes or nursing their wounds. In the wake of the Stoic tradition, Galen appealed both to conscious and to unconscious instinct, in his discussion of the use of parts.[71]

On the other side, Porphyry ascribed to reason the animal's knowledge of how to use its parts.[72] In the medieval Islamic tradition, Avicenna introduced a new concept, as we saw in Chapter Five. The estimative faculty (*vis aestimativa*, in the medieval Latin translations), to explain how the sheep knows the wolf is dangerous.[73] The estimative faculty already involves some power of abstraction, but is not tantamount to intellect.[74] Averroes, as we saw, denied any abstractive power to animals. Some people, he said, think that spiders' webs and bees' hexagonal cells display intellect, but, in fact, all they need is phantasms.[75] The debate on which animal skills are innate and which learned is still continuing today.[76]

Inference

Aristotle and the Stoics both had a hard time denying inference or reasoning to animals. Aristotle comes very close to conceding it in *On the Motion of Animals* ch. 7,[77] where he is talking about engaging in practical syllogism or reasoning (*sullogizesthai*). His main examples involve humans only, because they include such premises (*protaseis*) as 'I am a man', 'A house is a good thing', 'I need a cloak'. But towards the end he compares animals,[78] without any warning that theirs is a very different case. He does not explicitly use terms like 'syllogism' for

---

[70] Brad Inwood, 'Hierocles: theory and argument in the second century AD', *Oxford Studies in Ancient Philosophy* 2, 1984, 151-83.

[71] Galen *de Usu Partium* 1.3.

[72] Porphyry *Abstinence* 3.9-10.

[73] Avicenna Latinus *de Anima*, ed. S. van Riet, 86,99-3; 89,48-52.

[74] Avicenna op. cit. 118,6-119,25; 120,26-41.

[75] Averroes, *Short Commentary on Aristotle's de Anima*, explaining why Aristotle says that intellect is found in 'few', rather than 'only in man', translated into Spanish by Gomez Gonzalez, Madrid 1987, pp. 190-1.

[76] For bees, see J.L. Gould, *Ethology: The Mechanisms and Evolution of Behavior*, New York 1982; F.C. Dyer and J.L. Gould, 'Honey bee navigation', *American Scientist* 71, 1983, 587-97; J.L. Gould, 'The role of learning in honey bee foraging' in A.C. Kamil, J.R. Krebs and H.R. Pulliam, *Foraging Behavior*, New York and London 1987, 479-96.

[77] Aristotle *Mot.* 7, 701a6-b1.

[78] Ibid. 701a34.

what animals are doing, nor ascribe any premises to them, so he stops
short of contradicting himself. But the immediately preceding example
of a syllogism could apply to animals as well as humans, for the
premises would be accessible to animals, on Aristotle's own theory.
Appetite says 'I must drink' and perception says 'This is drink'. If
animals are to be denied practical syllogism, then, it will have to be
because they cannot *link* the premises and the conclusion in the right
way. But that linking is only a causal process, as appears from
Aristotle's discussion of human practical syllogisms in the *Nicomachean Ethics*. We can look at it like physicists (*phusikôs*), he says.
When the two premises fuse into one (*mia genêtai*) it is necessary
(*anangkê*) to draw the conclusion.[79] No reason is apparent why
animals should not be capable of such a causal process.

Some modern accounts of the process of inference agree that it is
causal. If a belief or appearance that my wife is at home is caused in
the right way by the right sort of thing, e.g. by seeing her gloves on the
table, that is an inference. There is only one strange thing about
Aristotle's practical syllogisms, and that is that *On the Motion of
Animals* tells us the conclusion (*sumperasma*) is not a belief or
appearance, but an *action*.[80] One drinks. But if it is once allowed for
the case of humans that there can be reasoning which culminates in
action, rather than belief, there is nothing to stop this being true of
animals too. If their appetite says 'I want drink', their perception 'This
is drink', and so they drink, that is just one more example of a practical
syllogism and Aristotle does not say how to avoid admitting it.
Sullogizesthai literally means reasoning; so the animals would reason.

It is sometimes asked whether Aristotle's practical syllogism merely
sets out the reasons one had in acting, or represents a deliberation one
'explicitly' went through.[81] But even if the first alternative is right,
Aristotle does not hesitate to describe this as a case of reasoning
(*sullogizesthai*). And I believe that we, too, can talk of the agent as
reasoning or drawing an inference. So even if animals do not 'explicitly'
go through a practical syllogism (and it may call for clarification what
that means), I do not think that is enough to justify the denial that
they reason.

Aristotle's *On the Soul* does offer a rationale for denying that
animals can deliberate (*bouleuesthai*). Choosing between different
courses of action involves applying a measure, and a measure must be
one single thing. So deliberation involves creating one single mental
image (*phantasma*) out of several. It is explicitly said that animals

---

[79] Aristotle *Nicomachean Ethics* 7.3, 1147a24-8.

[80] Aristotle *On the Motion of Animals* 7, 701a22.

[81] John Cooper interprets Aristotle's practical syllogism the first way, in *Reason and
Human Good in Aristotle*, Cambridge, Mass. 1975, and concludes from this that there
need be no actual deliberation, pp. 9-10.

cannot do this, but it is not explained why not.[82]

The Stoics run into difficulty over the same question of animal inference. Why is Chrysippus' dog at the crossroads only virtually reasoning (*dunamei logizesthai*)?[83] It cannot be urged that since the Stoics deny words and concepts to animals, an animal cannot have an 'if-then' appearance. For in several of the Stoic examples supplied by Sextus, human inferences do not involve an explicit use of 'if-then'. It is a Stoic logicians' reconstruction which insists that all inferences from signs depend for their validity on the corresponding 'if-then' formula.[84] It was actually urged by some of the Stoics' opponents that their analysis of inference from signs in terms of 'if-then' must be wrong, because farmers, navigators, dogs and horses all make use of signs, without having an 'if-then' appearance (*phantasia tou ei*),[85] that is an explicit one. But the answer is that for humans the Stoics admit this. Why then do animals not infer? The Stoics' best answer might be that they define reason (*logos*) as a collection of concepts, so reasoning (*logizesthai*) should involve the application of concepts, and they deny that animals have any.

If this would be their official answer, it raises two fresh questions. Whether animals really lack concepts will depend on what it is to have a concept. And whether the practical reasoning that leads to drinking in the earlier example from Aristotle really involves the application of concepts depends on whether perceiving 'this is drink' involves applying concepts. These issues were touched on in Chapter Three above.

The question whether Aristotle's drinking animal and Chrysippus' hound are reasoning could become a merely verbal one. We saw in Chapter Six that the ancient memorists, followed by Leibniz, reserved the name 'reason' for Aristotelian syllogising. Hume, however, allowed that the association of ideas employed by animals, and much of the time by humans, should be called 'reason' in one sense.

What distinguishes humans other than reason?

We have seen not everyone agreed that rationality was the distinguishing mark of humans, for many granted reason to animals. Those thinkers need to find another differentia for humans, one that might or might not imply reason, but which was not to be implied by it. Even an author like Aristotle, who does define humans as rational, is

[82] Aristotle *On the Soul* 3.11, 434a5-12.

[83] Sextus *PH* 1.69, discussed in Chapter Two above.

[84] Sextus *PH* 2.102; M 8.153. The point is made by Myles Burnyeat, 'The origins of non-deductive inference', 215-17, in J. Barnes, J. Brunschwig, M. Burnyeat and M. Schofield, eds., *Science and Speculation*, Cambridge 1982.

[85] Sextus *M* 8.269-71, also cited by Burnyeat.

prepared to cite such additional distinguishing marks as laughter,[86] the ability to learn grammar,[87] and others mentioned below. And we have noted above the new criterion proposed by Cheney and Seyfarth.

One author, who allowed reason to animals, was the Church Father Lactantius, writing in Latin early in the fourth century. What distinguishes humans, he says, quoting Cicero, is knowledge of God.[88] Like Augustine after him,[89] he thinks that this knowledge does imply reason. But it is, according to Lactantius, only one type of reason, not possessed by all rational beings, namely perfect reason, or wisdom (*sapientia*).

The claim that animals do not know God was resisted by some – we hear of worshipping elephants or tigers[90] – but many agreed that only humans have such knowledge.[91] Lactantius rejects not only the claims of reason to provide a differentia of man, but other claims too, and there were many. Animals have spoken communication (*colloqui*), foresight (*providentia, prudentia*) and laughter (*ridere*), he says.[92] These are only three out of a score or more of differentiae proposed in antiquity. Each of the three was opposed as well as proposed,[93] and the same is true of a number of the others.

Besides the debates already discussed over whether animals, or only men, know God, have speech, laughter, foresight with an associated knowledge of causes, preparation, memory, emotion, universals, or concepts, there were others over whether they can distinguish good

---

[86] Aristotle *PA* 3.10, 673a8; a28.

[87] Aristotle *Top.* 1.5, 102a18-22.

[88] Lactantius *Divine Institutes* 3.10 (cf. 7.9.10; *Epitome* 65.4), quoting Cicero *Leg.* 1.8.24.

[89] Augustine *Enarratio in Psalmos* 36.2.13: knowledge of God requires the human mind (*mens*). Cf. the converse, as one side of an argument, in Plutarch *Gryllos* 992E: reason (*logos*) implies knowledge of God.

[90] Xenocrates fr. 21 Heinze (= 220 Isnardi, from Clement *Stromateis* 5.13); Pliny *Nat. Hist.* 8.3; Plutarch *Sollertia* 972B; Aelian *Nat. Anim.* 4.10; 7.44; Dio Cassius *Roman History* 39.38.5; Philostratus *Life of Apollonius of Tyana* 2.28.

[91] Socrates according to Xenophon *Mem.* 1.4.13. Plato *Protagoras* 322A; ps-Plato *Menexenus* 237D; ps-Aristotle *Problems* 956a11-14; Cicero loc. cit.; 'Odysseus' in Plutarch *Gryllos* 992E; Justin Martyr *Dialogue with Trypho* 4; Lactantius loc. cit.; Calcidius in Tim. 191, 214, Waszink; Augustine *Enarratio in Psalmos* 36.2.13; cf. the Hermetic Asclepius 11 (= Corpus Hermeticum vol. 2, p. 309, Nock-Festugière, in the Budé series).

[92] Lactantius loc. cit.

[93] On laughter, Augustine *Lib. Arb.* 1.8.18.63, sides with Aristotle (loc. cit.) against Lactantius (loc. cit.). Pliny proposes grief and argues that laughter comes late, *Nat. Hist.* 7, proem 1-5. For speech, see above, this Chapter and for foresight Chapter Four.

and bad, just and unjust,[94] expedient and inexpedient[95] can be happy,[96] can achieve technical knowledge (*tekhnê*),[97] are political,[98] can count,[99] do geometry,[100] are born defenceless and naked,[101] have a sense of rhythm,[102] know shame,[103] have a face,[104] something which shows emotion and character, engage in sex at all seasons,[105] with their own sex,[106] or with other species.[107] In Chapter Nine, it will be seen that the Stoics were much more restrictive than Aristotle in denying animals voluntary behaviour, desire (*orexis*) and all its species.

Other distinguishing features suggested as unique to man were *parakolouthêsis* (a kind of understanding, especially introspectively

[94] Unique to man because of his speech (*logos*), according to Aristotle *Pol.* 1.2, 1253a9-18, but contrast *DA* 3.7, 431a10-12. Good not grasped, according to Seneca *Ep.* 124,1, yet they probably do have an appearance of injustice. Seneca *de Ira* 1.3. with 2.1.5. Unique to the human mind (*mens*), according to Augustine *Enarratio in Psalmos* 29.2.2; 36.2.13. But Aristotle's pupil Eudemus tells stories of moral sensibility in animals, Eudemus, ed. Wehrli, frr. 127-9 from Aelian *Nat. Anim.* 3.21; 4.8; 4.45.

[95] On expediency, Plato *Tht* 186C is ambiguous about whether any animals have reflections (*analogismata*) with a view to *ôpheleia*. Aristotle *Pol.* 1.2, 1253a12-18 probably wants to deny them awareness of *sumpheron* and *blaberon*.

[96] Unique to man, a sign it consists in philosophical contemplation (*theôria*), Aristotle *PA* 2.10, 656a5, 10. Outside rational nature (*rationalis natura*), we find none in mute animals, Seneca *Ep.* 124,15. Unique to man, Augustine *City* 8.17; 12.1. On the contrary, man's fate is the most burdensome, Plutarch *Gryllos* 986E, if *barupotmotaton* is the right reading.

[97] *Tekhnê* in animals Plutarch *Gryllos* 991E; Philo *de Animalibus* 23; Sextus *PH* 1.66. Unique to man, Anaxagoras fr. 21B (= Plutarch *de Fort.* 98F); Protagoras in Plato *Protagoras* 321D; 322A; Aristotle *Metaph.* 1.1, despite *tekhnikos HA* 9, 615a19; 616a4; 620b10; 622b23.

[98] Animals political: Aristotle *HA* 488a8-10; Cicero *Off.* 1.12; Basil of Caesarea *Hexaemeron* 8.4; Porphyry *Abstinence* 3.15. Aristotle *Pol.* 1.2, 1253a9-10 makes humans only *more* political than animals, but for the other side contrast Philo *de Animalibus* 65 with 91, and see Archelaus ap. Hippolytum *Ref.* 1.9 (= Diels- Kranz A4).

[99] Unique to man: Aristotle *Top.* 142b26; Plato according to ps-Aristotle *Problemata* 30.6, 956a13. But contrast Aristotle's pupil Eudemus on the Libyan animal which, though irrational (*alogon*), counted through a *natural* sense of arithmetic (*phusikê arithmêtikê*), according to Aelian *Nat. Anim.* 4.53.

[100] On the hexagonal cells of bees, see Aelian *Nat. Anim.* 5.13; Basil of Caesarea *Hexaemeron* 8.4, who, however, deny them reason or *tekhnê*.

[101] Anaximander fr. A10 Diels-Kranz (= *Dox. Gr.* 579); Plato *Protagoras* 320D-321C; Aristotle *PA* 687a23 ff; Epicurus ap. Lactantium *Opif.* 3.1; 6; Lucretius 5.222-34; Pliny *Nat. Hist.* 7, proem 1-5; Origen *Against Celsus* 4.78; Galen *de Usu Partium* 1.2.

[102] Only man: Plato *Laws* 653E-654A; 673C-D. Elephants: Aelian *Nat. Anim.* 2.2.

[103] Only man: Epictetus 3.7.27. Elephants: Pliny *Nat. Hist.* 8.5.5.

[104] Only man: Pliny *Nat. Hist.* 7, proem 1-5. Monkeys: Galen *de Usu Partium* Book 8, ch. 8, Kühn 2.690.

[105] Only man: Socrates ap. Xenophontem *Mem.* 1.4.12; Philo *de Animalibus* 49; Plutarch *Gryllos* 990D; *de Amore Prolis* 493F; Pliny *Nat. Hist.* 10.83.171; Macrobius *Sat.* 2.5.10. Contrast Oppian *Cyn.* 3.146 ff; Clement *Paedagogus* 2.10.83.3.

[106] Only man: Plato *Laws* 836C; Philo *de Animalibus* 49; Plutarch *Gryllos* 990D; ps-Lucian *Affairs of the Heart* 22; ps-Phocylides *Sentences* 190. Contrast ibid. 990E; Pliny *Nat. Hist.* 10.83.172; Aelian *Nat. Anim.* 15.11; *Varia Hist.* 1.15.

[107] Never beasts: Plutarch *Gryllos* 991A. Contrast Aelian *Nat. Anim.* 15.14; Basil *Hexaemeron* 5.7.18.

directed),[108] deliberately reminding oneself (*anamnêsis*),[109] deliberation (*bouleusis*),[110] deliberate action (*praxis*),[111] the ability to appreciate order or beauty,[112] knowlege of grammar,[113] upright posture,[114] assenting to fate,[115] love of independence,[116] the search for truth,[117] rational control of the sexual urge,[118] competitiveness,[119] possessing hands.[120] Plato offers the contrived etymology for 'man' (*anthrôpos*) as signifying the only being who reflects on what he sees (*anathrei ha opôpe*).[121] Lists of man's unique disadvantages are supplied above all by Pliny,[122] who adds to those already mentioned grief, post-coital sadness, love of luxury, ambition, avarice, anxiety about life and death and aggression towards conspecifics.[123]

Some of the proposed differentiating features are thought of as implying reason.[124] Others are not: Aelian concedes that Eudemus' counting animal is irrational, but describes it as having a natural sense

---

[108] In Epictetus *passim* (see the excellent account by David Hahm, in 'A neglected Stoic argument for human responsibility', *Illinois Classical Studies* (17.1,1-26); Ammonius *in Int.* 30,23 ff. *Parakolouthêsis* implies reason, in Origen *On Prayer* 6,1-2 (312,5-14) = *SVF* 2.989.

[109] Aristotle *Mem.* 2, 453a8-14 (because it is, as it were, a sort of reasoning); *HA* 1.1, 488b24-6.

[110] Aristotle *HA* 1.1, 488b24-6 (similarly for the mental imagery required for deliberation *DA* 3.11, 434a5-12); Philo *de Animalibus*, contrast 45 with 80; 97.

[111] Aristotle *NE* 6.2, 1139a20. Eve Cole wonders whether Theophrastus' reference to animal *praxis* at the opening of *Historia Plantarum* is casual, or a conscious disagreement: 'Theophrastus and Aristotle on animal intelligence', *Rutgers Studies in Classical Humanities* 5, ed. W. Fortenbaugh, Dimitri Gutas. The Stoics also deny action (*prattein, praxis*: same word as Aristotle uses) to irrational beings, as will become clear in Chapter Nine, but on the different ground that it requires not deliberation but rational assent.

[112] Cicero *Off.* 1.4.14 as a product of reason (from Panaetius); Augustine *contra Julianum* 4.73 (only a rational animal can appreciate corporeal beauty).

[113] Aristotle *Top.* 1.5, 102a18-22.

[114] Aristotle Protrepticus fr. 11; *PA* 4.10, 686a27. Plato *Timaeus* 91E-92A; Socrates ap. Xenophontem *Mem.* 1.4.11. Philo *de Animalibus* 11; Cicero *Leg.* 1.9.26; Seneca *de Otio* 1.4; Minucius Felix *Octavius* 17; Basil of Caesarea, *Hexaemeron* 9.2; Lactantius *Divine Institutes* 3.10; Augustine *Gen. ad Lit.* 6.12.22; *de Diversis Quaestionibus* 51; *Trin.* 11.1.1; Boethius *Consolation* 5, poem 5. From Greek Philosophy the point reached an Islamic treatise, *The Case of the Animals versus Man Before the King of the Jinn*, by the Ikhwân al-Safâ, translated by L.E. Goodman, Boston 1978.

[115] Marcus Aurelius *Meditations* 10.28.

[116] Cicero *Off.* 1.13, as a product of reason.

[117] Ibid., as a product of reason.

[118] Julian of Eclanum ap. Augustinum *Opus Imperfectum contra Julianum* 4.41.

[119] Augustine *Lib. Arb.* 1.8.18.63; cf. Hobbes *Leviathan*, part 2, ch. 17.

[120] Socrates ap. Xenophontem *Mem.* 1.4.11; Aristotle *PA* 687a7 ff, citing Anaxagoras; Galen *de Usu Partium* 1.2-3.

[121] Plato *Cratylus* 399C.

[122] Pliny *Nat. Hist.* 7, proem 1-5; 10.83.171.

[123] For further details, see Urs Dierauer, *Tier und Mensch*, and on the unfavourable human characteristics, George Boas, 'The superiority of the animals', in Arthur Lovejoy and George Boas, *A Documentary History of Primitivism and Related Ideas*, vol. 1, Baltimore 1935.

[124] See the footnotes above in this Chapter and in Chapters Three to Five.

of arithmetic (*phusikê arithemêtikê*).[125] Sometimes there is a debate not only on whether the proposed feature is unique to man, but also on whether it implies reason, as we saw in the case of preparation and foresight in Chapter Four.

My own impression on attempts to draw a boundary between humans and animals is that it is very easy to find things well beyond the compass of animals, like advanced mathematics, but very difficult to find the supposed border itself.

Modern animal ethology

Is there any parallel in modern science to the Aristotelian and Stoic inhibition on ascribing rationality to animals? For a long time behaviourist theory has deterred researchers from ascribing conscious states to animals, or explaining their behaviour by propositional attitudes. That is, they could speak of salivation when an ox was presented at such and such a distance, but could not join Aristotle or the Stoics in saying that the lion perceives, or has the perceptual appearance, that the ox is near. Now that the tide is beginning to turn against behaviourism,[126] however, there are ethologists willing to go beyond the Stoics and treat animals as rational. What they study is the various rational strategies animals have.[127] The areas where animals now appear deficient are quite different and unexpected ones, for example their understanding of each other's mental states, as opposed to each other's behaviour.[128] But whether these findings apply to apes as well as monkeys, and whether they apply to all animals is a matter of investigation. One suggestion is that failure to recognise each other's mental state differentiates animals from humans.[129]

The influence of animal considerations on the Philosophy of Mind

We can now look back and see the extent to which animal considerations influenced ancient Philosophy of Mind. It can hardly be

---

[125] Aelian *Nat. Anim.* 4.53.

[126] Important is the work of Donald R. Griffin, *The Question of Animal Awareness*, New York 1981; *Animal Thinking*, Cambridge, Mass. 1984.

[127] e.g. Richard W. Byrne and Andrew Whiten, eds., *Machiavellian Intelligence: Social Expertise and The Evolution of Intellect in Monkeys, Apes and Humans*, Oxford and New York 1988.

[128] e.g. Dorothy L. Cheney and Robert M. Seyfarth, *How Monkeys see the World*, Chicago 1990.

[129] e.g. Byrne and Whiten op. cit., ch. 16, 'The manipulation of attention in primate tactical deception', by the editors; ch. 13 'Does the chimpanzee have a theory of mind?' by David Premack. By contrast, Cheney and Seyfarth have hypothesised that ignorance of other minds may characterise all non-human animals: lecture at Wolfson College, Oxford, 18 June 1992.

denied that the Stoic redefinitions of memory, preparation and anger were driven by these considerations and that the Stoic accounts of appearance, speech and self-consciousness were influenced by them. The same will turn out in Chapter Nine to be true of the Stoic treatments of voluntary action and impulse. But it may be less obvious that there were similar motivations at work already in Aristotle. One view might be that animal considerations certainly dominated the analysis of memory, but played no role in the expansion of perceptual content.[130] I think that view would be wrong. The analysis of perception, no less than the analysis of memory, forms part of a wider project. Aristotle describes this project in *On the Soul* as being to say what the souls of plant, animal and human each are.[131] It is no accident, then, that reference to animals permeates his discussions throughout the psychological works. But since it has come as a surprise to me too to notice how often this happens, I shall take a moment to give examples.

One of the central concerns of Aristotle's treatise *On Memory* is to show that memory, like appearance, belongs to the perceptual part of the soul, and so is available to animals, unlike deliberately reminding oneself. The chapter that distinguishes appearance from thought, belief and reason, *On the Soul* 3.3, mentions animals no less than four times. It does so in order to say that only some (humans) have thought (*phronein*); all perceive sensible qualities like cold, fluid and dry; most, though not all, have appearances; none other than humans have conviction, persuasion, belief or reason.[132] Aristotle works both ways, appealing to animals to throw light on mental capacities and to capacities to throw light on animals. This happens not only in the chapters just mentioned. It happens, too, with the discussion of the source of voluntary motion. This is not intellect, but desire, and desire belongs to the perceptual part of the soul,[133] although perception on its own is not enough to produce voluntary movement, as shown by the case of stationary animals.[134] Equally, Aristotle explains by reference to animal needs the functions of the five senses, and which animals have which.[135] The treatises *On Sleep* and *On Dreams* both begin, like the treatise *On Memory*, by asking which part of the soul is involved,[136] and *On Sleep* determines that all animals sleep.[137] The account in *Metaphysics* 1.1, of cognitive development (perception, memory,

[130] I am grateful to Jonathan Barnes for pressing this issue.
[131] Aristotle *DA* 2.3, 414b32-3 cf. 1.1, 402b3-8.
[132] Ibid. 3.3, 427b6-8; b13; 428a10; a21-4.
[133] Ibid. 3.9, 431a8-14; cf. 3.7, 431a13.
[134] Ibid. 432b19-26. Cf. 3.10, 433b29-3,11, 434a12: in animals, it is desire and one kind of appearance, but not deliberation, that is responsible for movement.
[135] Aristotle *DA* 3.12, 434a27-b29; *Sens.* 1, 436b10-437a3.
[136] Aristotle *Som.* 1, 453b13; *Insom.* 1, 458b1; 459a21-2.
[137] Ibid. 454b23-4.

intelligence, learning, appearance, experience, technical and scientific understanding) is built around the ascending mental capacities of animals and humans. The gradualist chapter, *History of Animals* 8.1, is careful to distinguish the temperaments we share with animals from intellectual capacities which we do not. In this regard, Aristotle's psychology is no different from his ethics, for there too the difference between man and animal is crucial for determining the character of human happiness,[138] and voluntary action is defined in such a way as to allow it to animals.[139]

Aristotle's Philosophy of Mind

I can now draw a general conclusion about Aristotle's Philosophy of Mind. With each new fashion in the topic, Aristotle has been hailed as its precursor. Behaviourism reduces psychological states to dispositions towards certain kinds of behaviour. Materialism reduces them to certain physiological states. Functionalism, in one of its guises,[140] is also reductionist: it reduces psychological states to whatever (physical) states are caused by certain stimuli and cause certain behaviour, although many different types of physical state are allowed to play the relevant causal role. Aristotle has been described both as a materialist[141] and as a functionalist.[142] Some of my own earlier remarks have been taken as favouring a functionalist interpretation.[143] But each of these modern theories, as so far described, is seeking to reduce mental states to something at a different level, to behavioural dispositions, or physiological processes, or physical states with a given causal function. Aristotle's procedure is different. He is

[138] Aristotle *NE* 1.7, 1097b33-1098a4.

[139] Ibid. 3.1, 1111a25-6; 3.2, 1111b7-9.

[140] What follows supersedes my 'Intentionality and physiological processes: Aristotle's theory of sense-perception', in M. Nussbaum and A. Rorty, eds., *Essays on Aristotle's de Anima*, Oxford 1992, which failed to consider non-reductionist functionalism.

[141] Thomas Slakey, 'Aristotle on sense-perception', *Philosophical Review* 70, 1961, 470-84; Wallace I. Matson, 'Why isn't the mind-body problem ancient?', in P.K. Feyerabend and G. Maxwell, eds., *Mind, Matter and Method*, University of Minnesota 1966. That Aristotle finished up a materialist against his will is argued by Bernard Williams, 'Hylomorphism', *Oxford Studies in Ancient Philosophy* 4, 1986, 189-99.

[142] For various functionalist readings I would refer to Edwin Hartman, *Substance, Body and Soul*, Princeton 1977; Kathleen V. Wilkes, *Physicalism*, London 1978, ch. 7; Martha Nussbaum, Aristotle's *de Motu Animalium*, Princeton 1978, 61-74, drawing on Hilary Putnam (the first) 'Philosophy and our mental life', repr. in his *Mind, Language and Reality, Philosophical Papers* vol. 2, Cambridge 1975, 291-303; Hilary Putnam and Martha Nussbaum, 'Changing Aristotle's Mind', pre-publication version of chapter in Martha Nussbaum and Amelie Rorty, eds., *Essays on Aristotle's De Anima*, Oxford 1992; at one time Christopher Shields in Johann Christian Smith, ed., *Historical Foundations of Cognitive Science* (now superseded).

[143] Myles Burnyeat, 'Is Aristotle's philosophy of mind still credible?', in M. Nussbaum and A. Rorty op. cit.; Kathy V. Wilkes op. cit.; Deborah Modrak, *Aristotle: The Power of Perception*, Chicago 1987, 2.

more like those modern philosophers (here I am risking a comparison myself) who compare and contrast the content of belief and of perception. Content is not where Aristotle's interest focuses, but he does think it throws light on perception to show that it differs from belief or reason, but relates to appearance. Moreover, he relates all these capacities, along with thought, memory, experience, concept-formation, emotion and desire to each other. Nor is he interested in just one type of relation, the causal, although this sometimes plays a role. Much less does he think that desire could be *anything* that exercised the right causal function. It is not the causal function, or any other relationship, that constitutes a mental state. But light can be thrown on each by taking other mental states and bringing out the large variety of relationships, including differences, amongst them.

Functionalism is the most flexible of the modern theories mentioned, because in other guises it allows that the causes and effects may themselves include psychological states. A given desire or pain may be described as the state caused by, or causing, such and such beliefs, among other things. Indeed, the causing of beliefs has been described as an important part of the functional role of pains and other feelings.[144] Nor is the causal relation the only one (although it is the main one) invoked. A given pain might be specified as the state that supplies rational reasons for a certain belief, whether or not it causes that belief in fact, and probably whether or not the reasons are appreciated.[145] These versions of functionalism are not in the same way reductionist, but they have a new disadvantage insofar as they make pains depend on the ability to form beliefs.[146] This is a disadvantage, because it at least looks as if many more animals fully share with us liability to pain than fully share with us the capacity for entertaining beliefs. Indeed, Aristotle allows the latter capacities to none of them. In any case, Aristotle's procedure of interrelating, comparing and contrasting mental states, does not put a premium on any one or two interrelations, such as the causal or the justificatory.

---

[144] Sydney Shoemaker, 'Qualia and consciousness', *Mind* 100, 1991, 507-24, at 510.

[145] I am indebted to David Charles for a report on, and discussion of, his correspondence with Robert Cummins.

[146] Sydney Shoemaker has kindly informed me by letter of a reply he is formulating to this difficulty.

CHAPTER EIGHT

Plants and animals

So far I have focused on the border between humans and animals. But the nature of animals also depends on their differentiation from plants, a borderline which Aristotle warns us is fuzzy. 'On which side do sponges fall?' he asks.[1] Before I move from the Philosophy of Mind to Ethics, I should consider this other border. It is relevant to Ethics, because of the popularity of the slide or sorites objection: if you spare animals, you'll have to spare plants too.

Plants

To start at the beginnings of Greek thought, some Presocratics and Plato thought of plants as sensitive. Our own denial of this stems once again from Aristotle. It is unclear which Presocratics to include, perhaps Anaxagoras, Democritus and Protagoras.[2] But certainly Empedocles declared that all things have a share of thought (*phronêsis*, *nôma*),[3] that he had in one incarnation been a bush, and that people can be reincarnated as laurels.[4] Plato, in describing plants as animate, used the word *zôïa* which in Aristotle became the standard word for animals. He described them (and in this he is followed among the Neoplatonists by Proclus and Damascius, but not Porphyry) as having appetite and pleasant and painful sensations,[5] and he spoke at

---

[1] Aristotle *HA* 8.1.

[2] See ps-Aristotle *de Plantis* 815a16; b16; put into the mouth of Protagoras by Plato *Theaetetus* 167B-C.

[3] Empedocles fr. 110, line 10, Diels-Kranz, taken by Sextus Empiricus to apply to plants, *M* 8.286; cf. Empedocles fr. 103.

[4] Empedocles fr. 117; 127.

[5] Plato *Timaeus* 77A-B. Proclus *Platonic Theology* 128,54-129,2 (French translation Saffrey and Westerink, English Thomas Taylor) and Damascius *Lectures on the Philebus* §163, lines 4-5 Westerink (with English translation) allow appetite (*epithumia*) to plants and consciousness (*sunaisthêsis*), although Damascius explains that this conscious appetite neither foresees nor remembers. Porphyry, by contrast, construes Plato's reference to sensations as being merely to physiological processes, *ad Gaurum* 4.1, ed. Kalbfleisch, *Abhandlungen der Königl. Akademie der Wissenschaften zu Berlin* 1895, French translation by Festugière in *The Revelation of Hermes Trismegistus* vol. 4.

one point as if it should be possible to give a single account for plants
and animals of what a good life would consist in.[6] On the other hand, a
plant lacked belief (*doxa*), reasoning (*logismos*) and intellectual insight
(*nous*). It was not self-conscious (*katidein* and *logisasthai* its own
things, *strephein* within itself about itself – *peri*), nor capable of
self-motion, in opposition to motion from without.[7]

Aristotle changed all this. He agreed with his teacher Plato that
plants were alive, and so had a soul (*psukhê*), since soul for him was no
more than the life-giving capacities. But consciousness (*aesthêsis*) was
the prerogative of animals.[8] And with perception went desire (*orexis*).[9]
The plant's soul consisted instead in the capacity to use food for
acquiring, maintaining and reproducing its distinctive structure.[10] In
maintaining structure, it held the plant together (*sunekhein*),
preventing the constituent elements from disintegrating.[11] The Stoics
were later to emphasise this holding-together role, but to distinguish it
from that of soul. The *pneuma* in bodies had two distinct roles: one was
to serve as the holding power (*hexis*) or cause which held each and
every body together (*sunekhein*). The other was to serve as the soul in
those bodies which had one.[12]

If talk of a plant soul sounds unfamiliar to us, this is partly due to
Descartes in the seventeenth century, who deliberately sought to
suppress the idea of the soul as having a nutritive function, an idea he
wrongly attributed to the ancients in general, not recognising it as
Aristotle's innovation. He wanted to connect soul only with
consciousness, and to reinforce this intention, he announced that he
would drop the word 'soul' (*anima*), and substitute 'mind' (*mens*), the
word which has become idiomatic for us.[13]

The Stoics are repeatedly said to deny a soul to plants,[14] although
Seneca may be an exception, since he cites it as a received opinion
(*placet*), with which he does not quarrel, that plants and trees have a
soul (*anima*).[15] In denying soul, the Stoics are denying impulse (*hormê*),

---

[6] Plato *Philebus* 22B.

[7] Plato *Timaeus* 77B-C.

[8] Aristotle *DA* 2.2, 413b1-10. Aristotle's innovation here is well brought out by F.
Solmsen, 'Antecedents of Aristotle's psychology and scale of beings', *American Journal of
Philology* 76, 1955, 148-64.

[9] Aristotle *DA* 2.2, 413b22-4; 2.3, 414b15; cf.3.7, 431a13.

[10] Ibid. 413a20-b10.

[11] Ibid. 1.5, 410b10-15; 2.4, 416a6-7.

[12] See Richard Sorabji, *Matter, Space and Motion*, London and Ithaca NY 1989, ch. 6.

[13] Reply to objections brought against the *Second Meditation* §4, in the 5th Objections,
translated by Haldane and Ross, vol. 2, p. 210.

[14] Aëtius 5.26.3 (*Dox. Gr.* 438a15-20; *SVF* 2.708); Galen *PHP* 6.3.7 (509M; 561K; Kühn
5.521; de Lacy p. 374, lines 18-19; *SVF* 2.710); Clement *Stromateis* 2.20 (p. 487, Pott.
Stählin vol. 2, p. 173, 16-25; *SVF* 2.714).

[15] Seneca *Ep.* 58.10.

perceptual appearance (*phantasia*), and some add perception (*aisthê-sis*). These are precisely the characteristics which they ascribe to all animals,[16] and which correspond to Aristotle's desire (*orexis*) and perception (*aisthêsis*). Some Stoics added that all animals also possessed self-consciousness from birth, Hierocles claiming that this was never interrupted even in sleep.[17] In making this addition, the Stoics may have been influenced by Plato, who had previously stressed self-consciousness as distinguishing animals from plants,[18] although the Stoics put the idea to the new purpose of explaining the skill of irrational animals at self-preservation, and accounting for the origins of the spread of fellow-feeling (*oikeiôsis*).

After the Stoics, Plotinus, the founder of Neoplatonism, and his fellow-pupil the Christian Origen both accepted the possibility of being reincarnated as plants.[19] Plotinus does so even though he follows Aristotle in allowing plants only a nutritive capacity, not sensitivity.[20] What they have is a soul, or echo of soul, which may only be a trace of the soul in the earth.[21] they do, however, have their own good, for example according to whether they bear fruit or not.[22] Plotinus' pupil Porphyry, by contrast, denies that plants can suffer any evil or harm, given that they lack sensitivity.[23] He treats vegetables as lacking soul, and contrasts the life of a plant with the life of what is 'ensouled',[24] a usage followed also by his Christian antagonist Eusebius.[25]

Porphyry and the Stoics were not the only ones to deny a soul to plants. The denial is found among the Stoics' rivals, the Epicureans, according to one source,[26] in the Jewish philosopher Philo of Alexandria,[27] and in certain Pythagorean notebooks, which grant life

---

[16] Philo *Quod Deus Sit Immut.* 9, 41-5 (*SVF* 2.450); Clement *Stromateis* 2.20 (p. 487, Pott. Stählin vol. 2, p. 173, 16-25; *SVF* 2.714).

[17] Hierocles, *Berlin Klassikertexte* 4, von Arnim, Berlin 1906, 1.39-5.7.

[18] Plato *Timaeus* 77B-C.

[19] Plotinus 3.4.2; Origen *On First Principles* 1.8.4.

[20] Plotinus 1.4.1; 3.3.3; 3.4.1; 4.4.22; 4.4.27; 4.4.28; 4.9.1; 5.2.2.

[21] Plotinus 4.4.22 (1); 4.4.27 (1). The earth soul should not be confused with the world soul, when it reappears in Themistius' commentary on *Metaphysics* Book 12, in the Latin version at *CAG* 5.5, p. 9, and in the earlier Arabic version preserved in Averroes' commentary on the same, translated by Genequand, p. 106 = Bouyges 1494.

[22] Plotinus 1.4.1 (16-27).

[23] Porphyry *Abstinence* 3.19.

[24] Different lives: Porphyry *Sentences* 12; cf. 10, which contrasts the ways in which plants and souls can be said to contain all things. *Abstinence* 1.46.2; 1.47.2; and probably 4.16 treat vegetables as lacking soul.

[25] Eusebius *Eccl. Hist.* 2.2.3 says that St James ate nothing that had a soul (*empsukhon*).

[26] Aëtius 5.26.3 (*Dox. Gr.* 438a15-20).

[27] Philo *de Animalibus* 94.

(*zôê*) to plants and even call them *zôia*, but deny them a soul (*psukhê*), which is thought of as being a piece of aether in part immortal.[28] The denial of soul was not, however, extended to animals,[29] even if Porphyry's successors Iamblichus and Proclus took a few first steps in this direction.[30]

Embryos

The discussion of embryos was related. There were disputes whether embryos had souls at all, if so, whether they were plant or animal souls, if animal, whether actual or potential, if potential, whether embryos were to be compared with those hibernating or in a faint, or whether they should be viewed neither as animal nor as non-animal, but as like the sleeping.[31] Much of the information is recorded by Galen and Porphyry.

Among the Presocratics, Empedocles denies, on the standard MS reading, that embryos are animals, until they are born and draw their first breath.[32] Plato does call them *zôia*,[33] Aristotle's word for animals. But his meaning is taken differently by Porphyry, since Plato applies the name to other things besides animals which he thinks of as living, both plants and the womb itself.[34] Plato also says that the soul which has contemplated most fully enters into the seed or generation (*gonê*) of a future lover of wisdom or beauty.[35] But Porphyry takes Plato to agree with his own view, that the animal soul (*zôiopoios psukhê*)[36] enters only at the time of birth, and that before that there is only a

---

[28] Diogenes Laertius *Lives* 8.28; cf. 8.30.

[29] Mary Midgley's excellent *Animals and Why They Matter*, p. 10, may represent a common misconception here, though her claim is about Christians, rather than Greeks.

[30] Both allowed animals only a non-rational soul. Going further, Iamblichus in Stobaeus *Ecl.* 1, 369.20 ff, Wachsmuth, interprets Plotinus as robbing soul of perception, apearance and memory and transferring these functions to body. Proclus, moving in the same direction, prefers to describe non-rational soul as merely an image of soul, *Platonic Theology* 3.6 (128, Portus). But then he makes the same point also about human souls, when embodied, *in Tim.* 3.330, Diehl; *Elements of Theology* 64; *De Malorum Subsistentia* 25, Isaac.

[31] Summarised by Galen *Def. med* (Kühn 19,451-2); Porphyry *ad Gaurum* 1, ed. Kalbfleisch, with excellent introduction switching the attribution from Galen to Porphyry, *Abhandlungen der Königl. Akademie der Wissenschaften zu Berlin* 1895, French translation by Festugière in *The Revelation of Hermes Trismegistus*, vol. 4. Some of the points are in Clement *Stromateis* 8.4; some in Aëtius 5.15.1-5, *Dox. Gr.* 425-6.

[32] Aëtius 5.15.3 (*Dox. Gr.* 425,23-426,4) Diels' deletion of *mê* (*not* an animal) is not justified by any conflict with Aëtius 4.22.1 (= Empedocles A 74, Diels-Kranz), since (a) this is about an earlier stage of zoogony, and in any case (b) it gives a similar account, if *brephos* means new-born baby.

[33] Plato *Timaeus* 91D.

[34] Ibid. 77A-B; 91B-D. Porphyry *ad Gaurum* 4.

[35] Plato *Phaedrus* 248D.

[36] Porphyry *ad Gaurum* 1.4.

nutritive soul (*phutikê psukhê*).[37] He therefore interprets Plato as referring merely to the birth of a lover of beauty, not to the preceding embryonic development. On his side Porphyry cites the Chaldaeans, who are said to hold that the soul enters only at birth.[38]

For the rival view that embryos have animal souls, Porphyry cites the Middle Platonist Numenius and the Neopythagoreans.[39] Such a position is also discussed by Clement of Alexandria,[40] and taken by the pseudo-Galenic *Whether the Embryo is an Animal*, and by Galen himself, who says that animal life begins with the first heart beat, superseding plant life.[41] In a conscious reply to Porphyry, the Christian Hermippus also insists that embryos are animals.[42]

The Stoics take an even more extreme view than Porphyry's, contrasting nature (*phusis*) with soul (*psukhê*). The *pneuma* in the embryo changes from being its nature to being its soul at the moment of birth, thus converting the creature into an animal for the first time. Previously, it had no soul at all.[43]

The best solutions were developmental, and well before Galen, Aristotle gave a detailed developmental account. The embryo at first lives the life of a plant, and only later becomes an animal with consciousness – which sets the limit for permissible abortion.[44] The first movement and the first differentiation of sexual parts appears in male embryos around forty days, and in females around ninety.[45] At first, the embryo has a plant soul only potentially, until it can draw the nourishment to itself within the womb. Similarly, when the conscious soul arrives, it, too, is at first possessed only potentially.[46] At first, the embryo's condition is not one of sleeping, but merely resembles sleep, since it is plant-like, and plants do not sleep. Later the embryo can be said to sleep and wake in the womb.[47] Some embryos get stuck at an incomplete stage of development, and may turn out to be a monstrosity, like an animal, but not like a human.[48] Anthony Preus, in assembling the relevant passages, has commented that the successive incarnations

---

[37] Ibid. 6.3; 14.2; cf. 17.1.
[38] Ibid. 16.5.
[39] Ibid. 2.
[40] Clement *Stromateis* 8.14.
[41] ps-Galen *Whether the Embryo is an Animal* (Kühn 19,158-81); Galen *On the Development of Embryos* (Kühn 4.670,12 ff); cf. *On the Use of Parts* (Kühn 4.238,4 ff).
[42] Hermippus *On Astrology* 2.17.
[43] Hierocles, *Berliner Klassikertexte* 4, 1.5 ff (translated Long and Sedley, *The Hellenistic Philosophers* 1, 53B2-3); Porphyry *ad Gaurum* 14,3-4.
[44] Aristotle *GA* 2.3, 736a34 ff; 2.4, 740a24-b12; 5.1, 779a1; *Pol.* 7.15, 1335b20 ff.
[45] Aristotle *HA* 7.3.
[46] Aristotle *GA* 2.3, 736a34 ff; cf. 2.1, 735a9.
[47] Ibid. 5.1, 778b30 ff; 779a21-4.
[48] Ibid. 4.3, 767b6; 769b8-14.

of Empedocles are here found in the development of each and every human.[49]

Slide arguments

The various differentiations of plants from animals ought to be useful in answering the old sorites or slide argument, that if you spare animals, you will have, absurdly, to spare vegetables. The argument is found as early as the Athenian statesman Solon (*c.* 640-558 BC), according to Plutarch.[50] It recurs in a collection stemming from the Platonist Heraclides Ponticus (388-310 BC).[51] After that, it is ascribed to the Peripatetics and Stoics,[52] repeated by Sextus Empiricus[53] and used by Augustine.[54] Philo of Alexandria offers a slide in the opposite direction from plants to animals: since it is by nature, not reason, that plants manage to do the right thing, why should not the same be true of animals?[55]

The most comprehensive reply is given by Aristotle's successor Theophrastus. As reported by Porphyry, he has five moves available to him. First, he avoids the slide at one point by converting Pythagoras' argument that we are made of the same elements as animals (which would apply also to plants) into an argument that we are made of the same tissues and fluids (which would not).[56] Secondly, he replies that plants are not unwilling (*akontes*) to shed their fruit, which they will do anyhow. Thirdly, the taking of fruit does not destroy them. Fourthly, they are more ours than animals are, because we plant and raise them. Nor are vegetables the only food we can take harmlessly and rightfully: we can enjoy some of the honey in recompense (*misthos*) for our labours, without harming the bees. Finally, vegetarian sacrifice is more economical, hence holier and more continuously sustainable.[57]

The tradition of Heraclides had objected that to take honey, milk, eggs and wool is at least theft. Porphyry does not reply to this, when he endorses Theophrastus' list of permitted foods, adding other plant cast-offs, such presumably as nuts.[58] But Theophrastus had already addressed himself to it, when he treated our share of the honey as a recompense, and plants as in a way ours, because of our planting and

---

[49] I am indebted to his paper delivered to the Society for Ancient Greek Philosophy, delivered around 1979: 'Animal and human souls in the Peripatetic School', printed in *Skepsis* 1, Athens 1990, 67-99.

[50] Plutarch *Sep. Sap. Conv.* 159B-C.   [51] Porphyry *Abstinence* 1.8.

[52] Ibid. 1.6.   [53] Sextus *M* 9.127.

[54] Augustine *City of God* 1.20.

[55] Philo *de Animalibus* 94-5; cf. 79.

[56] Porphyry *Abstinence* 3.25.

[57] Ibid. 2.13.

[58] Ibid. 1.21 (Heraclides/Clodius) and 3.26.12.

raising them. This should not be seen as a general justification, or it would sanction our eating our children. But it is relevant to the particular charge that what is going on is theft.

There were other responses to the slide. There were those, of course, who did, to varying degrees, spare plants. Pythagoras does tell us to be kind to them,[59] the Egyptian followers of Osiris spared cultivated trees,[60] and the Manichaean priests are ridiculed by Augustine for leaving the cutting of plants to their followers.[61] Plutarch makes the more conventional reply that plants lack thought (*phronein*).[62] Porphyry for the first time, unless he is drawing on Plutarch, makes use of the fact that they lack not only sensation, but also pain and terror.[63] As regards sensation, however, he has to reinterpret Plato's ascription to plants of pleasant and painful sensations (*aisthêseis*) as referring only to physical reactions.[64] Augustine answers his own use of the slide argument by saying that plants have no feelings.[65] And the Emperor Julian reports wise men as saying that fruit is lifeless and not full of blood, and that plants are not caused pain and distress.[66]

Conclusion

It is time to conclude the discussion of ancient Philosophy of Mind. I have maintained that a single decision in Aristotle, the denial to animals of reason and belief, led in Aristotle and the Stoics to a massive re-analysis of psychological capacities: of perception, of perceptual appearance, of belief, of concept-possession, of memory, of intention and preparation, of anger and other emotions, and of speech. On independent grounds, the concept of reason was itself repeatedly transformed. But the denial of reason to animals was contested, especially by Pythagoreans and certain Platonists and even by Aristotle's own immediate successors. The modern reader cannot reflect on this debate about whether animals are sharply differentiated from humans in their psychological capacities without being led to ethical conclusions about how we should treat animals. The flimsier the differentiation appears to be, the more anxious the reader will or should be about how we treat them. Aristotle's interest in the debate

[59] Diogenes Laertius *Lives* 8.23; Clement *Stromateis* 2.18.

[60] Plutarch *de Iside* 365B; Porphyry *Abstinence* 1.21, quoting Clodius and Heraclides Ponticus; Diogenes Laertius *Lives* 8.23; Porphyry *Life of Pythagoras* 39; Iamblichus *Life of Pythagoras* 99.

[61] Augustine *de Moribus (On the Catholic and Manichean Way of Life)* 2.17; *City of God* 1.20.

[62] Plutarch *Sollertia* 962F-963A.

[63] Porphyry *Abstinence* 3.19.

[64] Plato *Timaeus* 77A-C; Porphyry *ad Gaurum* 4.1.

[65] Augustine *City of God* 1.20.

[66] Julian *Or.* 5, 174A-B.

was very largely scientific. But for the Stoics and their opponents the ethical questions were extremely important, and the Stoic ethical stance, I believe, has exercised great, perhaps excessive, influence on our own Western Christian tradition. In antiquity, it was religious as well as ethical issues that were at stake, because of the practice of animal sacrifice. It is to the ethical and religious questions that the second half of the book will be devoted. We shall start by finding that the debate on animal abilities extended also to their capacity for voluntary action.

Part II

Morals

CHAPTER NINE

Responsibility, justice and reason

There were two main ethical questions. If animals lack reason, are they responsible for what they do (e.g. for attacking us), and the more important question: do we owe them justice, or are they not the sort of beings who can suffer injustice? I shall start with the question of responsibility.

The two questions were not straightforwardly connected with each other. For it was not normally maintained that only morally responsible agents could be victims of injustice. Where this idea occurs at all, it is usually only as an indirect consequence of other more consciously entertained views. On the other hand, perhaps only morally responsible agents could be subject to just punishment.

Responsibility in Democritus

As early as the Presocratic Democritus we can probably find a primitive version of the idea that animals are responsible and of the idea that that makes them subject to just punishment.[1] At least as usually interpreted, he said that certain animals might willingly do us an injustice or wrong (*adikein kai thelein adikein*), contrary to justice (*para dikên*). If so, in killing them, one would incur no penalty (*athôïos*, but have justice (*dikê*) on one's side. Moreover, criminals should be killed just like animals. Here the willingness (*thelein*) of animals to wrong us contrary to justice may be relevant to justice of killing them. Are animals capable of acting willingly? Here we have yet another question in the Philosophy of Mind which is of direct concern to ethics. The Democritus fragments run as follows:

> This is how it is with the killing or not killing of certain animals. He who kills the ones that do wrong and are willing (*thelein*) to do wrong (*adikein*) pays no penalty. Doing this contributes more than not doing it

[1] Democritus frr. 257-9, Diels-Kranz, from Stobaeus *Ecl.* 2.4.15-17. I have benefited from discussion with John Procope of his 'Democritus on politics and the care of the soul', *Classical Quarterly* 39, 1989, 307-31, at 311-12. But I see Democritus' words as a moral injunction that it is all right to kill animals that willingly wrong us, rather than a prudential one that it is wise to kill animals that are disposed to harm us.

to well being. ... One must kill the ones that do harm (*pêmainein*) contrary to justice (*para dikên*), all of them at all costs. And he who does this will in every social organisation have a greater share of contentment and justice (*dikê*) and courage and property.

In the case of humans it seems to me one should act in just the same way as has been described for foxes and reptiles. That is, to kill the hostile in accordance with ancestral laws in every social organisation where law does not forbid it.[2]

Responsibility without reason in Aristotle

On one point Aristotle would agree with Democritus. For he held that animals could act voluntarily (*hekousiôs*).[3] Voluntariness implies, as Aristotle says, being liable to (justified) praise or blame.[4] In other words, it implies moral responsibility. What interests me is that animal action can be classed as voluntary, and therefore morally responsible, despite Aristotle's denial of reason to animals. What is needed for voluntariness is not reason, but some much weaker requirements, which vary from one work to another in ways that I have analysed elsewhere.[5] We can abstract from the variations by saying that there is always a causal requirement, for example, the requirement that the origin of the action should be internal. It should be one's own desires or negligence, for example, rather than something external like a wind which carries one off course. Secondly, there is a requirement about knowledge or ignorance. For example, the agent must not act because of ignorance of what he or she is doing. Presumably, an animal that bites need not do so because of ignorance that it is biting. A third requirement is sometimes included in the definition of voluntariness,[6] and sometimes (although this has not always been noticed) made an implication of the internal origin requirement.[7] It is that it should be *up to* the agent (*ep' autôi eph' hautôi; eph' hêmin*) whether he or she acts or not. This implies not only that it depends on the agent, but that there was, at least originally, a genuine possibility of things happening either way. Aristotle never says that this dependence on the agent presupposes a *rational* agent. On the contrary, he implies that it can be up to a non-rational animal which of two opposite outcomes occurs, when he says that animal action is voluntary. There is a genuine possibility of either outcome which depends on the animal itself.

[2] Democritus frr. 257-9, Diels-Kranz, from Stobaeus *Floril.* 4.2.13.

[3] Aristotle *NE* 3.1, 1111a25-6; b7-10; *Mot.* 11, 703b2.

[4] Aristotle *NE* 3.1, 1109b30-4; 5.8, 1135a19-23; similarly for the related notion of an act being up to oneself (*eph' hautôi*) *EE* 2.8, 1223a11.

[5] Richard Sorabji, *Necessity, Cause and Blame*, London and Ithaca NY 1980, see index s.v. voluntariness. I refer chiefly to *NE* 3.1-5; 5.8; 7.3; *EE* 2.6-9.

[6] Aristotle *EE* 2.9, 1225b8 (cf. 2.10, 1226b31-3); *NE* 5.8, 1135a24.

[7] Aristotle *NE* 3.1, 1110a15-18; 3.5, 1113b19-23; 1114a18-19. See *Necessity, Cause and*

It has none the less been supposed that Aristotle makes dependence on the agent presuppose a *rational* agent. And the most striking evidence adduced is his discussion in the *Metaphysics* of non-rational capacities like the capacity of fire to burn.[8] Non-rational capacities are incapable of opposite outcomes, Aristotle says, whereas rational capacities such as the doctor's ability to heal can be used in opposite ways, either to restore or to withhold health. This might have encouraged Aristotle to conclude that only those actions are up to us which are exercises of a rational capacity like medicine, because only those capacities are capacities for opposite outcomes. But that would have been very restrictive. For then more humdrum behaviour that was not an exercise of a rational capacity would not be up to us. What is required for something to be up to us is not that we should actually have had the capacity for the very *opposite*, e.g. for *withholding* health, but merely that there should have been a possibility, depending on us, of *refraining*.

Where, then, does reason come in for Aristotle? Only with deliberate choice (*proairesis*). This is a choice of a means which reason has seen to be conducive to an end, for example the choice of a diet as conducive to health.[9] It is important to Aristotle not because it is needed for moral responsibility, but because it is prerequisite for genuine virtue,[10] and at least in some cases for vice.[11] And so what an agent deliberately chooses is rightly thought to be the best test of character.[12] Even when someone acts out of character, this presupposes reason.[13] Testing the agent's whole character goes far beyond testing whether the agent is morally responsible for an individual act. The idea is that a virtuous person has to think out what are the goals that most matter in life, and what policies will secure them, and see what is to be done in each individual situation in the light of these goals and policies. Deliberate choice comes in at two points, both in the selection of policies to secure goals and in the selection of goals as entering into the ideal life. The deliberate choice of humans is carefully distinguished from the merely voluntary acts of animals.

Although deliberate choice appears to be voluntary, then, it is not the same thing. The voluntary extends further. For both children and

---

Blame, 235.

[8] Aristotle *Metaph.* 9.2 and 5, cited by Walter G. Englert, *Epicurus on the Swerve and Voluntary Action*, Atlanta Georgia 1987, 96-101 at 97.

[9] Aristotle *NE* 3.2-3 and 6.2, discussed in Richard Sorabji, 'Aristotle on the role of intellect in virtue', *Proceedings of the Aristotelian Society* n.s. 74, 1973-4, 107-29, repr. in A. Rorty, ed., *Essays on Aristotle's Ethics*, Berkeley and Los Angeles 1980.

[10] Aristotle *NE* 2.4, 1105a31; 2.5, 1106a3; 2.6, 1106b36; 3.5, 1113b3-7; 6.2, 1139a22-3; 6.12, 1144a19.

[11] Aristotle *EE* 3.7, 1234a25; *NE* 3.1, 1110b31-2; 5.8, 1135b25; 7.4, 1148a17; 7.7, 1150a20; 7.8, 1150b30; 1151a7.

[12] Aristotle *NE* 3.2, 1111b5-6; 1112a1-2.

[13] Ibid. 7.3, 1147b5.

animals share in the voluntary, but not in deliberate choice.[14]

Finally, full-scale action (*praxis*), unlike the voluntary actions of animals, requires deliberate choice.[15] This point is important, because it means that in denying full action to animals, Aristotle is not denying that they may be praised or blamed.[16] And conversely in allowing their behaviour to be voluntary, he is not conceding them full action.[17]

Although the behaviour of non-rational animals is not based on deliberate choice, then, it is at least voluntary and up to them. This voluntariness is not the rationale that Aristotle gives, when he introduces the idea of a just war against wild beasts (*thêria*).[18] But one later author does connect these ideas. The philologist Clodius, or the early Platonist Heraclides Ponticus on whom he probably draws, defends the idea of a just war against wild beasts, basing it (*gar*) on their attacking men voluntarily (*hekontes*).[19]

The greatest elaborator of ancient Aristotelianism, Alexander of Aphrodisias, takes Aristotle differently from me as making rationality a prerequisite of moral responsibility. But he is, I believe, not true to Aristotle, and why should he be? Writing over five hundred years later, in a work which does not purport to be an exegesis of Aristotle, he has to develop Aristotelianism, in order to defend it against its main opponents, the Stoic determinists. Their determinism, he claims,[20] excludes actions being up to us (*eph' hêmin*). It is no good their pleading that they allow for actions being in accordance with impulse (*kath' hormên*), for a great deal more is required if the actions are to be up to us. It is required that there be genuine alternative possibilities and (as the Stoics themselves acknowledge) that the agent uses his reason to decide. And this is possible only for humans, who are capable of deliberate choice (*proairetikos*). Here Alexander has upgraded the idea of 'up to us' and moral responsibility, so that it involves reason, an upgrading already introduced by his Stoic opponents before him. It does not follow that the upgrading is yet to be found in Aristotle. In fact, we should be warned by the example already encountered in Chapter Three, where Alexander reads back into Aristotle the Stoic idea of rational assent as a criterion for distinguishing appearance from belief.

---

[14] Ibid. 3.2, 1111b6-9. Cf. *EE* 2.8, 1223b37-1224a4; 2.9, 1225a37; 2.10, 1226b30, for voluntariness distinguished from deliberate choice.

[15] Aristotle *NE* 6.2, 1139a31 (cf. 1139a18-20); *EE* 2.8, 1224a25-30 (cf. 2.6, 1222b18-21); *Phys.* 2.6, 197b1-8.

[16] Pamela Huby, 'The Epicureans, animals and free will', *Apeiron* 3, 1969, 17-19.

[17] William Fortenbaugh, 'Aristotle: animals, emotion and moral virtue', *Arethusa* 4, 1971, 145.

[18] Aristotle *Pol.* 1.8, 1256b23-6.

[19] ap. Porphyrium *Abst.* 1.14.

[20] Alexander *de Fato* 33, 205,8-206,5.

There have been several thoughtful and thought-provoking interpretations recently that have taken Aristotle quite differently. It has been said that Aristotle's *Nicomachean Ethics* Book 3, differs on the role of reason from the *Eudemian Ethics*. On one account, *NE* 3 draws a sharp distinction between the merely voluntary and the up to us. It is, on this account, only the latter (the up to us) that implies moral responsibility, and it already requires reason in the form of deliberate choice.[21] On another account, *NE* 3 intends an additional requirement for moral responsibility over and above the action's being voluntary and up to us. In addition, the agent should at least be capable of making a deliberate choice on the matter, even if he does not, in fact, do so.[22] On both accounts, animals, though acting voluntarily, are not responsible.

I am not myself persuaded by these accounts, but what are their grounds? One appears to rest on the premise that Aristotle would not consider animals responsible for their actions, even when he calls those actions voluntary.[23] But I do not know why Aristotle should not hold a dog responsible for biting. This would be in line with Democritus before him and Clodius or Heraclides Ponticus after him. Moreover, he explicitly connects voluntariness with praise and blame, and it is agreed that if he really means to withhold responsibility from animals, this is at any rate nowhere explicit. Another account overlooks the three passages which make the 'up to us' requirement an implication of the 'internal origin' requirement for voluntariness. Only so can it detect a sharp distinction between the voluntary and the up to us.[24] A third account does not overlook the passages, but seeks to treat them as elliptical.[25] We are to understand that it is only in rational beings that an internal origin implies things are up to the agent. The only new motive, however, for taking the passages in an elliptical way is the authority of Alexander of Aphrodisias. And we have seen that Alexander is not expounding Aristotle, but developing Aristotelianism with a view to refuting subsequent Stoic developments.

What I would accept from these interpretations, and it is very well brought out in some of them, is that there are reasons why one might wish to develop Aristotle's thought in the direction indicated. At least there are reasons, if what is to be required for moral responsibility is the mere *capacity* for deliberate choice, not an actual exercise of it. (To

[21] Waler Englert, ch. 5. The statement on p. 111 that the merely voluntary behaviour of animals is not responsible is, however, modified in n. 16, where it is allowed that in a *different* way non-rational animals do get praised and blamed.

[22] Terry Irwin, 'Reason and responsibility in Aristotle', in A. Rorty, ed., *Essays on Aristotle's Ethics*, Berkeley and Los Angeles 1980, 117-55. Cf. Roderick Long, 'Alexander of Aphrodisias and Aristotle on the conditions for moral responsibility', in preparation.

[23] Terry Irwin, p. 125.

[24] Walter Englert, op. cit.

[25] Roderick Long, op. cit.

require an actual exercise would allow us to escape responsibility simply by failing to use our reason.) But then equally I see nothing wrong with what I take to be Aristotle's position, that non-rational animals can sometimes be held responsible.

To return to the dog held responsible for biting, it might be objected that we would not hold an *untrained* dog responsible, because it has no idea that biting is wrong.[26] But what about a *trained* dog? Cannot it have the appearance (*phantasia*) that what it is doing is wrong? This, I believe, may correspond to the view of Vicki Hearne. On the one hand, she saved from the gallows an untrained dog which had been condemned to death for biting.[27] On the other hand, she describes a trained dog as having enough moral sense to restrain the over-aggressive police handler for whom it was working.[28] The exoneration of the untrained dog may seem more problematic, because in the case of humans, Aristotle refuses to allow that ignorance of what is wrong makes an action involuntary.[29] But it may be right to treat an untrained animal differently. For one thing, and this is Aristotle's point, ignorance of right and wrong in humans may itself be culpable. For another, if it ever does look like an inevitable product of the social environment, we may still, without bestowing blame, find the wrong values abhorrent, the more so when the people who hold them are closer to ourselves. Animals are more distant, and in most cases hold no values at all.

Responsibility and reason in the Stoics

It is, I think, the Stoics who first make moral responsibility depend upon reason. It has been said that the reconciliation of fate and moral responsibility is the dominant and characteristic problem of Stoic moral philosophy.[30] The belief in fate implied that whatever happened had all along been inevitable or necessary, and this raised the question how we could be morally responsible. A major Stoic line was to accept necessity, and argue that inspite of it, things could be 'up to us' (*eph' hêmin*), and so we could be praised and blamed after all. I have described this 'compatibilism' and my own inability to believe in it elsewhere.[31] Things remain 'up to us', according to the Stoics, because

[26] I thank Bob Heinaman for this point.

[27] 'A little vicious', POV film by Immy Humes for US public television, featuring Vicki Hearne, also published as Vicki Hearne, *Bandit: Dossier of a Dangerous Dog*, Harper Collins, 1991.

[28] Vicki Hearne, *Adam's Task*, London 1987.

[29] Aristotle *NE* 3.1, 1110b31-3; 3.5, 1113b30 ff.

[30] Brad Inwood, *Ethics and Human Action in Early Stoicism*, Oxford 1985, 66.

[31] Richard Sorabji, *Necessity, Cause and Blame*, London and Ithaca NY 1980, chs 4, with 2 and 15. See Cicero *de Fato* 41, 43 (*SVF* 2.974); *Acad.* 2.37-9 (where, however, the view of Antiochus grants assent to animals as well); Aulus Gellius *Attic Nights* 7.2.7-11

when we receive the appearance (*phantasia*) that we should act in such and such a way, impulse and action need not follow the appearance. The appearance is presented to our reason, and reason can withhold assent. Of course, the withholding of assent is as much necessitated, when it occurs, as the granting. But in the Stoic view, our capacity of withholding it makes our actions 'up to us'. Animals, by contrast, lack reason and so the capacity to withhold assent. Consequently, what they do is not 'up to them' and they cannot be praised or blamed.[32]

We have met the Stoic appeal to rational assent twice. First, as seen in Chapter Four, Seneca makes the voluntariness of anger depend on assent of the rational will. Secondly, Alexander was following the Stoics when, as we have just seen, he made rationality the condition for an act's being up to us. Thomas Aquinas was in this Stoicising tradition when he said in the thirteenth century that both choice (*electio*) and will (*voluntas*) depend on reason, and that animal behaviour is therefore voluntary only in a secondary sense.[33] Seneca, as well as Alexander, is relevant to this remark. For as we have seen in Seneca's case (ch. 4, p. 61), Latin connects *voluntarius* with *voluntas*, a *rational* will,[34] and Thomas was heir to the Latin tradition of Cicero, Seneca and Augustine.

When humans evaluate appearances, reason plays at least two roles, for the Stoics. Being a collection of concepts,[35] it makes it possible for the appearance to be presented in a conceptualised, and verbalised, form. Secondly, it is the instrument with which we evaluate. The Stoics do not allow a non-conceptualised evaluative procedure to be available to animals.

There are other ways, too, in which the Stoics rob animals of anything like human action, and these ways take the Stoics a long way beyond Aristotle. The apparent agreement with Aristotle may be largely verbal when they deny that irrational beings can engage in action (*prattein*; *praxis*).[36] For the activation (*energein*) which they do concede to animals in these contexts is not *voluntary* behaviour, such

---

(*SVF* 2.1000); Origen *On First Principles* 3.1.2-5 (*SVF* 2.988).

[32] Origen *On First Principles* 3.1.2-4 (*SVF* 2.988), translated G.W. Butterworth, Origen, *On First Principles*, London 1936 (repr. Gloucester, Mass. 1973) and with discussion, by Brad Inwood, op. cit., 78-91, who makes beautifully clear the Stoic differentiation between humans and animals on the question of moral responsibility.

[33] Thomas Aquinas *Summa Theologiae* II.I. q. 13, a. 2, ad 3; II.I. q. 6, a. 2, in corp., the second cited by Terry Irwin, op. cit. Cf. his 'Who discovered the will?', *Philosophical Perspectives* 6, 1992, Ethics, 453-73.

[34] The point is excellently made by Charles Kahn, 'Emergence of the concept of the will in ancient philosophy', in John Dillon and A.A. Long, eds., *The Question of Eclecticism*, Berkeley, Los Angeles, 1988.

[35] Galen *PHP* 5.3.1, p. 304 de Lacy (= *SVF* 2.841); cf. Aëtius 4.11.3-4 in *Dox. Gr.* 400,17-26 (= *SVF* 1.149; 2.83).

[36] Alexander *de Fato* 205,28 (*SVF* 2.1002, translation by R.W. Sharples, London 1983); Simplicius *in Cat.* 306,26 (reading *prattein* for *plattein*); cf. 318,18-19.

as Aristotle concedes to them. Furthermore, Aristotle's denial of *praxis* to animals is a denial that they can act on policies which have been deliberately thought out with a view to securing what matters in life. The Stoics' denial, by contrast, is based partly on their denial that animals can withhold the assent of reason from appearances about what to do.

But there is a still greater divergence from Aristotle. For the Stoics, unlike Aristotle, deny that animals can have desire (*orexis*). *Orexis* is treated as a *rational* impulse.[37] It is also treated as directed to the good, or to the apparent good,[38] and Seneca denies that dumb animals can grasp the good (*comprendere bonum*), despite his apparent recognition, argued in Chapter Four above, that they can have a (confused) appearance of injustice.[39] The lack of *orexis* means that animals can have none of its species or subspecies, as these are recorded by Arius Didymus and others.[40] They can have neither will (*boulêsis*) which is directed to the genuine good, nor appetite (*epithumia*) which is irrational (*alogos*), though not arational, and is directed to the merely apparent good.[41] Under the heading of will, animals cannot have choice (*hairesis*, *expetere*), pre-choice (*proairesis*), or unconstrained willing (*thelêsis*).

Can animals engage in the selection (*eklogê*, *selectio*; possibly wider terms: *lêpsis*, *sumere*) of natural objectives which fall short of being good and are indifferent, such as self-preservation?[42] On the one hand, Stoic 'selection' has been described in the modern literature as *rational* impulse.[43] On the other hand, irrational animals and plants are said to be able to exercise their proper functions (*kathêkonta*, *officia*), on the grounds that they are activated (*energein*) in conformity with their own nature,[44] presumably when they follow such natural objectives as self-preservation. And Cicero, speaking of humans, not only calls it a proper function to preserve oneself in one's own natural constitution. He also says that what is in accordance with nature is to be taken (*sumere*) and

---

[37] Stobaeus *Ecl.* 2.7 (Wachsmuth 2.87,2-3).

[38] Ibid. 2.7 (Wachsmuth 2.90,7-8; 2.97,18-19 as supplemented = *SVF* 3.91 and 3.39); Cicero *Tusc.* 4.11-12; discussion in Brad Inwood op. cit. 228; A. Bonhöffer, *Epictet und die Stoa*, Stuttgart 1890, 235.

[39] Seneca *Ep.* 124,1 on good; *de Ira* 1.3.7 with 2.1.3 on injustice.

[40] Esp. Stobaeus *Ecl.* 2.7 (Wachsmuth 2.87,14-22 = *SVF* 3.173). There is a very good discussion in Brad Inwood, op. cit., Appendix 2.

[41] Stobaeus *Ecl.* 2.7 (Wachsmuth 2.90,7-8 = *SVF* 3.91); Diogenes Laertius *Lives* 7.113; 116; Cicero *Tusc.* 4.11-12; ps-Andronicus *Peri Pathôn* 1.2-6, pp. 225-37, Glibert Thirry (*SVF* 3.391; 432); Augustine *City* 14.8.

[42] One important passage is Cicero *Fin.* 3.20. Further discussion in Chapter Eleven below.

[43] Brad Inwood, op. cit. p. 324, n. 44, but he kindly tells me that he is now open-minded on the subject.

[44] Diogenes Laertius *Lives* 7.107 (*SVF* 3.493); Stobaeus 2.7 (Wachsmuth 2.85,15-17 = *SVF* 3.494).

describes it as a selection (*selectio*) if one holds on to (*tenere*) what is in accordance with nature, and rejects (*pellere*) what is contrary to it.[45] What makes it possible for animals to exercise proper functions is that these functions are defined as things for which it is *possible* to offer a rationale (*eulogon iskhei apologismon, probabilis ratio reddi possit*).[46] But as in the case of an animal enjoying the appearance that it is day (Chapter Two), it is not required that the animal *itself* should be able to supply the rationale. At most *we* should be able to.

Responsibility in the Epicureans

Not everyone endorsed the connexion between moral responsibility and reason. Epicurus distinguishes between wild and tame animals. We exonerate (*kathairein*) wild ones, not admonishing them (*nouthetêtikos*) nor retaliating (*aparaitêtikos*). We treat tame animals differently, because we distinguish their original constitution from their subsequent development (*apogegennêma*), and so we do admonish them.[47] This may relate to the point I made above that trained animals can have a sense of wrong conduct. There is no suggestion that tame animals are differentiated from wild by the possession of reason. It was Aristotle who had in a different context raised the question whether rebuke (*nouthetêsis*) could be directed to the irrational, and decided that it implied the possession of reason in some sense.[48]

Lucretius' Latin exposition of Epicurus is different again. He allows a mind (*animus, mens*) to horses and a will (*voluntas* belonging to that mind, and he describes the will as wrested away from fate (*fatis avulsa voluntas*).[49] But again the concept of reason is not said to be decisive.

Responsibility and the law

In Roman law, a text ascribed to the third-century AD jurist Ulpian, and subsequently incorporated in Justinian's sixth-century *Digest*, may possibly make the connexion with reason. Even though, as we are told by a later text, natural law (*ius naturale*) is recognised by animals in the matter of procreation and rearing,[50] an animal cannot, according

[45] Cicero *Fin*. 3.20. Brad Inwood op. cit., p. 316, n. 73, takes *Sumere* as = *Selectio*, citing *inter alia* the same work of Cicero, *Fin*. 3.59; 4.30; 4.39.

[46] Diogenes Laertius *Lives* 7.107 (*SVF* 3.493); Cicero *Fin*. 3.58 (*SVF* 3.498).

[47] Epicurus *On Nature* Arrighetti 34,25, lines 22-34.

[48] Aristotle *NE* 1.13, 1102b33-1103a3; *Pol*. 1.13, 1260b3-7, translated below p. 135.

[49] Lucretius 2.257-271, discussed by Julia Annas, 'Epicurus on agency', in J. Brunschwig and M. Nussbaum, eds., *Passions and Perceptions*, Cambridge 1993. Her *Hellenistic Philosophy of Mind*, Berkeley and Los Angeles 1992, reached me too late to be used in this book.

[50] Ulpian (?) in Justinian *Digest*, 1.1.1.3-4; *Inst* 1.2 pr. Thomas Aquinas follows, *Summa Theologiae* I, IIae q. 94, a. 2.

to our text,[51] be guilty of a wrong (*iniuria*) because it lacks *sensus*. I take *sensus* here to mean not sense perception, which would be nonsensical. It may possibly mean reason.[52]

The question of animal responsibility, however, would not have interfered with those earlier trials of animals which were common in Athens at least in the fourth century BC. An animal could be exiled from the state borders for killing someone, but so too could a tile which fell on someone's head. The sentence did not depend on any idea that the animal or tile was morally responsible, but on the need to rid the state of pollution.[53] E.P. Evans finds an analogous belief in demoniacal possession influencing the Council of Worms' legislation in AD 864 on the treatment of bees that had stung someone to death. But many of the later cases of animal trials which he describes from the fourteenth to eighteenth centuries treat animals as much more like humans. They can be summoned to court and defended for non-appearance. How can the rats appear in court, when their enemies the cats might waylay them en route? They are thought to be subject to excommunications or removal orders, but only after suitable alternative territory has been found.[54]

Justice towards irrational beings?

I shall turn now from moral responsibility to justice, because this also got tied to rationality by the Stoics and Epicureans. It was not merely that one had to be rational in order to be just – many philosophers would have agreed with that. It also concerned the questions of whether justice was owed to animals, and of whether there could be such a thing as being unjust to them. One might have thought that justice was owed to all conscious beings, with rationality being relevant only at the margins. Rational beings may be subject to particular kinds of suffering (complex anxieties), or have particular needs (political rights). But in antiquity the requirement of justice to animals came to turn on whether animals were rational.

Some modern philosophers, though not particularly concerned with animal rationality, would agree that there could not be such a thing as injustice to animals. On the face of it, this is surprising, as may be made clear by taking in turn Aristotle's three types of justice, distributive, reciprocal and rectificatory.[55] If I were to distribute all the food, when food was scarce, to the dog named after me, or reserve all

---

[51] Ulpian in Justinian *Digest* 9.1.1.3.

[52] Cf. our expression, 'to take leave of one's senses'.

[53] See e.g. D.M. MacDowell, *Athenian Homicide Law in the Age of the Orators*, Manchester 1963.

[54] E.P. Evans, *The Criminal Prosecution and Capital Punishment of Animals*, London 1906, repr. London 1987.

[55] Aristotle *EN* 5.2-5.

the painful experiments for the dog named after my enemy, that would naturally be thought of as an injustice. It looks like an injustice of Aristotle's distributive kind. If someone shoots his old sheepdog as soon as it becomes less efficient at working for him, that would look like an injustice,[56] a violation of what Aristotle calls reciprocity. And if I punish all the dogs because one has stolen a biscuit, that, too, apears unjust. It seems to go against Aristotle's rectificatory justice. Our intuitions, then, suggest that some treatment of animals would be unjust and some just. If this is denied, as it was by Aristotle himself, this tended to be on the basis not of intuition, but of myth, or theory. But if theory clashes too much with intuitions, this will be so much the worse for the theory.

The denial of justice starts with a myth in the poet Hesiod, as early perhaps as the eighth century BC. For he said that Zeus gave justice (*dikê*) only to man, not to animals.[57] And this idea is elaborated in the myth which Plato puts into the mouth of the fifth-century sophist Protagoras. Zeus gave justice to men to protect them from each other. It is emphasised that the gift was not for the benefit of animals when we learn that the need for it only arose after men had banded together in cities, precisely in order to exclude animals. The banding together protected them from the external threat from animals, while justice protected them from the internal.[58] Without the reference to Zeus, the twofold account is endorsed as an anthropological story by Epicurus' successor Hermarchus in the third century BC. Men banded together against the animals and practised justice towards each other, but not towards animals. Both of these measures promoted their security.[59] The pseudo-Platonic Menexenus repeats that only man has justice.[60]

As for theory, I shall turn to the two most relevant Greek theories, the Stoic and Epicurean, in Chapters Ten to Twelve. Modern theory sometimes ties justice to rights, interests, or contracts, in such a way that those who do not have rights or interests, or who do not make contracts, are said not to be subject to justice or injustice. There are modern authors who deny that animals have interests of the relevant sort, and consequently deny that they have rights, or are owed justice. One argument is that they lack the desires and emotions necessary for interests, because they lack speech.[61] Another is that animals lack the self-consciousness required for having interests and this argument has been used in an influential place.[62]

[56] Plutarch *Marcus Cato* 5.2, 339A, is admittedly inclined to say it is kindness rather than justice which constrains us in this case.
[57] Hesiod *Works and Days* 277-9.
[58] Plato *Protagoras* 320C-322D.
[59] Porphyry *Abstinence* 1.10.
[60] ps-Plato *Menexenus* 237D.
[61] Notably R.G. Frey, *Interests and Rights: The Case Against Animals*, Oxford 1980. On contracts cf. Jan Narveson, 'Animal rights', *Canadian Journal of Philosophy*, 7, 1977.
[62] Peter Byrne, in Kenneth Boyd, ed., Working Party Report of the Institute of Medical

But not only does this violate intuition. There is in any case another reason why we might not have expected to find Greek authors denying that animals can be victims of injustice. For quite apart from our intuitions about justice and injustice, the corresponding Greek notions of *dikaiosunê* and *adikia* are wider than ours. Aristotle himself points out that in its wider sense *dikaiosunê* is not merely the virtue of justice strictly so called, but covers all those virtues which relate to other people.[63] Correspondingly, *adikia* can apply to the wronging of others in general, regardless of whether that wronging takes the particular form of an injustice. The mugger who attacks me in the street certainly wrongs me, although it is not very obvious that the wrong is an injustice exactly. Similarly, the killing of animals for food or medical research might well be regarded by some people as a wrong of some kind, without necessarily being regarded as an injustice. To say, then, that animals cannot be the subjects of our *adikia* or *dikaiosunê* may be to say that there is no such thing as wronging them, or treating them aright. And this is still more counter-intuitive. How, then, did those Greek authors who sided with such a view find it, or make it, plausible?

The denial of justice might be made more palatable by the compensating manoeuvre which is used by Plutarch in his *Life of Cato the Elder*. He there concedes to possible opponents that justice, taken in a narrow sense, may not be owed to animals. But he insists that at least *benevolence* forbids us to get rid of a faithful horse or dog, when it is too old to serve us.[64] Those who deny that justice is owed, however, (and elsewhere Plutarch shows he is not one of them), do not normally qualify their denial in this way.

Aristotle adds an argument in his *Ethics*. In a phrase which became standard, he says there is no such thing as justice in relation to (*oude dikaion pros*) horse or ox, the reason being that we have nothing in common (*koinon*) with them.[65] Aristotle does not contradict this denial, when in the *Politics* he claims that to hunt wild beasts is to wage a just war against them. For he does not mean that we are giving them their *just* deserts. The point is only that we are entitled to hunt them because they are intended by nature for us.[66] Again, it is not in order to establish our *justice* that he says that tame animals have a better nature and are better off being governed by us because we protect them. The conclusion intended is merely that to be subject to such dominion is natural and

---

Ethics.

[63] Aristotle *EN* 5.1.

[64] Plutarch *Life of Marcus Cato* 5.2, 339A.

[65] Aristotle *EN* 8.11, 1161b2-3. Bignone's view that Aristotle had a more favourable approach to animals in his early treatise *On Justice*, now fragmentary, is rejected by Paul Moraux, *À la recherche de l'Aristote perdu; le dialogue 'Sur la Justice'*, Louvain and Paris 1957, 100-8.

[66] Aristotle *Pol.* 1.8, 1256b15-26.

advantageous.[67]

But Aristotle cannot entirely escape contradiction.[68] For we have just seen him say that the acts of animals can be voluntary. This implies that a dog can not only be blamed for biting me, but also praised for successful progress in its training, or in carrying out its trained skills. What then if I kick the dog that has just saved the baby from the cliff top? It is agreed that I have violated its deserts. Have I not, then, done it an injustice?

Not everybody agreed with Aristotle that there is no such thing as justice or injustice to animals. Pythagoras and Empedocles, we shall see, decried our injustice to them and Democritus, we have seen, thought it was a matter of justice to kill those which acted unjustly and advocated treating criminals similarly. Even Aristotle's own successor Theophrastus contradicted him. So far from animals having nothing in common with us, an animal is akin to us (*oikeios*).[69] Among the things that make this true is the fact that, contrary to Aristotle's claim, animals can engage in reasonings (*logismoi*).[70] We can wrong (*adikein*) animals[71] and some of them wrong us. Only those that do may be killed; others may not. The harmful ones merely *seem* to show that we stand in no relation of justice to them (*dikaion pros*, ignoring Bernays' emendation). In fact not all animals, any more than all humans, are harmful.[72] There are other authors too who speak of our owing justice to animals,[73] but wronging them.[74]

Justice exercised by irrational beings

So far I have spoken of justice and injustice towards animals, but the Greeks also discussed whether animals themselves exercised justice or had a sense of it. The questions were not necessarily connected, as the Greeks did not on the whole share the Kantian view, expressed for example by Rawls, that we are not required to give strict justice to animals who lack a sense of justice.[75] The only case I have noticed of

[67] Ibid. 1254b6-13.

[68] I am grateful to Steve Marone for raising this as a question.

[69] Theophrastus ap. Porphyrium *Abstinence* 2.22; 3.25.

[70] Ibid. 3.25.

[71] Ibid. 2.12; 2.22; 2.24.

[72] Ibid. 2.22

[73] This is the theme of Porphyry *Abstinence* Book 3.

[74] Heraclitus is combined with Empedocles by Plutarch Soll. 964D. For Empedocles, see Sextus *M* 9.127-9; for Pythagoras, Sextus *M* 9.127; Porphyry *Abstinence* 3.26; Plutarch *Soll.* 964E-F.

[75] John Rawls, *A Theory of Justice*, Cambridge Mass. 1971, 512, to be further discussed in Chapter Ten. The claim has been reiterated in defence of Rawls' comparative neglect of animals; Michael S. Pritchard and Wade L. Robinson, 'Justice and the treatment of animals: a critique of Rawls', *Environmental Ethics* 3, 1981, 55-61; Alan E. Fuchs, 'Duties to animals: Rawls' alleged dilemma', *Ethics and Animals* 2, 1981,

such an argument is one attributed to the Stoics and Peripatetics (i.e. Aristotelians), that there can be no such thing as wronging those who do not exercise justice (*dikaiopragein*) towards us.[76] The point here is more one about the lack of reciprocity than about the lack of a sense of justice. None the less, despite the rarity of this line of argument, there is much discussion of animals wronging us,[77] or treating us justly.[78] The second is substantiated by the argument that a dog, in distributing favours and threats according to what is appropriate (*kat' axian*), satisfies the (Stoic) definition of justice.[79] The occurrence of justice or injustice among animals is offered as a proof of their rationality by some authors,[80] and the direction of the post-Kantian argument is reversed. It is their rationality, rather than their justice or injustice, which is thought to entitle them to just treatment.

Animals are said to exercise justice, or display a sense of justice and injustice, not only towards ourselves, but also towards each other. Aristotle had denied that animals had any sense (*aisthêsis*) of justice and injustice, because they did not have speech.[81] But his pupil Eudemus is credited with many examples to the contrary: with that of a lion taking vengeance on a bear for killing a friendly dog, or for killing its cubs – in that case recruiting the help of a woodcutter and treating him with consideration. One story concerns the foal which took vengeance on its unnatural human father.[82] All these examples seem to involve a sense of oneself or another being wronged. The introduction of such a sense into the 'wild boy of Aveyron', captured in the woods of France in 1799, was the high point of achievement for his educatior, Itard. The boy's resistance, when he was unjustly punished instead of rewarded, displayed, in Itard's view, his elevation from primitive man to moral man.[83] In crediting animals too with such a sense, Eudemus is closer to Plato than to Aristotle. For Plato compares the spirit (*thumos*) of a man

---

83-7

[76] Plutarch *Soll.* 964B-C. In order to ascribe a comparable view to Epicurus, one would have needlessly to emend the manuscript reading at *Kuriai Doxai* 32, with Usener, from *alla* to *allêla* (each other), so that it speaks of animals which have no contracts not to harm *each other*, and one would have to understand *pros tauta* in a roundabout way to mean that *we* owe them no justice, if *they* lack contracts with each other. All this seems to me unjustified.

[77] Clodius or Heraclides Ponticus in Porphyry *Abstinence* 1.14; 1.19; Pythagoras as represented by Ovid *Metamorphoses* 15, 103-42; Democritus frr. 257-60.

[78] Sextus *PH* 1.67; Porphyry *Abstinence* 3.12.

[79] Sextus *PH* 1.67.

[80] For various virtues and vices so used, see Philo *de Animalibus* 62; 64; 66-70; Plutarch *Sollertia* 966B; Sextus *PH* 1.67-8; Porphyry *Abstinence* 3.11-13 and 22.

[81] Aristotle *Pol.* 1.2, 1253a14-18.

[82] Eudemus ap. Aelianum *On the Nature of Animals* 3.21; 4.8; 4.45 (frr. 127-9 in Wehrli's *Eudemus*).

[83] Jean-Marc-Gaspard Itard, translated from the French of 1806 as *The Wild Boy of Aveyron*, New York 1962, 94-6.

who thinks himself wronged (*adikeisthai*) with a shepherd's dog.[84]

A sense of justice (*aequitas, divinatio iustitiae*) is displayed also by Pliny's elephants which refused to punish their fellows.[85] And a standard example of just behaviour is the storks which feed their aged parents.[86] I shall come later to the examples of quasi-contractual arrangements among animals, which even the Stoics recognised. The most spectacular example they acknowledged was that of an apparent act of ransom among ants, which is described as displaying the seeds (*spermata*) of justice.[87]

No justice towards irrational beings

It is time to turn to the two post-Aristotelian theories of justice that will be examined in the next three chapters. They both reinforce Aristotle's denial that there is such a thing as justice in relation to animals. And they do so by making, on different grounds, the alleged non-rationality of animals the barrier. Thus rationality becomes central to the ethical questions and not, as in modern utilitarian theory, sensibility to pleasure and pain. It is surprising how late in the philosophical texts the argument is first introduced on behalf of animals that they feel pain and terror. I shall return to this point in Chapter Fifteen.

The two rationalistic theories of justice which arose in the generation after Aristotle were the Epicurean theory of contract and the Stoic theory of *oikeiôsis*. I shall consider the Stoic theory first.

---

[84] Plato *Republic* 440C-D.
[85] Pliny *Natural History* 5.11; 8.11.
[86] The Chorus in Sophocles *Electra* 1058-62. (I thank Pat Easterling for the reference: the birds in question are not here identified as storks); Aristophanes *Birds* 1355; Aristotle *HA* 9.13; Pliny *NH* 10.32; Philo *de Animalibus* 61; Plutarch *Soll.* 962E; Aelian *Nat. Anim.* 3.23; 10.16; Basil of Caesarea *Hexaemeron* 8.5; Porphyry *Abstinence* 3.11; cf. ps-Plato *Alcibiades* 1 135E; Cicero *Fin.* 3.63.
[87] Plutarch *Soll.* 967D-E. Cf. Aelian 6.50.

CHAPTER TEN

Oikeiôsis and bonding between rational beings

The Stoic theory of *oikeiôsis*

The Stoic theory of *oikeiôsis* or belonging had two elements which eventually came to be amalgamated. The first element is the explicit discussion of *oikeiôsis* proper. The *oik-* part of this word involves the idea of what is one's own. The *oikos*, originally *woikos*, is one's own household, as is reflected in the Latin *vicus*, a village, and in English place names ending in *-wick*. *Oikeiotês* is a relation of belonging, literally of belonging in the same household. It is the opposite of alienation. The ending *-sis* implies a process, so that *oikeiôsis* is a process of coming to treat things as belonging. One may come to treat one's own person or one's nearest and dearest as belonging. The Stoics came to be interested in the possibility of extending this sense of belonging more widely to one's fellow humans in general.

The second element in Stoic theory arose from the fact that Zeno of Citium, the founder of Stoicism, wrote a *Republic*, now lost, which, in marked contrast to Plato's *Republic*, spoke of a world-wide city or community. We should not live by separate cities and laws, but should consider all men our fellow-citizens.[1] The reference to all men is presumably an ideal, since Zeno is reported as having said in the same work that only virtuous people are in fact fellow-citizens, while all others are enemies to each other.[2] In later Stoics, however, the world is taken as already forming a single city, and the gods are included in the community, along with men, because we are all rational beings.[3]

The references to *oikeiôsis* itself in Zeno are uncertain, because,

---

[1] Plutarch *On the Fortune of Alexander* 329A-B (*SVF* 1.262). Many Stoic (and Epicurean) texts can now be found in translation, with admirable commentary, in A.A. Long and D.N. Sedley, *The Hellenistic Philosophers*, vol. 1, Cambridge 1987. See their index of sources; the original texts are supplied in vol. 2.

[2] Diogenes Laertius *Lives* 7.32-3.

[3] Cicero *Leg.* 1.7.22-3; Cicero *ND* 2.154; Arius Didymus ap. Eusebium *Praep. Ev.* 15.15.3-5 (*SVF* 2.528); Dio Chrysostom *Or.* 36.23 (*SVF* 3.334); and (without reference to the gods) Marcus Aurelius *Meditations* 4.4; (without reference to reason) Cicero *Fin.* 3.64; Seneca *On Leisure* 4.1.

although his circle (*hoi apo Zênônos*) are said to have made *oikeiôsis* the source of justice,[4] *oikeiôsis* in another Zeno text may be directed towards nature rather than towards one's fellow-man.[5] The first clear statement of the theory in the relevant form is found in Chrysippus, the third and most important head of the school. In this form, the theory involves a sense of mutual belonging together which can be extended to other people. Chrysippus said that it is extended by humans and animals in two directions (he does not describe this like some later authors as two stages in a process) to their own bodily parts and to their own offspring.[6] By the time of Cicero, Stoic theory has us extend the sense of mutual belonging far wider to the whole of mankind. And this is connected with Zeno's idea of a world-wide city, but one to which all men, and not just the virtuous, belong, and the gods as well.[7]

The idea in Cicero's account is that it is in accordance with nature that we should extend the feeling, and that the wise man would do so. Moreover, the wise man would extend it to all men, not as in Zeno only to the virtuous, nor only to non-foreigners.[8] But there are different opinions about how readily we do in fact extend it. Hierocles describes a series of concentric circles, starting with our own mind (*dianoia*) and body and passing out through a series of relatives and fellow citizens to the whole of mankind. He warns that extension of the feeling to wider circles is a duty requiring effort from the adult.[9] In Diogenes Laertius' account, it is only in good parents that the love for children exists, or is natural.[10] Cicero, more optimistically, says that we are impelled (*impellimur*) by nature to want to benefit as many people as possible, especially by teaching.[11] Outside the Stoic school, the Platonist Antiochus was still more optimistic. He developed a theory about children automatically extending the sense of belonging by stages across ever widening circles, until eventually it covered the human race.[12]

The alienation of animals

How does this theory affect animals? *Oikeiôsis* is said by the Stoics to

---

[4] Porphyry *Abstinence* 3.19. For other evidence of *oikeiôsis* in Zeno, see Paul Vander Waerdt, 'Hermarchus and the Epicurean genealogy of morals', *Transactions of the American Philological Association* 118, 1988, 87-106, at 105-6.

[5] Cicero *Ac. Pr.* 2.131: but *conciliatio naturae* may mean natural *oikeiôsis*, rather than *oikeiôsis towards* nature.

[6] Plutarch *Sto. Rep.* 1038B.   [7] Cicero *Fin.* 3.62-8.

[8] Cicero *Off.* 3.6.27-8; *Fin.* 3.19.63.

[9] Hierocles ap. Stobaeum 4.671,7-673,11, Hense.

[10] Diogenes Laertius *Lives of Eminent Philosophers* 7.120. The attachment to children is not here described as *oikeiôsis*, but simply as a kind of love (*philostorgia*; others say *amare*). Cf. Plutarch *Sollertia* 962A; Cicero *Fin.* 3.62; but *oikeiousthai* in Plutarch *Sto. Rep.* 1038B.

[11] Cicero *Fin.* 3.65.   [12] ap. Ciceronem *Fin.* 5.65.

be the source (*arkhê, initium*) of justice.[13] And Chrysippus declares
that no relation of justice holds between us and animals (*mêden hêmin
dikaion pros; nihil iuris cum*).[14] The reason is repeatedly said to be
that animals are not rational.[15] The texts present rationality as both a
necessary and a sufficient condition of our standing in a relation of
justice to another,[16] and this in turn is connected with the view that
oikeiôsis is the source of justice.[17] The idea is that rational beings like
ourselves can extend *oikeiôsis* (and hence justice) only to other rational
beings. The lack of any relation of justice means that whatever we do to
animals, it will not be a wrong, or an injustice.[18] If alienation can be
called the opposite of *oikeiotês*, animals can be said to be alienated
from us. It is admitted that animals can extend *oikeiôsis* to their own
offspring, which in humans constitutes the origin of justice. But just as
mules cannot by copulating achieve the goal of reproduction, so
animals do not achieve any share in justice.[19] The killing of animals for
natural purposes, then, is not unjust.

But do the Stoics not find other reasons, apart from justice, for
treating animals well? I shall later ask the same question about the
Epicureans. Concerning the Stoics, one might expect them to reject the
killing of animals in shows and spectacles, given their idea that
happiness consists of living in accordance with nature. But the Stoics
themselves do not draw attention to that implication. Seneca
disapproves of the battles with elephants that Pompey staged. But it is
the killing of the humans, not of the animals, that he deplores.[20] It was
left to the Roman public to feel pity for the elephants and disgust at
Pompey, whom they cursed. Ironically enough, Cicero suggests a Stoic
motive for the public: it was as if they felt that the elephants had a
relation of belonging (*societas*) with the human race.[21] The public was
ahead of the philosophers.

---

[13] Porphyry *Abstinence* 3.19 (*SVF* 1.197); 3.26; Plutarch *Sollertia* 962A; Anonymous *in
Theaetetus* 5.18 ff (Diels-Schubart, *Berliner Klassikertexte* 2, Berlin 1905); Cicero *Fin.*
3.66-7. In the Platonist Antiochus, the feeling (*affectio*) has actually come *to be* justice,
not merely its source, Cicero *Fin.* 5.65.

[14] Plutarch *Esu* 999B (*SVF* 3.374); Diogenes Laertius *Lives* 7.129 (*SVF* 3.367); Cicero
Fin. 3.67 (*SVF* 3.371); Sextus *M* 9.130 (*SVF* 3.370).

[15] Sextus *M* 9.130 (*SVF* 3.370); Porphyry *Abstinence* 3.19 (based on a lost work of
Plutarch. This part is not included in the *SVF* excerpt.); Plutarch *Sollertia* 963F-964B,
repeated in Porphyry *Abstinence* 1.4 and 1.6 (*SVF* 3.373); Porphyry *Abstinence* 3.1;
Augustine *City* 1.20. Note also the reference to irrational animals (*aloga*) in Plutarch's
formulation of the Stoic principle that no relation of justice holds towards them, *Esu*
999B (*SVF* 3.374), although this may not be consciously chosen.

[16] First three texts cited.

[17] Porphyry *Abstinence* 3.19; Augustine *City* 1.20.

[18] Porphyry *Abstinence* 3.1.

[19] Plutarch *Sollertia* 962A-B; repeated Porphyry *Abstinence* 3.23.

[20] Seneca *de Brevitate Vitae* 13,6.

[21] Cicero *Letters to Friends* 7.1.3; Pliny *Nat. Hist.* 8.7.20-1; Dio Cassius *Hist.* 39,38,2-4.
Pliny's description runs as follows: 'But when Pompey's elephants lost all hope of escape,

There was an ascetic strain in Stoicism, which commended vegetarianism to some, though not from concern for animals,[22] and in Seneca's case this influence came from his Pythagorean teachers, rather than from Stoicism.[23] It was left to the Platonist Plutarch in his *Life of Cato*, not to any Stoic, to say that benevolence is owed to animals, even if justice is not.[24] I have not found this argument anywhere else. Although the Stoics poured out handbooks on every kind of issue in practical ethics, such as those excerpted and listed by Stobaeus, in no case, so far as I know, do they devote one to the need to treat animals well. Indeed, it is hard to see how anyone could have a benevolent attitude to animals, if, like Chrysippus, he regarded pigs as having a soul only as a culinary preservative.[25]

Bonding and imprinting

The ground covered by the theory of *oikeiôsis* is sometimes treated nowadays in terms of the ideas of bonding and imprinting. The infant animal or human forms bonds with a parent, and later with a mate, learns a language, song or cries and accepts the members of some species as its natural associates, according to who gives the right signal, or provides the right habits, at the crucial age. After that age has passed, it is difficult for it to learn or unlearn any of these things. The mechanism, at least in some cases, is known as imprinting, and it becomes clearest from cases where it has gone wrong. A goose, for example, accepts a human as parent, a nightingale has learnt to imitate frogs, or the sparrow has misidentified Catullus' mistress as its mate, and it is too late for it to learn other ways. The original choice of

---

they entreated the crowd, trying to win their compassion with indescribable gestures, bewailing their plight with a sort of lamentation, and created so much distress in the public that they forgot the commander and his munificence, exquisitely designed in their honour, and in tears they rose as one and invoked curses on Pompey for which he soon afterwards paid the penalty.'

[22] Zeno of Citium, the founder of Stoicism, rejected his doctor's advice to eat pigeon on ascetic grounds, according to Musonius Rufus *On Food*. The Stoic Musonius Rufus in the first century AD preached vegetarianism for ascetic reasons in *On Food*, fragments edited and translated by Cora Lutz, *Yale Classical Studies* 10, 1947. Fragments 18A and B are *On Food*. The position of Posidonius in the first half of the first century BC is hard to reconstruct. See Haussleiter, *Der Vegetarismus*, 854-6. Persius, the poet of the first century AD, who studied under the Stoic Cornutus, attacks animal sacrifice and meat-eating in his *Satire* 2, 26-51: I owe the reference to Danuta Shanzer.

[23] Seneca was persuaded by his teacher, the Peripatetic Sotion, who told him of the model of his own teacher the Pythagorean Sextius, and of Pythagoras himself, *Ep.* 108,13-22.

[24] Plutarch *Life of Marcus Cato* 5.2,339A.

[25] Porphyry *Abstinence* 3.20 (drawing on Plutarch); Cicero *ND* 2.60; *Fin.* 5.38; Philo *Opif.* 66 (*SVF* 2.722); Plutarch *Quaest. Conviv.* 685C; Pliny *Nat. Hist.* 8.207; Varro *de R.R.* 2.4.10; ascribed to Chrysippus' predecessor Cleanthes: Clement *Stromateis* 7.6.33; cf. 2.20.105.

parent affects the type of mate that will be chosen later and the species that will be taken as providing natural associates.[26]

A lot of evidence is offered in the ancient texts that our natural association does spread as wide as the whole human race. Arius Didymus, for example, asks, in discussing *oikeiôsis*, who would refuse help to a traveller who had lost his way (*planômenos*), or needed water. And Seneca gives the same examples.[27] When Aristotle said, in his earlier discussion of friendship, how evident we found friendship to be 'in our wanderings' (*en tais planais*), he may have been referring either to travelling, or more specifically, to losing one's way.[28]

The cases where the bonding mechanism has gone wrong illustrate the truth in the Stoic insistence on the separateness of animals from ourselves (we had better omit gods). For there is a real barrier between species; the individual who has accepted a parent, or mate, or language, or associates from the wrong species is very much deprived. This barrier is most perceptively discussed by Mary Midgley.[29] None the less, she raises objections to seeing the barrier as absolute, objections which would apply to Stoic theory too.

Objections to *oikeiôsis* theory

First, she points out, relations are formed naturally between species. The horse feels happier with a goat or cat in its field or stable. I myself have seen a dog that mothered every injured bird that cheeped. Moreover, humans have always lived with pets. It is by a just retribution that the satirist Lucian chooses a Stoic philosopher as the one who is forced by his sweetheart to cuddle her sick little lap dog who pees on him.[30] There may be a double joke here, since the Stoics not only defended killing animals, but also approved a (rather different) kind of falling in love.[31]

The idea that humans cannot naturally treat other species as

[26] The pioneering scientist is Konrad Lorenz. See first his book *King Solomon's Ring*, London 1952. For a survey of the many variations on his theme, see e.g. P. Colgan, *Comparative Social Recognition*, New York 1983.

[27] Arius Didymus on Aristotelian Ethics ap. Stobaeum, vol. 2, p. 121, line 5, Wachsmuth, translated by Herwig Görgemanns, 'Oikeiôsis in Arius Didymus', in W. Fortenbaugh, ed., *Rutgers University Studies in Classical Humanities* 1, New Brunswick 1983, 165-89, at 169-70. Seneca *Ep.* 95.51.

[28] Aristotle *NE* 8.1, 1155a21-2.

[29] Mary Midgley, *Animals and Why They Matter*, Harmondsworth 1983, and University of Georgia, chs. 9, 10: 'The significance of species', 'The mixed community'.

[30] Lucian *On Salaried Posts in Great Houses*, 34.

[31] The kind of educational homosexual relation described in Plato's *Phaedrus* is approved: Diogenes Laertius *Lives* 7.129-30 (*SVF* 3.716); Stobaeus *Ecl.* vol. 2, p. 65,15-66,13, Wachsmuth = *SVF* 3.717 (this passage adds that there is even an erotic virtue); *Ecl.* 2, 144,9-10, Wachsmuth; and Stobaeus *Florileg.* vol. 4, ch. 20, part 1, 31, p. 444, Hense (*SVF* 3.720); Cicero *Fin.* 3.68; *Tusc.* 4.72.

belonging is refuted from another direction by Cicero's account of the public's disgust at Pompey's staged slaughter of elephants in 55 BC. Moved by their piteous trumpetings, the spectators felt there was a certain community (*societas*) – the Stoic word – between elephants and man.[32]

Secondly, when we turn to the moral inferences drawn by the Stoics, we should take note of what Midgley says about later versions of the Stoics' concentric circles – for their idea of concentric circles survived long after them. The idea stacks the case against animals, who are relegated beyond the outermost ring. This ignores the fact that the injured bird you have found, or have yourself run over, is a subject of special need, or special responsibility. In particular circumstances, we may be bound to particular animals, and the considerations which bind us are many, not just the one consideration of the position of animals in a series of concentric circles. Besides special need and special responsibility, she mentions gratitude, admiration, fellowship and trust.[33]

In any case, justice ought not to depend, even if benevolence might, on a sense of belonging. Justice is supposed to be impartial, and whether or not I feel that someone belongs with me is not supposed to affect my treating that person justly.

The Stoic treatment of animals raises a special difficulty regarding their treatment of children. For they say that children are not rational until the age of 7 or 14.[34] How then can we extend *oikeiôsis* towards them? But here they might have an answer. The simplest reply would be that children are said to be *by nature born* for virtue, which is one kind of rationality, even though it takes them time to acquire it,[35] so that *oikeiôsis* can be extended to embrace them too. This modification of the basic theory fits also with the text which tells us that children share *by nature* in citizenship of the ordinary city, as humans share with gods in the universal city of reason.[36]

Two further objections were raised against the Stoics by the sceptical Platonist Carneades in 155 BC in a show performance in Rome with the representatives of rival schools.[37] For one thing, he

---

[32] Cicero *ad familiares* 7.1.3.

[33] For this particular point, see ch. 2, pp. 29-31; ch. 9, pp. 109-10.

[34] Aëtius 4.11.4 (*Dox. Gr.* 400; *SVF* 2.83; 1.149); Aëtius 5.23.1 (*Dox. Gr.* 434-5; *SVF* 2.764); Iamblichus *DA* ap. Stobaeum 1.317,21 (*SVF* 2.835; 1.149); Schol. ad Platonem *Alcib.* 1, 121E (*SVF* 1.149); cf. Diogenes Laertius *Lives* 7.55 (*SVF* 3, Diogenes of Babylon, fr. 17).

[35] *Anecdota Graeca* ed. Cramer, vol. 1, p. 171 (*SVF* 3.214); Lactantius *Div. Inst.* 6.9 (*SVF* 3.216); Simplicius *in Cat.* 242,12-15 (*SVF* 3.217); Seneca *Ep.* 49.11 (*SVF* 3.219); Cicero *Leg.* 1.9.27 (*SVF* 3.220); Clement of Alexandria *Stromateis* 1.6.34 (*SVF* 3.225).

[36] Dio Chrysostom *Or.* 36.23 (*SVF* 3.334).

[37] Cicero *Rep.* 3.5.8 announces that the arguments repeated by Philus come from Carneades. Philus had heard Carneades' speech (Cicero *de Oratore* 2.155), and Carneades is known to have attacked the Stoic derivation of justice from *oikeiôsis* (Cicero

argued that the Stoic definition of justice as giving each what is appropriate to him (*dignum*) raises the question whether we should not follow Pythagoras and Empedocles, rather than the Stoics, and avoid harming animals. The text breaks off short at this point, but Carneades may have exploited the idea that some things are appropriate to animals.[38] His second move was to present a life raft dilemma. If there are two people to be saved and a life raft that takes only one, those people cannot be both just and wise. If one person justly gives way, he will be a fool, while if he wisely pushes the other off, he will be unjust.[39] Carneades may have been attacking *oikeiôsis* theory by saying that justice, so far from being derived from, is incompatible with the sense of belonging that one extends to one's own person. The life-raft example is applied to the Stoic theory of *oikeiôsis* in another Platonist text. There are degrees of *oikeiôsis*, and the sense of belonging one feels for oneself is bound, in the life-raft situation, to be stronger than that which one feels for another. For that reason justice will need to be described not in terms of weak human nature, but in terms of God's nature, by reference to Plato's expression, an assimilation of oneself to God (*homoiôsis theôi*).[40] In another dilemma, animals are directly involved: one might have to choose between jettisoning an expensive horse in a storm, or a cheap slave.[41] It is not clear whether our belonging with the slave was an explicit factor in the original argument.

Oikeiôsis and Kantian duties

Can the Stoic theory of *oikeiôsis* be assimilated to Kant's theory of duties, or to other theories in the Kantian tradition? According to Kant, all rational beings must be treated as ends in themselves, whereas non-rational beings (so he claims) have only relative value as means. Ideally there will be a kingdom of ends, or a systematic union of

---

ad Atticum 7.2.4).

[38] Cicero *Rep.* 3.11.18-19 (following Carneades 3.8). J.L. Ferrary speculates that in the lacuna Carneades may have posed the dilemma that we would be reduced to the life of animals, if we did not kill them (an argument ascribed instead to Stoics and Peripatetics at Plutarch *Sollertia* 963F, repeated Porphyry *Abst.* 1.4), and may have continued with the Sorites objection (documented in Chapter Eight above) that we would have to spare vegetables next: 'Le discours de Philus (Cicéron *De Re Publica* 3.8-31) et la philosophie de Carnéade', *Revue des Études Latines* 55, 1977, 128-56, at 138-42.

[39] Cicero *Republic* 3.20.30 is fragmentary, but can be filled in from Lactantius *Div. Inst.* 5.16.9-10. Cf. Cicero *Off.* 3.90. Lipsius and Grotius in the sixteenth and seventeenth centuries, so I am told by Richard Tuck, interpreted Carneades' example the other way round as showing the justice of self-defence, and as providing a basis for a theory of just war. (Paper read to the Conference on Morality in War from Cicero to Saddam, held in London, March 1992.)

[40] Anonymous commentary on Plato's *Theaetetus*, 5.18-6.31, translated in A.A. Long and D.N. Sedley, *The Hellenistic Philosophers* 57H.

[41] Cicero *Off.* 3.89-90.

rational beings treating each other as ends. It is through being moral that a rational being is an end in himself and can be a member in a possible kingdom of ends.[42] Duties are owed directly only to rational beings. In a discussion which seems to echo Plutarch, Kant takes up Plutarch's question whether you should do away with your dog, when it is too old to serve you. According to Kant, what forbids you to shoot. the dog is not any direct duty to it. The prohibition comes only from a duty to your fellow human beings not to indulge in practices which may make you inhumane to them.[43] Plutarch's discussion is quite different. He refers to Kant's indirect duty in an 'if for no other reason' clause. We should keep the dog, if for no other reason, for the sake of practice in humanity (*philanthrôpon*) to our fellow-humans.[44] But it is clear that Plutarch is driven by other reasons for nurturing the old dog, and he is filled with indignation at his subject, Cato the elder, for treating his old horse otherwise.[45]

In the same vein as Kant, but talking of rights rather than duties, contemporary authors have said that the right to life belongs only to moral agents, or to those who can possess the concept of a self, or to those who can reason, or to members of a natural kind whose mature members are normally rational.[46] Similarly, it has been said that we owe strict justice only to those who have a sense of justice.[47]

It may seem on the surface that the Stoics' view is very like this in one respect. For they restrict the obligations of the just man to his dealings with other rational beings, beings who belong together in a union, and they exclude non-rational beings from the benefits of justice. But let me draw attention to just one of the differences that separate off the Kantian tradition. The Stoics are in the present context more interested in rationality than in moral agency. Only once do we find them arguing that because animals are not moral agents, or rather because they do not exercise justice (*dikaiopragein*) towards us, they are not owed justice.[48] It is in the other direction that the debate with the Stoics usually proceeds. If animals possess the moral virtues,

---

[42] Immanuel Kant, *Grundlegung* 2nd edition, pp. 64-5; 74-5; 77-9, translated by H.J. Paton, as *Groundwork of the Metaphysic of Morals*.

[43] Immanuel Kant, 'Duties to animals and spirits', in *Lectures on Ethics*, translated by Louis Infield, New York 1963, 239-41.

[44] Plutarch *Lives, Marcus Cato* 4.5, esp. § 5.

[45] Cato in *On Agriculture* 2.7 recommends selling sick or old slaves, an idea which Plutarch here deplores.

[46] See respectively A.I. Melden, *Rights and Persons*, Oxford 1977, 204; Michael Tooley, 'A defense of abortion and infanticide', in Joel Feinberg, ed., *The Problem of Abortion*, Belmont California 1973; Mary Anne Warren, 'On the moral and legal status of abortion' in Tom L. Beauchamp and LeRoy Walters, eds., *Contemporary Issues in Bioethics*, Encino and Belmont California 1978; Alan Donagan, *The Theory of Morality*, Chicago 1977.

[47] John Rawls, *A Theory of Justice*, Cambridge Mass. 1971, 512.

[48] Plutarch *Sollertia* 964B-C.

it is said, this shows that they are rational,[49] and it is the latter point, their rationality, not the former, their morality, which is taken to answer the Stoic denial that they are owed justice.[50]

Much the same is true of the Epicureans who will be considered in Chapter Twelve. Admittedly, those to whom justice is owed will, for the Epicureans, be moral agents. But the important point for the Epicureans is not their moral agency, but their ability to make contracts, for justice, on the Epicurean view, is a matter of contract. That contract-making presupposes moral agency is not something they advert to, and the moral agency does not supply the reason for our owing justice.

Oikeiôsis in rival schools

The Stoic idea of belonging entered in little-noticed ways into the theories of rival schools and underwent some twists and turns. Epicurus' immediate successor Hermarchus conceded to Stoic views that the prohibition of homicide was perhaps partly based on *oikeiôsis* and not wholly on utility.[51] And the later Epicurean Diogenes of Oenoanda looked forward to a situation like that which Zeno the Stoic associated only with wise men, in which earth will be a single native land for all and there will come to be no need for laws or walls.[52] The Neoplatonist Iamblichus gave the topic a new twist in the fourth century AD. There is indeed an *oikeiôsis* which binds divine powers to the animals which they create. But this, so far from recommending that we spare animals, makes them ideal subjects for sacrifice.[53]

But the most important case of Stoic influence is found in Augustine. He is usually associated with a gloomy view of man as permeated with original sin.[54] But in the *City of God*, drawing on Cicero, he makes use of Antiochus' adaptation of Stoic theory, to present a more cheerful account.[55] The *oikeiôsis* which Antiochus describes as uniting all mankind in friendship and justice, and as spreading even to the gods whom the Christians call angels, actually does bind together the members of the Christian church. The contrast with Augustine's later stress on man's total sinfulness will only be somewhat reduced, if the

[49] Philo *de Animalibus* 47-65; Sextus *PH* 1.67-8; Plutarch *Sollertia* 966B; Porphyry *Abstinence* 3,11-13.

[50] e.g. Plutarch *Sollertia* 963F-964B; Porphyry *Abstinence* 3.1; 3.19.

[51] Porphyry *Abstinence* 1.7. See Paul Vander Waerdt, 'Hermarchus and the Epicurean Genealogy of Morals', *Transactions of the American Philological Association* 118, 1988, 87-106. For a further possible influence on Epicureanism, see pp. 163-4 on Lucretius.

[52] Diogenes of Oenoanda new fragments (M.F. Smith) 21.1.4-14 (translated by A.A. Long and D.N. Sedley, *The Hellenistic Philosophers* 22S) and 25.2.3-11.

[53] Iamblichus *On the Mysteries of Egypt* 5.9; Julian *Against the Galileans* 418-20.

[54] H.A. Deane, *The Political and Social Ideas of St Augustine*, New York 1963.

[55] Augustine *City of God* Book 19, chs. 3, 4, 14, 17.

reference is confined to the *invisible* church consisting of the saints.[56] Augustine follows the Stoics again when he insists that animals are not included in the association of rational beings, and so we are free to kill them,[57] an idea to which I shall return in Chapter Fourteen.

Antecedents

The Stoic theory of *oikeiôsis* did not arise out of the blue. The question whether we belong together with the animals was put, though in somewhat different terms, at least as early as Pythagoras and Empedocles. Instead of talking of belonging (*oikeiotês*), the sources talk of kinship and of things in common (*koinônia, sungenês, homogenês, homophulos, homophuês*). At least three reasons are given for saying that we are akin to the animals. We are made of the same elements,[58] one breath permeates us all,[59] and we are quite literally akin, because the dog you are beating may be a friend, or presumably a relative, reincarnated. The last example is attested by an early source for Pythagoras,[60] but the reincarnation argument becomes much more prominent in Empedocles.[61] The opposite claim about Pythagoreans, that they stayed off fish because fish are *not* akin (*mê sumphulon*), is rejected by Plutarch in favour of the standard view that Pythagoras saw fish as belonging with us (*oikeia*).[62]

The modern analogue for the claim of literal kinship, which is implied by reincarnation, is to be found in Darwin, who defends his thesis of the Descent of Man from the apes, to the consternation of his Victorian contemporaries, by insisting that animals differ from man only in degree. No characteristic, he maintains, although not quite consistently, is unique to man, not emotion, curiosity, imitation, attention, memory, imagination, reason, progressive improvement, tool use, abstraction, self-consciousness, language, sense of beauty, belief in the supernatural, nor moral sense.[63]

I shall return to the subject of reincarnation in a later chapter. For now it should be noticed that both Plato and Aristotle paved the way for *oikeiôsis* theory, Plato by making the important point that we may treasure others because they belong with us or are akin (*oikeioi*), and

---

[56] So Deane, op. cit.

[57] Augustine *City of God* 1.20; *de Moribus (On the Catholic and Manichean Ways of Life)* 2.17.

[58] Iamblichus *Life of Pythagoras* ch. 24,108 and 30,169.

[59] Sextus *M* 9.127-9.

[60] Xenophanes ap. Diogenem Laertium *Lives* 8.36.

[61] Empedocles fr. 117; Plutarch *Esu* 997E; Sextus *M* 9.129.

[62] Plutarch *Quaest. Conv.* 729D-E.

[63] Charles Darwin *The Descent of Man* 1871, chs. 3-4. But ch. 11 treats language and the use of fire as unique. I am grateful to Jose Bernadete and Dale Jamieson for drawing my attention to the relevant chapters.

that this is different from treasuring them because they are *like* us. The value may lie in the unlikeness. He leaves it undecided which is the basis of friendship.[64] Pythagoras and Empedocles had appealed more to our kinship than to our likeness to animals, and where likeness is cited by them and later by Theophrastus it is typically only as evidence for kinship or belonging.

Aristotle's contribution was to maintain that friendship towards others is modelled on one's relation to oneself.[65] He provided an expanding sequence of examples of friendship. It holds naturally between parent and child, then among members of the same race, while the relations of friendship and belonging (*oikeioi*) among fellow-human beings are illustrated in travelling (or perhaps in losing one's way: *planai*).[66]

But it is Aristotle's successor Theophrastus in whom the most important antecedents are found. He contradicted Aristotle's claim that there can be no friendship, and by implication no relation of justice, towards horse or ox, because there is nothing in common (*koinon*).[67] On the contrary, a relation of belonging (*oikeiotês*) unites us with animals, because they have emotions and even (*pace* Aristotle) reasoning (*logismos*), and are closest of all to us in their sense perception. Moreover, they are (as Pythagoras and Empedocles said) made of the same elements, but here we should be more precise than they were and specify the humours, flesh and seed, because more fundamental elements, such as earth, air, fire and water, would be shared also by plants. The other grounds for kinship given by Pythagoras and Empedocles are dropped, notably the belief in reincarnation.[68]

The Stoic theory is a brilliant innovation quite distinct from that of Theophrastus. But in several ways the Stoics may have responded to him, first by rejecting his extension of *oikeiotês* and justice to animals. The Stoic Chrysippus may even have taken from Theophrastus, if he did not take from Aristotle, the expression, 'no justice in relation to animals'.[69] Theophrastus' further idea[70] that

---

[64] Plato *Lysis* 221E-222D.

[65] Aristotle *EN* 9.4 and 9.8.

[66] Ibid. 8.1, 1155a16-22. For *oikeios*, cf. 1161b22; 1167b34-1168a2.

[67] Ibid. 8.11, 1161a32-b3. It is hardly a concession when Aristotle acknowledges, as Lin Foxhall has pointed out to me, that for a poor the ox replaces the household servant (*oiketês*), despite the etymological link between *oiketês* and *oikeiotês*. *Pol.* 1.2, 1252b12.

[68] Theophrastus *On Piety*, cited by Porphyry *Abstinence* 2.22; 3.25. Part of the latter is translated in Chapter Thirteen.

[69] Chrysippus ap. Plutarchum *de Esu* 2.7, 999B (=*SVF* 3.374); Theophrastus ap. Porphyrium *Abstinence* 2.22.3. Without Bernays' needless emendation, the text means: the case of dangerous animals *seems* (*eoiken*) to show that we stand in no relation of justice to animals. But in fact other animals (*ta de*; cf. Theophrastus *Metaphysics* 11a24) are not dangerous, any more than all humans are criminals.

[70] Porphyry *Abstinence* 3.25, translated below, ch. 13.

oikeiotês extends far beyond common ancestry in ever widening circles to all humans may have influenced some of the later Stoics.

In the first century BC, Arius Didymus, epitomator and philosopher – friend of the Emperor Augustus, was able to amalgamate the Stoic and Aristotelian traditions. He takes the fact that children are loved for their own sake as entailing that the same relation of belonging holds towards people in varying degrees more distant, and he cites the Aristotelian example of help given to travellers who have lost their way or are in need of water.[71]

Antecedents for the other aspect of Stoic theory, the belief in a world-wide community, are better studied when we come to the Cynics in Chapter Twelve. But first I should address the idea that the Stoic theory was a theory of human rights. Examining this will reveal a great deal more about the Stoic outlook.

---

[71] Arius Didymus on Aristotelian Ethics ap. Stobaeum, vol. 2, pp. 118-21, Wachsmuth, translated by Herwig Görgemanns, '*Oikeiôsis* in Arius Didymus', in W. Fortenbaugh, ed., *Rutgers University Studies in Classical Humanities* 1, New Brunswick 1983, 165-89, at 169-70.

CHAPTER ELEVEN

Did the Greeks have the idea of human or animal rights?

Aristotle, Stoics and slavery

The Stoic theory has a very striking consequence: justice is owed even to a slave. Aristotle had expressed himself more guardedly:

> There is no such thing as friendship towards him qua slave, but qua human there is. For it is thought that for every human there is some relation of justice towards everyone who can partake in law and agreements – and hence there is friendship too, insofar as he is human.[1]

The Stoics are much more forthcoming.[2] If Zeno, the founder, did without slaves,[3] he may only have been following the personal asceticism of Diogenes the Cynic, of whom the same is reported.[4] But later Stoics class all subordination (*hupotaxis*) and all slave-owning (*despoteia*) as bad.[5] They do not propose to abolish the institution. But Seneca urges good treatment for slaves and claims to practise it,[6] and other Stoics recommend that slaves should study philosophy.[7] Epictetus insists that even a refractory slave is related to us (*sungenês*), and by nature a brother as the offspring of Zeus.[8] More striking still is a passage whose second half can be firmly associated with the Stoic Chrysippus, and whose first half rejects Aristotle's view that there are natural slaves, who play the same role as tame animals. 'No human is a slave by nature', comes the reply, 'irrational animals

---

[1] Aristotle *NE* 8.11, 1161b5-8.
[2] See Andrew Erskine, *The Hellenistic Stoa*, London 1990, 43-63; C.E. Manning, 'Stoicism and slavery in the Roman Empire', *Aufstieg und Niedergang der römischen Welt* 2.36.3, 1518-1543.
[3] Seneca *ad Helv.* 12.4 (*SVF* 1.15).
[4] Seneca *Tranq. An.* 8.7.
[5] Diogenes Laertius *Lives* 7.121-2 (*SVF* 3.355).
[6] Seneca *Ben.* 3.18-28; *Ep. Mor.* 47; *de Beata Vita* 24.
[7] Lactantius *Inst. Div.* 3.25 (*SVF* 3.253).
[8] Epictetus *Discourses* 1.13.4.

take the place of slaves'.[9] All Aristotle concedes is that natural slaves as humans differ from animals by sharing reason:

> The natural slave is one who is capable of belonging to another, which is why he does so belong, and who shares in (*koinônein*) reason (*logos*) to the extent of appreciating it (*aisthanesthai*), but not having it (*ekhein*). The other animals do not obey reason by appreciating it, but obey only their passions. And the use made of them differs little, since bodily help for basic necessities comes equally from slaves and tame animals.[10]

The distinction, which Aristotle repeats elsewhere,[11] is between being able to listen to another's reasoning (*epipeithes, katêkoös, peitharkhikos, peithesthai, akouein, akoustikos*), which slaves can do, and being able to reason things out for oneself, which natural slaves cannot. Sometimes, as here, Aristotle puts this in terms of having a share (*metekhein, koinônein*) in reason,[12] without having it (*ekhein*). But sometimes he says that this ability belongs to the part of the soul that has reason,[13] and that it actually is a case of having reason, in a secondary sense.[14] Consequently, it is wrong to deny reason to slaves, and this has anti-Platonic implications for how we should treat them:

> So it is clear that the master should be the cause of this kind of virtue in a slave, but not as having the master's art of teaching him his tasks. And that is why people are wrong to rob slaves of reason, and to say that one should only give them commands. Slaves should be given admonition (*nouthetêteon*) more than children.[15]

Aristotle, Stoics and the American Indians

These concessions were not sufficient for the Stoics, who have been seen by some people as the inventors of a theory of human rights. Indeed, their theory seems to have been used by those who defended the American Indians, at the time of the Spanish conquest of Latin America. The issue turned mainly on the ideas of Aristotle, who had said that some people were natural slaves, and that those who hunted down either natural slaves or animals were equally engaged in a just war. Of the two most relevant Aristotelian passages one has already been quoted in part:[16]

---

[9] *ekhei taxin*: Philo *de Spec. Leg.* 69 (= *SVF* 3,352). The part on animals is ascribed to Chrysippus by Cicero *Fin.* 3.67.

[10] Aristotle *Pol.* 1.5, 1254b20-4.

[11] Aristotle *EE* 2.1, 1219b27-31; *NE* 1.7, 1098a3-5; 1.13, 1102b30-1103a3.

[12] *EE* 2.1, 1219b27-31; *NE* 1.13, 1102b29-30; *Pol.* 1.5, 1254b21-4.

[13] *NE* 1.7, 1098a3-5.

[14] Ibid. 1.13, 1103a1-3.

[15] Aristotle *Pol.* 1.13, 1260b3-7, in opposition to Plato *Laws* 777E, which insists on commands, not admonition.

[16] Aristotle *Pol.* 1.8, 1256b15-26; 1.5,1254b6-26.

So similarly we must clearly think that after their birth, plants exist for the sake of animals, and the other animals for the benefit of men, the tame ones for service and for food, and the wild ones, if not all at least most, for the sake of food and other needs, so that clothes and tools may be made from them. If then nature makes nothing incomplete or pointless, it must have made all of them for the sake of men. And that is why the art of war will naturally be an art of acquisition in a way, for huntsmanship is part of it. And it is necessary to use this against wild animals and those men whose nature is to be governed, but who are unwilling, inasmuch as this war is by nature just.

In this it is evident that it is natural and advantageous for the body to be governed by the soul, the passionate part by the intellect and part that has reason, whereas equality or the opposite rule is harmful for all. Again, it is the same in humans and in the other animals. For tame animals have a better nature than wild ones, and for all of them, it is better to be governed by humans, since in that way they come by security. Further, male is naturally related to female as better to worse, and as governing to governed, and it must be the same way with all humans too. So then all those who differ from each other as much as soul from body and human from beast (and such is the distance of all those whose function and best activity is to use their bodies) – all those are slaves by nature. For them it is better to be governed in the way described, if that is better for the others we have mentioned. The natural slave is one who is capable of belonging to another, which is why he does so belong, and who shares in (*koinônein*) reason to the extent of appreciating it (*aisthanesthai*), but not having it (*ekhein*). The other animals do not obey reason by appreciating it, but obey only their passions. And the use made of them differs little, since bodily help for basic necessities comes equally from slaves and tame animals.

Cicero had borrowed these ideas in his *Republic*, to put them into the mouth of Laelius and direct them against Carneades. It was just, so Laelius is made to argue, for Rome to subjugate the provinces, because it was in their interest that wrongdoers should be controlled, and that they should be governed (here is the Aristotelian echo) in the way that God governs humans, the soul governs the body and reason governs lust.[17] The discussion was transmitted to later ages by Isidore of Seville,[18] and is repeated in the sixteenth century by Sepúlveda against the American Indians. Supúlveda held that the American Indians were natural slaves, and if they resisted enslavement, it would be a just war that was waged against them.

On the other side of the American Indian debate, in 1539 Francisco

---

[17] This bit of Cicero's lost *Republic* is summarised by Augustine *City* 19.21. It reflects in part Aristotle *Politics* 1.5, 1254b4-10. The use by Sepúlveda was brought to my attention by Anthony Pagden. That the argument is Cicero's own is maintained by Paul Vander Waerdt, *The Theory of Natural Law in Antiquity*, Ithaca NY, forthcoming 1993, ch. III iv.

[18] The route of transmission is supplied by Vander Waerdt loc. cit.

de Vitoria argued that the American Indians corresponded not to Aristotle's description of natural slaves, but to his description of children,[19] and so required only temporary tutelage from the Spanish crown. These claims were reinforced in 1550-51 by Bartoleméde Las Casas in a great debate with Sepúlveda, arranged by Charles V of Spain. The builders of such cities, it was argued *inter alia*, could certainly plan things for themselves, unlike natural slaves.

What is interesting for present purposes is that the defenders of the American Indians sometimes drew on the Stoic ideas recorded by Cicero. Vitoria argued for the American Indians that their capacity for social life proved them citizens of 'the whole world which in a certain way constitutes a single republic'. The idea of the world as a single republic surely expresses the Stoic view, and Las Casas evidently drew on this as well, when he cited Cicero's account of the Stoic world community, in defence of the native Americans:

> All the peoples of the world are men, and there is only one definition of each and every man, and that is that he is rational.[20]

This is not a direct quotation from Cicero's *de Legibus* 1, to which Las Casas refers, but it does correspond roughly to some of the sentiments.[21]

I do not know if the defenders of the American Indians, Vitoria and Las Casas, were expressing the idea of human rights. A case has been made for Vitoria, who has also been seen as a precursor of the idea of animal rights.[22] On the other hand, they were in practice less liberal about African than about American Indian slaves.[23] Las Casas did not deny that there might be individual natural slaves, and argued only that nature would not allow a whole people to be such.[24] None the less, if they did approach any idea of human rights, its formulation will

---

[19] See Lewis Hanke, *Aristotle and the American Indians*, Chicago 1959; J.H. Elliott, *The Old World and The New, 1492-1650*, Cambridge 1970, 45-8; Anthony Pagden, *The Fall of Natural Man: the American Indian and the Origins of Comparative Ethnology*, Cambridge 1982, esp. pp. 104-5 on Vitoria's *de Indis*. For Aristotle's treatment of children, see *Pol.* 1.13.

[20] J.H. Elliott, loc. cit., citing Vitoria *De Potestate Civili*, ed. Teófilo Urdánoz, p. 191, and Las Casas *Apologética Historia* ch. 48, *Obras Escogidas* 3, 165-6.

[21] See Cicero *Leg.* 1.7.22-3; 1.9.29-30; 1.12.33.

[22] According to Daniel Deckers *Gerechtigkeit und Recht*, Fribourg, Vienna 1991 at 168-9, Vitoria went along with John Gerson and Konrad Summenhart, though not thinking it strictly correct, in allowing that animals have some *dominium* (= *ius*) over the things they eat, as well as among themselves where they have leaders, and this frees some of their actions from the charge of injustice. Whether this gives them rights is unclear, although elsewhere in the book Deckers argues for an adumbration of the idea of human rights.

[23] See Pagden op. cit. 32-3.

[24] Ibid., ch. 6.

have owed a little to the Stoics. Whether the Stoics themselves had a theory of human rights, however, is a different question.

Oikeiôsis and human rights

The most recent follower of the human rights interpretation is also the most illustrious: the former British Prime Minister, Mrs Thatcher. In 1989 the French people celebrated the two-hundredth anniversary of their revolution. Mrs Thatcher sought to dampen their ardour by saying on French television that they had no claim on the concept of human rights. For, she maintained, that had been invented by the ancient Greeks. A subsequent article in *The Times* of London by Mr Kilroy Silk took it that she had the Stoics in mind. The Stoic theory of the community of rational beings might indeed be described in one of Mrs Thatcher's favourite expressions as a theory of 'one-of-us-ness'. We are to treat another as 'one of us', not in her sense of belonging to the same political persuasion, but as belonging to the community of rational beings. But does the theory imply human rights? Mrs Thatcher's intervention in the study of Ancient Philosophy is to be welcomed, and the question she has raised is difficult. I shall offer six reasons for thinking that the Stoic theory is not one of human rights, and I shall then explore two ways in which these reasons need themselves to be heavily qualified, before asking what the final verdict ought to be.

The case against

First, the theory was not in its original form a theory of humans, because in Zeno's version, only virtuous humans are members of the world-wide community. Other humans are instead enemies.[25] Moreover, others besides humans belong to the rational community, namely the gods, and this continues to be the position.[26] But admittedly later in Cicero and Seneca we find an emphasis on humans belonging together just because they are human,[27] an emphasis which may have derived from Antipater (died *c.* 129 BC), whom Cicero reports in somewhat similar terms.[28] This is one of the two qualifications that I shall explore below.

A second reason for doubting that we have here a theory of human

[25] Zeno ap. Diogenem Laertium *Lives* 7.32-3.

[26] e.g. Cicero *Leg.* 1.7.22; Cicero *ND* 2.154; Cicero *Fin.* 3.64; Seneca *On Leisure* 4.1; Arius Didymus ap. Eusebium *Praep. Ev.* 15.15.3-5 (*SVF* 2.528); Dio Chrysostom *Or.* 36.23 (*SVF* 3.334).

[27] Cicero *Leg.* 1.12.33, *Off.* 3.6.27-8; *Fin.* 3.19.63; Seneca *Ep.* 95,52-4; *de Beata Vita* 24.3. I thank Th. G. Sinnige and Phillip Mitsis for drawing my attention to some of these references.

[28] Cicero *Off.* 3.51-5.

rights emerges when we ask what would be the goal or *telos* of the good Stoic in his dealings with his fellow humans. If you are a just Stoic employer, you will probably give your workers a decent living wage. But as regards your goal or *telos* in doing so, the Stoics' goal is defined as follows:

> The [Stoics] say that being happy (*eudaimonein*) is the goal (*telos*), for the sake of which everything is done, while it is not done for the sake of anything else. And this consists in living in accordance with virtue, in living in agreement and again in accordance (which is the same thing) with nature.[29]

Is one of these goals, being happy, living in accordance with virtue, or in accordance with nature, an ultimate goal? Panaetius, the successor of Antipater, goes further than his predecessors in picking out being happy:

> All the virtues make being happy the goal, which consists in living in agreement with nature.[30]

But we are told that the virtues are ends as well as means (*telika agatha* as well as *poiêtika*), for they are parts (*merê*) of happiness, as well as generating it (*apogennân*).[31]

The important point for our purposes is that you can reach the goal, whether or not your actions succeed,[32] in our example whether or not the money reaches your employees, provided it fails to reach them through no fault of your own. The definition of the goal as living in accordance with nature is refined by Antipater and his predecessor Diogenes of Babylon, to bring this point out. Antipater defines it as doing everything in your power to obtain the natural objectives, which would include health and money both for yourself and for your workers. Diogenes of Babylon defines it as being rational in your selection (*eklogê*, a term to be explained below) of such natural objectives.[33] The point of both definitions is that actual success in getting them is not part of the goal. The *telos* is to aim right, whether or not you hit. The comparison with an archer aiming is actually used both for and against

---

[29] Stobaeus 2.77.16-27 W (= *SVF* 3.16).
[30] Panaetius ap. Stobaeum 2.7 (Wachsmuth 2.63-4 = Panaetius fr. 109 van Straaten). Contrast Seneca *BV* 9, who says that virtue has no further goal.
[31] Stobaeus 2.71.15-2.72.6 (= *SVF* 3.106).
[32] Cicero *Fin.* 3.22 (*SVF* 3.504).
[33] Stobaeus 2.76.9-15 (*SVF* 3 Diog. 44; Antip. 57); Clement of Alexandria *Stromateis* 2.21 (*SVF* 3 Diog. 46); Diogenes Laertius *Lives* 7.88 (*SVF* 3. Diog. 45); Cicero *Fin.* 3.22 (*SVF* 3.18); 5.20 (*SVF* 3.44); Plutarch *CN* 1070F-1071E (*SVF* 3.195); 1072E-F (*SVF* 3 Antip. 59).

the Stoics,[34] and it has been conjectured that it was introduced by Antipater. The just Stoic employer aims at doing everything in his power to give the workers the just wage. But, to use an English expression, 'the game's the thing', not whether he scores; not in other words whether the money actually reaches them. Money is described as part of the subject matter (*hulê, materia*) of virtuous action;[35] it is not the goal (*telos*). I doubt if a believer in human rights could take this attitude. If a living wage is a human right, its delivery will be a goal, not merely the subject matter in pursuit of some other goal, one's own virtue. Indeed, treating delivery as a mere subject matter may seem to us a rather repulsive attitude. The Stoics' own rationale, we shall see shortly, has to do with the fact that delivery may not be under one's control. But it may help to make their position more acceptable to us to recall that their philosophy is often at its most helpful for those who are in a difficult corner. If, for example, delivery of the just award were at great personal cost, we could understand people bringing themselves to deliver it by reminding themselves that it matters that they should be just.

The attitude of the employer will become clearer, if we turn, thirdly, to the perspective of the workers and ask whether they have a right to the basic necessities for subsistence. No, at least not on the face of it. For life, health, pleasure, beauty, strength, well-functioning sense organs, wealth, reputation and their opposites, death, disease, pain, ugliness, frailty, disablement, poverty, low repute and ignoble birth are said to be matters of indifference (*adiaphora*) – the Stoics' own word.[36] The only thing that really matters is whether people are virtuous, and the wise Stoic will be virtuous while starving.

Admittedly, life, health and the rest are natural objectives ('in accordance with nature').[37] Admittedly, we prefer them (they are *proêgmena*).[38] They excite our impulses and are not indifferent in relation to that.[39] Admittedly, we select them (*eklegsthai, seligere*), and they are normally to be taken (*lêpta*), although it would do them too

---

[34] Plutarch *CN* 1071C; Cicero *Fin.* 3.22 (*SVF* 3.18). The superb article by A.A. Long, 'Carneades and the Stoic telos', *Phronesis* 12, 1967, 59-90, reports also the earlier contributions to the subject. For later literature, see the bibliography in A.A. Long and D.N. Sedley, *The Hellenistic Philosophers* vol. 2, Cambridge 1987, and Gisela Striker, 'Following nature: a study in Stoic ethics', *Oxford Studies in Ancient Philosophy* 9, 1991, 1-73.

[35] Plutarch *CN* 1069E (*SVF* 3.491); 1071B; Cicero *Fin.* 3.60 (*SVF* 3.763).

[36] Diogenes Laertius *Lives* 7.101-5; Sextus *M* 11.61-3; Stobaeus 2.79-80 W.

[37] Stobaeus 2.79-80; 2.82.11 ff W; Plutarch *CN* 1071A (*SVF* 3.195); Cicero *Fin.* 3.22; Epictetus 2.6.9 (*SVF* 3.191).

[38] Cicero *Fin.* 3.51-2; Stobaeus 2.84.21 ff W (*SVF* 1.192; 3.128); Diogenes Laertius *Lives* 7.105-6 (*SVF* 3.126; 3.127); Alexander *Mantissa* 163.4 ff (*SVF* 3.192); Sextus *M* 11.62.

[39] Stobaeus 2.79; 2.80; 2.83.2 ff W.

much honour to say that they are to be chosen (*haireta, expetenda*).[40] Admittedly, they are regarded by most Stoics as having some value, or more exactly *selective* value (*axia eklektikê*),[41] although Aristo denies them any value at all[42] and in Epictetus it is their indifference that is stressed rather than their value.[43] None the less, I think we have to take seriously the Stoics' refusal to say that the natural objectives are actually good (*agatha*), or a benefit (*ôpheleia*), or their opposites bad.[44] The only beneficial thing for the workers would be to use their wages or their starvation in the right way.[45] The wages are not themselves good, nor starvation bad.

This doctrine of indifference throws further light on the employer's perspective. His hitting the target and getting the money to the workers is not good, nor his missing it bad. And this has to be, if the wise employer and the wise worker alike must, for the Stoics, be free of passions. There must be neither grief nor exultation. What is admitted, we have seen, is that receiving the money, or hitting the target is 'preferred'. Seneca describes how he prefers having a lot of money, but he insists that it would not matter to him if he lost it.[46] It is also admitted that there are involuntary reactions to suffering apparent injustice, to imminent death, or to pain: reactions such as reddening, pallor, or crying out. But these are not themselves proofs of passion, so long as reason does not assent that real evil has been suffered.[47] If once the indifferents were admitted to be genuinely good or bad, employer and worker alike would be subject to hope, despair, exultation, grief and fear, according as they seemed to be securing their natural objectives or not.

If the Stoic insistence on freedom from all passion sounds strange, it becomes intelligible when it is remembered that, in the absence of tranquillisers, every self-respecting school in the period after Aristotle had to offer a recipe for personal tranquillity, even if tranquillity was differently conceived in different schools, and had different names. Seneca says that his Latin *tranquillitas* corresponds to the Greek *euthumia* (good cheer),[48] as opposed to *ataraxia* (freedom from

---

[40] Stobaeus 2.79.15-16; 2.75; 2.82-3; 2.85, 1-4 W; Cicero *Fin.* 3.31 (*SVF* 3.190); 3.22; Epictetus 2.6.9 (*SVF* 3.191); Plutarch *CN* 1071A (*SVF* 3.195); 1071E; Alexander *Mantissa* 164.7 (*SVF* 3.193); 163.32 and 164.32 (*SVF* 3.194).

[41] Stobaeus 2.83-4 (*SVF* 3.124); 2.79; 2.80 (*SVF* 3.136); Sextus *M* 11.62ff (*SVF* 3.122); Alexander *Mant.* 163-4 ff (*SVF* 3.192); Plutarch *CN* 1071B; Seneca *BV* 22.4.

[42] Sextus *M* 11.64-7 (*SVF* 1.361); Diogenes Laertius *Lives* 7.160 (*SVF* 1.351).

[43] Epictetus *Discourses* 3.3; 3.26.

[44] Diogenes Laertius *Lives* 7.103; Sextus *M* 11.22 (*SVF* 3.75) Cicero *Fin.* 3.50; 3.53.

[45] Cicero *Fin.* 3.3 (*SVF* 3.15); Diogenes Laertius *Lives* 7.104; Seneca *Ep.* 92.11-13; and descriptions of the end cited above from Diogenes of Babylon and Antipater.

[46] Seneca *BV* 22.

[47] Cicero *Tusc.* 2.61; 3.83; Seneca *On Anger* 2.2-4; Aulus Gellius 19.1, partly reporting Epictetus, and partly reported by Augustine *City* 9.4.

[48] Seneca *Tranq.* 2.3. See Christopher Gill, 'Peace of mind and being yourself:

disturbance), and says that the happy life is perpetual *tranquillitas*.[49] Some of the recipes for achieving tranquillity were rather drastic. The Stoics said you should give up the idea that anything mattered that was not in your control.[50] The one thing that was in your control was your character – whether you were virtuous, as they put it – and this meant that your happiness was in your control,[51] even if the misfortunes of Priam should befall you.[52] The Stoics then cannot afford to admit that money is actually important, or the tranquillity of the wise Stoic cannot be guaranteed.

For our purposes the upshot is that a living wage does not appear to be being treated as a human right, because someone who regarded it that way could hardly treat it as a matter of indifference. I shall later have to qualify the claim that the Stoics regarded such things as wholly indifferent. That will be the second of two kinds of qualification to be explored below. But for the moment I wish to pass to a fourth reason for doubting that the Stoics are offering a theory of human rights.

If justice requires you to pay a living wage, nothing follows, for the Stoics, about a right to it. Modern definitions of justice are often couched in terms of rights. The same may appear to be true of the Stoics because of the misleading habit of English translators of rendering the Stoic definition of justice as a disposition to distribute things to people according to their *due*.[53] The English notion of *due* does suggest entitlement and so perhaps right. But the Stoic phrase is once again according to *axia*, or in Latin *dignum*.[54] This time, I think the meaning is according to what is appropriate. Another meaning that has been canvassed is according to desert.[55] Neither appropriateness nor desert implies the idea of rights, or entitlement. Desert is connected with merit, and if justice considers only the workers'

Panaetius to Plutarch', forthcoming in *ANRW* 2.36.

[49] Seneca *Ep.* 92.3.

[50] Epictetus *Discourses* 3.3; 3.8.

[51] Cicero *Tusc.* 5.40-1; 5.81-2.

[52] Stephanus *in Rhet.*, *CAG* 21.2, 325,15.

[53] Bury translating Sextus *PH* 1.67; Keyes translating Cicero *Republic* 3.18. The same translation is offered in some of the writings from which I have learnt most: Gisela Striker, 'Following nature ...', loc. cit., p. 42. Similarly Paul Vander Waerdt, 'Philosophical influence on Roman jurisprudence? The case of Stoicism and Natural Law', *Aufstieg und Niedergang* 2.36.6, 1992 understands *dignitas* in the definition of justice as one's *right* (part V, text relating to n. 157).

[54] Stobaeus 2.59.4 (*SVF* 3.262); 2.84.4 (*SVF* 3, Diogenes of Babylon 47); Philo *Leg. Alleg.* 1.87 (*SVF* 3.263); Plutarch *Sto. Rep.* 1034D (*SVF* 1.563); Galen *PHP* 7.2 (*SVF* 1.374, Aristo); Andronicus *Peri Pathôn*, p. 19, Schuchardt, p. 241, Glibert-Thirry (*SVF* 3.266); Cicero *Rep.* 3.18-19; *Off.* 1.42; *de Inventione* 2.160. Cf. without reference to the Stoics, Sextus *PH* 1.67; ps-Plato *Definitions* 411E.

[55] Long and Sedley, translation of 61H = Stobaeus *Ecl.* 2.59.4 (*SVF* 3.262). The same is implied by Andrew Erskine, *The Hellenistic Stoa*, London 1990, 114-20, who translates *axia* as *worth*.

deserts, it may find that some are undeserving, while others may deserve punishment, and yet others may deserve supererogatory bonuses which, being supererogatory, still do not yield an actual entitlement to pay.

One Stoic, Diogenes of Babylon (died *c.* 152 BC) actually offers a definition of what is meant by *axia* in the Stoic definition of justice. It means *to epiballon*, what is appropriate.[56] *To epiballon* may have two meanings in Stoic texts, duty[57] and the appropriate,[58] although all of the cases could be brought under the second meaning. It is in any case the second meaning that is relevant here, since justice is not a matter of distributing duties.

I see no justification for the translation of the Stoic definition of justice as distributing what is due. Appropriateness is a much broader notion, since entitlement is only one possible way in which a distribution may become appropriate. There is no suggestion that entitlement is the source of the appropriateness, and in fact, it is unlikely in many cases to be so. For in the case of punishment, the Stoics were concerned above all with reform.[59] The just punishment would therefore distribute what was appropriate for purposes of reform (reward, if necessary), rather than what was due. Concern with what is due belongs rather to a retributive theory of punishment. Other grounds which Cicero mentions as a basis of distribution, although admittedly not in connexion with the definition of justice, are need and closeness of relationship.[60]

A fifth consideration reduces the motives for the Stoics to invent for the first time a theory of human rights. They believe in a divine providence, which extends even,[61] selectively, to individual humans. In connexion, therefore, with those of our needs which are fully met, they have no incentive to invent a theory of human rights. Admittedly, there can be other motives, apart from needs, for developing such a theory, and some of the motives that have been attributed to Grotius in the seventeenth century are decidedly curious.[62] Admittedly, too, the Stoics

[56] Stobaeus *Eclogae* 2.84.4 (*SVF* 3, Diogenes 47).

[57] Plutarch *Sto. Rep.* 1036A (*SVF* 2.137). Chrysippus said it is a duty (appropriate?) for sceptics to argue on both sides of a case, but for teachers not to. Ibid. 1034D (*SVF* 1.563); Cleanthes analysed virtues as a tension in the soul adequate for performing duties (Long and Sedley 61C prefer the other meaning: what is fitting).

[58] Plutarch *Sto. Rep.* 1047A (*SVF* 2.297): appropriate modulations of the voice. Stobaeus *Ecl.* 2.7.11, 99.3 Wachsmuth (*SVF* 1.216): Zeno said the good man has the appropriate height and strength. Stobaeus *Florilegium* LXVII, *Peri Gamou* 25, Wachsmuth and Hense, vol. 4, pp. 507-12 (*SVF* 3, p. 255, 1. 6): Antipater speaks of marriage as appropriate to nature.

[59] See Seneca *de Ira* 1.6; 1.15.1-2; 1.16.1-4; 1.19.7; 2.31.8, for reform and deterrence. I thank Myles Burnyeat for reminding me of this, although his own conclusion was a different one.

[60] Cicero *Off.* 1.49; 1.50; 1.59.

[61] Cicero *ND* 2.164-7.

[62] Grotius, according to Richard Tuck (lectures in London 1990, 1991), was partly motivated by a concern to protect the rapacious conduct of members of the Dutch East

recognised that there was evil in the world, so needs were not utterly eliminated by providence, even if the only true evil and the only true need would have to be a lack of virtue.

There is a sixth reason for doubting that we are being given a theory of human rights. The Stoics compare the individual to a finger or leg, or stone in an arch, which cannot successfully flourish at the expense of the whole.[63] The intention is to show that it is more in accordance with nature to put the common advantage before one's own (*communem utilitatem nostrae anteponere*).[64] Antisocial conduct prevents us being held together (*contineri*) and pulls society apart (*distrahere*).[65] This stress on the whole is found in some of the passages which have been thought most clearly to express the idea of the rights of others. But it has an unexpected consequence. If it is natural that I should put the interest of the whole before my own, it is equally natural that the interest of the whole should come before the interests of other individuals. And this does not accord well with the idea of human rights, for human rights accrue to individuals or sub-groups.[66] The preference for whole over part recurs also in the discussion of providence and evil. The grace (*kharis*) of the whole comedy, says Chrysippus, may require that there be a few vulgar (*phaula*) lines.[67]

Qualifications: humanity and indifference

It is time to qualify the contrast with human rights theories. The first of two areas in which qualification is required has been outlined already. In Cicero and Seneca, perhaps following the lead of Antipater, there is a new stress on being human and on considering others just because they are human.

Cicero says:

> If nature prescribes that a human should want to consider another human (*homo homini consultum velit*), whoever he is, just because he is a human ...

He goes on to insist that it destroys the divinely established community (*societas*) of the human race, if you deny that account is to be taken (*rationem habendam*) of foreigners.[68] Elsewhere he maintains:

India Company from the control of the Dutch government, when he developed the idea of the right to self-defence.

[63] Cicero *Fin.* 3.63-4; *Off.* 3.22; Seneca *Ep.* 95.52; Hierocles ap. Stobaeum 3.732,1-13.
[64] Cicero *Fin.*, 3.64; *Off.* 3.22-33.
[65] Cicero *Off.* 3.27-8.
[66] I am grateful to Tad Brennan for this observation.
[67] Plutarch *CN* 1065D-E (cf. *Sto. Rep.* 1050F); Marcus Aurelius 6.42 (all in *SVF* 2.1181). Cf. Augustine *City* 11.23 (and 17); a beautiful picture requires shadows; Plutarch *On Tranquillity* 474A: a melody needs worse notes as well as better.
[68] Cicero *Off.* 3.6.27-8.

This gives birth to the result that there is also a natural and communal concern (*commendatio*) of humans for each other, such that a human ought not to be seen as alien from another human (*oporteat hominem ab homine non alienum videri*), and that because of the very fact that he is human.[69]

There is an echo here of the comic playwright Terence (died 159 BC), who is explicitly quoted both by Cicero in his *de Legibus*[70] and in the next passage, which comes from Seneca. Seneca is talking of human duties (*officium, praeceptum*) to humans. He cites rescuing the shipwrecked, guiding the lost traveller, sharing bread with the starving. All things human and divine are members of one great universal body, he says, and Nature made us all relatives (*cognati*), because she made us all out of the same materials and into the same kinds of being. Nature implanted love, sociability and justice, and so constituted us that it is more wretched (*miserius*) to harm than to be harmed. By her command our hands are prepared for giving help. We should remember Terence's verse:

> I am a human: nothing human do I think alien from me (*homo sum, humani nihil a me alienum puto*).

Our community (*societas*) depends on that, and would collapse like an arch without that mutual support.[71]

Several things are new here. There is a stress not just on the agent, but on the recipient: the recipient's humanity is the reason why he or she ought to be considered. And this stress on the recipient gets us a little closer to a human rights theory, because a right imposes a duty on agents not just because of something about the agents (their need to be virtuous or happy) but because of something about the recipients. The new stress also means that the welfare of the recipient looks a little less like the mere subject matter of the agent's exercise in virtue, and a little more like an end in itself.

But we must be cautious. The agent's ultimate end is still that he himself should be living in the right way. Moreover, there is no search for needs under threat and needing protection. Rather, both Cicero and Seneca give stock examples of needs we respond to anyway: shipwreck, lost travellers, starving neighbours and, Cicero says, providing for our children after our death. Cicero chooses as his star example teaching and handing on the principles of prudence, and of this he says that we are impelled (*impellimur*) by nature to do it, and that it is hard to find anyone who would not.[72] The point is that these particular needs are

---

[69] Cicero *Fin.* 3.19.63.
[70] Cicero *Leg.* 1.12.33.
[71] Seneca *Ep.* 95, 52-3, quoting Terence *Heautontimorumenos* 77.
[72] Cicero *Fin.* 3.65-6.

perceived as catered for already through the providence of nature, and so they supply little incentive to invent a theory of human rights.

There are other caveats too. It is in these passages that Cicero and Seneca are particularly insistent that the whole should take precedence over the part, which we have seen does not fit well with the rights of individuals. And further the question remains whether the rescue of the shipwrecked, the lost traveller, or the starving neighbour is still in the end a matter of indifference. I think it will therefore be more profitable to turn from the texts on humanity to the second remaining topic, the thesis of indifference, and consider the extent to which it came to be qualified over the course of time.

Two reports in Diogenes Laertius are unfortunately hard to rely on. They concern two later Stoics, Panaetius (*c.* 185 – *c.* 110 BC) and Posidonius (*c.* 135 – *c.* 50 BC). The claim that Posidonius put wealth and health in the class of things good, not indifferent, is contradicted by Seneca and probably by Cicero. And the statement that both Stoics rejected the claim of virtue to be sufficient for happiness and desiderated health, strength and provisions (*khorêgia*) as necessary, is at any rate unknown to Cicero.[73]

The thesis of indifference may seem to be more clearly compromised by the recognition that the Stoic is sometimes justified in committing suicide. Surprisingly, Cicero tells us[74] that the decision should turn on whether one has, or even foresees having,[75] the preferred indifferents, indeed a preponderance (*plura, in maiore parte*) of them. It should not turn on whether one has the only thing that is good, virtue, or the only thing that is evil, vice.[76] Does this give a new importance to the indifferents? No, on the contrary, it emphasises the importance of the act of selection and the unimportance of the things selected, including life itself. The point has been made by others. Selecting death can itself be a rational and virtuous exercise, while life which is disselected is indifferent.[77]

I think the attitude manifested by some later Stoics is different. Instead of totting up, in a rather calculating way, where the preponderance lies, they came to list certain rather extreme circumstances

---

[73] Diogenes Laertius *Lives* 7.103 (contradicted by Seneca *Ep.* 87,31-2; 35; and possibly by Cicero *Tusc.* 2.61) and 7.128 (ignored in Cicero *Fin.* 3). The passages are discussed in Ian Kidd, 'Stoic intermediates and the end of man', in A.A. Long, ed., *Problems in Stoicism*, London 1971, ch. 7; M. Griffin, *Seneca, A Philosopher in Politics*, Oxford (1976), 1992, p. 296, n. 5. See also her ch. 11 for the next topic: suicide.

[74] Cicero *Fin.* 3.60-1.

[75] Cf. Diogenes Laertius *Lives* 7.28; 7.176; Seneca *Ep.* 58.34; 70.3; 104.21.

[76] Cf. Stobaeus *Ecl.* 2.110,9-15W; Plutarch *Sto. Rep.* 1042D; *CN* 1063D-E; Alexander *DA* 159,16-22; 160,20-31; 168,1ff (=*SVF* 3.758; 759; 767; 766; 764).

[77] John Cooper, 'Greek philosophers on euthanasia and suicide', in Baruch Brody, ed., *Suicide and Euthanasia*, Kluwer 1989, with a gloss by Tad Brennan.

that could justify suicide.[78] Suicide is permitted to save one's country, to avoid a disgraceful deed imposed by a tyrant, or (these are the relevant cases) to avoid senility, incurable disease, or poverty. The inclusion of poverty as a reason is dubious.[79] Diogenes Laertius omits poverty, but adds severe pain and mutilation.[80] We need to ask whether in this list freedom from senility, pain, disease, mutilation and perhaps poverty have gained a new importance and ceased to be matters of indifference. Seneca gives an answer completely different from the other Stoic one. He might by suicide put an end to senility, illness, or pain, not, however, to avoid the pain, but only if the pain were an impediment to all that he lived for,[81] perhaps progressing, or in the case of a sage even aiming aright. This rationale provides a different method of making virtue the important thing and treating pain as indifferent. Admittedly, there could be a human right to something indifferent if it was a necessary means to something important. But Seneca does not make that point. Moreover, most of the items on the list befall people unavoidably, so could not be the subject of a right. Again, to the person who has reached perfection, its cessation in death should be indifferent, since perfection is in no way increased by prolongation.[82]

A new attitude to indifferents might emerge, if we concentrate on the ordinary person, not the wise Stoic. Consolations are addressed by the Stoics to ordinary people, and not all of them agree with Cleanthes' approach of insisting on the indifference of loss. Chrysippus thinks the main thing (*caput*) is rather to attack the belief that it is *right* to grieve,[83] and even then Cicero thinks that that treatment needs postponing.[84] Seneca goes further. In his *Consolation to Marcia*, he puts into practice a good number of the techniques described by Cicero. But the indifference of loss is not merely passed over in silence, as in Chrysippus' technique. It seems by implication almost to be denied. For Seneca emphasises the magnitude of loss, in the case of two parallel examples he chooses, by describing the virtues of other sons who died prematurely.[85] This is, in fact, a far more effective preparation for other techniques, such as that of denying the duty to

---

[78] Olympiodorus, *Commentary on Plato's Phaedo* 1.8, ed. and transl. Westerink; Elias *CAG* 18.1, 14.15-15.22 (= *SVF* 3.768); David *CAG* 18.2, 32.11-33.26 (transl. from Armenian version, Bridget Kendall and Robert W. Thomson, Chico California 1983), ps-Elias *in Isag.* 13,1-17.

[79] For the case against poverty, see Plutarch *Sto. Rep.* 1039E-F; *CN* 1069D-E; Diogenes Laertius (next ref.) and Westerink on Olympiodorus *ad loc.*

[80] Diogenes Laertius *Lives* 7.130 (*SVF* 3.757).

[81] Seneca *Ep.* 58,35-6.

[82] Seneca *Ep.* 32; 93.7; 101.8-9; cf. Cicero *Fin.* 3.61 on the prolongation of wickedness.

[83] Cicero *Tusc.* 3.75-7 summarises the rival techniques. See Stephen A. White, 'Cicero and the therapists', in J.G.F. Powell, ed., *Cicero the Philosopher*, forthcoming.

[84] Cicero *Tusc.* 3.79.

[85] Seneca *Cons. ad Marc.* 2.3; 3.1.

grieve. But it does not seem true to the Stoic idea that such loss is indifferent.

If, however, this is a modification of the Stoic idea that loss is indifferent, it still does not create room for the idea that there is any right to avoid loss. On the contrary, Seneca uses the technique already ascribed by Cicero to the Cyrenaics,[86] though he uses it in a retrospective version: one should have expected loss. It is ubiquitous and almost inevitable.[87]

There is a special group of ordinary people who may be more strongly affected by indifferents than other people, namely those who are progressing (*prokoptôn, proficiens*) towards virtue, without having reached it. Many Stoics refused to treat them as an intermediate category between the virtuous and the vicious. The man just under the surface is drowning no less than the man five hundred fathoms below.[88] But Seneca claims to be progressing, and urges that those who are progressing may be already as good as free, certainly better, and like a racer compared with a cripple.[89] He claims, in defending his own wealth, that such people need some indulgence from fortune (*aliqua fortunae indulgentia*),[90] in contrast to Panaetius, who appears to be more severe on them.[91] He concedes, in another context, that they need food and the liberal arts, although his main point is that these are merely necessary preconditions for reaching virtue, not a positive aid (*adiutorium*) or means (*per*).[92] He insists that someone making progress needs not only the right ethical theory, but also precepts (*praecepta*), or rules of thumb, supplied by a qualified mentor. The path must be shown (*demonstranda*).[93] Again, he claims that the wealthy man can give to those whom he can make into good people.[94] Later Epictetus acknowledges what in Cicero is merely raised as a problem for the Stoics that those who are progressing should be grieved (*algein, agônia*) at their own failings.[95]

This does suggest that those making progress have special needs,

---

[86] Cicero *Tusc.* 3.28-31; 52-9: keep anticipating trouble.

[87] Seneca *Cons. ad Marc.* 9-11. The retrospective version (you should *have* anticipated) may feature at Cicero *Tusc.* 3.76.

[88] Plutarch *CN* 1063A-B (*SVF* 3.539); *On Moral Progress* 75C (*SVF* 3.539); Diogenes Laertius *Lives* 7.127; Alexander *de Fato* 199,14-22 (*SVF* 3.658).

[89] Seneca *BV* 16.3; 17.3; 17.4; 24.4.

[90] Ibid. 16.3.

[91] Seneca *Ep.* 116,5 (= Panaetius, fr. 114): whether or not falling in love is all right for the wise Stoic, it certainly is not for the one who has not reached wisdom.

[92] Seneca *Ep.* 88.31.

[93] Seneca *Epp.* 94-5. I am indebted to discussion with Phillip Mitsis and to his admirable article 'The Stoics on action, rules and moral development', in J. Brunschwig and M. Nussbaum, eds., *Passions and Perceptions*, Cambridge, 1993.

[94] Seneca *BV* 23.5.

[95] Cicero *Tusc.* 3.77-8; Epictetus 3.19.1; 3.23.30 and 37; 4.9.10; 4.10.3, discussed by A. Bonhöffer, *Epictet und die Stoa*, Stuttgart 1890, 302-3.

and that those who can further their progress have a special obligation to do so. For the acquisition of virtue cannot be treated as a matter of indifference. But it still does not open up the idea of the person progressing enjoying a human right to have their needs satisfied. For one thing, such people are too small a group for any right to be viewed as a *human* right. It is only the most worthy (*dignissimi*) whom the wealthy person can hope to make good.[96] And Seneca confines the group who can benefit from precepts to those who have a chance of acquiring wisdom,[97] who have learnt philosophy first,[98] and who are of a certain social class – Seneca envisages them as having slaves,[99] and at least a small (*parvum*) amount of property,[100] while the opponent of precepts is made to give examples applicable only to a certain class of society.[101] The Stoics were deeply concerned with education, of course, as shown by the passage in Cicero which treats it as something providentially catered for.[102] Still later, in the second century AD, the Stoic Musonius Rufus insists that by and large the same education should be extended to women as to men, and certainly in philosophy.[103] This is because they have the same need of and capacity for virtue, and require the same virtues. But the discussion is still not couched in terms of rights.

There is another ingredient missing. Although Seneca stresses the recipient's need for precepts, there is no stress on the teacher's duty.[104] The context is not one of exhorting a reluctant teacher, as it might be in a theory of rights, even though Seneca himself was a most reluctant teacher of the Emperor Nero.

Seneca does not list the giving of precepts at *Ep.* 95.51 among the things we owe to humans as humans, like rescuing the shipwrecked, directing the lost traveller, or sharing a crust with the starving. The giving of precepts is not presented as a duty and while these other things are so presented, they are not treated as a human right. Since the shipwrecked, lost and starving are not being envisaged as progressing towards virtue, there is no qualification to the claim that what happens to them is in the end indifferent.

There is one more context in which the thesis of indifference comes

---

[96] Seneca *BV* 23.5.

[97] Seneca *Ep.* 94.52; 95.1.

[98] Ibid. 95.11-12; 34; 37-40; 44-6; 58-64.

[99] Ibid. 94.54.

[100] Ibid. 94.72.

[101] Ibid. 94.14-16.

[102] Cicero *Off.* 3.65.

[103] Musonius Rufus *That Women Should Do Philosophy* and *Whether Daughters and Sons Should Get Similar Education*, Teubner edition, ed. Hense, 9-19, translation by Cora Lutz, *Yale Classical Studies* 10, 1947. I am grateful to Martha Nussbaum for the reference.

[104] *Demonstranda* at 94.50 probably refers to the need for the path to be shown, rather than to the duty to show it.

under pressure, although it involves special pleading. As already mentioned, Seneca undertakes in the *de Beata Vita* to defend his colossal wealth. He does so not only by drawing attention to his status and that of some of his beneficiaries as progressing towards virtue. He claims that the poor can exercise only the one virtue of fortitude, while the rich can practise moderation, liberality, economy, orderliness and magnificence.[105] It is not clear why the poor cannot be generous with a crust of bread, moderate, orderly or economical. But in any case, Seneca is here contradicting the standard Stoic view that if you have one virtue, you have them all.[106] Seneca claims also to use his wealth in pity (*misereri*) for others, if they do not deserve to be dragged down (*deducere*) by poverty.[107] This does not in the usual Stoic manner treat poverty altogether as indifferent, nor eschew pity as an unwanted emotion.[108] I believe that Seneca's case can be discounted for our purposes, and not only because it is a piece of special pleading not endorsed by other Stoics. More to the point, nobody could possibly suggest that wealth of the kind Seneca is defending was a human right. How could that be attained, and what room would be left for liberality if it were?

I have looked at two kinds of modification to Stoic theory: the new stress on humanity and pressures on the thesis that everything is indifferent except virtue. Though modifications are to be found, they are still not such, I believe, as to let in a theory of human rights.

There were schools which took over the Stoic theory of *oikeiôsis*, while dropping the Stoic idea of everything being indifferent except virtue. This would be true of the Aristotelian school as described by Arius Didymus,[109] and of the Platonist Antiochus.[110] Both are thus rid of one obstacle to the formulation of a theory of human rights. But they still treat *oikeiôsis* as something that spreads naturally, rather than as an unfulfilled obligation which answers to an unmet need.

Natural law

The idea of human rights has also been thought to come from another direction, from the Stoic idea of natural law. The conception of natural law would have seemed an oxymoron to the sophists of the fifth century BC. For, although some of them treated *justice* as natural,[111] they

---

[105] Seneca *BV* 22.1.

[106] Plutarch *Sto. Rep.* 1046E (*SVF* 3.299; 3.243); Stobaeus 2.63,6-24 (*SVF* 3.280).

[107] Seneca *BV* 24.1; cf. *deprimere* 22.1.

[108] Cf. Seneca *de Beneficiis* 6.29.1. But for pity as a fault, see *On Anger* 2.15.3.

[109] Arius Didymus ap. Stobaeum 2, 118-21, Wachsmuth, translated Görgemanns, loc. cit.

[110] For Antiochus see Cicero *Fin.* 5.

[111] Alcidamas (schol. ad loc.) does not use the term justice. But see Antiphon fr. 44, Diels-Kranz, and Anonymus Iamblichi = no. 89 in Diels-Kranz, *Die Fragmente der*

contrasted law with nature as something variable with something invariable.[112] But Aristotle in the fourth century speaks of a natural law (*nomos kata phusin*) even without community (*koinônia*) or contract (*sunthêkê*) and gives three examples of its upholders: Sophocles' Antigone, who defied the ban on burying her brother, Gorgias' pupil Alcidamas, an opponent of natural slavery, and Empedocles. Empedocles himself had only spoken in terms of a universal law (*nomimon*) the law against killing animals. It is Aristotle who describes Empedocles' law as *natural*.[113]

The classic Stoic statement of natural law is put by Cicero into the mouth of the Stoic Laelius. Instead of the different laws that hold in different times and places, there is a single universal and eternal law in accordance with nature.[114] This is a development of the idea of the founder Zeno, in the third century BC that we should not live by separate cities and laws, but should consider all men our fellow citizens.[115] Moritz Voigt argued in the nineteenth century that it led to the *ius gentium*, the law of nations in Roman law, which was supervised by separate officials, and applied to dealings with foreign nations. It was later said to be established by natural reason.[116] The *ius gentium* was sometimes identified with *ius naturale*, natural law, but sometimes distinguished on the ground that natural law extended beyond nations even to animals.[117] Voigt connected these Roman legal conceptions with human rights, and saw Stoic natural law as leading to them.

These ideas have been adequately answered by others.[118] First, the emphasis in these theories is on obligations, not on rights. This is especially clear in the Stoics' case, where the reference is to the

---

Vorsokratiker.

[112] The pioneering work is Felix Heinimann, *Nomos und Phusis*, Basel 1945. On how nature came to be thought of as lawful, see Klaus Reich, 'Der historische Ursprung des Naturgesetzbegriffs' in H. Diller and H. Erbse, eds., *Festschrift Ernst Kapp*, Hamburg 1958. But the present interest is in how law came to be thought of as natural, even though in the Stoics the scientific and the juridical questions are closely related, because justice depends on the nature of the universe.

[113] Aristotle *Rhet.* 1.13, 1373b4-17.

[114] Cicero *Republic* 3.33 (*SVF* 3.325).

[115] Plutarch *On the Fortune of Alexander* 329A-B (*SVF* 1.262), as above.

[116] Moritz Voigt, *Das ius naturale, aequum et bonum, und ius gentium der Römer*, vol. 1, 267-344, Leipzig 1865. The reference to natural reason was introduced in the 2nd century AD by the jurist Gaius, in the view of Paul Vander Waerdt, 'Philosophical influence on Roman jurisprudence? The case of Stoicism and Natural Law', part IV, in *Aufstieg und Niedergang der römischen Welt (ANRW)* 2.36.6, 1993.

[117] For this distinction, see Ulpian (?) in Justinian's *Institutes* 1.2 pr. and *Digest. init.* 1.1.1.3-4. Thomas Aquinas also brings animals under natural law, *Summa Theologiae* 2, part 1, q. 94, a. 2. But Grotius *de jure belli ac pacis* 1.1.11.1 rejects the extension to animals (I owe the reference to Paul Vander Waerdt).

[118] M. Colish, *The Stoic Tradition from Antiquity to the Early Middle Ages*, Leiden 1985, 356-64; Paul Vander Waerdt, *The Stoic Theory of Natural Law*, Ph.D. Diss, Princeton 1989, esp. pp. 18-28; 270-83.

practices a person must adopt, if he is to progress towards the end which nature intends for man. It was, some would say, although the champions of Vitoria would disagree,[119] a seventeenth-century development, either in Hobbes, or in Grotius, that drew attention away from the ambitious idea of obligations directed to the end of self-perfection to the minimalist idea of rights, notably the right of self-preservation.

Secondly, it is true that the Roman *ius gentium* was devised for foreigners by the relevant praetors on the basis of laws widely accepted among Mediterranean peoples. But once formulated, it was incorporated into civil law, or alternatively, in the case of a conflict, was overridden by civil law, as for example in connexion with the legal status of children born out of wedlock, and with the requirement of legal guardianship for adult women. Slaves could therefore not appeal from the civil law to the law of nations, since civil law would take precedence. In any case, the law of nations itself endorsed slavery, and if natural law was ambiguous on the point, it was not this law that prevailed.[120]

Criteria

It may be useful to gather together the criteria I have used for detecting the invention of a theory of human rights. For the first *invention* of a theory of human rights, more criteria must be considered than are recognised in discussions of what a human right is. The rights I am concerned with are natural, not legislated, and the idea of naturalness is indeed found in the Stoics, though in connexion with law, not rights. I have been looking for a theory that applied to humans rather than others, and to all or most humans – the recent suggestion that holidays with pay is a human right has provoked ridicule. The Stoics did extend justice to all humans. The right should be something that it is important to receive, because it answers a major need or confers a significant good. By this criterion, the Stoic doctrine of indifference diverged from a human rights theory. There should be a duty on others to help if possible, or at least not to interfere, but the stress should be on the recipient. The duty is imposed because of something about the recipient, not just because of something about the agent. Here the Stoics' 'because' in 'because they are human' did supply the required stress. The receipt of the needed thing should be an end in

---

[119] Grotius is selected by Richard Tuck (lecture to the King's College, London, Centre for Philosophical Studies, May 1990). Daniel Deckers' dissenting case for Vitoria in *Gerechtigkeit und Recht* reached me too late for proper consideration.

[120] M. Colish, loc. cit.; Paul Vander Waerdt, *ANRW*, 1993, part IV.

itself, a criterion not sufficiently satisfied by the Stoics. The recipients should be entitled to it, another unsatisfied criterion. There may be little motive to invent a theory of human rights initially in connexion with needs that are already well catered for, as the Stoics supposed many of our needs to be. Human rights cater for the needs of the individual rather than, as with the Stoics, for the needs of the community as a whole. Finally, there cannot be a human right to something wholly unattainable, as immunity from bereavement is, and still more clearly was in the Stoic era.

Ius

The impression that the Stoics are talking of rights is reinforced by the common practice of using this term in English translations, especially of the word *ius*. This word sometimes refers to legal rights, but it does not necessarily do so. One context in which it clearly does not refer to rights is that in which a Latin author says that there is no *ius* connecting us with animals (*nihil iuris cum*). This is a Latin rendering of the Greek idea, bequeathed by Aristotle to the Stoics, that there is no such thing as justice in relation to animals (no *dikaion pros*). As the Greek word *dikaion* shows, the point is one about justice, not about rights.[121]

Rights

On the other hand, we must not go too far in the opposite direction and deny that the Greeks and Romans had any concept of rights. They did not have a special word, but they did express the concept. Indeed, the concept of legal rights must be present, whenever the law says that someone is permitted to do something and others are obliged to allow it. The only room for dispute is over which examples of legal rights are genuine. Myles Burnyeat has rightly claimed that the Greeks had the concept of rights, and not just of legal rights either. His proffered example is that Socrates claimed the right to know.[122] Julius Tomin has replied that Socrates claimed only the duty to know, the right to question.[123] Over this particular example, I am inclined to be more cautious still. Socrates was claiming only the duty to question, but he recognised that the Athenians had the right to shut him up. It may

---

[121] See e.g. Cicero *de Finibus* 3.67, where *ius* and *iniuria* are often translated in terms of rights.

[122] Myles Burnyeat, 'A question of origins', *Times Literary Supplement*, 15-21 June 1990, 643, a forceful defence of the Classics, which led to a joint seminar on the subject of human rights.

[123] Julius Tomin, 'The right to question', *Oxford Magazine*, Noughth Week, Hilary Term 1991, 5.

have been unjust for them to do so, but they had a right to pass a verdict, even if unjust.

But an example of legal rights, without the name, is provided by the laws of slavery of Gortyn in Crete, which set out what slaves were allowed to do, including the circumstances, more liberal than in Athens, in which they could marry. Aristotle treats masters as having rights over slaves, and he could even be said, in a sense, to regard these rights as natural, because they are based on the different nature of slaves, who need someone to plan their lives for them.[124] Of course, these are not natural rights in the modern sense of human rights based on the nature of man as a whole.[125] If we were to look for an example of human rights in Aristotle, it might be one almost opposite to the kind that interests modern theorists. Humans might be said to have the right to hunt animals,[126] although this will be a rather non-standard right, like the right sometimes now recognised of the starving to be fed. These rights are non-standard because they do not correlate in any obvious way with anyone else's duty, unless it be the duty not to interfere. Aristotle's human right to hunt animals is curious in another way, that it is coupled with a right to hunt for natural slaves, which cannot be a human right, since it is available only to natural masters. None the less, the right to hunt animals is still recognised as a natural right (*ius naturale*), the one liberty of all, by Gratian in the twelfth century, drawing on Isidore from nearly six centuries earlier.[127]

Justice and rights

The question has already arisen whether the very idea of justice implies the idea of rights. Certainly, the most discussed modern account of justice has been said to be based on the idea of rights.[128] But there are very few Greek definitions of justice which hint at any idea of rights. The main Stoic definition turned instead, as we saw, on appropriateness. Plato considers in the *Republic* an account of justice which he elicits from the poet Simonides, that justice is giving to each what he is owed (*to opheilomenon*). But any expectation that the notion of rights would thus be tied to justice is dashed, when Plato rejects the definition, after first deliberately reinterpreting what is owed as meaning merely what is appropriate (*prosêkon*).[129] At most Plato reinforces his idea that justice is a matter of different parties *doing*

---

[124] Aristotle *Pol.* 1.2; 1.4-8; 1.13.

[125] Jeremy Waldron, ed., *Nonsense Upon Stilts*, London 1987, 7; 163.

[126] Aristotle *Pol.* 1.8, 1256b20-6.

[127] Gratian *Decretum*, Dist. 1, c. 7. See Brian Tierney, 'Tuck on rights: some medieval problems', *History of Political Thought* 4, 1983, 429-41.

[128] R. Dworkin, *Taking Rights Seriously*, London 1977, ch. 6, 169-83, commenting on John Rawls, *A Theory of Justice*, Cambridge Mass. 1971.

[129] Plato *Rep.* 331E; 332B-C.

their own job by appealing to a commonplace that not only the *doing* of one's own (job) but also the *possession* (*hexis*) of what is one's own (*oikeiou, heautou*) is justice. Plato's rulers will give legal judgments (*dikazein*) with a view to nobody being robbed of their own (*tôn hautôn*).[130] The reference to one's own here does imply the idea of what one has a right to, yet Plato does not incorporate this aspect of the commonplace in his own definition of justice.

Aristotle brings in a notion connected with rights, but only with reference to one kind of justice, and that the most unexpected kind, namely the corrective justice which is exercised in punishment. We might have thought that punishment at least for homicide, which is one of Aristotle's examples, cannot be intended to restore anyone's rights. But Aristotle points out that people (presumably, the relatives of the victim in this case) speak in terms of getting their own back (*ekhein to hautou*).[131] So in the corrective kind of justice, but not in all, the notion of rights is suggested by the notion of one's own. And the idea of giving to each his own (*suum cuique tribuere*) recurs in Roman law in the enumeration of the three precepts of justice attributed to Ulpian in the third century AD, but possibly interpolated later.[132] But this text may in any case be based on Cicero's Stoicising definition of justice as *suam cuique tribuens dignitatem*, or as disposed *tribuere id cuique quod sit quoque dignum*, in other words as giving to each what is *appropriate* or *deserved*, rather than what is due, and in that case it need not hint at the idea of rights at all.[133] In other definitions, there is no reference to what is due, not, for example, in the two definitions of justice favoured by Platonists, as an inner psychological state in which each part of the soul does its own job, with reason in command, or alternatively as an assimilation of oneself to God, nor in the many definitions of justice offered in the pseudo-Platonic *Definitions*.[134]

The Stoic influence

Although my conclusion is that the Stoics did not have a theory of human rights, this is not as important as two other facts. First, they did have a theory which was benign as regards human beings, and this may have had a benign influence on later ages. Rights are not the only medium for being humane. Secondly, their theory was needlessly disadvantageous to animals, and this, as we shall see in Chapter Fourteen, influenced later generations too.

[130] Plato *Rep.* 443E; 6-10. I owe the reference to David Robinson.
[131] Aristotle *EN* 5.4, 1132a28; 1132b17.
[132] Ulpian Justinian's *Digest* 1.10.1-2.
[133] Cicero *de Inventione* 2.160, cited by Paul Vander Waerdt, *ANRW*, 1993, n. 157, and Cicero *Off.* 1.42; *Republic* 3.11.18. The abbreviated version is found at Cicero *Leg.* 1.19; *Off.* 1.15.
[134] ps-Plato *Definitions* 411D-E.

Animal rights

A particularly hard question is whether any Greeks express the idea of
animal rights. Porphyry devotes Book 3 of *On Abstinence from Animal
Food* to our owing justice to animals. And we owe justice not, as in the
Stoic case, because it is good for us to be just, but because of something
about the animals themselves. Part of the argument is that animals
are rational, but the background to this is not the idea that rationality
confers a right, any more than it is in the Stoic theory. Rather, the
Stoic theory is taken as given, that justice extends to all and only
rational beings, and animals are argued to qualify as rational. It may
seem more promising when, in 3.25, Porphyry goes back to a pre-Stoic
assertion of animals belonging (*oikeioi*). Aristotle's successor Theophrastus had claimed that they belong with us because they are made of
the same tissues, and like us have appetites (*epithumiai*), anger
(*orgai*), reasoning (*logismoi*), and are most similar of all to us in respect
of their perceptions (*aisthêseis*). Exactly how Theophrastus used these
claims is not said, though elsewhere in the treatise, Porphyry shows
that Theophrastus was concerned with justice to animals.[135] But
whatever Theophrastus may have said, Porphyry makes use of his
materials in an interesting way. He treats these similarities in
animals not as parts of some technical theory of justice, like the Stoic
one, but simply as relevant reasons for our treating them justly. It is
this emphasis on the animals themselves that makes his call for justice
look more like an assertion of their rights. But even here what he is
emphasising about the animals, like Pythagoras and Empedocles
before him, is their relation to *us*, their *belonging*. *Oikeiotês* is a
relational term and so the emphasis may not be so purely on the
animals themselves as to provide an unmistakable appeal to rights.

In the case of Pythagoras and Empedocles, the appeal to our kinship
with animals sometimes treats them not as animals but as our friends
and relatives, who happen to be reincarnated in animal form.
Admittedly, there are other grounds too for the claim of kinship: the
common breath we draw and elements we are made of. But it remains
a little unclear to what extent the appeal is to our duty as kin and to
what extent it is, as in a theory of animal rights, to the nature of the
animals themselves. Talk of animal rights, in the case of Pythagoras,
Empedocles and Theophrastus may not be totally out of place, but I
think it is safer to couch the discussion in terms of justice.

One thing, however, is striking. Even if animals are being granted
only quasi-rights, these quasi-rights are at least natural ones, based
not on society, but on the nature of things. And what is interesting is
that two of the earliest discussions of such natural rights, or

---

[135] Porphyry *Abstinence* 2.12; 2.22; 2.24.

quasi-rights, concern *animals*. The first, as Myles Burnyeat has quite rightly pointed out,[136] is Empedocles' insistence that it is a universal law (*nomimon*), valid for everyone not to kill living things (*to empsukhon*). The second is Aristotle's riposte, which equally grounds in *nature* the entitlement of humans to domesticate, hunt and kill animals.[137] It was the Stoics who raised the idea of a *natural* law to the highest point, in the theories we have been looking at. But in the next chapter we shall see they were drawing on the Cynics in doing so, and that even the Epicureans insisted there was something natural to just arrangements, although only so long as they were expedient.

---

[136] Empedocles, as reported by Aristotle *Rhetoric* 1.13, 1373b4-18. That the earliest example concerns animals has been pointed out by Myles Burnyeat, talk on Radio 3, 9 April 1992.

[137] Aristotle *Pol.* 1.5, 1254b10-26; 1.8, 1256b15-24.

CHAPTER TWELVE

Anarchy and contracts between rational beings

There is a great difference, it may seem, between the Stoics' belief in a world-wide community and the Cynics' rejection of all existing communities. The second would be compatible with living as a hermit. Yet the two ideas are connected.[1] When Zeno, the founder of Stoicism, wrote his *Republic* speaking of a world-wide community of the wise, he was still a pupil of the Cynic philosopher Crates[2] and was influenced by the Cynic belief that civilisation is bunk.

Cynicism

The first Cynic, Diogenes of Sinope in the fourth century 38 BC, rejected civilisation, preferring the simplest, often ascetic and usually shocking, ways of satisfying needs. The sources say that he allowed all sorts of sexual practice – free love, homosexuality, incest and, as being least trouble, masturbation in public.[3] He allegedly advocated cannibalism, even eating one's parents.[4] He is said to have despised religious practice with its temples, sacrifices, initiations, purifications and votive offerings.[5] There are even more famous stories about him: that he lived in a tub,[6] and – this one much illustrated – that he rebuffed Alexander the Great's offer 'Ask me for anything you like' with the reply 'Stand out of my light'.[7]

[1] John Moles has even argued that the Cynics had the first of these two ideas, but I am not entirely convinced. 'Le cosmopolitisme Cynique', in M. Goulet Cazé, ed., *Le Cynisme et ses prolongements*, CNRS Paris, forthcoming 1992-3.

[2] Diogenes Laertius *Lives* 7.4. The testimony on the Cynics is usefully collected in Gabriele Giannantoni, ed., *Socraticorum Reliquiae, Naples* 1983, vol. 2.

[3] Diogenes Laertius *Lives* 6.46; 6.56; 6.69; 6.72; Dio Chrysostom *Or.* 6.17; Lucian *Lives for Sale* 10; Augustine *City of God* 14.20; Plutarch *Sto. Rep.* 1044B; Galen *de loc. affect.* 6.15; Athenaeus *Deipnosophists* 4.158F; Theodoretus *Graec. affect. cur.* 12; Clement of Rome *Hom.* 5.18

[4] Diogenes Laertius *Lives* 7.121; Theophilus *ad Autolycum* 3.5 (*SVF* 3.750).

[5] Diogenes Laertius *Lives* 6.39; 6.42; 6.59; 6.73; Julian *Orations* 199B.

[6] Diogenes Laertius *Lives* 6.22-3, and texts collected by Giannantoni, vol. 2, 483 ff.

[7] Diogenes Laertius *Lives* 6.38, and texts collected by Giannantoni, vol. 2, 422 ff.

More important for our purposes, Diogenes was an anarchist: he rejected the state. He claimed to lack city (*apolis*) and country (*patris*)[8] other than the cosmos,[9] which was the only true state (*politeia*),[10] there being no city or law of which we have knowledge.[11] The law (if this is the meaning of the relevant passage) is a mere refinement.[12] He was bound by no law and engaged in no civic duties.[13] He regarded armies as useless,[14] and rejected coinage in favour of knucklebones.[15] The word *apolis*, lacking a city, had been used by Aristotle with almost opposite implications, when he said that the man who by nature was unsuited to a city was either savage or superhuman.[16]

Diogenes was, in fact, an exile from his native Sinope, and is said to have quipped, 'I condemned the Sinopians to stay there.'[17] Two later writers on exile, the Platonist Plutarch and the Stoic Musonius Rufus, used as a consolation his idea that their country was the whole world.[18]

Crates agreed with Diogenes: his country (*patris*) was disgrace and poverty, his citizenship (*politês*) not the legal one, but the same as that of Diogenes.[19] One of his tragic characters is made to declare that his country (*patra*) and citadel (*polisma*) extends across the earth.[20] We can see that it was only existing communities that he rejected, if we may judge from his wistful lines about a city (*polis*) bearing only thyme, garlic, figs and loaves, which attract neither greed, nor aggression, and require no armies.[21]

We can see how Zeno came by his view that we should not reside by cities (*poleis*) or by parishes (*dêmoi*), each distinguished by its own system of right and wrong (*dikaia*).[22] Plutarch's testimony on Zeno here has been doubted,[23] because the view he goes on to associate with Zeno's *Republic*, that *all* men should be seen as fellow citizens, and

[8] Diogenes Laertius *Lives* 6.38; Epictetus *Discourses* 3.24.66.

[9] Diogenes Laertius *Lives* 6.63; 6.72; Epictetus *Discourses* 3.24.66; Dio Chrysostom *Orations* 4.13; Lucian *Lives for Sale* 8.

[10] Diogenes Laertius *Lives* 6.72. If we can believe Cicero *Tusc.* 5.108, this idea goes back to Socrates.

[11] Philodemus *On the Stoics* col. 10.

[12] Diogenes Laertius *Lives* 6.73. On the meaning see D. Tsekourakis, *Studies in the Terminology of Early Stoic Ethics*, Hermes Einzelschriften 32, Wiesbaden 1974; Malcolm Schofield, *The Stoic Idea of the City*, Cambridge 1991, Appendix G *asteion*.

[13] Maximus of Tyre *Philosoph.* 36.5.

[14] Philodemus *On the Stoics* col. 14.

[15] Athenaeus *Deipnosophists* 4, 159C; Philodemus *On the Stoics* col. 14.

[16] Aristotle *Pol.* 1.2, 1253a3-10.

[17] Plutarch *On Exile* 602A.

[18] Plutarch *On Exile* 600E; Musonius Rufus fr. 9, translated Cora Lutz, *Yale Classical Studies* 10, 1947.

[19] Diogenes Laertius *Lives* 6.93.

[20] Ibid. 6.98.

[21] Ibid. 6.85.

[22] Plutarch *On the Fortune of Alexander* 329A-B.

[23] H.C. Baldry rejects it in *The Unity of Mankind in Greek Thought*, Cambridge 1965, 158-63.

that there should be one life and one cosmos, as for a single flock, appears to conflict with other evidence, if it is taken to be about present possibilities. For at present many men are not good and these, according to Zeno's *Republic*, are not citizens, or friends, or free men, and do not belong (*oikeioi*).[24] But at least the first part of Plutarch's attribution is not compromised, and it is confirmed by Zeno's not wanting there to be law courts, or currency for exchange or travel.[25] Zeno's pupil Aristo of Chios still insists that by *nature* we have no fatherland,[26] and the third head of his school, Chrysippus, wrote in the same vein as Diogenes on the uselessness of armies.[27]

The Cynics' condemnation of civilisation had its own implications for animals. On the one hand, Diogenes ate a raw octopus, and was later defended by the Emperor Julian for doing so.[28] This was part of his indifference to what he ate,[29] and went along with his advocacy of cannibalism, an advocacy which was to be given qualified support by Chrysippus and other Stoics.[30] On the other hand, he rejoiced in the nickname of dog which he was given for his rejection of civilised living, and turned it to a number of witty purposes.[31] Moreover, it was this nickname (*kuôn*) which was transferred to the whole Cynic sect (*kunikoi*). Along with this went Diogenes' insistence that animals were, in fact, *superior* to humans.[32] Such a view had already been expressed in relation to the stork by the chorus in Sophocles' *Electra*,[33] had been hinted at by Democritus,[34] and is ascribed to the cranes in Plato's myth in the *Statesman*.[35] Diogenes' claims for animals may have been answered in the third century BC by the third head of the Epicurean school, Polystratus, in his treatise *On Irrational Contempt*.[36] But their ultimate defence is supplied by the Platonist Plutarch in the first century AD. In his treatise *That Irrational Animals Use Reason*, he takes up the story of the witch Circe who turned Odysseus' crew members into pigs, while she and Odysseus 'mingled in sweet sleep'. But in Plutarch's version, the pigs' spokesman Gryllos, or Grunter, refuses to be turned back into a man. 'We animals

---

[24] Diogenes Laertius *Lives* 7.33.

[25] Ibid.

[26] Plutarch *On Exile* 600E.

[27] Philodemus *On the Stoics* col. 14.

[28] Plutarch *Esu.* 995C-D; Julian *Orations* 6.

[29] Pophyry *Abstinence* 1.42.

[30] Diogenes Laertius *Lives* 7.121; 7.188; Theophilus ad Autolycum 3.5 (*SVF* 3.750); Sextus *PH* 3.207; 3.247; *M* 11.192; 11.194; Epiphanius *Against Heresies* 3.39 (*Dox. Gr.* 593,1; *SVF* 3.746).

[31] The evidence is collected by Giannantoni, vol. 2, pp. 474-83.

[32] See esp. Dio Chrysostom *Orations* 6.13-33; 10.16; Diogenes Laertius *Lives* 6.22.

[33] Sophocles *Electra* 1058-62. I owe the reference to Pat Easterling.

[34] Democritus frr. 154; 198.

[35] Plato *Statesman* 263D.

[36] Papyrus frr. ed. Indelli, Naples 1978.

are much happier and better than you men,' is his line, 'and you are a fool, Odysseus, to ask us to sail away with you, instead of becoming a pig like us.'

Among other arguments, Gryllos claims that animal virtues are better, precisely because they involve no toil,[37] and animal skills, because they are untaught.[38] Courage indeed is natural in animals, not in humans, as is shown by the fact that in animals, but in them alone, both sexes possess it equally.[39] Earlier in the century, Philo of Alexandria had put into his nephew's mouth the argument that the spider's skill is the more remarkable for not depending on tools,[40] and elsewhere Plutarch argues against the Epicureans that animals have more pleasurable lives, because they do not need to be relieved of anxiety.[41] Philo and Plutarch display traces of a more favourable attitude to women as well as to animals. Philo, in debate with his nephew, has the nephew say that our contempt of animals is like man's contempt of woman.[42] Plutarch makes the remark about female lions in his own person, and further wrote a treatise *The Virtues of Women*.

The praise of animals as superior may be compared with the Greek tradition of the noble savage which hymns people both real, like the Scythians, and imaginary like the Hyperboreans.[43]

The superiority of animals was to be maintained again by Rorarius and Montaigne in the sixteenth century, on the basis of the Greek originals, with Montaigne adding in the virtues of cannibalism. I shall return to this in Chapter Fourteen. Neither went so far as the early-thirteenth-century Pope Innocent III, who made even plants superior to man, in his treatise *On Contempt for the World*.[44]

Epicureanism

It was the Cynic viewpoint that led to Zeno's theory in the *Republic* of justice as involving a natural law that governed all rational beings alike. The main rival theory in that period, Epicurus' theory of justice as contract differing from one society to another, may have been evolved, it has been suggested, in response to Zeno.[45] Theories of social contract were as old as the Sophists of the fifth century BC, and had

---

[37] Plutarch *That Irrational Animals Have Reason* 986F-987B.
[38] Ibid. 991D; 992A.
[39] Ibid. 987F-988C.
[40] Philo *de Animalibus* 19.
[41] Plutarch *A Pleasant Life Impossible* 1091E-1092D.
[42] Philo *de Animalibus* 11. I thank David Runia for making the point.
[43] George Boas, 'The noble savage in antiquity', in Arthur Lovejoy and George Boas, *A Documentary History of Primitivism and Related Ideas*, vol. 1, Baltimore 1935.
[44] *De Contemptu Mundi, sive de miseria humanae conditionis*.
[45] Paul Vander Waerdt, 'The justice of the Epicurean wise man', *Classical Quarterly* 37, 1987, 402-22, at 404-5.

been subjected to criticism in Plato's *Republic*.[46] None the less Epicurus should not be seen as merely copying earlier versions. Nor should his successor Hermarchus be taken as merely following Democritus in his treatment of animals.[47] For Democritus, we have seen, included noxious animals within the system of criminal justice, whereas Hermarchus excluded animals from any system of justice, on the grounds that they could not make contracts.

Two preconditions are laid down by Epicurus as requisite for anything's being just.[48] First, there must have been a contract or agreement (*sunthêke*) to avoid causing or suffering harm. Secondly, in order to be just, the thing must be expedient, and it will remain just only so long as it is so. The second requirement of expediency is meant to provide a natural, alongside the conventional, element in all cases of justice, but it does not produce the Stoic result that the same things will be just for everyone, and independently of contract.

The consequence for animals is drawn explicitly. There is no such thing as justice or injustice in relation to those animals or tribes (*hosa tôn zôïôn, tôn ethnôn hosa*) which do not make agreements to avoid causing or suffering harm. This formulation leaves it open whether there might be any non-human animals which did make such agreements.[49] And Epicurus' expositor, Lucretius, suggests that animals are positively eager to be domesticated, by way of protection.[50] But if Epicurus leaves this possibility open, his immediate successor Hermarchus closes it. If it had been possible, he says, to make agreements with animals about their not killing us and our not indiscriminately killing them, it would have been good to push justice this far, because it would have extended our security. But that was not possible because they do not have reason (*logos*). Thus Epicurean theory reaches the same point as Stoic theory by denying justice to animals on the grounds that they are not rational. Hermarchus' intends to oppose Empedocles' extension of justice to animals, and his treatise is called *Against Empedocles*:[51]

> It would have been good to push justice this far, if they had been able to make a contract (*sunthêkê*) with the other animals just as with humans about not killing and not being indiscriminately killed by us. It would have constituted an increase in security. But since it was impossible for animals that do not possess reason (*logos*) to participate in law, it was not possible to achieve our interest in security from other living things by

[46] Plato *Republic* 358E-362C.
[47] Contrast J. Haussleiter, *Der Vegetarismus in der Antike*, Berlin 1935, 285.
[48] Epicurus *Principal Doctrines* 31-8, in Diogenes Laertius *Lives* 10.150-3.
[49] This fact is exploited by Victor Goldschmidt, *La doctrine d'Épicure et le droit*, Paris 1977, 43-57.
[50] Lucretius *de Rerum Natura* 5.855-77, esp. 868.
[51] Porphyry *Abstinence* 1.12.5-6. The title is established by Dirk Obbink, 'Hermarchus, Against Empedocles', *Classical Quarterly* n.s. 38, 1988, 428-35.

such means any more than from inanimate things. Only from getting the option which we do now have of killing them is it possible to have attainable security.

But if the Epicureans denied justice to animals, we must still ask the same question as we asked about the Stoics. Did they not have other reasons, apart from justice, for treating animals well? They did indeed believe, for the sake of tranquillity, in pursuing only natural and (for preference) necessary desires.[52] Hence Epicurus banned fish and meat as luxuries, and is consequently praised, unlike the Stoics, by Porphyry in his treatise *On Abstinence from Animal Food*.[53] On the other hand, if he spared animals, that was not, of course, out of concern for them.

The Epicurean denial of justice to animals, like the Stoic denial, needs to face the difficulty of how justice is to be extended to children who cannot make contracts. Like the modern contract theorist Jan Narveson,[54] the Epicureans can presumably appeal to contracts between adults in respect of third parties. One could have an agreement with one's neighbour not to harm each other's children. And such a contract could be extended to each other's domestic animals as well. We cannot afford to be shocked that such a theory offers only indirect protection to children. The US Supreme Court recognised children as persons under the Bill of Rights only in 1967.[55] But there is still a weakness in such indirect protection. For neither contract nor expediency would prevent a father killing his own children. This was indeed allowed by Athenian law, but only during the first nine days of life, after which time the father had to decide whether to recognise the child as his own.

The Epicurean solution is given by Lucretius. By their blandishments (*blanditiis*) children broke the proud spirit of their parents. Stammering, they indicated by voice and gesture that it is right for everyone to have pity on the weak. So people commended (*commendare*) children to care, and the result is called a contract (*foedus*).[56] Even here there is an irony, however, for *commendare* is the word used by Cicero (*Fin.* 3.16) to describe the Stoic process of *oikeiôsis* by which a newborn animal accepts its own person as *belonging* to it.[57] So just as Hermarchus, Epicurus' successor, gives *oikeiôsis* along with

[52] Epicurus *Letter to Menoeceus* 127-8; *Vatican Sayings* 21; cf. Cicero *Fin.* 2.28. I have benefited here from Paul Vander Waerdt, 'The justice of the Epicurean wise man', *Classical Quarterly*, n.s. 37, 1987, 402-22, at 408-16.

[53] Epicurus *Letter to Menoeceus* 132; Porphyry *Abstinence* 1.48-54.

[54] Jan Narveson, 'Animal rights', *The Canadian Journal of Philosophy* 7, 1977.

[55] Sue Halpern, *New York Reivew of Books*, 29 March 1990.

[56] Lucretius 5.1011-27. I am indebted to Paul Vander Waerdt for the solution to this problem and for the two following references.

[57] So J. Pigeaud, 'Épicure et Lucrèce et l'origine du langage', *Revue des Études Latines* 61, 1983, at 138-42.

expediency as a reason for the introduction of laws against homicide,[58] so Lucretius may be appealing to *oikeiôsis*, rather than to expediency as ordinarily understood, as the basis for the contract that protects children. The Epicurean solution leans on Stoicism.

The case of children is not the only difficulty for Epicurean theory. Another is that contract ought to be considered only one of many considerations relevant to justice. And expediency is only one of many motives. On the second point, it has recently been shown,[59] the Epicureans are less vulnerable than some contract theorists, including Hobbes. For they do not assume that humans are motivated chiefly by aggression, or by the lust for power. They allow that there were people in the past and might be in the future who recognise the advantage of mutual co-operation without the constraints of law. None the less, it remains true that, as the Stoics' concentric circles reduced our relationship with animals to one, so the Epicurean theory oversimplifies the springs of justice.

Several features of Epicurean theory reappear in the seventeenth century in Thomas Hobbes' defence of sovereignty.[60] Without a covenant there is no such thing as injustice, which is the non-performance of covenant. Expediency is also relevant: obligations to the sovereign, whom men have set up by covenant with each other, lapse when the sovereign cannot fulfil the original purpose of providing protection. Covenants with animals are said to be impossible. At most it is conceded that the ants and bees discussed by Aristotle, which lack reason and speech, have a natural agreement with each other. But this (as Aristotle would again agree)[61] is not a covenant, since a covenant is something artificial. At least one modern proponent of contract theory has drawn out the implications for animals more explicitly. Because they cannot make agreements to restrict behaviour and enforce them, they have no rights and we owe them no protection from suffering, unless that happens to suit our own interests.[62] It has rightly been objected that

[58] Hermarchus ap. Porphyrium *Abst.* 1.7.1, discussed by Paul Vander Waerdt, 'Hermarchus and the Epicurean Genealogy of Morals', *Transactions of the American Philological Association* 118, 1988, 87-106.

[59] Philip Mitsis, *Epicurus' Ethical Theory* 79-92. For the past see Lucretius 5,925-1457; Hermarchus in Porphyry *Abstinence* 1.7-9; for the future, Diogenes of Oenoanda new fragments (M.F. Smith) 21.1.4-14 (translated by A.A. Long and D.N. Sedley, *The Hellenistic Philosophers* 22 S) and 25.2.3-11.

[60] Thomas Hobbes *Leviathan* (1651) Part I, chs. 14-21.

[61] Aristotle *Int.* 2, 16a26-9 animals make no *sunthêkê*; *Pol.* 1.2,1253a9-18 they lack speech. Aristotle's denial to them of reason was documented in Chapter One.

[62] Jan Narveson, op. cit. Some writers have also offered this as the justification of Rawls' comparative neglect of animals: Michael S. Pritchard and Wade L. Robinson, 'Justice and the treatment of animals: a critique of Rawls', *Environmental Ethics* 3, 1981, 55-61; Alan E. Fuchs, 'Duties to animals: Rawls' alleged dilemma', *Ethics and Animals* 2, 1981, 83-7. But I doubt if Rawls would welcome this rationale.

such a theory is likely to threaten some humans as well.[63]

The most influential current theory of social contract is that of John Rawls. The duties required by justice on this theory might be described as those that would be agreed by a group of rational beings who knew that they were going to be incarnated in the society they were devising, but did not know what position they would occupy in that society.[64] Do these contractors envisage that they might be incarnated as animals? That is what Plato's God envisages when he instructs rational souls before they are incarnated.[65] Since Rawls' legislators do not envisage this, they would seem to have discriminated against animals quite arbitrarily,[66] unless there is some impossibility in the idea of a rational being turning into an animal. But if there is an impossibility, that would imply that the technique proposed for discovering what justice requires was not competent to assess the question of justice to animals. Rawls does allow that we have duties of compassion and humanity towards animals,[67] but his whole focus is on duties of justice, so that his denial of these is far more prominent than his parenthetical concession of others.

Whether animals do, in fact, make agreements was a subject of discussion in other ancient schools. The Stoic Cleanthes recognised a case of ants accepting a grub as if it were a ransom (*hôsper lutra*) for the corpse of a dead comrade. And Plutarch, who records this, may be using a Stoic term when he says that animals display seeds (*spermata*) of justice.[68] Another Stoic, Hierocles, recognises truces (*anokhai*) and as it were (*hoion*) indissoluble agreements (*sumbaseis*) among animals.[69] But these descriptions are presented only as similes. Less cautious, to judge by the translation from the Armenian, is the view which Philo of Alexandria ascribes to his nephew that pilot fish have lasting agreements,[70] but Philo himself rejects his nephew's views.

Those who wished to reject the Stoic and Epicurean conclusion that we owe no justice to irrational animals had two obvious routes open to them. One was to deny that animals were irrational. But another was to appeal to alternative theories of justice. Porphyry takes the second

[63] Tom Regan, *The Case for Animal Rights*, London 1984, 56-163.

[64] John Rawls, *A Theory of Justice*, Cambridge, Mass. 1971.

[65] Plato *Timaeus* 41E-42D.

[66] For the controversy on this, see Donald van De Veer, 'Of beasts, persons and the original position', *Monist* 63, 1979, 368-77; Michael S. Pritchard and Wade L. Robinson, 'Justice and the treatment of animals: a critique of Rawls', *Environmental Ethics* 3, 1981, 55-61, with reply by Robert Elliot, 'Rawlsian justice and non-human animals', op. cit. 95-106; Alan E. Fuchs, 'Duties to animals: Rawls' alleged dilemma', *Ethics and Animals* 2, 1981, 83-7; Brent Singer, 'An extension of Rawls' theory of justice to environmental ethics', *Environmental Ethics* 10, 1988, 217-31.

[67] Rawls op. cit., 512.

[68] Plutarch *Soll.* 967D-E; Aelian 6.50.

[69] Hierocles, *Berliner Klassikertexte* 4, Berlin 1906, 3, 19 ff.

[70] Philo *de Animalibus* 60, translated by A. Terian.

route when he invokes the account of justice given by Plato.[71]

Species and individuals

Although the Stoic and Epicurean theories of justice confine themselves to the human species, they are concerned with the welfare of individual members of that species, and only indirectly with that of the species itself. But in the modern debate, the question has arisen whether we should not be concerned with species, at the expense of individuals. Should an endangered species be conserved, even though this almost always disadvantages individual members of a more plentiful one? Is the factory farming of animals justified because it keeps the species in being, however much it harms the individuals? I shall return to these questions in Chapter Fifteen.

There was discussion in antiquity of the welfare of species, as opposed to individuals. I am not thinking of Plato's idea that we seek vicarious immortality through offspring, because we cannot have it for ourselves.[72] That is still concerned with a vicarious benefit for the individual. Rather the ancient discussion, unlike the modern one, took place in the context of theology. It was sometimes said that God's providence extended to species, not to individuals, precisely because the universe is organised for the preservation only of species. This was the view taken by the Aristotelians against the Stoics and Maimonides ascribes it to the Aristotelian Alexander of Aphrodisias.[73] Consonant with this is the view found, for example, in Plato's *Timaeus* and Maimonides, that God's purpose in creating the physical world was plenitude: the realisation of as many different species as was possible.[74] Plotinus and many other Neoplatonists agreed that God's providence did not extend to individuals, and the first recorded Neoplatonist to extend divine providence to all individuals was Proclus in the fifth century AD, drawing on Iamblichus from the fourth century.[75] He is followed, of course, in the sixth century by Boethius in the *Consolation of Philosophy*. Maimonides' view in the thirteenth century was different again. God's providence extends to individual humans, but only to species of animal. The passage is worth quoting at

[71] Porphyry *Abstinence* 3.26.

[72] Plato *Symposium* 208A-B.

[73] Maimonides *Guide for the Perplexed* 3.17, tr. M. Friedländer. Stoic providence, by contrast, extends selectively to individuals (Cicero *ND* 2.164-7), although the Stoics still admit much evil in the universe (*SVF* 2.1168-1186).

[74] Plato *Timaeus* 41B-C; Maimonides *Guide for the Perplexed* 3.25. The fullest discussion is in Arthur Lovejoy, *The Great Chain of Being*, Cambridge, Mass. 1936.

[75] Plotinus 4.3.25 (20-4). Proclus *Prov.*, chs. 62-5; *de Dec. Dub.* q. 1, chs. 2-5; *Plat. Theol.* 1.21; *in Parm.* (Cousin) 958,30-961,18. Proclus extends divine providence by exploiting Iamblichus' idea that the gods can have changeless knowledge of the changeable, definite knowledge of the indefinite, and so on. See further A.C. Lloyd, *The Anatomy of Neoplatonism*, Oxford 1990, 159-63.

length, the more so as it will become relevant again in Chapter Fourteen. Here it is in the translation of M. Friedländer. Maimonides gives his own view, preceded by an idiosyncratic interpretation of Aristotle and Alexander:[76]

> *Second Theory.* Whilst one part of the Universe owes its existence to Providence, and is under the control of a ruler and governor, another part is abandoned and left to chance. This is the view of Aristotle about Providence, and I will now explain to you his theory. He holds that God controls the spheres and what they contain: therefore the individual beings in the spheres remain permanently in the same form. Alexander has also expressed it in his writings that Divine Providence extends down to, and ends with, the sphere of the moon. This view results from his theory of the Eternity of the Universe; he believes that Providence is in accordance with the nature of the Universe: consequently in the case of the spheres with their contents, where each individual being has a permanent existence, Providence gives permanency and constancy. From the existence of the spheres other beings derive existence, which are constant in their species but not in their individuals: in the same manner it is said that Providence sends forth (from the spheres to the earth) sufficient influence to secure the immortality and constancy of the species, without securing at the same time permanence for the individual beings of the species....
>
> All other movements, however, which are made by the individual members of each species are due to accident; they are not, according to Aristotle, the result of rule and management; e.g., when a storm or gale blows, it causes undoubtedly some leaves of a tree to drop, breaks off some branches of another tree, tears away a stone from a heap of stones, raises dust over herbs and spoils them, and stirs up the sea so that a ship goes down with the whole or part of her contents. Aristotle sees no difference between the falling of a leaf or a stone and the death of the good and noble people in the ship; nor does he distinguish between the destruction of a multitude of ants caused by an ox depositing on them his excrement and the death of worshippers killed by the fall of the house when its foundations give way; nor does he discriminate between the case of a cat killing a mouse that happens to come in her way, or that of a spider catching a fly, and that of a hungry lion meeting a prophet and tearing him. In short, the opinion of Aristotle is this: Everything is the result of management which is constant, which does not come to an end and does not change any of its properties, as e.g., the heavenly beings, and everything which continues according to a certain rule, and deviates from it only rarely and exceptionally, as is the case in objects of Nature. All these are the result of management, i.e., in a close relation to Divine Providence. But that which is not constant, and does not follow a certain rule, as e.g., incidents in the existence of the individual beings in each species of plants or animals, whether rational or irrational, is due to chance and not to management; it is in no relation to Divine Providence....
>
> My opinion on this principle of Divine Providence I will now explain to

[76] Maimonides loc, cit., tr. M. Friedländer, 2nd edition, Routledge and Kegan Paul, London 1904.

you. In the principle which I now proceed to expound I do not rely on demonstrative proof, but on my conception of the spirit of the Divine Law, and the writings of the Prophets. The principle which I accept is far less open to objections, and is more reasonable than the opinions mentioned before. It is this: In the lower or sublunary portion of the Universe Divine Providence does not extend to the individual members of species except in the case of mankind. It is only in this species that the incidents in the existence of the individual beings, their good and evil fortunes, are the result of justice, in accordance with the words, 'For all His ways are judgment.' But I agree with Aristotle as regards all other living beings, and *a fortiori* as regards plants and all the rest of earthly creatures. For I do not believe that it is through the interference of Divine Providence that a certain leaf drops (from a tree), nor do I hold that when a certain spider catches a certain fly, that this is the direct result of a special decree and will of God in that moment; it is not by a particular Divine decree that the spittle of a certain person moved, fell on a certain gnat in a certain place, and killed it; nor is it by the direct will of God that a certain fish catches and swallows a certain worm on the surface of the water. In all these cases the action is, according to my opinion, entirely due to chance, as taught by Aristotle. Divine Providence is connected with Divine intellectual influence, and the same beings which are benefited by the latter so as to become intellectual, and to comprehend things comprehensible to rational beings, are also under the control of Divine Providence, which examines all their deeds in order to reward or punish them. It may be by mere chance that a ship goes down with all her contents, as in the above-mentioned instance, or the roof of a house falls upon those within; but it is not due to chance, according to our view, that in the one instance the men went into the ship, or remained in the house in the other instance; it is due to the will of God, and is in accordance with the justice of His judgments, the method of which our mind is incapable of understanding. I have been induced to accept this theory by the circumstance that I have not met in any of the prophetical books with a description of God's Providence otherwise than in relation to human beings.

But the condition of the individual beings of other living creatures is undoubtedly the same as has been stated by Aristotle. On that account it is allowed, even commanded, to kill animals; we are permitted to use them according to our pleasure.

The Christian tradition is different. Christ said: 'Are not two sparrows sold for a penny? And not one of them will fall to the ground without your Father's will.' (Matthew 10.29; Luke 12.6) Augustine cites this in arguing that God cares for individual animals,[77] even though, we shall see in Chapter Fourteen, he directs human concern more to the species than to the individual.

Animal irrationality

We have seen that the Stoic and Epicurean theories made possession

---

[77] Augustine *Enarratio in Psalmos* 145.13-14; 34.1.6.

or lack of reason the crucial test for how animals were to be treated. In Chapter Fourteen it will appear how Augustine and the Christian tradition seized on this line of thought.

CHAPTER THIRTEEN

Religious sacrifice and meat-eating

In the next two chapters, I shall consider the religious background to the philosophical debate on the treatment of animals, although only insofar as religion affected the philosophical debate. Animal sacrifice was an even more important feature of Greek life than animal experimentation is for us. Moreover, it was intimately connected in a two-way link with the eating of meat. For it was the normal Greek practice not to burn up the sacrificial victim (that would be called a holocaust), but to eat it after sacrifice. Conversely, if you bought meat from the butcher, or were served it by a friend, you could not be sure that it had not been sacrificed. Indeed, for reasons of hygiene, the butcher might well prefer such meat,[1] and there is a surviving inscription recording purchases from the priests.[2] Even if there are records of people having a choice,[3] and even if the spread of Christianity could make sacrificed meat scarce,[4] we know that some early Christians were encouraged to eat sacrificed meat. For in his Epistle to the Corinthians,[5] Saint Paul tackles the question whether Christians should eat meat that may have been sacrificed to idols. His answer is that it is all right, provided you do not *know* that it has been sacrificed. His rationale is that to Christians the procedures of sacrifice are meaningless in themselves. A problem arises only if possible converts are put off by seeing you eat sacrificed meat knowingly:

Whatsoever is sold in the shambles, that eat, asking no question for conscience sake. If any of them that believe not bid you to a feast, and ye be disposed to go, whatsoever is set before you eat, asking no question for conscience sake.

[1] I am grateful to Fred Brenk for this point.
[2] F. Sokolowski, *Lois sacrées des cités grecques* 154B 39-40.
[3] ps-Aristotle *Oeconomica* 1349b10, drawn to my attention by Simon Pulleyn; M. Isenber, 'The sale of sacrificial meat', *Classical Philology* 70, 1975, 271-3.
[4] Pliny, Letter to Trajan, 10.96.10.
[5] Epistle to the Corinthians 1.8 and 1.10 (19-31: quotation from verses 25 and 27 in the Authorised Version).

There is even a third type of link. It was not allowed to pagans to eat unsacrificed meat. Hercules is described as first sacrificing the ox which he stole from a farmer on Lindos, even though he was in a hurry to eat.[6] An inscription in Pisidia reveals that someone called Meidon was struck dumb, when his servants ate unsacrificed meat. He put up the inscription to record his recovery.[7] Again, Proclus' pupil Asclepiodotus refused the doctor's order to eat unsacrificed (*athutos*) meat,[8] at a later date when Christianity had made sacrificed meat scarce. Evidently, you could not say that you shared in traditional religion, but did not eat meat, or that you ate unsacrificed meat. And conversely, you could not say as an early Christian that you repudiated the city's religion, but liked a nice piece of beef.

Animal sacrifice had an importance which it is hard for present-day readers to imagine. When Aristotle discusses what makes a city state (*polis*) as opposed to a mere conglomeration of people, one major part of his answer is the possibility of communal sacrifices.[9] He also claims, to the consternation of at least one modern critic,[10] that the conduct of public sacrifice is one of the offices essential to a city state. The opportunity for rich sacrifice is given by Xenophon as one of the main advantages of being a landowner.[11] In times of persecution for Christians, sacrifice became even more significant, since refusal to engage became a litmus test of Christianity as opposed to paganism.[12] Where a different test was administered, it is still recorded that the decline in Christianity renewed the demand for animals for sacrifice.[13] Conversely, when Christianity had gained the upper hand, Theodosius I forebade sacrifice in AD 391. The physical evidence of sacrifice will also have been pervasive. Even if Gunther Zuntz admits that 'we have in some points gone beyond what is commonly accepted', we may listen to his description, when he says: 'The glorious city in its continuous worship must have resounded with the shrieks of dying animals; its air reeking with the stench of blood and burning carcasses.'[14]

Eating and sacrifice were the two uses of animals most discussed in philosophical texts, although there were many others and animals were more ubiquitous than in our society. Besides food, there was dress and adornment, and these uses did not have to be lethal: the

[6] ps-Apollodorus *Bibl.* 2.5.11.

[7] P. Herrmann, *Das Testament des Epikrates*, Sitz. öst. Akad. philos.-hist. Klasse 265,1, Vienna 1969, 58 ff.

[8] Suidas, ed. Asmus 80 (= Damascius fr. 216, Zintzen).

[9] Aristotle *Pol.* 3.9, 1280b37.

[10] Aristotle *Pol.* 6.8, 1322b26-31, criticised by Jonathan Barnes, in 'Aristotle and political liberty', in Günther Patzig, ed., *Aristoteles' 'Politik'*, Göttingen 1990.

[11] Xenophon *Oeconomicus* 5.

[12] See e.g. Tertullian *ad Scap.* 4, 1-4; *Apologeticus* 28-9; Cyprian *Ep.* 20 Eusebius *Martyrs of Palestine*; PE 8-9, and (for Origen) 6.39.5; Julian *Against the Galileans*.

[13] Pliny *Epp.* 10.96-7.

[14] G. Zuntz, *Persephone*, Oxford 1971, 183-4.

philosophers point to the use of animals for wool, milk, eggs and honey.[15] There was also the non-lethal use of animals for haulage and transport. But Porphyry does condemn the use of animals for divination through entrails,[16] and he records that Plotinus refused medicines with animal ingredients.[17] Medicine used animals also for diet (pp. 125, 171) and for anatomical dissection or vivisection. But even here we find Galen recommending that a pig may be substituted for a monkey in demonstrations, because the monkey's face shows emotions like a human's.[18] There was cavalry, and there is an entertaining description by Lucretius of experiments, some disastrous, with bulls, lions and boars in warfare. This is often derided, but why?[19] There were hunting and racing; there were guard dogs, sheep dogs and vermin-catchers. There were zoos, aviaries and fishponds. The philosophers refer to circus animals.[20] There was cock-fighting and quail-fighting, and the huge public entertainments with animals displayed and often killed by each other, or by humans. There were animals kept as ornaments and from earliest times an enormous variety of species kept as pets.[21] These are particularly hymned by the poets, but we have met them in philosophical contexts with supposedly talking birds and peeing lapdogs, and in refutation of the alleged barrier between humans and other species.

It should not be thought that food was the sole purpose of hunting. The excitement of the chase is such that Montaigne describes it as more irresistible than sexual temptation,[22] and Augustine gives it as an example of his subservience to curiosity that he cannot help watching, if he sees a dog chasing a hare while riding in the country.[23] Equally from Xenophon's instruction in the care of hounds, if it is his, the excitement of controlling a pack is vividly apparent and modern opponents of hunting need a strategy which takes the excitement into account.[24]

Pythagoreans

To oppose animal sacrifice or meat-eating was especially tricky, because it was necessary to make clear that one did not oppose

[15] Porphyry *Abstinence* 1.21, reporting the tradition of Heraclides Ponticus; 2.13 citing Theophrastus; 3.26 in his own person.

[16] Porphyry *Abstinence* 2.48; 51-3.

[17] Porphyry *Life of Plotinus* 2.

[18] Galen *On the Use of Parts*, Kühn 2.690.

[19] Lucretius 5,1297-1349. At a later date, lions were allegedly released into the Syrian desert by Decius (Emperor AD 249-51) to discomfort the Bedouin tribes.

[20] Philo *de Animalibus* 23-4; Plutarch *Gryllos* 992A-B; Porphyry *Abstinence* 3.15.

[21] See the very useful short article by W.R. Halliday, 'Animal pets in ancient Greece', in *Discovery* 3, 1922, 151-4, a journal of popular knowledge, and more recently Jocelyn Toynbee, *Animals in Roman Life and Art*, London 1973.

[22] Montaigne *Essay on Cruelty*.

[23] Augustine *Confessions* 10.35.

[24] Xenophon *Cynegeticus*.

religion. There were before Pythagoras sects which favoured the use of barley cakes, honey, or oil, rather than of animals, in sacrifice. Many of them were called Orphic, or followers of Orpheus, while others had local names.[25] But Pythagoras from some time after 530 BC is the first identifiable philosopher, so far as we can trust our sources on him, to have favoured this. His advocacy did not impose on ordinary citizens, partly because his closest followers are said to have lived apart in groves, or outside cities,[26] and partly because he is said to have endorsed different practices for different classes of people.[27] Since he left no writings, we have only later stories and conjectures about his reasons for sparing animals. One reason ascribed is the idea of our kinship to the animals, already discussed in Chapter Ten. We are made of the same elements,[28] one breath permeates us all,[29] and (this report at least is early and reliable) animals may be reincarnated humans.[30] Pythagoras is also supposed to have forbidden anyone to sacrifice or eat the labouring ox.[31] This might suggest not so much our kinship as our debt to it. (In others the reason would be economic.) He is credited with the argument that cruelty to animals leads to cruelty to fellow-humans.[32] This 'indirect' duty as regards animals is the only one recognised by Clement of Alexandria,[33] by Maimonides,[34] by Thomas Aquinas,[35] by Kant, and by some modern philosophers, and is held by others to be all too relevant to the training of medical students who may become dehumanised through animal dissection. Pythagoras is represented by Ovid as pointing out that, even if we are entitled to kill dangerous animals, it does not follow that we may eat them.[36] Some arguments retrospectively associated with Pythagoras' concern our relation to the gods (some animals are sacrosanct; the wrong food

[25] On local cults, see Nancy Demand, 'Pindar's *Olympian 2*, Theron's faith and Empedocles' *Katharmoi*', *Greek, Roman and Byzantine Studies*, 16, 1975. On the Orphics, J. Haussleiter, *Der Vegetarismus in der Antike*, Berlin 1935.

[26] Porphyry *Abstinence* 1.36; but a different story in Iamblichus *Life of Pythagoras* 21,96. In any case Demand points out that archaeology has found animal and non-animal sacrifice in juxtaposition.

[27] Iamblichus *Life of Pythagoras* 18.85; 28,150 (but Iamblichus denies it was our Pythagoras who prescribed meat for athletes, 5.25); Porphyry, *Life of Pythagoras* 15; Diogenes Laertius, *Lives* 8.12; Porphyry *Abstinence* 1.26. See M. Détienne, *Les Jardins d'Adonis*, Paris 1972, 78-113.

[28] Iamblichus *Life of Pythagoras* 24,108; 30,169.

[29] Sextus *M* 9,127-9.

[30] Diogenes Laertius *Lives* 8.36, quoting the words of Xenophanes.

[31] Iamblichus *Life of Pythagoras* 28,150; Diogenes Laertius *Lives* 8.20.

[32] Clement of Alexandria *Stromateis* 2.18; Plutarch *Sollertia* 959F; *On Benefiting from Enemies* 91C; *Quaest. Conv.* 729E-730B; Iamblichus Life of Pythagoras, ch. 30, 168 and 186.

[33] Clement loc. cit.

[34] Maimonides *Guide for the Perplexed* 3.17.

[35] Thomas Aquinas *Contra Gentiles* 3.112; *Summa Theologiae* 2.1, q. 102, a. 6, reply obj. 8.

[36] Ovid *Metamorphoses* 15.110.

severs our kinship with the gods).[37] Others concern our own dietary welfare (the right food promotes virtue, health, reason and prophetic power, and shortens sleep).[38]

Empedocles

When we come to Empedocles in the next century (*c.* 495 – *c.*435 BC), we have fragments of his own verses left. He speaks of a past age when the Goddess of Love prevailed and men sacrificed myrrh, incense and honey, neither eating, nor sacrificing animals. They gave the goddess, he suggests, not live animals, but *grapta zôïa*, which may mean drawn pictures or, more charmingly, drawn animals.[39] In those days, animals were tame and friendly.[40] The sacrifices he mentions would not even involve destroying plants, and this may be because he claims himself to have been reincarnated not only as boy, girl, bird and fish, but even as a plant,[41] and because plants have intelligence and thought (*phronêsis*, *noêma*), at least as Sextus interprets his words.[42]

He laments his own past crime of shedding blood[43] and eating.[44] The sacrificing of bulls and eating of limbs is the greatest pollution among men.[45] Whenever one of the divine spirits (*daimones*) engages in slaughter in this way, he is exiled from the blessed for 30,000 years and reincarnated in many shapes. And this is what Empedocles himself is now, a fugitive from God and a wanderer (*phugas theothen*, *alêtês*).[46] This theme of man as an exile from his divine home is taken up by Plotinus and Porphyry,[47] is repeated in a different sense by Augustine[48] and is used by Plutarch as one of the consolations for political exile.[49]

Empedocles' case that we are wronging animals and that we owe

---

[37] Iamblichus *Life of Pythagoras* 24,106; Diogenes Laertius *Lives* 8.34.

[38] Photius, Anonymous *Life of Pythagoras* 439a24 ff. (Bekker); Iamblichus *Life of Pythagoras* 3,13; 16,68; 24,106; 30,186; 31,187. The arguments are surveyed by J. Haussleiter, op. cit. 127-44.

[39] Empedocles fr. 128, Diels-Kranz.

[40] fr. 130

[41] fr. 117

[42] fr. 110, as Sextus *M* 8.286 interprets the reference to 'all things'; cf. 103.

[43] fr. 115

[44] fr. 139

[45] fr. 128

[46] fr. 115. *Phobôi* (fear) in line 3 is a very understandable corruption of *phonôi* (slaughter).

[47] Plotinus 1.6.8 (16); Porphyry *Abstinence* 1.30.

[48] Augustine *City* 1 preface; 18.51; 19 *passim*. There is a basis in Psalm 28.13, echoed by the 1st Epistle of Peter 2.11, and ps-Paul Epistle to the Hebrews 11.13. There is also an analogue in the exile from the garden of Eden, which is taken up by Paul in 2 Corinthians 5.6. See Gerhart B. Ladner, 'Homo Viator: medieval ideas on alienation and order', *Speculum* 42, 1967, 233-59.

[49] Plutarch *On Exile* 607C.

them justice is based on our kinship with them. A common breath pervades us,[50] and reincarnation means that we are literally slaughtering our kin: we are in effect devouring each other, and it is one's son, in a changed form, or one's mother or father that one kills.[51]

Will you not cease from bellowing slaughter? Do you not see
That you are feasting on each other through the heedlessness of your
  thought?

The father will lift his dear son changed in form
And slay him as he prays, great fool. And the sacrificers
Bring the pleading son. But the father, deaf to his reproaches,
Slays him in his home and prepares an evil feast.
In the same way, son takes father and children their mother,
And robbing them of life's breath, eat the beloved flesh.

Theophrastus

The third pre-Christian philosopher to have left us a major case against the sacrifice of animals is Aristotle's pupil and successor, Theophrastus. Sizeable portions of his treatise *On Piety* are preserved by Porphyry.[52] It is wrong to see this as directed only against sacrifice, not against meat-eating,[53] given the connexion between the two, which he emphasises.[54] In fact he explicitly condemns eating meat.[55] He is concerned with justice to animals.[56] Eating normally involves killing for the purpose, even if there was some discussion of the legitimacy of eating animals that were already damaged.[57]

Theophrastus, like Empedocles, presents animal sacrifice as a deviation from earlier custom, and like Empedocles describes it as attended by guilt.[58] He claims it was brought on by famine and war, which led first to cannibalism, and only then (as in the story of

---

[50] Sextus *M* 9.127-9; Aristotle *Rhet.* 1373b6-17.

[51] Empedocles fr. 136; 137; Sextus *M* 9.127-9; Plutarch *Esu.* 997E.

[52] There is a modern translation in William Fortenbaugh, Pamela Huby, Robert Sharples, Dimitri Gutas, eds., *Theophrastus of Eresus, Sources*, part 2, Leiden 1992, pp. 404-37. The extract at 3.25 may or may not be from the same work.

[53] U. Dierauer, *Tier und Mensch*, Amsterdam 1977, 177, with further references at n. 22; Simon Pembroke, '*Oikeiôsis*', in A.A. Long, ed., *Problems in Stoicism*, London 1971, 114-49, at 136; J. Bernays, *Theophrastos Schrift über Frommigkeit*, Berlin 1866, 121.

[54] 2.25-9.

[55] 2.28.4.

[56] Porphyry *Abstinence* 2.12; 22; 24.

[57] Plutarch *Esu.* 998B suggests that at first people may have eaten only damaged fish and birds. The Pythagoreans forebade eating damaged animals. Diogenes Laertius *Lives* 8.33; *Anon. Pyth. Sent.* 41 (Mullach 1.507). Ps-Phocylides also forbids this, *Sentences* 147-8, ed. van der Horst, but he draws on Jewish sources notably Exodus 22.30. Cf. Leviticus 17.15; 22.8; and Deuteronomy 14.21, which are discussed by Philo, *On the Special Laws concerning the 8th, 9th and 10th Commandments*, and Maimonides *Guide for the Perplexed* 3.48.

[58] Porphyry *Abstinence* 2.9 and 2.29.

Abraham) to the substitution of animal for human victims.[59] In other cases, it was introduced through an accident or fit of temper.[60] The implication is, presumably, that it was unnatural. If the motive were religious, he further complains, and not gluttony, the Greeks could follow the Jews, whom he describes as refraining from eating the sacrifice.[61] There are three reasons for sacrifice: to show honour, or gratitude, or to get a favour. But one cannot show honour or expect a favour through being unjust, and one cannot show gratitude by taking another's property.[62]

Theophrastus tackles the argument that God gave animals as much as fruits for our use, and replies that killing them is not holy, as sacrifice is required to be, because it is unjust. It is unjust because it harms them by robbing them of life.[63] The point is important. It goes beyond Jeremy Bentham's utilitarianism and beyond current UK animal legislation in recognising loss of life, and not just suffering, as a harm. Theophrastus' teacher Aristotle had already seen that you can be harmed by what happens even if you are not conscious of it and even if you are dead. We can imagine the frustration of a person's life work of which they are ignorant either because they are living in a fool's paradise, or because they have died.[64] It should be still more obvious that a painless and unanticipated early death is a loss, whether to a human or an animal.

Theophrastus goes on to confront the slide argument that we also rob plants of something and gives the most comprehensive answer extant.[65] He replies first that plants are not unwilling to shed their fruit, which they would drop anyhow. Secondly, taking their fruit does not kill them. Thirdly, whereas animals belong to the gods, plants are, like honey, more ours because we contribute to the labour of cultivating them, and can take something for our pay. Fourthly, vegetable sacrifice, as more economical, is holier and more continuously sustainable. A fifth argument, based on the difference of plant tissues, will be encountered below.

He also gives a new twist to the arguments about cannibalism. Pythagoras is reported as holding that vegetarianism will deter us from cannibalism,[66] and Empedocles, if not Pythagoras, had urged that killing animals actually was killing your reincarnated kin.[67] Theophrastus' contemporary the Platonist-turned-Aristotelian Heraclides, or

[59] Ibid. 2.9; 2.12; 2.27. In the story of Abraham in Genesis 22, an animal victim was substituted for the sacrifice of his son.   [60] Ibid. 2.9 and 2.29.

[61] Porphyry *Abstinence* 2.26.   [62] Ibid. 2.24.

[63] Ibid. 2.12. Contrast Jeremy Bentham, *Introduction to the Principles of Morals and Legislation*, 1789 (NY 1948, p. 311 note).

[64] Aristotle *NE* 1.10, 1110a18-30; Thomas Nagel, 'Death', *Nous* 4, 1970, repr. in his *Mortal Questions*, Cambridge 1979, 1-10.

[65] Porphyry *Abstinence* 2.13.   [66] Ibid. 1.23-4.

[67] Empedocles frr. 136, 137 DK; Plutarch *Esu.* 997E-F; Sextus *M* 9.129.

Clodius drawing on him, actually turned Pythagoras' argument round. If we spare animals as Pythagoras requires, we shall lose our crops, and that is what may force us to attack each other.[68] Theophrastus' contribution is to exploit the horror which even Heraclides and Clodius feel at cannibalism, and to turn it against meat-eating and animal sacrifice. Even if meat-eating is not, as it is for Empedocles, literally cannibalism, it results from cannibalism and human sacrifice[69] and is equally unnatural.

Theophrastus may have been in conflict with Heraclides also on the argument from dangerous animals which can legitimately be killed. This makes it *seem* (*eoiken*) that no justice is owed to animals (we need not emend the text).[70] Theophrastus answers that the same applies to certain criminals, even though these are akin (*oikeioi*) to us, but nothing follows about the other (*ta de*) safe animals or humans. Further, the dangerous animals are not in any case appropriate for sacrifice.

But Theophrastus' most important philosophical contribution is his insistence, against his teacher Aristotle, that animals enjoy kinship (*oikeiotês*) with us, so that it is unjust to kill them.[71] He supports the claim of kinship in a different way from Empedocles: kinship does not depend, as the reincarnation argument might suppose, on ancestry alone, but on other criteria which extend it in widening circles, until it covers all humans. (Later Stoics – see p. 123 – may have benefited from this idea, although they all rejected the extension to animals.) Further, the Pythagorean argument[72] that we have the same elements as animals would apply also to plants. The refinement we need is that with animals we share even fluids and tissues. Again, we are alike not only in appetites, emotions and perceptions, but also, contrary to Aristotle's whole theory of the nature of man, in reasonings (*logismoi*), even if the likeness is closest in respect of the five senses. The text runs:

Theophrastus uses in addition an argument of this kind. We say that those born from the same people, I mean father and mother, are naturally akin (*oikeioi*) to each other. Similarly, therefore, we think that those generated from the same forebears are also akin to each other. Yet we also think that fellow citizens are akin through sharing in land and in interaction with each other. For we no longer judge such people to be akin to each other through having sprung naturally from the same people, unless some of their first forebears were the same natural founders (*arkhêgoi*) of the race, or were descended from the same people.

In this way, too, I think, we say Greek is akin (*oikeios*) and related to (*sungenês*) Greek, barbarian to barbarian and all humans to each other

---

[68] Porphyry *Abstinence* 1.23-4.   [69] Ibid. 2.27.

[70] Ibid. 2.22.3, without Bernays' emendation (see ch. 10, n. 69 above) may be in reply to Heraclides/Clodius, as reported at 1.14.

[71] Ibid. 2.22.

[72] Iamblichus *Life of Pythagoras* ch. 24,108 and 30,169.

through one of two things: either through having the same forebears, or through sharing the same food, habits and race.

In this way, too, we class all humans as related both to each other and to all animals. For their bodily origins (*arkhai*) are by nature the same. By this I do not mean to refer to the primary elements, since plants also are made of these, but for example skin, flesh and the type of fluids that are natural to animals. And much more are they related through their souls being no different in nature, I mean in their appetites (*epithumiai*), anger (*orgai*), and again in their reasonings (*logismoi*) and above all in their senses (*aisthêseis*). But as with their bodies, some animals have souls more finely tuned, others less so, but they still all by nature have the same origins. And this is shown by their passions (*pathê*) being akin (*oikeiotês*).[73]

Platonism and Plutarch

The early Academy of Plato was divided, because, as so often, Plato had supplied some material for either side in the debate. The third head, Xenocrates, and his successor, Polemo, were vegetarian,[74] and I shall say more about Xenocrates in Chapter Fifteen. But the arguments of Xenocrates' Platonist rival, Heraclides of Pontus, are preserved by Porphyry. It looks as if the same issues are taken up from the opposite point of view by a later Platonist, Plutarch in the first century AD, although he does not always address Heraclides' arguments.

Heraclides, or Clodius the philologist who either excerpted him or added arguments of his own, concedes that eating raw meat is unnatural. But he concludes that meat-eating is natural from its being universal since the discovery of fire.[75] Plutarch by contrast in *On the Eating of Meat* points to the need for fire and spices, to show that meat-eating is unnatural. He cites our lack of suitable organs, challenging his opponents to catch animals with their teeth and eat them alive.[76] Heraclides (or Clodius) borrows Aristotle's idea that we wage a just war against animals, because wolves and lions attack us.[77] Theophrastus, we have seen, had already answered this, but Plutarch adds that it is not wolves and lions that we eat.[78] Heraclides/Clodius pleads that the prowess of carnivorous animals shows meat not to be bad for soul or body.[79] Plutarch maintains that it is.[80] Heraclides/ Clodius says it is no objection to meat-eating, if human souls are reincarnated in animal bodies. For to kill the animals would be to

---

[73] Ibid. 3.25.
[74] Clement *Stromateis* 7.32.9.
[75] Porphyry *Abstinence* 1.13.
[76] Plutarch *Esu.* 993E; 994F-995A.
[77] Porphyry *Abstinence* 1.14.
[78] Plutarch *Esu.* 994B.
[79] Porphyry *Abstinence* 1.15.
[80] Plutarch *Esu.* 995C-E; 998C.

hasten the soul's return to human existence.[81] Plutarch says that this would be cannibalism.[82]

Plutarch wrote two other treatises in defence of animals. In one, *Gryllos*, or *That Irrational Animals Have Reason*, he sides with the Cynic claim of animal superiority, perhaps in opposition to an Epicurean treatise, Polystratus' *On Irrational Contempt*. This is where he presents Odysseus' crew members as preferring to be pigs rather than men. In the other, *On the Cleverness of Animals*, he compiles a large collection of arguments for animal rationality, and replies to a claim, which he takes from the Stoics and Aristotelians, but which is also argued on slightly different grounds by Heraclides/Clodius,[83] that civilisation would break down if justice required us to spare animals. Plutarch replies that Pythagoras had found a middle way. Dangerous animals can be killed, others domesticated as our helpers, but not killed. Civilisation will thus be preserved with no injustice.[84]

Christianity

The situation was decisively changed by the new Christian attitude to animal sacrifice. St Paul opposes animal sacrifice in the First Epistle to the Corinthians.[85] The rationale is given in the pseudo-Pauline Epistle to the Hebrews.[86] It had absolutely nothing to do with kindness to animals, as we shall see in the next chapter, nor in St Paul was pagan sacrifice yet seen as horrifying, so much as meaningless.[87] The point was rather that Christ has with his blood made the one sacrifice that counts, so all other blood sacrifice is otiose. Paul's attitude is new for him, since he had earlier condoned the stoning of Stephen for his attack on animal sacrifice and other Jewish practices.[88] The attack on animal sacrifice is concerned with pagan Greek practice in the Epistle to the Corinthians and with Jewish practice in the Epistle to the Hebrews. But after AD 80, when the Jewish temple in Jerusalem was destroyed, animal sacrifice became less central a feature of Jewish practice. It had in any case been possible for the Epistle to the Hebrews[89] to appeal to Jewish texts of the Old Testament for the idea that what God requires is not blood sacrifice, but spiritual sacrifice.

[81] Porphyry *Abstinence* 1.19
[82] Plutarch *Esu.* 997E; 998C.
[83] Plutarch *Sollertia* 963F-964C; repeated by Porphyry *Abstinence* 1.4 and 6; cf. 1.16 and 24.
[84] Plutarch *Sollertia* 964E-965B.
[85] Paul 1 Corinthians 8 and 10 (19-31).
[86] Hebrews 9.6-10.22.
[87] The meaninglessness is suggested in the Epistle to the Corinthians. In later centuries, there is evidence of Christians crossing themselves, or rioting, in face of pagan sacrificial ritual.
[88] Acts 7.42 and 8.1.
[89] Hebrews 13.15-16.

The most notable such texts are perhaps Psalms 50 and 51. As Psalm 51 says:

> The sacrifices of God are a broken spirit: a broken and a contrite heart, O God, thou wilt not despise.[90]

Of course, Christian practice was never made uniform. The traveller to Greece even nowadays may be startled to read in the *Michelin Guide to Greece*, of the island of Lesbos:

> The feast of St Michael the Archangel, patron saint of the island, is celebrated on the third weekend after Easter at Mandamádos (34km – 21 miles – northwest of Mytilene). On Saturday afternoon a bull and several goats and sheep, decorated with flowers, are sacrificed beneath a great plane tree in the courtyard of the monastery. The spectators dip their handkerchieves in the blood and mark their foreheads to protect themselves from illness. A service including the baptism of children is held in the church in the presence of the Archbishop. ... On the following day, after more ceremonies, the meat is distributed.
>
> A similar celebration takes place in the last week in May near the town of Agia Paraskevi in the centre of the island. The procession on the Saturday, where horses and mules decorated with plumes parade to the sound of music, attracts the greater crowd. The bull is sacrificed on Saturday evening and on Sunday, after the church service and the distribution of the meat, there is horse-racing.

Other accounts describe how the bull is got to kneel inside the church, before being taken out to be killed. This is particularly interesting because of the apparent analogy with the ancient practice of getting the ox to nod assent by sprinkling it with a libation.[91] Similar sacrifices are conducted in Greece at Sparta and Kalivia. And German idiom reflects sacrificial practice when it speaks of someone as 'decked like an ox at Pentecost'.[92]

Porphyry and Iamblichus

Porphyry (AD 232-309) was the most effective philosophical critic of Christianity in Antiquity. His attack in *Philosophy From Oracles*, and in a work later known as *Against the Christians*, is lost. But fragments survive. Many of the leading Church Fathers felt obliged to defend themselves against it. It was suppressed under Constantine by AD 325,

[90] Psalm 51.17, in the Authorised Version. Christian attitudes are discussed by Frances M. Young, *The Use of Sacrificial Ideas in Greek Christian Writers from the New Testament to John Chrysostom*, Cambridge, Mass, 1979.

[91] Plutarch *Quaest. Conv.* 729F. This practice was re-enacted in effigy during the Townsend Lectures at Cornell. The bull in one of the Lesbos festivals is allowed to eat from people's gardens on the way to the sacrifice. I do not know whether it thereby acquires guilt, as the ox that originated the Athenian *bouphonia* was guilty of eating the sacred cakes from the altar: Theophrastus ap. Porphyrium *Abstinence* 2.29.

[92] So W. Burkert *Homo Necans* tr. Berkeley and Los Angeles 1983 from the German of Berlin 1972.

according to one source, and was burnt in AD 448 under Theodosius II.

As regards animals, Porphyry made two points against the Christians. In the collection of fragments controversially assigned to *Against the Christians*, he says that Christ was not much of a saviour. He cast the devils out of the man possessed by devils. So far, so good. But why could he not banish them from the universe altogether? All he did was to transfer them from a party he did care about (*phrontizein, kêdesthai*) to the swine whom he didn't. The well-known result was that the swine plunged over a cliff to their deaths.[93] Augustine, we shall see in Chapter Fourteen, was to accept the case of the Gadarene swine as showing a lack of concern for animals.

As regards Porphyry's second point, he approved of the Christian preference for spiritual, rather than blood, sacrifice, and advocated this himself in his treatise *On Abstinence from Animal Food*:

To the gods the best first offering (*aparkhê*) is a pure intellect and an untroubled soul.[94]

But in the fragments assigned to *Against the Christians*,[95] he questions whether the Christians were really so spiritual after all. What are we to make of the Gospel according to St John? There Christ says:

Except ye eat the flesh of the Son of man and drink his blood, ye have no life in you.[96]

Porphyry describes it as more bestial (*thêriodes*) than any bestiality that humans should eat each other's flesh and drink each other's blood and thereby have eternal life. He is aware that the saying may be taken 'allegorically', and his attack is more subtle than the earlier ones which accused the Christians of literally killing and eating babies at their assemblies.[97] It also contains an extra irony, in that in *Abstinence* Porphyry urged the unnaturalness of animal sacrifice and meat-eating by recording Theophrastus' account of it as a development from the much more obviously unnatural human sacrifice and cannibalism.

Porphyry's own view on spiritual sacrifice was actually more

---

[93] Porphyry *Against the Christians* fr. 49 (Harnack), from Makarios Magnes *Apokritikos ê Monogenês* 3.4, referring to Matthew 8.28-34; Mark 5.1-17.

[94] Porphyry *Abstinence* 2.61. Pötscher, however, treats this as a fragment (no. 8) from Theophrastus. There are, admittedly, pagan antecedents before Porphyry. Richard Price has drawn my attention to Cicero *ND* 2.71; Seneca *Ep.* 115.5; *Ben.* 1.6.3; fr. 123 in the Teubner edition of Haase.

[95] Porphyry *Against the Christians*, fr. 69 (Harnack); from Makarios Magnes 3.15. I thank Christos Evangeliou for drawing my attention to this.

[96] John 6.53, from the Authorised Version.

[97] Justin *Apology* 1.26; Athenagoras *Legatio* 35; Tertullian *Apology* 2 (1-5); 7; 9; Minucius Felix *Octavius* 30. I thank Christopher Stead for references.

nuanced than I have said. It is for the supreme God that purely spiritual sacrifice is appropriate. Nothing material is pure to the immaterial, not voice, not even internal speech, but only pure thoughts.[98] To the divine heavens, however, sacrifice of hymns may be offered.[99] Animal sacrifice is appropriate only to evil demons, and should be avoided, even if cities find it necessary to sacrifice to such beings.[100]

Porphyry was an independent spirit, who questioned not only Christianity, but also (though this is less commonly recognised) the religion of the Egyptians and of his fellow Greeks. Egyptian religion was questioned in a respectful *Letter to Anebo*, which again survives only in fragmentary form, and to which I shall return. But Greek religious practice, as regards animals, was challenged in his admirable treatise *On Abstinence from Animal Food*, which survives.[101] Porphyry may have been converted to vegetarianism after he came to Rome in AD 263, and joined the circle of Plotinus, whom he describes as a vegetarian.[102] *On Abstinence* is divided into four books. In the first, Porphyry reports the anti-animal arguments of Stoics, Aristotelians, of Heraclides of Pontus the Platonist, and of Hermarchus the Epicurean. His reply constitutes a good introduction to the ascetic ideals of the Neoplatonist way of life. Vegetarian diet is a necessary prerequisite for a personal ascent to God. In Book 2, he attacks the practice of animal sacrifice. In Book 3 he argues that justice requires us to spare animals, *inter alia* because they are rational. In Book 4 he supplies an anthropology of vegetarian nations. Of Phoenician descent himself, he shows no preference for the Greek-speaking over the 'barbarian' peoples. In attacking animal sacrifice, he has to be careful not to seem to be attacking state religion. And accordingly he protests that he is not challenging the law.[103] But the law is written for ordinary people and does not consider how a contemplative life is to be conducted. Such a life is superior to any written law designed for the common man, since it follows the unwritten law of God.[104] Porphyry is addressing not the ordinary man, but the philosopher.[105] All this is caution: in fact, if his arguments are sound, they ought to affect the ordinary man. And his pupil Iamblichus may be replying when he says that in the city all citizens must engage in worship of the gods, which is based on

---

[98] Porphyry *Abstinence* 2.34; 2.45; 2.61.

[99] Ibid. 2.34.

[100] Ibid. 2.42-3.

[101] Nineteenth-century English translation by Thomas Taylor; better French translation by Bouffartigue in the Budé series.

[102] Porphyry *Life of Plotinus* 2.

[103] Porphyry *Abstinence* 2.33.

[104] Ibid. 1.28.

[105] Ibid. 2.3; 4.18. For other relevant comments see 2.43 (already mentioned); and Porphyry *Letter to Marcella* 25-7.

sacrifice.[106]

Porphyry attacks animal sacrifice not only in *On Abstinence from Animal Food*, but also in the *Letter to Anebo*, in the *Letter to Marcella* (his wife), and even in the fragmentary *Philosophy from Oracles*. If this last supplies the details of sacrificial practice,that does not mean it endorses them,[107] as the following references will show. The objections which Porphyry assembles had for the most part been used by others, both pagan and Christian, the biggest single source being Theophrastus.

Porphyry cites Theophrastus' rejection of the three possible purposes of animal sacrifice: honouring the gods, expressing gratitude, and gaining some benefit.[108] He complements Theophrastus' arguments with many further reasons why the third motive, securing benefits, will not work. The gods have no needs.[109] If we nourished them they'd be our inferiors.[110] It is we who stand to benefit, but not through animal sacrifice. Rather we purify and divinise ourselves, if we seek to know God and imitate him through virtue.[111] The gods cannot be won over by sacrifice, for the good is always good, while bad demons are always bad.[112] And animal sacrifice merely attracts bad demons,[113] who should be hated.[114] There is another reason why the gods can neither be won over, nor be angry with us, and that is that they cannot be affected by anything (they are *apatheis*).[115] Moreover, they are not subject to anything involuntary like anger.[116]

Porphyry is opposed not only to sacrifice, but also to other uses of animals. Though he believes in prophecy, he opposes divination by means of swallowing or inspecting the entrails of animals,[117] and he rejects all eating of meat. It impedes ascetic progress to union with God,[118] and is unjust to animals.[119] It is incompatible with the inner

---

[106] Iamblichus *On the Mysteries of Egypt* 5, introduction: the connexion is suggested by H.D. Saffrey, 'Les livres 4 à 7 du *de Mysteriis* de Jamblique relus avec le *Lettre* de Porphyre *à Anebon*', in H.J. Blumenthal et al., Proceedings of the International Conference on Iamblichus, held at Liverpool, Sept. 24-26, 1990.

[107] *Pace* J. Bidez, *Vie de Porphyre*, Leipzig 1913, repr. Hildesheim 1980.

[108] Porphyry *Abstinence* 2.24.

[109] Ibid. 2.33; 2.37; *Oracles* quoted by Augustine *City* 19.23 (= Wolff, pp. 185-6).

[110] *Anebo* (reported and discussed Eusebius *PE* 5.10, 197D; Iamblichus *Myst.* 5.10, 213,8-214,3); *Letter to Marcella* 18.

[111] Porphyry *Oracles* quoted by Augustine *City* 19.23 (= Wolff, pp. 185-6).

[112] Porphyry *Abstinence* 2.39; 2.41.

[113] Ibid. 2.42-3; *Oracles* ap. Eusebium *PE* 4.22.16 (= Wolff, pp. 147-9).

[114] Porphyry *Oracles* quoted by Augustine 19.23 (= Wolff, pp. 185-6).

[115] Porphyry *Anebo*, reported and discussed by Iamblichus *Myst.* 1, 11-13; 8.8; Eusebius *PE* 5.10, 199A.

[116] Porphyry *Letter to Marcella* 18.

[117] Porphyry *Abstinence* 2.48; 2.51-3.

[118] Ibid. 1.28-57; 2.44-50; 3.26 (10-13); 3.27; 4.18 (end).

[119] Ibid. Book 3; cf. 2.22; 2.24, drawing on Theophrastus.

spiritual sacrifice which the gods require,[120] and if they had required animal sacrifice, it still would not follow that the sacrificed animals should be eaten.[121]

As regards injustice to animals, Porphyry's arguments in Book 3 on animals possessing reason and being in other ways akin to us have been considered in other chapters. They draw to a considerable extent on Theophrastus and Plutarch, but Porphyry introduced his own replies to the denial of animal speech and learning, as was seen in Chapter Seven. He may have been the first, if he was not following Plutarch, to appeal to animal pain and terror as a reason for treating them differently from plants,[122] and he certainly had to reinterpret Plato's ascription of sensation to plants in his embryological treatise *To Gaurus*.[123]

Porphyry also gave the best answer to the old argument[124] that animals must be culled, or we would suffer from overpopulation and loss of crops or even plague from the corpses of animals that starved to death. Porphyry replies that nature is self-regulating, and that other animals will correct overpopulation.[125] The self-regulation of nature has been similarly invoked in the modern literature as more benign than intrusive conservation of species, at least in a context where the rights of individual animals are respected.[126] As for the mutual killing of animals, this has been cited in the opposite sense in modern discussions, as a defence of our killing animals, and for still other purposes in the ancient literature.[127]

Iamblichus (*c.* AD 250 – 317/325) is normally taken to have been a pupil of Porphyry, on the assumption that *akêkoa* means he had heard him, not merely heard of him.[128] The standard characterisation of

---

[120] Ibid. 2.45.

[121] Ibid. 2.2; 2.4; 2.26; 2.44; 2.53; 2.57, partly drawing on Theophrastus.

[122] Ibid. 3.19.

[123] Porphyry *ad Gaurum* 4.1, ed. Kalbfleisch, *Abhandlungen der Königl. Akademie der Wissenschaften zu Berlin* 1895, French translation by Festugière in *The Revelation of Hermes Trismegistus*, vol. 4. The reference is to Plato *Timaeus* 77A-C.

[124] Hermarchus the Epicurean urged that this was true of all killable animals, however innocent they might appear (Porphyry *Abstinence* 1.11). Heraclides the Platonist, or Clodius drawing on him, added that failure to cull would lead to plague, as the animals died, and to cannibalism, as we ran out of food (Porphyry *Abstinence* 1.16; 1.24). Even Plutarch accepted that the ancients had been reluctantly forced to kill animals despite Pythagorean beliefs, although he deplores the luxurious eating of fish, and reports that Neo-Pythagoreans had objected to Chrysippus' arguments for culling cocks (Plutarch *Quaest. Conv.* 729F-730A; *Sto. Rep.* 1049A-B).

[125] Porphyry *Abstinence* 4.14.

[126] Stephen Clark, 'The rights of wild things', *Inquiry* 22, 1979, 171-88. By contrast Iamblichus makes Pythagoras turn the Daunian bear into a vegetarian (*Life of Pythagoras* 13.60). This is the intrusive approach.

[127] For Plotinus 3.2.15 (16-33), see below.

[128] Iamblichus *de Anima* ap. Stobaeum 1.49.37, p. 375,24, Wachsmuth. The 'heard of' meaning must apply where an author speaks of a distant predecessor, rather than of contemporary; see D.M. Schenkenveld, 'Prose usages of akouein, to read', *Classical*

Iamblichus' extant work as superficial and of Porphyry as an unimportant thinker is overdue for revision.[129] Totally unconvinced by Porphyry, Iamblichus became the leading exponent of pagan belief and practice, including animal sacrifice, at a time when persecution of Christians was succeeded by persecution of pagans. When the Emperor Julian some years later tried to reinstate pagan religion during his brief reign (AD 361-3), and restored sacrifice as his first act, he took the writings of Iamblichus as his guide, and, according to the archaeologists, he installed the splendid mosaics at Apamea, in Syria, where Iamblichus appears to have taught. I have interpreted these mosaics elsewhere.[130] The one which displays Socrates teaching represents the Neoplatonist philosophy school, but the other, which shows a young lady disrobing, represents, in my opinion, the rhetoric school. To see her as the emblem of the philosophers, we must take it that she is removing the robe of the body to reveal her soul, but that does not appear to be what she is revealing. She is named in the mosaic as Cassiopeia, the figures of persuasion (*peithô*) and judgment (*krisis*) are standing by, and Cassiopeia is being crowned in the presence of Poseidon. I believe this advertises the teaching practices of rhetoric schools, which used to set their pupils a theme from mythology and require them to argue that the verdict should have gone the other way. In the original story, Cassiopeia was not crowned in the beauty contest, but disqualified by Poseidon, angered at the challenge to his sea nymphs. Here in the mosaic it is shown how, with the help of persuasion, judgment can be given in the opposite direction. This in turn throws light on the fate of the school. The rhetoric faculty will have continued after Iamblichus' death, when many of the philosophers left. And Julian will not have been placing his mosaics in a dead memorial to his late philosophical hero, but encouraging a continuing school to resume its classes in pagan philosophy.[131]

We are helped to imagine the atmosphere of the school under Iamblichus by Eunapius, who portrays him sacrificing at dawn in one of his several suburban villas, accompanied by members of his school who had earlier urged him to admit them to his private rites.[132]

Quarterly n.s. 42, 1992, 129-41.

[129] E.R. Dodds, drawing on Bidez for Porphyry, in the *Oxford Classical Dictionary*, 2nd ed. s.v. 'Iamblichus', 'Porphyry'.

[130] Richard Sorabji, 'The ancient commentators on Aristotle' in *Aristotle Transformed: The Ancient Commentators and Their Influence*, London and Ithaca NY 1990, 1-30, at 9-10; Jean-Charles Balty, 'Julian et Apamée, aspects de la restauration de l'Hellénisme et de la politique antichrétienne de l'empéreur', *Dialogues d'histoire ancienne* 1974, 267-304; Janine et Jean-Charles Balty, 'Un programme philosophique sous la cathédral d'Apamée; l'ensemble néoplatonicien de l'empéreur Julien', in *Texte et Image, Actes du colloque international de Chantilly (13-15 Octobre 1982)*, Paris 167-76.

[131] The same lecturers could often teach both subjects. The philosopher Syrianus, for example, also wrote on Rhetoric, as Steven Strange reminds me.

[132] Eunapius *Lives of the Sophists* 458-9.

Iamblichus replies to the questions which Porphyry had posed in his *Letter to Anebo* for Egyptian religious practice. The magisterial answer purports to come from Anebo's teacher (Anebo is the *mathêtês*).[133] That piece of one-up-manship against Porphyry is augmented by another if the hypothesis is right that the teacher's name, Abamon, meant in Egyptian Father of God.[134] Elsewhere Iamblichus expresses actual disdain, despite Porphyry having dedicated a book to him (*On 'Know Thyself'*). Iamblichus is recorded as saying that Porphyry speaks neither Platonically (*Platonikôs*) nor with truth, and that his manner is not philosophical, but full of barbarian pretension.[135] The actual author of Abamon's words is Iamblichus himself and the treatise is called *On the Mysteries of the Egyptians*.[136] Iamblichus preserves some fragments of Porphyry's lost *Letter to Anebo*. He has Abamon address Porphyry as 'you', and explain that he is offering arguments addressed to the intellect on Porphyry's account, although he does not himself think that this is the most appropriate approach.[137]

Iamblichus agrees with Porphyry on divination, rejecting divination through physical techniques,[138] and insisting, through the mouth of Pythagoras, on the importance of a strict diet for prophecy.[139] As regards sacrifice, he concedes to Porphyry that there are gods at different levels, who call for different kinds of sacrifice, but he holds that the material gods require material sacrifice, inlcuding blood.[140] He acknowledges Porphyry's reminder that the gods do not need our sacrifice.[141] But he insists that we ourselves benefit, and not only as Porphyry said from a pure life, but from the rituals of theurgy. The invocations can raise us to union with God.[142] In giving this power to invocations, Iamblichus disagrees not only with Porphyry, but also with Plotinus, who had said that after the intellectual effort of ascending to union with the Intellect, one must simply wait as for the sunrise for union with the One.[143] Porphyry is right that the gods cannot be affected (are *apatheis*). But they can still act, not by being affected, but through their will (*boulêsis*).[144] Moreover, when we speak

---

[133] Proclus *in Tim* 1.152.29; 153.9.

[134] Iamblichus *On the Mysteries of Egypt* 1.1, p. 2,7-14.

[135] H.D. Saffrey, 'Abamon, pseudonyme de Jamblique', in Robert B. Palmer and Robert Hamerton-Kelly, eds., *Philomathes, Studies and Essays in Memory of Philip Merlan*, The Hague 1971.

[136] There is a convenient Budé edition with French translation by Des Places (1966), English translations by Thomas Taylor (1821), A. Wilder (1881-5).

[137] Iamblichus *Myst.* 1.2, p. 6,10; p. 7,6; cf. 5.13, 216,16-217,2.

[138] Ibid. 6.4.

[139] Iamblichus *Life of Pythagoras* 24,106.

[140] Iamblichus *Myst.* 5.17; 5.19; cf. 5.14,218, 5-10; 5.24,234,18-235,9.

[141] Ibid. 5.10-11.

[142] Ibid. 1.12.

[143] Plotinus 5.5.8 (3-7).

[144] Iamblichus *Myst.* 1.12.

of them as angry, this is still not a case of their being affected, but is a metaphor for our stepping into the shade.[145] Sacrifice can secure us benefits because of a sympathy (*sumpatheia*) that connects the whole universe.[146] Moreover, the belonging (*oikeiôsis, oikeiotês*) which in Theophrastus united us to the animals and in the Stoics estranged us from them, is here used in a third way. It is said to connect animals to their creators, the demons and, more indirectly, to the gods and the supreme god. By an irony, however, this produces an almost Stoic result. It makes animals suitable material for sacrifice, because it enables us to set in motion all these divinities.[147] It also reverses the usual order by making animals in one way intermediate between gods and humans.

There could hardly be a greater contrast with Porphyry's description, in his *Life of Plotinus*, of how two live birds were used, when Plotinus' personal god was conjured up by an Egyptian priest.[148] The birds were not to attract demons, but rather for protection, presumably the protection of those participating, against evil demons. But the birds were (misguidedly) strangled, and this, so far from setting divinities in motion, actually stopped the god speaking. The story has been connected with Porphyry's point in the treatise on *Abstinence* that one must abstain from all birds, if one wants to be rid of terrestrial beings and become established with the celestial gods.[149]

Iamblichus has one more surprise in store for us. He appeals to Aristotle's brilliant defence of tragedy and comedy in the *Poetics*. They should not be expelled from the state as dangers in the way that Plato recommended in *Republic* Book 10, for according to Aristotle they perform the valuable function of arousing pity and fear and so purging us (*katharsis*) of 'such' emotions.[150] We should expect this theory to be discussed again and again, but in fact the strict Aristotelian idea virtually disappears,[151] until it reappears here in Iamblichus' defence of ritual. This, too, can purge us of emotions. Iamblichus extends the theory to invocations (*klêseis*) and to obscene sights and sounds in

---

[145] Ibid. 1.13.

[146] Ibid. 5.7.

[147] Ibid. 5.9; 6.3.

[148] I am grateful to Rebecca Resinski for drawing the contrast: Porphyry *Life of Plotinus* 10.

[149] Porphyry *Abstinence* 4.16, cited by E.R. Dodds, *The Greeks and the Irrational*, Berkeley and Los Angeles 1951, Appendix 2.3.

[150] I shall argue in a later study that 'such' must include not only pity, but also grief, the companion emotion felt by 'The part that hungers for tears' in the Platonic passage that Aristotle is answering (*Republic* 606A-B). Pity reduces grief.

[151] For the fragmentary references in Philodemus *On Poems* V, see Richard Janko, 'From catharsis to the Aristotelian mean', in A. Rorty, ed., *Essays on Aristotle's Poetics*, Princeton 1992. Cf Theophrastus fr. 716 W.H.S.G.; Plutarch *Quaest. Conv.* 657A; *On Control of Anger* 455C. The summary of Aristotle in the *Tractatus Coïslinianus* is later (sixth century AD). See Richard Janko, *Aristotle Poetics*, Indianapolis 1987.

religious rituals.[152] He refers to the setting up of phalli and the uttering of obscenities (*aiskhrologia*; *tôn aiskhrôn rhêsis*).[153] His idea is that a moderate exercise (*metrios energeia*) of our emotions can first make them moderate,[154] which is the Aristotelian ideal, and then rid us of them (*apallagê*), as required by the Stoics.

The contrast with Porphyry is again striking.[155] Both authors are agreed that persuasion (*peithô*), rather than force (*bia*), is the best way to remove the emotions.[156] Porphyry connects freedom from emotion not with the Aristotelian term *katharsis*, but with cognate terms, with purity (*katharotês*), purifying (*kathareusai*)[157] and with the purifications (*katharmoi*) required by Empedocles after the pollution (*miasma*) induced by killing animals.[158] But Porphyry's method of persuasion is to avoid all experience of temptations, for example to avoid the sight of things like food which arouse the passions and to attend to things of the intellect.[159] His idea is the Pythagorean one, that if you are merciful[160] to animals, you will be humane to your fellow-humans.[161] This is almost the opposite of Iamblichus' suggestion, that an actual exercise (*energeia*)[162] of the emotions, if moderate, can rid us of them. The two philosophers even give the same example of obscene language (*aiskhrorhêmosunê* in Porphyry), to illustrate their opposite theories.[163]

The denial of transmigration

I suspect that at this period the debate on the transmigration of souls between men and animals was also partly driven by the need to justify animal sacrifice. At any rate, it was relevant to the status of animals. Those two fellow-students, if fellow-students they were,[164] Plotinus the Neoplatonist and Origen the Christian both allowed that human souls might transmigrate into animals or even plants.[165] The idea was

---

[152] Iamblichus *Myst.* 1.11, 38,13-40,8; 1.12, 41,18-42,1.

[153] Ibid. 1.11, 39,14-40,8; 41,18-42,1. His alternative explanation is that the obscenities work as an aversion therapy, 1.11,39,3-12.

[154] Ibid. 1.11, 40,1; 4-5; 9-10.

[155] I am again indebted to Rebecca Resinski for several of the following suggestions, and to Terry Irwin for discussion of the Iamblichan passage.

[156] Porphyry *Abstinence* 1.32.1; 1.38.2; Iamblichus *Myst.* 1.11, 40,2.

[157] e.g. Porphyry *Abstinence* 2.34; 2.45; 2.61 and (for purifying) 1.35.

[158] Ibid. 2.31.

[159] Ibid. 1.32; 1.35; 1.37; 1.45.3.

[160] *Praotês* at 3.20.7 means mercifulness, not, as at Aristotle *NE* 1125b26 ff, moderation in temper.

[161] Porphyry *Abstinence* 3.20.7; 3.26.6-7; rejected by Heracleides of Pontus at 1.23.

[162] Iamblichus *Myst.* 1.11, 39,16.

[163] Porphyry *Abstinence* 1.34.2; Iamblichus *Myst.* 1.11, 38,14-39,13. I hope in a future book to consider ancient views on what to do with your feelings.

[164] The doubts of H. Dörrie are now reinforced by Mark Edwards, 'Ammonius, tutor of Origen', *Journal of Ecclesiastical History* 1992.

[165] For plants, see Plotinus 3.4.2; Origen *On First Principles* 1.8.

welcome to Plotinus, as helping to solve the problem of the apparent evil of animals eating each other. This is all right, because they are like actors who will change their clothes and reappear on the stage.[166] Transmigration was similarly used in the Islamic and Jewish traditions, both to justify our own killing of animals,[167] and to explain present animal suffering as expiation for the sins of a past incarnation.[168]

The Greek Neoplatonists after Plotinus, however, possibly Porphyry (but see below), certainly Iamblichus followed by Hierocles of Alexandria, denied there was any transmigration of human souls into animals. They took Plato's references to transmigration metaphorically: a man acquires a beast-like character, which can happen both in this life and in the next incarnation.[169] Iamblichus further attributed to Pythagoras the view that there was no transmigration of human souls into *sacrificial* animals[170] – a hint that he saw the transmigration issue as relevant to sacrifice. Transmigration must be denied, or sacrifice will involve killing our kin. If he thought this way, it was no doubt the sacrifice, not the meat-eating that he sought to defend. The extreme abstemiousness of his admirer Proclus is recorded in the Life of him by Marinus, yet he, too, thought it necessary to taste the sacrifice.[171]

The metaphorical reading of Plato is very strained, and consequently another interpretation began to flourish, an interpretation which I see as adventurously different.[172] Aeneas of Gaza thinks it began with Syrianus and Proclus, while Proclus cites as the inventor an earlier figure, Iamblichus' pupil Theodore of Asine, who, he says, convinced him. It further convinced Sallustius and Hermeias of Alexandria.[173]

---

[166] Plotinus 3.2.15 (16-33).

[167] Râzî (AD 865-925) *On the Philosophic Life*, translated by A.J. Arberry, *Asian Review* 1949, 703-13, at 707-8 (reference supplied by Thérèse-Anne Druart).

[168] This argument is opposed in the first half of the eleventh century AD by Yûsuf al-Basîr, *Refutation of the Supporters of Transmigration*, translated into French by Georges Vajda, in Robert B. Palmer and Robert Hamerton-Kelly, eds., *Philomathes, Studies and Essays in Memory of Philip Merlan*, The Hague 1971, 281-90.

[169] For the controversial case of Porphyry, see below. For Iamblichus, see Nemesius *Nature of Man* 2.18 (115-118M). The same view appears to be taken by Hierocles of Alexandria, *Commentary on the Golden Verses*, Teubner ed. Koehler, 96,24-97,5.

[170] Iamblichus *Life of Pythagoras* 85,18.

[171] Marinus *Life of Proclus* 12 and 19.

[172] Here I agree with Smith against Dörrie, who sees it as only a variant on Porphyry's metaphorical interpretation. Heinrich Dörrie, 'Kontroversen um die Seelenwanderung im kaiserzeitlichen Platonismus', *Hermes* 85, 1957, 165-92, repr. in his *Platonica Minora*, Munich 1976: see p. 438. Andrew Smith, 'Did Porphyry reject the transmigration of human souls into animals?' *Rheinisches Museum* 127, 1984, 277-84. See also Werner Deuse, *Untersuchungen zur mittelplatonischen und neuplatonischen Seelenlehre*, Akad. d. Wiss. u. Lit. zu Mainz, Abh. d. Geistes- u. Sozialwiss. Kl., Wiesbaden 1983, 129-67; and his earlier *Theodoros von Asine* 158, n. 298; Wilhelm Purpus, *Die Anschauungen des Porphyrius über die Tierseele*, Inaugural Dissertation, Ansbach 1899, p. 63.

[173] Theodore ap. Proclum *in Remp.* 2,310,15; Syrianus and Proclus ap. Aeneam Gaz.,

According to this theory, human souls can animate animals, but by remote control, without entering their bodies. This had the advantage of coming closer to Plato's belief in literal transmigration, while still presumably enabling Iamblichus' successors to ward off criticism of animal sacrifice: your granddam's soul cannot be inside the sacrificed animals. The verb *eiskrinesthai* means that the human soul is allotted to an animal, not that it actually enters the animal,[174] which would defeat the purpose of the theory.

As a matter of fact, a theory of remote association, of a rather different kind, is anticipated in still earlier writings. Already in the first century AD, Plutarch's *On the Daemon of Socrates* describes how there is something in contact with the head that supports (*anekhei*) the soul like a buoy (*akroploun*). The vulgar call it intellect (*nous*), but in fact, being external, it is a daemon.[175] Plutarch is echoing Plato's *Timaeus*, where it is said that the highest part of the soul resides at the top of the body, and suspends (*anakremmanun*) our head by rooting it in the heavens.[176]

After Plutarch, but still before Theodore, we find Plotinus considering two possibilities: either the human soul does not enter (*eisedu*) the animal at all, or it is present without being present or belonging to the animal. If it does not enter the animal at all, the animal is generated by some illumination (*ellampsis*) from universal soul.[177] Another Plotinian passage written earlier, tells us more.[178] The illumination (*ellampsis*) from the soul of the All is like an outline in matter. A person is described in what precedes as having several souls, but if the soul that was joined to the person when it was human (the rational soul?) follows (*sunepesthai*) the (sensory?) soul that has chosen the nature of a beast, it gives it the *logos* (rationale) of a beast, a *logos* that it contains within itself. It does so by tracing the illumination or outline left by the soul of the All in matter. It thus not only makes, but, like a dancer on the stage, becomes what it shapes. The later of the two passages says:

> And how does living animal include beasts? First, if, as is said, there are in beasts human souls that have erred, the separable part of the soul does not come to belong to the beasts, but is present, without being present to them. Their consciousness includes the image of soul with

Theophrastus PG 85, 896B-897A; Proclus *in Tim.* 3.294,22 ff, Diehl; *in Remp.* 2,309,28 ff; 334,14, Kroll; Sallustius *On the Gods* 20.1; Hermeias *in Phaedr.* 170,16, Couvreur.

[174] Smith p. 279.

[175] Plutarch *On the Daemon of Socrates* 591D ff. I owe the reference to Ian Kidd.

[176] Plato *Timaeus* 90A.

[177] Plotinus 1.1.11 (9-15).

[178] Plotinus 6.7.6-7. I am grateful to John Dillon for this extra reference. The interpretation of the two souls as rational and sensory is confirmed by Pierre Hadot, *Plotin, Traité 38*, Éditions du Cerf, Paris 1988, 226-8.

body. A body like that is then made by an image of soul. Alternatively, if the soul of a human has not entered (*eisedu*), the beast becomes a living animal of that kind by illumination from the universal soul.

It is doubtful that the non-entry alternative could still qualify as transmigration. And the other alternative gives us transmigration only in a qualified form. This may help to account for the disagreement in our sources as to whether Plotinus' pupil Porphyry accepted transmigration into animals. We are emphatically told by Augustine that Porphyry rejected the transmigration of human souls into animals.[179] But Nemesius, in a passage that elsewhere shows signs of confusion, implies that Porphyry accepted transmigration.[180] What are we to think? Two scholars have accommodated Nemesius' view, by finding support for it in a quotation from Porphyry in two sources which refer to humans being reincarnated in a new bodily shape (*tên tôn sômatôn morphên*, Aeneas), or body (*sôma*, Stobaeus).[181] I do not think this conclusive on its own, for are the new bodies animal ones? On the contrary, they sound rather like *human* ones, because the surrounding text is offering the metaphorical interpretation according to which humans in the next incarnation are merely *like* animals. They do not change their *essential* nature (*phusis*, Aeneas), although they do take on the character (*phusis*, Stobaeus 447,19) of a lion or wolf. Would not a change into animal bodies be an *essential* change? Admittedly, we cannot be sure that it would, so so far the issue remains open.

May the solution not be that because Porphyry learnt two theories from Plotinus, both of which make the human soul's association with beasts remote in varying degrees, it was not clear to readers whether to count this as genuine transmigration into animal bodies? Plotinus and Porphyry would presumably have been more concerned that their accounts should be faithful to Plato than that they should merit the label 'transmigration'. The conflicting interpretations of Porphyry may have been further provoked by Iamblichus' report that Porphyry was in two minds on a related issue. He was tempted (not in the extant writings, but perhaps in lectures, if that is what Iamblichus means by 'I heard') by the more extreme view, which Iamblichus went on to develop from him, that animals have a non-rational soul of a different substance from the human soul.[182] Iamblichus wanted to withdraw

---

[179] Augustine *City of God* 10.30.

[180] Nemesius *Nature of Man* 2.18, 115-118M. Porphyry's view at 117M that all soul is rational is connected at 115M with the view that there is transmigration.

[181] Smith and Deuse using Stobaeus *Ecl.* 1.445 f and Aeneas of Gaza *Theophrastus* 893A-B.

[182] Iamblichus in Stobaeus *Ecl.* 1, 365,17-21; 375,24-8; 458,12-14. Dörrie, p.434 accepts that Porphyry distinguishes non-rational souls, and even suggests that he denies soul to animals.

rationality from animals altogether. I shall conclude by explaining this development.

The withdrawal of rationality

It is emphatically not Porphyry's intention in the extant writings to deny a rational soul to animals, a denial which he would have seen as disadvantageous to them. Porphyry, as we know from the treatise on *Abstinence*, regards animals as having rational souls. Indeed, there is much to be said for Nemesius' view that Porphyry makes *all* soul rational.[183] For in the *Sentences* (if we ignore the embryo stage), Porphyry appears to deny a soul to plants,[184] and to describe soul, without exception, as containing things in a rational way (*logikôs*).[185] The only person to cast doubt on this interpretation of Porphyry is Iamblichus, in the passage already mentioned which portrays Porphyry as tempted, possibly in his lectures, to postulate a non-rational soul for animals, different from the human soul and of a different substance. But if we take Porphyry's extant writing, both in the *Sentences* and in *Abstinence*, we find him very emphatic that animal souls are rational. He resists the suggestion that we need to contrast rational with non-rational souls. The only thing that needs to be contrasted with the rational is what lacks soul altogether.[186] It is dialectically inept, he says, quoting Plutarch, to expect a person to grant that some ensouled things are irrational, when that person holds (here Plutarch travesties the Stoics) that all sense perception involves understanding (*sunesis*), and there is no animal which lacks belief (*doxa*) and reasoning (*logismos*).[187] Even birds and fish have reasoning.[188] It is only their bodies which make it more or less prominent,[189] but, in fact, animals differ from man only more or less, that is as a matter of degree, and not in substance.[190]

How different from this is Iamblichus' view that animal souls are non-rational.[191] And this claim was exploited in order to generate a very different kind of remote control theory. It draws a sharp distinction between the soul which the animal already has, without needing any human soul, and the human soul which may come to be added to it. The animal soul is described as non-rational and the

---

[183] Nemesius *Nature of Man* 2.18 (115-118M). For embryos, see p. 101.
[184] Porphyry *Sentences* 12.
[185] Ibid. 10.
[186] Porphyry *Abstinence* 3.21.2.
[187] Ibid. 3.21.4, direct quotation from Plutarch *Sollertia* 960D-E.
[188] Ibid. 3.9.4.
[189] Ibid. 3.8.6. Cf. the Pythagoreans, ap. Aëtium, 5.20 (*Dox. Gr.* 432a15 ff).
[190] Ibid. 3.7.1.
[191] Iamblichus erroneously linked with Porphyry ap. Aeneam Gaz. *Theophrastus* 893A-B. Cf. Iamblichus ap. Simplicium (?) *in DA 3* 187,35 ff (cf. 211,1 ff) contrasting our rational perception with (their?) irrational perception.

human soul as rational.[192] The same description is found in the metaphorical interpretation, according to which humans merely become *like* a wolf or lion. The reason for denying in this case, as in the remote control theory, that the human soul actually enters the animal is that a rational soul cannot become a non-rational one.[193] Porphyry's view that all soul is rational would remove this barrier to transmigration. The view that animal souls are *non*-rational is one on which we saw Plato wavering in Chapter One. But it is endorsed by Iamblichus, Proclus, Sallustius, Hermeias and Simplicius,[194] although the source that couples Porphyry with Iamblichus is presumably wrong.

It is Iamblichus who departs from Porphyry in this way and makes the animal soul irrational. So Nemesius should not be criticised for saying that Iamblichus 'runs in the opposite direction' from Porphyry.[195] The departure is indeed a major one, and we have seen that Nemesius may have been right in a sense in attributing to Porphyry another difference: the acceptance of the transmigration of human souls into animals, even if Augustine had some justification for denying the attribution.

Iamblichus goes even further in his departure from Porphyry. He takes Plotinus to be removing the irrational capacities (*alogoi dunameis*) of sense perception, appearance and memory from the soul altogether and assigning them to the body.[196] This would take us back to a position like that of Plato's *Phaedo*, where non-rational functions were ascribed to the body. It was only later that Plato hit on the theory of the *Republic*, *Timaeus* and *Phaedrus* that there are non-rational parts of the soul, to accommodate the irrational functions. Proclus is also attracted by the idea that Plato's non-rational parts of the soul,[197] and more generally human souls as embodied,[198] are not properly soul, but rather mere images (*eidôla*) of soul. But on the other hand, he is in the same breath willing to say that those irrational animals who have sense perception, appearance and memory, do partake of intellect

---

[192] Proclus *in Remp.* 310,4; Hermeias *in Phdr.* 170,17-18; Sallustius *On the Gods* 20. Nemesius is presumably wrong when he diverges from these sources by saying that Theodore makes all souls rational, *Nature of Man*, 2.18,117M.

[193] Aeneas *Theophrastus* 893A-B; Proclus *in Tim.* 3.294,25-6; cf. for the remote control theory Sallustius loc. cit.

[194] Proclus *Platonic Theology* 3.128; Hermeias *in Phdr.* 170,17; Sallustius *On the Gods* 20; Iamblichus (and Porphyry) ap. Aeneam Gaz. *Theophrastus* 893A-B; Simplicius (?), endorsing Iamblichus, *in DA 3* 187,35 ff; cf. 211,1 ff (if Simplicius, rather than Priscian, is the author of these passages). Cf. further attributions without names in Nemesius 2.18,115-118M (Platonists) and Proclus *in Tim.* 3.294,25-6.

[195] Nemesius *Nature of Man* 2.18 (115-118M), criticised by Dörrie, 434.

[196] Iamblichus in Stobaeus *Ecl.* 1, 369,20 ff, Wachsmuth.

[197] Proclus *Platonic Theology* 3.128; *On the Subsistence of Evils* 25,223-4.

[198] Proclus *Platonic Theology* 3.6, Saffrey and Westerink 23,23, offering a rather contrived interpretation of Plato *Philebus* 21A-D.

(*nous*), as opposed to reason. This is not because of any admiration for animals, but for the purpose of expanding the empire of intellect. Proclus gives as the ground for his decision that when Plato's *Philebus* imagines a life bereft of intellect, he robs it of all cognition (*gnôsis*).[199]

To sum up, Iamblichus was a crucial figure. He suppressed the earlier Platonic tradition, so prominent in Plutarch and Porphyry, of granting animals reason. And his pupil, Theodore of Asine, found an even more effective way than his of denying the transmigration of human souls into animal bodies. Earlier, Plotinus, perhaps followed by Porphyry, had considered ways of associating the human rational soul with the animal that were more or less remote. Iamblichus denied transmigration outright, because on his view of things, it would involve a rational human soul becoming non-rational. But how then to square the text of Plato? The metaphorical interpretation was one way. But Theodore's remote control theory was another, which fully incorporated Iamblichus' denial of a rational soul to animals. This persuaded most of the Neoplatonists who followed. Most important of all, Iamblichus defeated Porphyry's attempt to steer Neoplatonism away from animal sacrifice.

---

[199] Proclus *in Tim.* 3.330, Diehl; *Elements of Theology* 64; *De Malorum Subsistentia* 25, Isaac.

CHAPTER FOURTEEN

Augustine on irrational animals and the Christian tradition

Although Christians were against animal sacrifice, this was not out of kindness to animals, but, as observed in Chapter Thirteen, because Christ had already made the great sacrifice. St Paul notoriously reinterprets the Old Testament when he quotes Deuteronomy 25.4:

Though shalt not muzzle the mouth of the ox that treadeth out the corn.

In other words, the ox should be allowed to eat a little. St Paul's comment is

Doth God take care for oxen?[1]

And he goes on to give a metaphorical interpretation of the saying instead.

This reversed the meaning of the original, and Augustine had to reassure people that God did take providential care for their oxen, despite St Paul's remark.[2] As seen in Chapter Twelve, Augustine's God takes care of individual animals, not merely of species.

Augustine

Augustine does, however, continue the harsher new tradition started by St Paul in two important passages. In a treatise of AD 388 *On the Manichaean and Catholic Ways of Life*,[3] he takes up the challenge which we have found in Porphyry on Christ's lack of concern for the Gadarene swine, although he may be unaware that Porphyry is associated with the challenge.[4] It is perfectly true that Christ did not

---

[1] 1 Corinthians 9.9.

[2] Augustine, *Enarr. in Psalmos* 145.13-14; cf. 34.1.6. I owe this reference to Henry Chadwick, who takes it that Augustine is reassuring farmers who concluded only the pagan gods would care for their beasts.

[3] Augustine *de moribus ecclesiae catholicae et de moribus Manichaeorum* 2.17.54.

[4] In *Ep.* 102 Augustine knows of some of Porphyry's arguments against the Christians,

spare them, and that is because Christ was a Stoic as regards animals. That in effect is what Augustine is saying. For he ascribes to Christ the Stoic theory that animals cannot be brought within the community of just dealings, because they lack reason.[5]

> And first Christ shows your abstention from killing animals and tearing plants to be the greatest superstition. He judged that we had no community in justice (*societas iuris*) with beasts and trees, and sent the devils into a flock of swine, and withered a tree by his curse, when he had found no fruit in it. ...

The Manichaean holy men did not eat meat and did not themselves pluck the vegetarian food which they ate. Augustine invokes the Stoic theory against them a second time, when he says that he would at least regard them as observant if their motive were (as it was not) that animals die with pain. But, in fact, we disregard even this consideration, on the (Stoic) ground that animals do not belong to the legally protected community, because they lack reason:

> And from this killing you debar even your followers, for it seems to you worse than that of trees. Here I do not much disapprove of your senses, that is of your physical senses. For we see and appreciate from their cries that animals die with pain. But man disregards this in a beast, with which, as having no rational soul, he is linked by no community of law (*societas legis*).[6]

The Manichaean holy men were motivated by the belief that by eating vegetarian food they could release the divine trapped in it, so that god could return to his kingdom. Augustine asks if they would not release soul more quickly, if they spent their time cutting down trees and killing wolves.[7] He returns to Manichaean practices in the *City of God* Book 1, written by AD 413. If you will not kill animals, then you should not kill plants either. But that is the error of the Manichaeans.[8] Parallel arguments had already been recorded in Porphyry's treatise *On Abstinence from Animal Food*. It has been doubted that Augustine knew of this,[9] and there is no necessity to suppose he did, although

---

but only from a correspondent. He speaks again of this correspondent's information in *Retractations* 2.31, but adds that the arguments must be by a different Porphyry from the philosopher, whom he indeed treats with respect as a worthy opponent in the *City of God*. I thank Gerard O'Daly for the information.

[5] This is not actually gainsaid in the interesting passage to which Gillian Clark has helpfully drawn attention (Augustine *Gen. Lit.* 3.8, discussed in her 'The Fathers and the Animals: the rule of reason?' in Andrew Linzey, ed., *Animals on the Agenda*) where Augustine allows that birds and even fish have a life close to reason.

[6] Augustine *de moribus Manichaeorum* 2.17, 59.

[7] Augustine *de moribus* 2.17.58-9.

[8] Augustine *City* 1.20.

[9] Aemilius Winter, *de doctrinae Neoplatonicae in Augustini Civitate Dei vestigiis*, diss.

Eusebius had read it earlier and Augustine's contemporary Jerome made the fullest use of it.[10] Porphyry attributes the sorites argument ('we'll have to spare plants next') first to the Stoics and Peripatetics, and then to the philologist Clodius, who may be drawing on the early Platonist Heraclides Ponticus (388-310 BC).[11] He also attributes to Clodius/Heraclides the argument that animals should like being killed, because their souls will be released for reincarnation into men. In this version, it is added that animals would be glad to become young again.[12]

The *City of God* 1.20 discusses the commandment, 'Thou shalt not kill', and insists that it forbids suicide. But some people had raised the question whether the commandment did not forbid killing animals too. It is then that Augustine asks, 'Why not apply it to plants?' and he replies that it should be applied to neither. For plants have no feelings, and as regards animals, he invokes the Stoic doctrine once again. Animals lack reason, and so have no rational community with us:

> It is the more evident that a man may not kill himself since in the text 'Thou shalt not kill', which has nothing added after it, no one may be taken as exempted, not even he to whom the commandment is addressed. Hence some people try to extend this commandment to beasts and cattle also, so that it does not even allow any of them to be killed. Why not then extend it to plants and to anything fixed by its roots in the earth, and nourished by it? For even this class of things is said to be alive, although it does not feel, and so it can die too, and thus be killed when violence is done to it. And so the Apostle, speaking of seeds of this kind, says, 'What you sow does not come to life, unless it dies'. And in the Psalm is written, 'He kills their vines with hail'. But do we for this reason infer, when we hear 'Thou shalt not kill', that it is wrong to clear brushwood, and subscribe as if completely mad to the error of the Manichaeans?
>
> Rather we set these ravings aside, and if when we read 'Thou shalt not kill', we do not on that account accept that this is said of thickets, since they have no feelings (*sensus*), neither do we accept it is said about irrational living things, whether flying, swimming, walking, or crawling, because they are not associated in a community (*sociantur*) with us by reason (*ratio*), since it is not given to them to have reason in common (*communis*) with us. Hence it is by a very just ordinance of the Creator that their life and death is subordinated to our use.[13]

Freiburg im Breisgau 1928, not currently available to me. But Augustine's familiarity with *Abst.* is assumed by Georges Folliet, 'Deificari in otio: Augustin, Epistula 10,2', *Recherches Augustiniennes* 2, 1962, 225-36, who cites in the same vein W. Theiler, *Porphyrios und Augustin*, Halle 1933, 8.

[10] For Eusebius, see K. Mras, *Eusebius, Praeparatio Evangelica* 2, Berlin 1956, 459-61; J. Sirinelli, in Eusèbe de Césarée *La Préparation Evangelique* 1, *Sources Chrétiennes* 206, Paris 1974, 28-34. For Jerome, Ernestus Bickel, *Diatribe in Senecae Philosophi Fragmenta*, vol. 1 Fragmenta de Matrimonio, Leipzig 1915, 395-420.

[11] Porphyry *Abstinence* 1.6; 1.18.

[12] Porphyry *Abstinence* 1.19. Cf. Râzî *On the Philosophic Life*, translated A.J. Arberry, *Asian Review* 1949, 703-13, at 707-8: this is the only justification for killing domestic animals (Reference from Thérèse-Anne Druart).

[13] Augustine *City of God* 1.20.

We can see here the point at which the Stoic insistence on human reason as the prerequisite for receiving justice became irrevocably embedded in the Christian tradition of the Latin West. In the thirteenth century, Thomas Aquinas quotes Augustine's Stoic argument from *City of God* 1.20, when he reaffirms that it is permissible to kill animals.[14] We shall see that the insistence on reason had not been a settled position among Christian writers in Latin before Augustine.

Augustine concludes the discussion by appealing to Genesis. Because of the Stoic point in *City of God* 1.20 about reason and community, God is just in subordinating animals to us. Once again, Thomas Aquinas repeats the point and quotes Augustine's words.[15] But Augustine's claim that the death of animals, as well as their life, was subordinated to our needs, is an oversimplification of Genesis, an oversimplification recently repeated by the British Minister of Agriculture, Mr Selwyn Gummer, exhorting us to eat beef during an epidemic of mad cow disease. It telescopes together several distinct stages in the story. For, as Thomas Aquinas acknowledges,[16] it was only after the Fall of Man, when things had already gone badly wrong, that man was allowed to kill animals. The dominion granted to man over animals before the fall did not involve killing them. Food was vegetarian.[17] After the fall, Adam and Eve were provided with the skins of animals (not necessarily killed),[18] and it was only in a later generation that Abel became a shepherd and his sacrifice of animals was preferred to Cain's vegetarian sacrifice.[19] It was later still that God made a new covenant with Noah, and that only after Noah had protected all kinds of animals, even unclean ones, from the flood by preserving them in the ark. Noah then made a burnt offering (not for eating) of animals, and God explicitly extended his original provisions, by allowing man to eat animals as well as green plants.[20] It is on this second agreement that Augustine's account needs to rely. It was still later again that the threat of human sacrifice arose, when Abraham was commanded to kill his son, but then allowed to substitute a ram.[21]

Animals for man before Augustine

Augustine's view that animals exist for humans was in line with a long

---

[14] Thomas Aquinas *Summa Theologiae* 2.2, q. 64, a. 1.

[15] Thomas Aquinas *Summa Theologiae* 2.2, q. 64, a. 1; cf. *contra Gentiles* 3.112; *de Caritate* a. 7, ad. 5.

[16] Thomas Aquinas *Summa Theologiae* 2.1, q. 102, a. 6, ad. 2 refers to the time after the Flood.

[17] Genesis 1.26-30.   [18] Genesis 3.21.   [19] Genesis 4.3-5.

[20] Genesis 8.20-9.4   [21] Genesis 22.

earlier tradition, which can be copiously illustrated from pagan and Christian sources alike.[22] The earliest attribution to a Greek philosopher that I have noted is Xenophon's ascription of the view to Socrates.[23] This takes us back to the fifth century BC. Aristotle asserts that animals exist for humans and infers that there is such a thing as a just war. This concept, here introduced for the first time into Western Philosophy, is surprisingly applied in the first instance to hunting animals, and in the second to capturing those who are naturally slaves.[24] The most extreme elaboration of the idea that animals are for man is found in the Stoics. According to Chrysippus, bugs are useful for waking us up and mice for making us put our things away carefully. Cocks have come into being for a useful purpose too: they wake us up, catch scorpions, and arouse us to battle, but they must be eaten, so that there won't be more chicks than is useful (*khreia*).[25] As for the pig, it is given a soul in place of salt, to keep it fresh for us to eat.[26] Philo not only takes over into Jewish philosophy the idea of animals,[27] except snakes and suchlike,[28] being for man, but declares it sacrilege to question Providence by denying this.[29]

But there was opposition. Aristotle's successor Theophrastus shows his independence again. He is aware of the argument that God has given animals for our use. But he insists that they are still not ours, and so not suitable for sacrifice.[30] The sceptic Carneades replies to the Stoics that if it is the natural function (*telos*) of the pig to be eaten, it ought to benefit from being eaten, because that is what function implies.[31] Not all of the Christian fathers were uncompromising. Basil of Caesarea insists that animals live not for us alone, but for themselves and for God.[32] And John Chrysostom points out that animals exist not necessarily for our use, but to proclaim the power of

---

[22] Some, but not all, of the examples are cited in A.S. Pease's note to Cicero *de Natura Deorum* 2.154 (cf. his 'Caeli enarrant', *Harvard Theological Review* 34, 1941, 163-200; J. Haussleiter, *Der Vegetarismus in der Antike*, Berlin 1935, 247-8; H. von Arnim, *SVF* 2.1152-67.

[23] Xenophon *Mem.* 4.3.9-10.

[24] Aristotle *Pol.* 1.8, 1256b15-26.

[25] Plutarch *Sto. Rep.* 1044D; 1049A.

[26] Porphyry *Abstinence* 3.20 (drawing on Plutarch); Cicero *ND* 2.160; *Fin.* 5.38, Philo *Opif.* 66 (*SVF* 2.722); Plutarch *Quaest. Conv.* 685C; Pliny *NH* 8.207; Varro *de RR* 2,4,10; ascribed to Chrysippus' predecessor, Cleanthes: Clement *Stromateis* 7.6.33; cf. 2.20.105.

[27] Philo *Quod deus sit immutabilis* 4,74-8; *Questions on Genesis and Solutions* 94.

[28] Philo ap. Eusebium *Praep. Ev.* 8.14, 397B-D.

[29] Philo *de Animalibus* 100.

[30] Theophrastus ap. Porphyrium *Abstinence* 2.12-13.

[31] Porphyry *Abstinence* 3.20. Carneades here overlooks a second, related meaning of 'function', to refer to the intentions of the designer or user; Richard Sorabji, 'Function', *Philosophical Quarterly*, 1964.

[32] Basil *Liturgy*.

the Creator.[33] In the twelfth century, the medieval Jewish philosopher Maimonides was to insist that since we could have been created without most other things, although perhaps not without plants, those other things cannot exist for us.[34] Moreover, God's goal in creation is not the production of mankind, but of as many species as possible – the principle of plenitude.[35] But Maimonides does make a concession: God's Providence is concerned with us, not with individuals below the human level. And in evidence he again reinforces the importance of reason, because he says that man is the only species endowed with intellect.[36]

It is not at all obvious why it should be supposed that animals exist for us, and for us not merely to admire, but to kill. Our superiority of intellect is hardly relevant to the latter. But two further arguments were introduced, the utility of animals to us, and the naturalness of our using them. Unfortunately, these arguments cut both ways. The argument on utility is best set out in the pages of Origen's treatise *Against Celsus* and of Porphyry's *On Abstinence from Animal Food*, at a point where he is again drawing from Plutarch.[37] In reply to the utility argument, the Platonists Celsus and Porphyry object that flies are not useful to us, whereas we are very useful to crocodiles.

Origen's position is an extreme one. He does not accept, as Basil was later to do, that animals exist also for their own sakes. On the contrary, he identifies himself with the Stoics who maintain, he says, that irrational animals are made primarily (*proêgoumenôs*) for rational beings. Rational beings have the value of children, irrational the value of the afterbirth (*khorion*) which is created with the child.[38]

On the question of natural equipment, Celsus again shows that the argument cuts both ways: crocodiles are very well equipped to eat us. One might add that bacteria are much better adapted to survive mankind than mankind is to survive bacteria.[39] Origen replies to Celsus that God has given us intelligence to protect us. But Celsus complains that before man developed cities, arts and weapons, he was unprotected. This last point was later to be endorsed by a Christian, Arnobius the teacher of Lactantius, in his reply to those pagans who gave too divine a status to the human soul.[40] There had in fact been a history of discussing the idea that man alone is born defenceless and naked.[41]

[33] John Chrysostom *Homily on Genesis* 7.11-12.
[34] Maimonides *Guide for the Perplexed* 3.13.
[35] Ibid. 3.25.
[36] Ibid. 3.17, translation in Chapter Twelve.
[37] Origen *Against Celsus* 4,74-80, esp. 78-80; Porphyry *Abstinence* 3.20.
[38] Origen *Against Celsus* 4,74; cf. Porphyry *Letter to Marcella* 32, where the embryo's outer covering is for the sake of its development, but is later discarded.
[39] James Lovelock, *Gaia*.
[40] Arnobius *Adversus Nationes* 2.18.
[41] Anaximander A.10 Diels-Kranz (= *Dox. Gr.* 579); Plato *Protagoras* 320D-322A; Aristotle, reporting others, *PA* 4.10, 687a23 ff; Epicurus ap. Lactantium *Opif.* 3.1; 6; Lucretius 5,222-34; Pliny *Nat. Hist.* 7, proem 1-5; Galen *de Usu Partium* 1.2.

There were other contributions, too, to the debate on the naturalness of our using animals. Aristotle argues that just as it is natural for the soul to rule the body, so it is natural for man to domesticate animals, and the domesticated ones have a better nature.[42] Theophrastus and Plutarch, by contrast, represent the sacrificing and eating of animals as a decline from earlier practice and one brought on by war, famine, hunger and poverty.[43] Plutarch challenges anyone who thinks meat-eating natural to kill an animal with his teeth and eat it raw.[44] Clodius, however, again drawing probably on Heraclides Ponticus, had earlier pleaded, rather implausibly, that eating *cooked* meat at least was natural, as shown by its universality.[45]

The Christian appeal to irrationality as ethically crucial

In the Latin West it was Augustine above all who stamped the test of rationality into Christian discussions of how to treat animals. We have seen two examples of how Augustine, followed by Aquinas, accepted the Stoic view that animals can be killed, because, lacking reason, they do not belong in our community. There is an even more far-reaching conclusion in Thomas Aquinas. Citing Aristotle as his authority, Thomas says that intellectual understanding (*intelligere* = *nous*) is the only operation of the soul that is performed without a physical organ, and infers that the souls of brute animals are not immortal like ours.[46] Here the alleged irrationality of animals makes the difference between them and us a chasm, for it is the difference between mortal and immortal souls. Augustine did not go as far as this explicitly. At most, he took a step in this direction, in that some of his proofs of the immortality of the human soul presuppose its rationality.[47] But the idea that the non-rational parts of the soul are mortal is already found in Plato's *Timaeus*,[48] though implicitly denied in his *Phaedrus*, where the immortal gods have the non-rational parts of the soul.[49] It is not surprising, therefore, that Platonists disagreed on whether non-rational soul is immortal.[50] This would have implications for animals

[42] Aristotle *Politics* 1.5.

[43] Theophrastus ap. Porphyrium *Abstinence* 2.9; 2.12; 2.27; Plutarch *Esu.* 1.2, 993C-994B.

[44] Plutarch *Esu.* 1.5.

[45] Porphyry *Abstinence* 1.13.

[46] Thomas Aquinas *Summa Theologiae* 1, q. 75, a. 3, *respondeo* (citing Aristotle *DA* 3.4, 429a24); *Contra Gentiles* 2.82.

[47] Augustine *Soliloquia* 2.22; 2.24; *de Immortalitate Animae* 8-9, with Gerard O'Daly, *Augustine's Philosophy of Mind*, London 1987, 75.

[48] Plato *Timaeus* 69C.

[49] Plato *Phaedrus* 246A-247C.

[50] No: Albinus(?) *Didaskalikos* 25, 178,19; 21-5, Hermann; Porphyry and Proclus ap. Damascium *Comm. on Phaedo* 124,13-20. Yes: Xenocrates, Speusippus, Numenius, Plotinus, Iamblichus, Plutarch of Athens, according to Damascius, loc. cit.

when, from Iamblichus onwards, the Neoplatonists denied them rational souls (see Chapter Thirteen).

Before Augustine, the linkages between animals, reason and immortality were by no means settled. Admittedly, Eusebius had anticipated him to the extent of saying that our souls are immortal and quite unlike those of irrational animals (*aloga zôïa*), despite the views of the philosophers with their raised eyebrows.[51] But Lactantius, who like Augustine wrote in Latin, had not even accepted that animals lack reason (*ratio*). They have reason, can converse (*colloqui*), laugh (*ridere*) and exercise foresight, perhaps perfect foresight (*perfecta providentia*). The only way in which man differs is not through reason, but through what Cicero mentioned, knowledge of God. This knowledge is perfect reason (*ratio perfecta*), or wisdom (*sapientia*), and we are given an upright posture, to look at the heavens, solely for religious reasons.[52] Lactantius further uses our knowledge of God, reminding us that it is (almost) the only thing that distinguishes us from animals, as one of the proofs of the soul's immortality.[53] Our reason forms no part of the proof, and indeed elsewhere Lactantius says that reason has been given to us because of our soul's immortality,[54] not immortality because of our reason. In comparison with this, Augustine has taken a big step towards Thomas Aquinas' view that our rationality implies the immortality of human souls alone.

Lactantius' teacher Arnobius, another Christian writing in Latin, had taken a similar view. Answering pagans who speak of our souls as divine (he refers to followers of Plato, Pythagoras and Hermes Trismegistus),[55] he replies that we are little different from the animals. In many men there is not much sign of reason, whereas in animals there are images of reason and wisdom which we cannot copy, and if they had had hands, they would have produced new works of art.[56]

Some early Christians had taken another tack. Not accepting the rationality of animals, Origen none the less sometimes accepts the transmigration of human souls into animals,[57] and the eventual salvation of all souls, evidently even of those that were in animals.[58] Basil of Caesarea speaks in one of his prayers of God having promised to save both man and beast.[59] Admittedly, the relevant Biblical passages were often interpreted in a different sense. When Isaiah

[51] Eusebius *Demonstratio Evangelica* 3.3, 106C-D in PG 22, 193C.
[52] Lactantius *Divine Institutes* 3,10, citing Cicero *Leg.* 1.8.24.
[53] Lactantius *Divine Institutes* 7,9,10; *Epitome* 65,4.
[54] Lactantius *Opif.* 2.9.
[55] Arnobius *adv. Nationes* 2.15.
[56] Ibid. 2.17.
[57] Origen *On First Principles* 1.4.1; 1.8.4; but contrast *Contra Celsum* 8.30.
[58] Origen *On First Principles* 3.6.5-6.
[59] Basil *Liturgy*.

prophesies that the leopard shall lie down with the kid,[60] and Paul tells us that the creature shall be delivered from corruption,[61] these passages are sometimes connected, and taken to refer not to an afterlife for animals, but to the last thousand years of this earth when Christ will reign, the devil be punished and the just, who will be resurrected first, will judge the living.[62]

Pro- and anti-animal strands in Christianity

I have dwelt on the anti-animal tendency in the Christian tradition. It would be wrong to ignore other strands, and I am grateful to Margaret Atkins for emphasising and illustrating them to me. There was the theme of the goodness of the animal creation, and there was the tradition of individual saints returning to paradisal relations with the animals, communing with them and curing them. This latter tradition is found already in the desert fathers,[63] and is praised by John Chrysostom in the fourth century, who himself spent ten years in the desert.[64] It is followed later by the Celtic Saints,[65] and celebrated in the Franciscan tradition, notably by St Bonaventure and Raymond Sebond,[66] though even on St Francis' example caveats have been entered.[67]

Praise of the animal creation is well exemplified in the fourth century in Basil of Caesarea's *Hexaemeron* and more briefly in John Chrysostom's *Homily on Genesis*.[68] Both themes are taken up by Augustine: the recovery by individuals of pre-lapsarian immunity from dangerous animals[69] and the beauty and order to be found in animals.[70] I shall leave the details to Margaret Atkins.[71]

[60] Isaiah 11,6-9.

[61] Romans 8.21.

[62] Irenaeus *adv. Haereses* 5.32.1; 5.36.3; Lactantius *Divine Institutes* 7.24.7. This is the probable meaning also of Tertullian *adv. Hermogenem* 11.3.

[63] See e.g. N. Russell, *Lives of the Desert Fathers*, 43-4; 110.

[64] John Chrysostom *Homily* 39.35 on the Epistle to the Romans.

[65] See Helen Waddell, *Beasts and Saints*.

[66] This is well discussed by J. Glacken, *Traces on the Rhodian Shore*, Berkeley and Los Angeles 1967, 214-16; 237-40.

[67] John Passmore ('The treatment of animals', *Journal of the History of Ideas* 36, 1975, 195-218, at 243 *Man's Responsibility for Nature*, London 1974) repeats a story from *The Life of Brother Jonathan*, ch. 1, in *The Little Flowers of Saint Francis*, which represents the saint as objecting to the violation of property, not the callousness, when the trotters are cut off a living pig.

[68] Basil *Hexaemeron*, Homilies 7-9; John Chrysostom *Homily on Genesis* 7,11-12.

[69] Augustine *Gen. Lit.* 3.15.24.

[70] Augustine, e.g. *Gen. Lit.* 3.14.22; *Reply to the Epistle of the Manichaeans called Fundamental* 37; *de Vera Religione* 77; *de Genesi contra Manichaeos* 1.16.26. The fullest account of this side of Augustine is in Clarence J. Glacken, *Traces on the Rhodian Shore*, Berkeley and Los Angeles 1967.

[71] Margaret Atkins, work in preparation, shows that Augustine is answering the Manichean view that the world of matter is evil, and that it is not merely with respect to

Even so there are heavy qualifications. Animals are to be admired not for their own sake, but as pointers to God. We must not let the creature take hold of us, so that we forget the Creator.[72] Even the suffering of animals serves this purpose of pointing the way to God. It reminds us that he implanted the urge to struggle against disintegration and emulate his own unity.[73] Moreover, in the very same breath in which Augustine speaks of animal beauty he reminds us that a weeping man is better than a happy worm, and that though mice are better than bread and fleas than gold, men are still higher in the scale of value.[74] This would be compatible with caging a lion, to remind us of its Creator.

We should take a warning from the case of Aristotle, who speaks of the beauty of animal studies, without thinking we owe them justice, when he defends zoology as a subject against astronomy, by reminding us of Heraclitus' saying that there are gods even in the kitchen.[75] A further warning is supplied by the Cynics, who dwell on the cleverness of animals, not in order to urge kindness to them, but in order to contrast the folly of human practices.[76]

Much the same situation can be found in Thomas Aquinas. He, too, maintains that the creation is good and animals beautiful, while insisting on the hierarchy that puts humans above them.[77] At most there are two passages in which a more radical modification has been detected: animals exist for their own sake, as well as for humans.[78]

One point, however, which has been made by Margaret Atkins,[79] is that although the arguments in praise of the Creation do not protect individual animals, they are the sort of arguments that can be used to support the conservation of species. In that case, the attitude to be recommended to humans is opposite to that which Augustine ascribes to God. For we have seen that Augustine makes God's providence extend to animals as individuals.

By and large, despite some opposing tendencies, my impression is that the emphasis of Western Christianity was on one half, the anti-animal half, of a much more wide-ranging and vigorous ancient Greek debate. And I think this helps to explain why until very recently

---

our need, pleasure, comfort, or convenience (Augustine *City* 11.16; 12.4) that animals are to be admired.

[72] Augustine *Enarratio in Psalmos*, 39, verse 8.

[73] Augustine *Lib. Arb.* 3.23.232-9; *Gen. Lit.* 3.16.25.

[74] Augustine *de Vera Religione* 77; *City* 11.16.

[75] Aristotle *Parts of Animals* 1.5, 645a7-31.

[76] See Chapter Twelve above.

[77] Thomas Aquinas *Summa Theologiae* 1, q. 75, a. 2; 1, q. 70. a. 1.

[78] Thomas Aquinas, *de Veritate* q. 5, a. 3; *in 2 Sent.* d. 1, q. 2, a. 3, as interpreted by John Wright, *The Order of the Universe in the Theology of St Thomas Aquinas*, Rome 1957, 145-7.

[79] Contribution to the symposium on animals held by the Classical Association in Oxford, April 1992.

we, or at least I myself, have been rather complacent about the treatment of animals.

The re-emergence of Ancient Greek arguments for animals: Ikhwan al-Safâ, Montaigne, Leibniz

The pro-animal side of the Greek debate was maintained chiefly by Platonists, Pythagoreans and some Aristotelians. It gets things the wrong way round to suggest that Platonism is to blame for overthrowing a kindly Biblical tradition, and even to name those two Platonist champions of animals, Celsus and Porphyry, as if they were opponents.[80]

The Greek case for animals does re-emerge at various later times. One interesting example is a text from a rather isolated group of perhaps four tenth-century Islamic thinkers, the Ikhwan al-Safâ, or Brethren of Purity. In *The Case of the Animals Versus Man Before the King of the Jinn*, the animals are allowed to put their case before an impartial third party for being liberated from man, and they draw on Ancient Greek arguments.[81]

The superiority of animals was to be promulgated to a wide literary public in the sixteenth century by Montaigne. In the *Apology for Raymond Sebond*, first published in 1580, he took up the case of ancient scepticism, with a view to promoting Christian faith over reason. Montaigne often followed Plutarch on animals, and, given this, there is no need to doubt that animal superiority, not merely animal goodness, was what he was maintaining.[82] He also introduced a new sceptical theme based on the opening up of the American continent: the superiority of the noble savage, although this theme is more fully taken up by Rousseau.[83] Plutarch was not Montaigne's only source. Sextus Empiricus was another, and his remarks on animal language may suggest at least an indirect acquaintance with the ideas of Porphyry's treatise *On Abstinence from Animal Food*.[84] In his later *Essay on Cruelty*, Montaigne after all accepted the Stoic view that we owe no justice to animals. But, like Plutarch,[85] he insisted that we owed humanity, and not only to animals, but also to plants. And with animals that are close to us he recognised the existence of mutual obligations.

[80] C.W. Hume, founder of the Universities Federation for the Welfare of Animals, in one of their publications, *The Status of Animals in the Christian Religion*, London 1956.

[81] Translation by L.E. Goodman, Boston, Mass, 1978.

[82] George Boas is hesitant in *The Happy Beast*, Baltimore 1933.

[83] For these various themes, see *Apologie de Raimond Sebond*, in P. Villey ed., *Les Essais de Michel de Montaigne*, vol. 2, Paris 1922, 186-214; 218; 329-49. There is a new translation into English by Michael Screech, London 1991.

[84] On language, see Sextus *PH* 1.73-7; Porphyry *Abstinence* 3,3-6.

[85] Plutarch *Marcus Cato* 5.2.

Montaigne's ascription of reason to animals helped to provoke the backlash of the Cartesian position that animals have no feeling at all, whether that was Descartes' own meaning, or only the interpretation of his followers.[86] Descartes explained his motivation in the *Discourse on Method* of 1637. If we do not recognise the enormous difference between ourselves and animals, we may fancy that we, like them, will not be liable to punishment after death. Conversely, once we do realise how much the animals differ, we can understand much better the arguments proving that our souls are independent of the body's death.[87] Descartes' denial of feeling and soul to animals went beyond anything found in the Greeks. I do not know whether the extreme character of his position was partly due to the need to counteract Montaigne.

There was another sixteenth-century reader of the Greeks whose work proved influential, in that it brought Leibniz into the debate. In 1544 Rorarius wrote a treatise, *That Brute Animals Possess Reason Better than Man*, in two books. A manuscript of this was printed in 1648, thus provoking a whole article on Rorarius by Pierre Bayle in his *Dictionary*, coupled with reflections of Bayle's own concerning Rorarius, the Cartesians, the Aristotelians and Leibniz.[88] Leibniz replied to the version of 1702.[89] He objects that Descartes is wrong to deny that animals have sense perception. They do, and hence their souls are immaterial, and so indestructible. Ordinary opinion would unwittingly rob of us immortality, either by allowing (for the case of animals) that conscious beings could be wholly material, or by denying (in the case of animals) that immaterial souls are indestructible. Although animal souls are as indestructible as ours, Leibniz avoids Rorarius' mistake of sapping the foundations of religion by denying any specific difference. The differences are very important, and here Leibniz reimposes a rationalistic view. First, animals have only memory, not reason, and so can attain only to universals based on induction or experience, which we saw Aristotle granting to animals in Chapter Three above. They are like the empiricist doctors of antiquity (the ones described in Chapter Six above as memorists), who have no understanding of cause and effect, but merely expect good or harm from the same thing in similar circumstances. Humans, by contrast, can use their reason to attain to the universal necessary truths and

[86] The latter, according to John Cottingham, ' "A brute to the brutes"? Descartes' treatment of animals', *Philosophy* 53, 1978, 551-9.

[87] Descartes *Discourse on Method*, end of part 5.

[88] See O. Kristeller, 'Between the Italian Renaissance and the French Enlightenment', *Renaissance Quarterly* 32, 1979, 41-72; George Boas, op. cit.; Leonora Rosenfield, *From Beast-Machine to Man-Machine*, Oxford 1941.

[89] Leibniz, 'Extrait du Dictionnaire de M. Bayle, article "Rorarius", p. 2599 sqq. de l'édition de l'an 1702, avec mes remarques', in Gerhardt, ed., *Philosophische Schriften* 4, 524-54, at 524-9.

deductive syllogisms of Aristotelian Science: just the capacity which we saw the memorists dismissing as useless. Further, the souls of beasts are not spirits, because they have no understanding of reasons and so no freedom. Moreover, they do not preserve their personality, because they have no knowledge of self, and such knowledge is necessary for reward or punishment after death. Thus the religious doctrine of reward and punishment which Descartes saw as threatened if animals were conscious, and Bayle if their souls were like ours, is safely preserved by Leibniz. In summarising Leibniz, Bayle says that the moral status of human souls makes them citizens of the City of God.

Leibniz expounds more fully in his *Monadology* of 1714 a theory to which he alludes only briefly here. The souls and bodies of animals and men were made and united together at the time of the Creation, and will last for ever, but in changing sizes. Animal bodies will be shrunk to microscopic size at death, so that they can live, for example, on a particle of dust. And birth is only an expansion of their microscopic bodies, which are fully organised within the seed.[90]

[90] Leibniz *Monadology*, translated Latta, pp. 114-16.

CHAPTER FIFTEEN

The one-dimensionality of ethical theories

I have emphasised how the post-Aristotelian debate and the subsequent Christian tradition focused on whether animals have reason. The other side of the coin is how astonishingly late in the philosophical texts we find the first explicit statement that the pain and terror felt by animals is a reason for treating them justly. The point arises as a defensive one in reply to the sorites objection that if we start sparing animals, we will have to spare vegetables next, which is absurd. Porphyry (AD 232-309) answers in a passage apparently drawn from a lost discussion by Plutarch (c. AD 46-120), that there is no comparison, because animals are conscious (*aisthanesthai*), can feel pain and terror (*algein, phobeisthai*), be harmed (*blaptesthai*), and so unjustly treated (*adikeisthai*).[1]

It is in this context of plants that animal pain normally gets mentioned. After Porphyry Julian, the pagan emperor, reports it as the view of many wise men that fruit can be picked, because this causes no pain or distress,[2] though this does not stop him himself from promoting animal sacrifice, and elsewhere praising Diogenes for eating a raw octopus. Augustine entertains the sorites argument about sparing vegetables, but answers by saying that plants have no feelings and animals no reason. He accuses the Manichaeans of misplaced consideration for both plants and animals, and says he would have understood if their motive concerning animals had been that animals die with pain. But it is not, and, in fact, we consider more relevant than pain the fact that animals do not belong to our legal community (*societas legis*), because of their lack of reason.[3] Neither Julian nor Augustine, then, takes animal pain as a decisive consideration.

In emphasising the lateness of the philosophical texts which mention animal pain as a reason for treating them justly, I should not overlook the very early testimony that Pythagoras in the sixth century BC stopped someone beating a dog, because he claimed to recognise in it the voice of a reincarnated friend.[4] But pain is not mentioned, and what matters is that it is a friend being beaten. Lucretius clearly

---

[1] Porphyry *Abstinence* 3.19.

[2] Julian *Or.* 5,174A-B.

[3] Augustine *City* 1.20; *On the Manichaean and Catholic Ways of Life* 2.17.59.

[4] As reported by Xenophanes, fr. 7 Diels-Kranz, from Diogenes Laertius *Lives* 8.36.

thinks that the mother's anguish is a bad thing, when the calf is removed for sacrifice.[5] But his immediate point is only that the calf has a distinctive, recognisable shape, and what he is out to criticise is the evils of religion, not the injustice to animals. An even better case for him is the sacrifice of Agamemnon's daughter, Iphigeneia, which occasions the resounding line:

tantum religio potuit suadere malorum[6]
(So much evil could religion induce)

The Platonist Apuleius gives a vivid depiction of an animal's suffering in *The Golden Ass*. But this is a *human* turned animal, and the message is not one of animal welfare in general. Where animal pain or grief is treated as a major consideration, this can turn out to be, as in the case of the twelfth-century Jewish philosopher Maimonides, merely because inflicting pain corrupts our character and makes us cruel.[7]

If we are to find purer examples of concern for animals as animals, we might turn to the poet Bion around 100 BC, who says that boys throw stones at frogs for fun (*paizontes*), but the frogs die not for fun.[8] Or again, we might look to Xenocrates, head of Plato's Academy from 339 to 314 BC, who records that the Athenians punished a man for flaying a ram alive,[9] and who is said to have rescued a sparrow which fled to him from an eagle, stroked it (*katapsân*), and declared that a suppliant must not be betrayed.[10] He is further concerned whether there were motives of kinship (*homogenes*) at work, or merely economic or other motives, when Triptolemus forbade animal sacrifice to the Athenians.[11] These stories suggest a variety of concerns, including perhaps pain or terror, although this is not explicitly spelled out in the surviving fragments.

In antiquity the focus was much more on animal reason. A decisive shift away from this was made in the eighteenth century by the British philosophers Hume and Bentham. In two works Hume has sections entitled, 'Of the reason of animals', in which he argues that reason is found in man and animals alike and is no more than an instinct, which arises from past observation and experience and carries us along a certain train of ideas. It is custom alone that makes us, from something perceived, infer its usual attendant. There is no process of reasoning or

[5] Lucretius *de Rerum Natura*, 2.349-66: I thank Georgia Nugent for the reminder.
[6] Lucretius 1.82-101.
[7] Maimonides *Guide for the Perplexed* 3.17; 3.48; interpreting Numbers 22,32; Leviticus 22,28.
[8] Plutarch *Sollertia* 965A-B.
[9] Plutarch *Esu.* 996A. I thank Kate Emmett for picking out this reference.
[10] Diogenes Laertius *Lives* 4.10.
[11] Porphyry *Abstinence* 4.22.

argumentation by which, for example, we entertain the idea that unexperienced objects will resemble experienced ones.[12] The downgrading of reason to a function of memory is like the denial of reason by the ancient memorists, which was referred to in Chapter Six above. Hume not only downgrades reason; he also upgrades the passions, when he says that 'reason is and ought only to be the slave of the passions'.[13] On the usual interpretation, morality for him is a matter of feeling and sympathy, not of reason.

Bentham, while maintaining that a dog or horse was rational, shifted the ethical question by writing of animals:

> The question is not, can they reason? Nor, can they talk? But can they suffer?[14]

This was an expression of his utilitarian ethics, according to which action should aim at the greatest happiness of the greatest number, and animals, as capable of suffering, were included in that number.

In the nineteenth century, Schopenhauer conceded that animals lacked reason, but deplored our denying them rights on that account. He saw the English, who in 1839, when he wrote, had recently introduced a Society for the Prevention of Cruelty to Animals, as a happy exception:

> We see this English nation of fine feelings distinguished above all others by a conspicuous sympathy for animals, which appears at every opportunity and has been strong enough to induce the English, in spite of the cold superstition which otherwise degrades them, to repair by legislation the gap that religion has left in their morality.[15]

A further challenge to the focus on reason came in 1871, when Darwin defended his evolutionary theory, by arguing in *The Descent of Man*, though not with perfect consistency,[16] that there is no psychological attribute of humans which is not also found in animals to some degree, reason included.

---

[12] Hume, *A Treatise of Human Nature*, 1739, 1.3.16, pp. 176-9 in Selby-Bigge; *Enquiry Concerning Human Understanding*, Section 9,82, in Niddich 104-8. For virtues and passions in Hume's animals, see Annette Baier, 'Knowing our place in the animal world', ch. 8 in her *Postures of the Mind*, London 1985, repr. from H.B. Miller and W.H. Williams, eds., *Ethics and Animals*, Clifton NJ 1983.

[13] David Hume, *A Treatise of Human Nature*, book 2, part 3, sec. 3, p. 415 in Selby Bigge; 3.1.1, pp. 457-8.

[14] Jeremy Bentham, *Introduction to the Principles of Morals and Legislation* 1789, ch. 17.

[15] I thank Mark Migotti for the references: Arthur Schopenhauer, *On the Fourfold Root of the Principle of Sufficient Reason* 1839, ch. 5, §§26-8; cf. *The Foundation of Ethics*, §19,4-9.

[16] Charles Darwin, *The Descent of Man* 1871, chs. 3-4. Darwin does, however, allow in Chapter Eleven that language and the use of fire are unique to humans.

In contemporary philosophy, there have been two main defences of animals.[17] One, developing Bentham's utilitarianism, is the position of Peter Singer; the other is the theory of animal rights of Tom Regan. Reason does not play a central role in either, although the capacity for belief comes in at the margins of Regan's theory. These are both theories that make us think more deeply, and that is the most important thing in philosophy, not whether one happens to agree, since philosophers are trained to disagree with each other.

Peter Singer's *Animal Liberation*[18] is unique among works of modern analytic philosophy, for the social revolution it has produced with effects on the economics of the meat industry and on practices in scientific and medical research. It would be hard for any reader not to be affected by the empirical chapters describing the treatment of animals in scientific research and in factory farming. Yet while it convinces that we must change our treatment of animals, the moral basis offered for a new outlook is not to me persuasive. The moral theory, if I can say this without disrespect, has a one-dimensional aspect, in that only one thing is thought to matter: the satisfaction of preferences. Most animals, it is said, have preferences, with such possible exceptions as molluscs. Elsewhere Singer handles the problem of molluscs by suggesting that with those animals which lack self-consciousness the one thing that matters is not preferences, but pleasure and pain.[19] It is a further part of his view that similar interests should be given equal consideration, whether they are those of a human, or of a non-human animal. Singer considers a test case: if it is really true that we are obliged to conduct medical or scientific experiments on living beings, we should be ready to do so on an orphaned imbecile with few preferences rather than on a vivacious animal with many. For that will maximise preference satisfaction.

In expressing my support for Singer's aims, I am assuming that the point about imbeciles was made in the expectation that right-minded people would recoil in horror and think again about animals, not that they would go looking for imbeciles. If animals are still chosen rather than imbeciles, according to Singer, then we are guilty of speciesism. This is a term coined by Richard Ryder[20] to draw a parallel with racism and sexism,[21] attitudes that are widely abhorred. How does speciesism differ?

[17] There are other defenders who take neither line. I shall be drawing attention to Mary Midgley. Another is Stephen Clark, *The Moral Status of Animals*, Oxford 1977.

[18] Peter Singer, *Animal Liberation*, London 1975; second edition 1990. Singer's work was preceded by letters and writings of Brigid Brophy, Stanley and Roslind Godlovich, John Harris and Richard Ryder.

[19] Peter Singer, *Practical Ethics*, Cambridge 1979.

[20] In 1970; see his *Animal Revolution*, Oxford 1989, p. 328.

[21] For the comparison of speciesism with sexism, cf. Philo *de Animalibus* 11, discussed in Chapter Ten.

Tom Regan, who shares Singer's admirable benevolence towards animals, has provided the main alternative moral theory in modern philosophy in his book, *The Case for Animal Rights*.[22] Higher animals, at least the mammals, and perhaps many others, are argued to have certain value-giving attributes. The list, which starts with the possession of beliefs, can best be given in a footnote.[23] But all these animals are said to have inherent value, and this value admits of no degrees, but is equal and demands respect wherever it is found. Consequently all of them equally have the right not to be harmed. Inherent value thus replaces preference-satisfaction as the solitary moral consideration. Regan concedes that it can occasionally be overridden, but so far as he can, he seeks ruthlessly to exclude other considerations, for example that of endangered species. If there are only two honey buzzards left, they have no more right to protection than a dog, because rights belong to individuals, not species. And he would sacrifice them for the dog, if necessary.[24] This preference for the individual is going to make species conservation difficult, given that the conservation of one species is almost always going to have adverse effects on the individuals of another.[25]

Regan, like Singer, sets himself a test case, and it is parallel to that pressed in antiquity against the Stoic theory of belonging (*oikeiôsis*), as discussed in Chapter Nine. It is the case of the life-raft. Suppose there are on a life-raft three humans and a dog, but room for only three of the four. If one is to be sacrificed, does Regan's principle of equal inherent value imply that lots should be drawn and one of the humans possibly jettisoned, rather than the dog? At this Regan demurs. Death is a greater loss to a human than to a dog.[26] This has the merit of introducing a further consideration, and one, it should be said, that

[22] Tom Regan, *The Case for Animal Rights*, London 1984.

[23] The attributes are listed on p. 243: beliefs and desires; perception, memory and a sense of the future, including their own future; an emotional life together with feelings of pleasure and pain; preference and welfare-interests; the ability to initiate action in pursuit of their desires and goals; a psychophysical identity over time; and an individual welfare in the sense that their experiential life fares well or ill for them, logically independently of their utility for others, and logically independently of their being the object of anyone else's interests.

[24] Regan, op. cit. 359.

[25] I am grateful to Margaret Atkins for sharpening the difficulty in this way and referring me to the modern literature below. I say 'almost' always, because a conservationist farmer who chooses a rare breed of cow, in place of more common ones which have the same diet, may not disadvantage existing individuals of another species. But such cases are rare. For the conflict, see J. Baird Callicott, 'Animal Liberation: a triangular affair' and Alastair Gunn, 'Why should we care about rare species?', both in *Environmental Ethics* 2, 1980, 311-38 and 17-38 respectively. For possible responses, see Mary Anne Warren, 'The rights of the non-human world', in Robert Elliot and Arran Gare, eds., *Environmental Philosophy*, Open University, Milton Keynes 1983, 109-34; Stephen Clark, 'The rights of wild things', *Inquiry* 22, 1979, 171-88, with whom compare Porphyry *Abstinence* 4.14 on the Essenes.

[26] Regan op. cit. 9.1, 351-3.

Regan has carefully prepared us for in advance.[27] But I am not sure that it is the right consideration. Is confidence in the greater loss justified? It depends on the human; it depends on the dog. What if one of the humans is senile and the dog bounding with life? Or what if the fourth passenger is not a dog, but a Martian with a far richer life than our own? Singer further objects that the principle of greater loss opens the floodgates to medical experimentation on animals, if it is necessary for saving the lives of humans, for whom death is a greater loss.[28]

I can now state my chief doubt about the two principal modern theories, and that is that they take only one main consideration into account: preference satisfaction (supplemented by pleasure and pain equations) or inherent value. But there are so many other considerations. About Singer's orphaned imbecile one may want to say that it has suffered a tragedy. But is there room for the idea of a tragedy in his theory? Of course, within the chosen dimension of preference satisfaction, many different considerations can be raised by a sophisticated theorist. It might be argued, for example, although it is not by Singer, that allowing experimentation on humans will tempt people to more violations of human or animal preference in the end than allowing experimentation on animals. But even if this difficult claim could be made out, it would only spare the orphaned imbecile for the sake of others, not for his or her own sake, and so it does not get at the reasons which should motivate us.

The idea of tragedy would also have helped explain why we value human imbeciles who lack Regan's value-giving characteristics, a question he excludes as beyond the scope of his book.[29] As regards Regan's life-raft, one wants to ask, 'Are some of the passengers one's dependants, or members of one's own family?' If there is a Martian on board, did he come there as an intruder, or as a friend? Regan does, in fact, allow close family ties or friendship as an extra overriding consideration.[30]

But there are many more. Mary Midgley, whose admirable defence of animals is free of one-dimensionality, draws attention to special need and special responsibility: the fledgling fallen from its nest, the injured rabbit one has oneself run over.[31] Concerning Regan's

[27] Ibid. 307-10.

[28] Peter Singer, Review of Regan's book, and subsequent correspondence with him, *New York Review of Books* 1985, 17 Jan., pp. 46-52; 25 April, pp. 57-8. On both the last two points, discussion is carried further by Dale Jamieson, 'Rights, justice and duties to provide assistance: a critique of Regan's theory of rights', *Ethics* 1990, pp. 349-62, at 359-60.

[29] Regan op. cit. 246-7; 319-20. On the other hand, he does refer to tragedy, to insist, rightly, that an animal death can still be a harm, even if it cannot be called a tragedy, 102-3.

[30] Regan op. cit. 315-17.

[31] Mary Midgley, *Animals and Why They Matter*, University of Georgia and Harmondsworth 1983, 29-31.

endangered species, we may compare, without necessarily believing in
a Divine Artist, how much worse it is to lose the whole of an artist's
work than to lose the individual pieces. The charge of speciesism was
in effect discussed in Chapter Ten. But it gains its force from ignoring
yet other consideration which make species a less penetrable frontier
than race or sex. Midgley points out that we cannot intermarry or have
children with any other known species, or farm children out for
adoption by them, while those who have been adopted by other species
have been deprived.[32] By contrast, some of the deepest relationships
cross the frontier of race or sex. If there were Martians with whom we
could relate as deeply as with humans, this would indeed affect our
duties towards them. Conversely, if such relations were not possible
with the Martians, we would have to accept that they had some
justification for preferring themselves to us. This is the reverse side of
the coin, and would work to our disadvantage, if they needed to eat
us.[33] But not all relationships between species are of this adversarial
kind. Good relationships are both natural and common, as was
illustrated in Chapter Ten.

The other relevant considerations, in many cases, though not in all,
concern our very numerous relationships with animals, both with
species and with individuals. These are every bit as important as
preference satisfaction and inherent value. I do not entirely agree with
those animal supporters who see no value in the preference for pets
over other animals: one describes a lady serving meat sandwiches
while doting over her pet dog.[34] But what we should remember is that
in another culture (this is a real example) it may be cows rather than
dogs that are pets,[35] and the possibilities of relationship, as well as
actual relationships, should carry some weight. The consideration of
relationships has the unexpected consequence that it puts more onus
on the farmer who knows his animals than on the huntsman who
cannot know his quarry. And a fifth-century Latin poem by the
Christian Prudentius does advocate that we should accept the fish and
birds provided by nature, rather than slaughter cattle for the table.[36]
Gratitude is another relevant relationship. Pythagoras, and to some
extent Attic as well as Phrygian law, are said to have given special

[32] Mary Midgley, op. cit. 99; 104-7.

[33] Similarly Robert Nozick, Review of Regan's book, *New York Times Review*, 27 Nov.
1983, p. 29. Role reversal, in which humans are judged in the way they normally judge
animals, has been a recurrent theme: Plato *Statesman* 263D; Apuleius *The Golden Ass*;
The Case of the Animals Versus Man Before the King of the Jinn, tenth century by the
Ikhwân al-Safâ, translated by L.E. Goodman, Boston 1978; Cyrano de Bergerac, *Les
estats et empires de la lune*, 1657.

[34] Peter Singer, preface to the first edition of *Animal Liberation*.

[35] In India cows behave more like pets because they are treated as such. Some English
farmers, protesting against farm closures, have said the same.

[36] Prudentius *The Daily Round* 3,58-60.

protection to the labouring ox.[37] Was this gratitude as Ovid suggests,[38] or, as Porphyry asks about a similar case,[39] mere economics? At any rate, Plutarch says a good man will care for his horse or dog, when it is worn out with age, though he sees this as a matter of benevolence (*euergesia*, *kharis*), rather than justice, which he regards as not extending to animals.[40]

Relationships are of many different kinds: we enter into a relationship even with the rabbit we have injured. Pets are literally *oikeioi* – members of the household. Others may be *oikeioi* by being akin in other ways. Plato performed a service in insisting that to treasure another as akin (oikeios) is not the same as to treasure another as being like oneself[41] – the unlikeness may be part of the pleasure, and all these considerations are different.

It is the absence of other considerations which could lead to throwing one's grandmother off the life-raft, or experimenting on an orphaned imbecile, and sparing the imbecile, if at all, only because of calculations about the effect on *others*. I am not saying that either Regan or Singer intended this, but that the logic of their positions must allow in the possibility. Preference satisfaction might be maximised by experimenting on an ophaned imbecile; it certainly might be reduced by choosing a dog instead. The jettisoned grandmother might suffer less loss than a puppy. These unacceptable results flow simply from an artificial parsimony in the considerations admitted. And Singer has been led by his principles to allow the killing of newborn haemophiliacs and Mongoloid children, if the parents intend to replace them with a happier child and there is no possibility of adoption.[42]

We found the same parsimony in ancient theories. The Stoic idea of animals as occupying a single circle beyond the outermost limit of concern overlooked the variety of connexions we may have with them. The idea that all just dealing depended on contract and expediency overlooked the many other springs of justice. Moral theories may seek to make things manageable by reducing all considerations to one. Insofar as they do, this is so much the worse for them.

Before I leave the modern theories, I will refer briefly to two outstanding issues. Singer tackles the objection that without factory farming, many domestic species would die out. On this issue, I am inclined to say that the welfare of a species is not independent of the welfare of its members. We cannot claim to be promoting the welfare of

---

[37] Pythagoras: Diogenes Laertius *Lives* 8.20; Iamblichus *Life of Pythagoras*, 28, 150; Attica: Plato *Laws* 873E; Aelian *Varia Historia* 5.14; Phrygia: Aelian *Nat. Anim.* 12.34. See also Schol. Aratus *Phain.* 132, p. 138, Martin.

[38] Ovid *Metamorphoses* 15,122-6.

[39] Porphyry *Abstinence* 4.22.

[40] Plutarch *Cato the Elder*, 4.5.

[41] Plato *Lysis* 221E-222D.

[42] Peter Singer, *Practical Ethics*, Cambridge 1979, 131-8.

a species, if we allow most of its members to be miserable. The same mistaken justification might be offered for breeding a race of slaves, that otherwise the enslaved race would dwindle.

Finally, I have two particular difficulties with Regan's view that inherent value is equal and admits of no degrees.[43] First, it creates a sharp frontier that denies right to animals who lack the value-giving characteristics. So Regan has to seek special arguments to protect non-adult mammals, for example frogs, baby seals and foetuses.[44] Secondly, the claim that the value-giving characteristics do not themselves admit of degrees seems far from obvious. For it may be in a less rich sense that certain mammals can be said to have beliefs. In that case, will not the postulated inherent value, like the value-giving characteristic (possession of belief), admit of degrees? For although the possession of such characteristics is not to be confused with inherent value,[45] it is said to be relevant.[46]

Singer and Regan have made the problems clear. If I do not see them as yet providing the right solution, I can fairly be asked what I would say instead. I began my reading with only a historical interest in the large, and largely uncharted, ancient debate on human and animal psychology. But I was led to appreciate that there was a real, live moral problem by the badness of the arguments for a major difference between animals and man. It sounded grand enough when Aristotle and the Stoics declared that man had reason and animals did not. But as the debate progressed, it began to appear that animals might lack only certain kinds of reasoning, and a stand was taken on their not having speech. When this defence too began to be questioned, a retreat was made to the position that they lacked syntax. 'They lack syntax, so we can eat them', was meant to be the conclusion. It was amazing to find that modern discussions had reached exactly the same point as the ancient ones. As described in Chapter Seven, the debate on the ability of chimpanzees to use sign language has come down to the question whether they can string the signs together syntactically. This is a point of the highest scientific interest, but of absolutely no moral relevance whatsoever.

But now there is a problem. How are we to treat animals, if none of the main moral theories available has convinced us? I am not persuaded by the two ancient theories of useful contract or of belonging (*oikeiôsis*), nor by the two modern ones of preference satisfaction or inherent value. What is the right approach? Politically, the language of rights is effective, and evokes a response. I am therefore glad if its use can do something to redress the appalling imbalance which currently

[43] Tom Regan, op. cit. 358; 366-9; 390-2.
[44] Ibid. 244-5.
[45] Ibid. 240-1.
[46] Ibid. 244.

penalises animals. But from a philosophical point of view, I do not think we have to adopt any moral theory at all, and certainly not any moral theory of this unifying type which seeks, as far as possible, to boil down all considerations to one. So long as I am speaking not to moral sceptics, but to moral people who have no wish to hurt their fellow human beings, why should I not speak as follows? *Whatever* protects our fellow humans (and I have no theory to tell me what does), the same will protect animals, to the *extent* that they do not differ in morally relevant ways.[47] We should then study the ways in which other species do differ, and be ready to consider whether these ways are, or are not, morally relevant. The relevant differences, I have suggested, will include possible relationships to us.

I deliberately mention differences between humans and animals, rather than similarities, because no number of similarities can prove the point, so long as the thought is lurking that somewhere there is a huge and relevant difference. But it may be objected that I cannot avoid espousing some moral theory, to decide, for example, what differences are morally relevant. I think this is not so. To discover a theory of moral relevance that was actually correct would be a harder task than the one on which we were already embarked, whereas to find areas of agreement on moral relevance with our interlocutors may not be hard at all. We could agree at once, for example, that a lack of syntax, which I declared morally irrelevant, would be morally relevant after all, if it could be shown that syntax was a necessary prerequisite for depression or fear. Depression induced by caging or lighting conditions, fear induced by slaughterhouse procedures, would be agreed by many to be morally relevant. Where we do not agree on the moral relevance of an alleged analogy, we may still agree that the onus is on us to find a morally relevant disanalogy.[48] Or where agreement is missing on the moral relevance of one point, either party can look for another. This is not to say that agreement on moral relevance will always be possible. It may not be, if like Porphyry we are arguing with a community that believes in animal sacrifice. But failure to agree would not be cured by invoking a moral theory, for that theory would be no easier to commend to the opposition. Philosophical argument proceeds by exploiting areas of agreement in other branches of philosophy too, not only in ethics. In ethics, the difference may only be that the issues are morally important.

The challenge to find morally relevant differences is a severe one,

[47] A similar 'whatever' strategy is used for the question of the right to liberty by James Rachels in 'Do animals have a right to liberty?' in T. Regan and P. Singer, eds., *Animal Rights and Human Obligations*, Englewood Cliffs 1976.

[48] A visitor to India, shocked by seeing animals dying on the streets, may be reminded that we do not offer euthanasia to our elderly relatives, even if they ask for it. The onus is then on him or her to discuss the differences.

when lack of syntax will not count. But where there are morally
relevant differences, there will still be further considerations to take
into account. How great are the differences and what is our purpose in
using or killing the animals? Unfortunately, where the purpose is most
serious, as for medical research,[49] the relevant animals may display
the smallest differences. And where the differences are large, the
purpose, be it food or even cosmetics, may be less pressing. We must
ask whether the use of animals is necessary, or whether substitutes
can be used. We must consider what is to count as harm, only
suffering, as Bentham maintained, or also loss of life, as was held by
Theophrastus, and later by the poet Bion ('Boys throw stones at frogs
for fun; the frogs die not for fun, but in reality').[50] There is no reason to
think we can foresee a finite list of considerations, although it may be
possible to classify the many considerations into some broad general
types. Already in this chapter, attention has been paid to a large
number of concerns. It is in terms of such multiple considerations that
argument and reflexion needs to be conducted, rather than in terms of
a theory that supplies one master consideration.

The need for multiple considerations in ethics has already been very
well put by more than one contemporary philosopher.[51] But it may be
objected that that issue needs first to be settled in the abstract, before
any conclusions can be drawn about how to treat animals. I believe, on
the contrary, that the present order of discussion is the right one. The
concrete case of animals makes clearer than an abstract discussion
why multiple considerations are needed, and why elaborations of the
one-dimensional theories do not seem to get at the reasons that move
us, even if they help those theories to reach more acceptable verdicts.

Some supporters of multiple considerations have cited Aristotle as a
model of what is wanted.[52] It is true that what I am suggesting is
partly in the spirit of Aristotle. In his *Nicomachean Ethics*, Aristotle
recommends that we should first identify the various things that
matter in life. He recognises that these are multiple, and when it
comes to particular decisions one needs not theory, but a perceptive
eye, to see how to achieve what matters.[53] He does, however, think that

[49] Yet Plotinus refused medicines based on wild animals, saying that he didn't even
want to eat domestic ones, Porphyry *Life of Plotinus* 2.

[50] Quoted by Plutarch *Sollertia* 965A-B.   [51] See next note.

[52] e.g. Tom Nagel, 'The fragmentation of value', in his *Mortal Questions*, Cambridge
1979, revised from an article of 1977, cites Aristotle. Cf. Charles Taylor, 'The diversity of
goods', in Amortya Sen and Bernard Williams, eds., *Utilitarianism and Beyond*,
reprinted in Taylor's *Philosophical Papers*, vol. 2, Cambridge 1985. That values are not
only multiple, but also liable to conflict, has been a major theme of Isaiah Berlin's work,
and is further discussed by Bernard Williams, 'Conflicts of values', in Alan Ryan, ed., *The
Idea of Freedom: Essays in Honour of Isaiah Berlin*, Oxford 1979, repr. in Williams' *Moral
Luck*, Cambridge 1981.

[53] Aristotle *NE* 2.9, 1109b20-3; 4.5, 1126b2; 5.10, 1137b27-32; 6.8, 1142a26-9; 6.11,
1143a35-b14; 6.13, 1144b1-17; with discussion in my 'Aristotle on the role of intellect in

a finite list of ultimate types of concern can be assembled, and he gives some weight to theory, none explicitly to imagination, in assembling the list. What I have been suggesting is still less theoretical than that. For I have been appealing to the reader's own values, rather than offering theoretical support for any values.

The role of theory in Aristotle's ethics can be illustrated by his treatment of slavery, and the modern debate on the treatment of animals has, in fact, reached the same point as the ancient debate on slavery in Aristotle's time. Aristotle himself compares the status of slaves and animals at *Politics* 1,7-8. In the previous century, Athenian citizens, on an unsuccessful military expedition to Sicily, had been taken slaves. So the public knew that not all slavery could be right as it stood. Some felt uneasy, and it was time for an arbiter. That arbiter came along and his name was Aristotle. 'You are right to be uneasy,' he said in effect, 'for not all slavery is justified. But I will draw a philosophical distinction and tell you which practices are right and which are wrong. The world is divided into those who can plan their own lives and those who cannot, but can only follow the plans of others. The latter are the ones for whom it is natural to be slaves.'[54] This is an example of theory; it would take not a theory, but an eye to recognise the natural slave.

I entirely agree with Aristotle's premise that the world is divided into those who can plan their own lives and those who cannot. But if his conclusion followed that the latter ought to be slaves, then I fear that some very distinguished philosophers might find themselves on the wrong side of the division.

Theory is, however, attractive, and I think the public would welcome a new arbiter to tell them whether it is all right to eat fish, or to use animals for research into cancer. He or she would tell them that they were right to feel uneasy, but would offer to draw a philosophical distinction or distinctions. Perhaps the new Aristotle will be reading the words on this page at this very moment. But if so, I doubt if a single distinction, or a unifying theory can give the right answers. I hope that what will be drawn from Aristotle is the need for a multiplicity of considerations, not the possibility of applying a single criterion.

The implication of this is that, although we ought to make major changes in our treatment of animals in the more prosperous countries, many considerations, including our own serious needs, have to be taken into account. There is no simple criterion for condemning what we presently do. On the other hand, I suspect that a more complex consideration will still find a very great deal that is unjustifiable.

---

virtue', *Proceedings of the Aristotelian Society* 74, 1973-4, 107-29, repr. in A. Rorty, ed., *Essays on Aristotle's Ethics*, Berkeley and Los Angeles 1980.
[54] Aristotle *Politics* Book 1, chs. 2; 4-7; 13.

Principal Protagonists

Presocratics
Pythagoras, fl. late sixth century BC
Empedocles, c. 495-435 BC
Democritus, fl. c. 435 BC

Plato and Older Academy
Plato, c. 427-348 BC
Xenocrates, head 339-314 BC
Heraclides of Pontus, left Athens when
    defeated by Xenocrates for chair

Aristotle and Peripatos
Aristotle, 384-322 BC
Eudemus of Rhodes, fourth-century pupil
Theophrastus, head 322-287 BC
Strato, head 287-269 BC

Cynics
Diogenes of Sinope, mid-fourth century
Crates of Thebes, pupil of Diogenes

Epicureans
Epicurus, 341-271 BC
Hermarchus, head from 271 BC
Polystratus, next head, mid-third century
Lucretius, c. 99 – c. 55 BC
Philodemus, first century BC

Stoics
Zeno, founded Stoa c. 300 BC
Chrysippus, c. 280 – c. 206 BC
Diogenes of Babylon, died c. 152 BC
Antipater, head, c. 152 – c. 129 BC
Posidonius, 135-51 BC
Seneca, c. 4 BC – AD 65
Musonius Rufus, taught Epictetus
Epictetus, c. AD 55 – c. 135
Hierocles, fl. c. AD 100

Sceptics
Sextus Empiricus, fl. c. AD 190

Neopythagoreans
Sotion, taught the teacher of Seneca (q.v.)
Apollonius of Tyana, first century AD

Jewish philosophers
Philo of Alexandria c. 30 BC – c. AD 45
Maimonides, AD 1135-1204

Middle Platonists
Plutarch, c. AD 46-120
Didaskalikos, c. AD 150
Celsus, opposed by Christian Origen (q.v.)

Platonist Eclectic
Galen, c. AD 129-199

Neoplatonists
Plotinus, c. AD 205-260
Porphyry, AD 232-309
Iamblichus, c. AD 250-319/325
Theodore of Asine, pupil of Iamblichus
Proclus, c. AD 411-485
Hermeias of Alexandria, fifth century AD
Priscian of Lydia, left Athens in the AD 529
    exodus
Simplicius, wrote after AD 529
Olympiodorus AD 495/505-after 565

Christians
Origen, AD 185-284
Lactantius, early fourth century AD
Augustine, AD 354-430
Thomas Aquinas, c. AD 1225-1274

Islamic thinkers
Râzî, AD 865-925
Ikhwân al-Safâ, tenth century AD
Avicenna (Ibn Sina), c. AD 980-1037
Avempace (Ibn Bajja), died AD 1138

Post-medieval thinkers
Montaigne, Michel de, 1533-1592
Descartes, René, 1596-1650
Hobbes, Thomas, 1588-1679
Leibniz, Gottfried Wilhelm, 1646-1716
Hume, David, 1711-1776
Kant, Immanuel, 1724-1804
Bentham, Jeremy, 1748-1832
Darwin, Charles, 1809-1882

Select Bibliography

1. Ancient thought on animals
J. Haussleiter, *Der Vegetarismus in der Antike*, Berlin, 1935
Urs Dierauer, *Tier und Mensch im Denken der Antike*, Amsterdam, 1977.

2. Later thought on animals
E.P. Evans, *The Criminal Prosecution and Capital Punishment of Animals*, London, 1906; repr. London, 1987.
Helen Waddell, *Beasts and Saints*.
George Boas, *The Happy Beast*, Baltimore, 1933.
O. Kristeller, 'Between the Italian Renaissance and the French Enlightenment', *Renaissance Quarterly* 32, 1979, pp. 41-72.
Leonora Rosenfield, *From Beast-Machine to Man-Machine*, Oxford, 1941.
John Cottingham, ' "A brute to the brutes"? Descartes' treatment of animals', *Philosophy* 53, 1978, pp. 551-9.
John Passmore, *Man's Responsibility for Nature*, London, 1974.
J. Glacken, *Traces on the Rhodian Shore*, Berkeley and Los Angeles, 1967.
Keith Thomas, *Man and the Natural World, Changing Attitudes in England 1500-1800*, London, 1983.

3. Main ancient philosophical texts relating to animals
By far the most important is Porphyry *On Abstinence from Animal Food*, Budé edition with French translation and introductions, vols. 1 and 2, J. Bouffartigue, Paris, 1977 and 1979; vol. 3. Alain Segonds, Paris, 1993; English translation by Thomas Taylor, 1823, repr. Centaur Press, London and Fontwell, 1965. This incorporates extensive arguments by:
Heraclides of Pontus, 1.13-26;
Hermarchus, the Epicurean, 1.7-12;
Plutarch, esp. Book 3; and
Theophrastus, the last available in a modern translation as: Theophrastus of Eresus, *Sources*, ed. Fortenbaugh, Huby, Sharples, Gutas, frr. 531, 584-8.
Empedocles, *Purifications*, frr. 112-59, Diels-Kranz, translated e.g. Kathleen Freeman, *Ancilla to the Pre-Socratic Philosophers*, Oxford, 1971; M.R. Wright, Empedocles, *The Extant Fragments*, New Haven 1981. *See also* G. Zuntz, *Persephone*, Oxford, 1971.
Lives of Pythagoras: the somewhat apocryphal *Lives* by Iamblichus and Porphyry are conveniently collected with other material in K.S. Guthrie, *The Pythagorean Sourcebook and Library*, 1920; repr. Phanes Press, Grand Rapids, Michigan, 1987.
Philo of Alexandria, translated from the Armenian version, with introduction, by Abraham Terian, *Philonis Alexandrini de Animalibus*, Scholars Press, Chico, California, 1981.
Plutarch *de Sollertia Animalium, Bruta Animalia Ratione Uti* (or *Gryllus*), *de Esu Carnium*, translated by William C. Helmbold, in Loeb Classical Library, Plutarch *Moralia*, vol. 12, as *Whether Land or Sea Animals are Cleverer, Beasts are Rational* and *On the Eating of Flesh*.
Sextus Empiricus *Outlines of Pyrrhonism*, 1.62-78, translated by R.G. Bury in Loeb

Classical Library, vol. 1, and, with other material, and comments in Julia Annas and Jonathan Barnes, *The Modes of Scepticism*, Cambridge 1985, pp. 31-53.
Origen *Against Celsus*, 4.74-80, translated by Henry Chadwick, *Origen Contra Celsum*, Cambridge, 1953.
Augustine, *City of God*, 1.20, translated e.g. by Henry Bettenson in Penguin Books, and *de Moribus*, 2.17.54-9, translated as *The Catholic and Manichaean Ways of Life*, New York, 1966.

4. Other Ancient philosophical texts
Plato *Theaetetus*, 184-6. There is an introduction by Myles Burnyeat to the translation of M.J. Levett, as revised, Indianapolis, 1990.
Aristotle *de Anima (On the Soul)*; *History of Animals*, 8-9; *Posterior Analytics*, 2.19; *Metaphysics*, 1.1.
A.A. Long and D.N. Sedley, *The Hellenistic Philosophers*, a collection of fragments with masterly commentary, covering Stoics, Sceptics and Epicureans, 2 vols., Cambridge, 1987, translations in vol. 1.
Cynic fragments are conveniently collected, without translation, in Gabriele Giannantoni, ed., *Socraticorum Reliquiae*, vol. 2 with comments in Italian vol. 3, Bibliopolis, 1983 and 1985.
Apuleius, *The Golden Ass*.
Iamblichus, *On the Mysteries of Egypt*, Budé edition with French translation, English translations by Thomas Taylor, 1821, Alexander Wilder 1911, with fragments of Porphyry *Letter to Anebo*, to which it is a reply, conveniently collected in Stephen Ronan, ed., *Iamblichus On the Mysteries*, Chthonios Books, 1989.

5. Later philosophical and scientific texts relating to animals
Ikhwân al-Safâ, *The Case of the Animals Versus Man Before the King of the Jinn*, translated by L.E. Goodman, Boston, 1978.
Maimonides, *Guide for the Perplexed*, 3.17; M. Friendlander's translation is on pp. 167-8 above. Translated also by S. Pines, Chicago, 1963.
Thomas Aquinas, *Summa Theologiae*, 1, q.75, a.3, *respondeo*; 2.2, q.64, a.1.
Montaigne, *An Apology for Raymond Sebond* and *On Cruelty*, both translated by Michael Screech in *The Essays of Michel de Montaigne*, London, 1991.
Descartes, *Discourse on Method*, Introduction.
Hobbes, *Leviathan*, Part 1, chs. 14-21.
Leibniz, 'Extrait du Dictionnaire de M. Bayle, article "Rorarius", p. 2599, sqq. de l'edition de l'an 1702, avec mes remarques', in Gerhardt, ed., *Philosophische Schriften* 4,525-6.
Hume, *Enquiry Concerning Human Understanding*, 82-5; *A Treatise of Human Nature*, 1.3.16.
Kant, *Groundwork of the Metaphysic of Morals*, tr. of *Grundlegung* by H.J. Paton.
Kant, 'Duties to animals and spirits' in *Lectures on Ethics*, tr. by Louis Infield, N.Y., 1963.
Bentham, *Introduction to the Principles of Morals and Legislation*, ch. 17.
Darwin, *The Descent of Man*.

6. Animal marvels
Pliny the Elder, *Natural History*, 8-11.
Aelian, *On the Nature of Animals*.

7. Ancient texts on hunting
Xenophon, *Cynegeticus*.
Arrian, *Cynegeticus*.

8. Presocratics on animals
G. Zuntz, *Persephone*, Oxford, 1971 (for Empedocles).
John Procope, 'Democritus on politics and the care of the soul', *Classical Quarterly* 39, 1989, pp. 307-31.
Catherine Osborne, 'Boundaries in nature: eating with animals in the fifth century BC', *Bulletin of the Institute of Classical Studies* 37, 1990, pp. 15-29.
See also Solmsen, under Plato.

9. Plato
John Cooper, 'Plato on sense-perception and knowledge: *Theaetetus*, 184-6', *Phronesis* 15, 1970, pp. 123-46.
Myles Burnyeat, 'Plato on the grammar of perceiving', *Classical Quarterly* 26, 1976, pp. 29-51.
Michael Frede, 'Observations on perception in Plato's later dialogues', in his *Essays in Ancient Philosophy*, Minneapolis, 1987.
Eve Cole, 'Plato on the souls of beasts', circulated to Society for Ancient Greek Philosophy, 1991.

10. Aristotle
Terence Irwin, *Aristotle's First Principles*, Oxford, 1988.
Martha Nussbaum and Amelie Rorty, eds., *Essays on Aristotle's de Anima*, Oxford, 1992.
William Fortenbaugh, 'Aristotle: animals, emotion and moral virtue', *Arethusa* 4, 1971, pp. 137-65.
Christopher Gill, 'Is there a concept of person in Greek philosophy?', in Stephen Everson, ed., *Psychology, Companions to Ancient Thought*, 2, Cambridge, 1991.
F. Solmsen, 'Antecedents of Aristotle's psychology and scale of beings', *American Journal of Philology* 76, 1955, pp. 148-64.
Paul Vander Waerdt, 'Aristotle's criticism of soul division', *American Journal of Philology* 108, 1987, pp. 627-43.

11. Theophrastus
William Fortenbaugh, *Quellen zur Ethik Theophrasts*, Amsterdam, 1984, pp. 262-85.
Anthony Preus, 'Animal and human souls in the Peripatetic school', *Skepsis* 1, Athens, 1990, pp. 67-99.
Eve Cole, 'Theophrastus and Aristotle on animal intelligence', in William Fortenbaugh and Dimitri Gutas, eds., *Theophrastus, his Psychological, Doxographical and Scientific Writings, Rutgers University Studies in Classical Humanities* 5, 1992.
Elisabetta Matelli, *'Endiathetos* e *prophorikos logos*, note sulla origine della formula e della nozione', *Aevum* 1, 1992, pp. 43-70.
Dirk Obbink, 'The origin of Greek sacrifice: Theophrastus on religion and cultural history', in William Fortenbaugh and Robert Sharples, eds., *Theophrastean Studies, Rutgers University Studies in Classical Humanities* 3, 1988, pp. 272-95.

12. Cynics
George Boas, 'The superiority of animals', in Arthur Lovejoy and George Boas, *A Documentary History of Primitivism and Related Ideas*, vol. 1, Baltimore, 1935.

13. Epicurean philosophy of mind
Julia Annas, *Hellenistic Philosophy of Mind*, Berkeley, Los Angeles, 1992.
Julia Annas, 'Epicurus on agency', in J. Brunschwig, M. Nussbaum, eds., *Passions and Perceptions*, Cambridge, 1993.
Julia Annas, 'Epicurean emotions', *Greek, Roman and Byzantine Studies* 30, 1989, pp. 145-64.

Pamela Huby, 'The Epicureans, animals and free will', *Apeiron* 3, 1969, pp. 17-19.
David Glidden, 'Epicurus on self-perception', *American Philosophical Quarterly* 16, 1979, pp. 297-306.
See also Epicurean ethics.

14. Stoic philosophy of mind
Brad Inwood, *Ethics and Human Action in Early Stoicism*, Oxford, 1985.
A. Bonhöffer, *Epictet und die Stoa*, Stuttgart, 1890.
Julia Annas, *Hellenistic Philosophy of Mind*, Berkeley, Los Angeles, 1992.
Christopher Gill, 'Is there a concept of person in Greek philosophy?' in Stephen Everson, ed., *Psychology, Companions to Ancient Thought* 2, Cambridge, 1991.
See also Emotions, *Oikeiôsis*, World community, Natural law, The Stoics on what matters, Suicide.

15. Sceptics
Michael Frede, 'Des Skeptikers Meinungen', *Neue Hefte für Philosophie* 15-16, 1979, pp.102-29, repr. as 'The Skeptic's beliefs' in his *Essays in Ancient Philosophy*, Minneapolis, 1987.
Myles Burnyeat, 'Can the Sceptic live his scepticism?' in M. Schofield, M. Burnyeat, J. Barnes, eds., *Doubt and Dogmatism*, Oxford, 1980.
Jonathan Barnes, 'The beliefs of a Pyrrhonist', *Proceedings of the Cambridge Philological Society* n.s. 28, 1982, pp. 1-29.
Tad Brennan, 'Does the Sceptic have beliefs?', *Bulletin of the Institute of Classical Studies* n.s. 1, 1993, forthcoming.
Michael Frede, 'An empiricist view of knowledge: memorism', in Stephen Everson, ed., *A Philosophical Introduction to Ancient Epistemology*, Cambridge, 1990.

16. Middle Platonism
Larry Schrenk, 'Faculties of judgment in the *Didaskalikos*', *Mnemosyne* 44, 1991, pp. 347-63.
For Celsus, *see* Origen under Main ancient philosophical texts relating to animals.

17. Plutarch
D. Tsekourakis, 'Pythagoreanism or Platonism and ancient medicine? The reasons for vegetarianism in Plutarch's *Moralia*', in *Aufstieg und Niedergang der römischen Welt* 2.36.1, pp. 366-93.

18. Pliny and philosophical background
M. Beagon, *Roman Nature: The Thought of Pliny the Elder*, Oxford, 1992, ch. 7, 'Man and the animals'.

19. Porphyry
D.A. Dombrowski, 'Porphyry and vegetarianism: a contemporary philosophical approach', in *Aufstieg und Niedergang der römischen Welt* 2.36.2, pp. 774-91.
Anthony Preus, 'Biological theory in Porphyry's *de Abstinentia*', *Ancient Philosophy* 3, 1983, pp. 149-59.
H.D. Saffrey, 'Les livres 4 à 7 du *de Mysteriis* de Jamblique relus avec le *Lettre* de Porphyre à Anebon', in H.J. Blumenthal et al., Proceedings of the International Conference on Iamblichus held at Liverpool, 24-26 September, 1990.
See also Transmigration.

20. Iamblichus
H.D. Saffrey, *as under* Porphyry.
H.D. Saffrey, 'Abamon, pseudonyme de Jamblique', in Robert B. Palmer and Robert Hamerton-Kelly, eds., *Philomathes, Studies and Essays in Memory of Philip Merlan*, The Hague, 1971.
On the mosaics at his school, *see* Jean-Charles Balty, 'Julian et Apamée, aspects de la restauration de l'Hellénisme et de la politique antichrétienne de l'empéreur', *Dialogues d'histoire ancienne*, 1974, pp. 267-304.
Janine et Jean-Charles Balty, 'Un programme philosophique sous la cathédral d'Apamée; l'ensemble néoplatonicien de l'empéreur Julien', in *Texte et Image, Actes du colloque international de Chantilly, (13-15 Octobre, 1982)*, Paris, pp. 167-76.
Richard Sorabji, 'The ancient commentators on Aristotle' in his, ed., *Aristotle Transformed: The Ancient Commentators and Their Influence*, London and Ithaca, N.Y., 1990, 1-30, at 9-10.
Janine Balty, 'Les Thérapénides d'Apamée', in *Dialogues d'Histoire Ancienne* 18, 1992, pp. 281-91.
See also Transmigration.

21. Augustine on animals
Matthias Baltes, Dieter Lau, 'Animal' in *Augustinus-Lexikon*, vol. 1, fasc. 3, 1988.
Gillian Clark, 'The fathers and the animals: the rule of reason?', in Andrew Linzey, ed., *Animals on the Agenda*, forthcoming.
Catherine Osborne, 'Topography in the *Timaeus*: Plato and Augustine on man's place in the natural world', *Proceedings of the Cambridge Philological Society*, 1989.

22. Perceptual content in modern philosophy
Gareth Evans, *The Varieties of Reference*, Oxford, 1982.
Christopher Peacocke, 'Analogue content', *Proceedings of the Aristotelian Society*, supp. vol. 60, 1986, pp. 1-17.

23. Intentionality in Greek thought
Victor Caston, 'Towards a history of the problem of intentionality', *Proceedings of the Boston Area Colloquium in Ancient Philosophy* 8, 1992.

24. *Phantasia*
M. Frede, 'Stoics and Sceptics on clear and distinct impressions', in Myles Burnyeat, ed., *The Skeptical Tradition*, Berkeley, California, 1983, repr. in his *Essays in Ancient Philosophy*, Minneapolis, 1987.
Jean-Louis Labarrière, '*Phantasia* et *logos* chez les animaux', in J. Brunschwig and M. Nussbaum, eds., *Passions and Perceptions*, Cambridge, 1993.
Jean-Louis Labarrière, 'Imagination humaine et imagination animale chez Aristote', *Phronesis* 29, 1984, pp. 17-49.
Gerard Watson, *Phantasia in Classical Thought*, Galway, 1988.
A.A. Long, 'Representation and the self in Stoicism', in Stephen Everson, ed., *Psychology, Companions to Ancient Thought* 2, Cambridge, 1991.

25. Self-consciousness
A.C. Lloyd, 'Nosce teipsum and conscientia', *Archiv für Geschichte der Philosophie* 46, 1964, pp. 188-200.
Peter Lautner, 'Rival theories of self-awareness in late Neoplatonism', *Bulletin of the Institute of Classical Studies* n.s. 1, 1993, forthcoming.
David Hahm, 'A neglected Stoic argument for human responsibility', *Illinois Classical Studies* 17.1.1-26.

Brad Inwood, 'Hierocles: theory and argument in the second century AD', *Oxford Studies in Ancient Philosophy* 2, 1984, pp. 151-83.

David Glidden, 'Epicurus on self-perception', *American Philosophical Quarterly* 16, 1979, 297-306.

Paul Rabbow, *Seelenführung, Methodik der exerzitien in der Antike*, Munich, 1954.

Pierre Hadot, *Exercises Spirituels et Philosophie Antique*, Paris, 1981.

26. Emotions

Two outstanding books are:

Martha Nussbaum, *The Therapy of Desire: Theory and Practice in Hellenistic Ethics*, Princeton, 1994.

Paul Rabbow, *Antike Schriften über Seelenheilung und Seelenleitung*, Teubner, 1914.

Also in preparation:

Martha Nussbaum, *Need and Recognition, A Theory of the Emotions*, Gifford Lectures, 1993, which will supersede Martha Nussbaum, 'Poetry and the passions: two Stoic views', in J. Brunschwig and M. Nussbaum, eds., *Passions and Perceptions*, Cambridge, 1993.

See further:

Stephen A. White, 'Cicero and the therapists' in J.G.F. Powell, ed., *Cicero the Philosopher*, forthcoming.

Julia Annas, 'Epicurean emotions', *Greek, Roman and Byzantine Studies* 30, 1989, pp. 145-64.

Ian Kidd, 'Posidonius on emotions', in A.A. Long, ed., *Problems in Stoicism*, London, 1971.

J. Filion-Lahille, *Le de Ira de Senèque et la philosophie Stoicienne des passions*, Paris, 1984.

A. Glibert-Thirry, 'La théorie Stoicienne de la passion chez Chrysippe et son évolution chez Posidonius', *Revue Philosophique de Louvain* 75, 1977, pp. 393-435.

William Fortenbaugh, *Aristotle on Emotion*, London, 1975.

M. Frede, 'The Stoic theory of the affections of the soul' in M. Schofield and G. Striker, eds., *The Norms of Nature*, Cambridge, 1986.

A.C. Lloyd, 'Emotion and decision in Stoic psychology' in J. Rist, ed., *The Stoics*, Berkeley and Los Angeles, 1978.

27. Speech and communication

In modern philosophy:

Paul Grice, 'Meaning', *Philosophical Review* 66, 1957, pp. 377-88.

Paul Grice, 'Utterer's meaning, sentence meaning and word meaning', *Foundations of Language* 4, 1968, pp. 1-18.

Jonathan Bennett, *Linguistic Behaviour*, Cambridge, 1976.

Noam Chomsky, *Language and Mind*, N.Y., 1968.

In ancient philosophy: *see* Matelli, under Theophrastus

In modern animal studies:

Konrad Lorenz, *King Solomon's Ring*, London, 1952.

R.A. Gardner and B.T. Gardner, 'Teaching sign language to a chimpanzee', *Science* 165, 1969, pp. 664-72.

H.S. Terrace, 'Animal cognition: thinking without language', *Philosophical Transactions of the Royal Society of London* B 308, 1985, pp. 113-28.

Irene M. Pepperberg, 'Comprehension of "absence" by an African grey parrot: learning with respect to questions of same and different', *Journal of the Experimental Analysis of Behaviour* 50, 1988, pp. 553-64.

E. Sue Savage-Rumbaugh, James L. Pate, Janet Lawson, S. Tom Smith, Steven Rosenbaum, 'Can a chimpanzee make a statement?', *Journal of Experimental Psychology*, General 112, 1983, pp. 457-92, with replies pp. 493-512.

D. Premack, *Intelligence in Ape and Man*, Hillsdale, N.J., 1976.

Dorothy L. Cheney and Robert M. Seyfarth, *How Monkeys see the World*, Chicago, 1990.
Daniel Dennett, *The Intentional Stance*, Cambridge, Mass., 1987, ch. 7 and appendix (comment on preceding).
Carolyn A. Ristau, ed., *Cognitive Ethology, The Minds of Other Animals*, Hillsdale, N.J., 1991.
Richard W. Byrne and Andrew Whiten, *Machiavellian Intelligence: Social Expertise and the Evolution of Intellect in Monkeys, Apes and Humans*, Oxford, 1988.

28. Further modern animal studies
Wolfgang Koehler, *The Mentality of Apes*, London, 1925.
Konrad Lorenz, *Man Meets Dog*, London 1954, translated from the German of 1953.
P. Colgan, *Comparative Social Recognition*, N.Y., 1983.
Donald R. Griffin, *Animal Thinking*, Cambridge, Mass., 1984.
Jane Goodall, *In the Shadow of Man*, Boston, 1971.
Vicki Hearne, *Adam's Task*, London, 1986.
Marc Bekoff and Dale Jamieson, *Interpretation and Explanation in the Study of Animal Behaviour*, vol. 1, Oxford, 1990.

29. Further discussions of animals in modern philosophy
Norman Malcolm, 'Thoughtless brutes', Presidential Address to the American Philosophical Association, repr. in his *Thought and Knowledge*, Ithaca, N.Y., 1977.
Jonathan Bennett, 'Thoughtful brutes', Presidential Address, *Proceedings of the American Philosophical Association*, 1987.
Gareth Matthews, 'Animals and the Unity of Psychology', *Philosophy*, 53, 1978, pp. 437-54.
Donald Davidson, 'Rational animals', *Dialectica* 36, 1982, pp. 318-27, repr. in E. Lepore and B.P. McLaughlin, eds., *Actions and Events: Perspectives on the Philosophy of Donald Davidson*, Oxford, 1985.
Stephen P. Stich, 'Do animals have beliefs?' *Australasian Journal of Philosophy* 57, 1979, pp. 15-28.

30. Rationality
Michael Frede, 'An empiricist view of knowledge: memorism', in Stephen Everson, ed., *A Philosophical Introduction to Ancient Epistemology*, Cambridge, 1990.
H.J. Blumenthal, 'Simplicius and others on Aristotle's discussions of reason', in *Gonimos, Neoplatonic and Byzantine Studies Presented to Leendert G. Westerick at 75, Arethusa*, Buffalo, N.Y., 1988.
Jonathan Bennett, *Rationality*, London, 1964.
Robert Solomon, 'Existentialism, emotions and the cultural limits of rationality', *Philosophy East and West* 42, 1992, pp. 597-621.

31. Intellect
Stephen Clark, 'Reason as Daimon', in Christopher Gill, ed., *The Person and the Human Mind*, Oxford, 1990.
Richard Sorabji, 'Myths about non-propositional thought', in his *Time, Creation and the Continuum*, ch. 10.
A.C. Lloyd, 'Non-propositional thought in Plotinus', *Phronesis* 31, 1986, pp. 258-65 (a reply to preceding).
A.C. Lloyd, *The Anatomy of Neoplatonism*, Oxford, 1990.

32. Abstraction and universal concepts in Neoplatonism
Ian Mueller, 'Aristotle's doctrine of abstraction in the commentators', in Richard Sorabji,

ed., *Aristotle Transformed: The Ancient Commentators and Their Influence*, London and Ithaca, N.Y., 1990.
A.C. Lloyd, *Form and Universal in Neoplatonism*, Liverpool, 1981.

33. Ancient ascriptions of intelligence to animals
Jean-Louis Labarrière, 'De la phronèsis animale' in P. Pellegrin et al., *Actes du colloque d'Oleron (29 Juin – 3 Juillet, 1987) sur Biologie, Logique et Metaphysique chez Aristote*.
G.E.R. Lloyd, *Science, Folklore and Ideology*, Cambridge, 1983, pp. 18-35.
M. Pohlenz, 'Intelligenz tierische und menschliche bei Posidonius', *Hermes*, 1941, pp. 1-13.
S.O. Dickerman 'Some stock examples of animal intelligence in Greek psychology', *Transactions of the American Philological Association* 42, 1911, pp. 123-30.
Marcel Detienne, *Cunning Intelligence in Greek Culture and Society*, tr. Harvester Press, 1978, from the French of Paris, 1974.
See also Fortenbaugh under 'Aristotle', Cole under 'Theophrastus', Boas under 'Cynics'.

34. The modern debate on the treatment of individual animals
Peter Singer, *Animal Liberation*, London, 1975, 2nd ed. 1990.
Tom Regan, *The Case for Animal Rights*, London, 1984.
Tom Regan and Peter Singer, eds., *Animal Rights and Human Obligations*, Englewood Cliffs, 1976.
Peter Singer, Review of Regan and correspondence with him, *New York Review of Books*, 17 January and 25 April, 1985.
Mary Midgley, *Animals and Why They Matter*, University of Georgia and Harmondsworth, 1983.
Mary Midgley, *Beast and Man*, Ithaca, N.Y., 1978.

35. The modern debate on species conservation
J. Baird Callicott, 'Animal Liberation: a triangular affair', *Environmental Ethics* 2, pp. 311-38, 1980.
Alastair Gunn, 'Why should we care about rare species?', ibid., pp. 17-38.
Mary Anne Warren, 'The rights of the non-human world', in Robert Elliot and Arran Gare, eds., *Environmental Philosophy*, Milton Keynes, 1983, pp. 109-34.
Stephen Clark, 'The rights of wild things', *Inquiry* 22, 1979, pp. 171-88.

36. John Rawls on justice to animals
John Rawls, *A Theory of Justice*, Cambridge, Mass., 1971.
Michael S. Pritchard, Wade L. Robinson, 'Justice and the treatment of animals: a critique of Rawls', *Environmental Ethics* 3, 1981, pp. 55-61.
Robert Elliot, 'Rawlsian justice and non-human animals', ibid., pp. 95-106.
Alan E. Fuchs, 'Duties to animals: Rawls' alleged dilemma', *Ethics and Animals* 2, 1981, pp. 83-7.
Donald van De Veer, 'Of beasts, persons and the original position', *Monist* 63, 1979, pp. 368-77.
Brent Singer, 'An extension of Rawls' theory of justice to environmental ethics', *Environmental Ethics* 10, 1988, pp. 217-31.

37. Modern philosophy on rights
Jeremy Waldron, ed., *Nonsense Upon Stilts*, London, 1987.
Ronald Dworkin, *Taking Rights Seriously*, Oxford, 1977.
Joel Feinberg, 'The nature and value of rights', *Journal of Value Inquiry* 4, 1970, pp. 243-57.

Joel Feinberg, 'Duties, rights and claims', *American Philosophical Quarterly* 3, 1966, pp. 137-44.
J.L. Mackie, 'Can there be a rights-based moral theory?', *Mid-West Studies in Philosophy* 3, 1978, pp. 350-9.
J. Raz, *Morality of Freedom*, 1986, chs. 7-8.
J. Finnis, *Natural Law and Natural Rights*, Oxford, 1980, ch. 8.
The Monist 70, 1987, *Animal Rights*.
David Lyons, ed., *Rights*, Belmont, CA, 1979

38. History of the concept of rights
Richard Tuck, *Natural Rights Theories*, Cambridge, 1979.
Lewis Hanke, *Aristotle and the American Indians*, Chicago, 1959.
J.H. Elliott, *The Old World and the New, 1492-1650*, Cambridge, 1970.
Anthony Pagden, *The Fall of Natural Man: the American Indian and the Origins of Comparative Ethnology*, Cambridge, 1982.
Daniel Deckers, *Gerechtigkeit und Recht*, Fribourg, Vienna, 1991.
Brian Tierney, 'Tuck on rights: some medieval problems', *History of Political Thought* 4, 1983, pp. 429-41.

39. Voluntariness and moral responsibility in ancient thought
Richard Sorabji, *Necessity, Cause and Blame*, London and Ithaca, N.Y., 1980.
Brad Inwood, *Ethics and Human Action in Early Stoicism*, Oxford, 1985.
Terence Irwin, 'Reason and responsibility in Aristotle', in A. Rorty, ed., *Essays on Aristotle's Ethics*, Berkeley and Los Angeles, 1980.
Terence Irwin, 'Who discovered the will?', *Philosophical Perspectives* 6, 1992, Ethics, pp. 453-73.
David Furley, *Two Studies in the Greek Atomists*, Princeton, 1967, Study 2.
Walter G. Englert, *Epicurus on the Swerve and Voluntary Action*, Atlanta, Georgia, 1987.
Phillip Mitsis, *Epicurus' Ethical Theory*, London and Ithaca, N.Y., 1988, ch. 4.
Charles Kahn, 'Emergence of the concept of the will in ancient philosophy', in John Dillon and A.A. Long, eds., *The Question of Eclecticism*, Berkeley, Los Angeles, 1988.

40. *Oikeiôsis*
Simon Pembroke, 'Oikeiôsis', in A.A. Long, ed., *Problems in Stoicism*, London, 1971.
C.O. Brink, '*Oikeiôsis* and *oikeiotês*: Theophrastus and Zeno on nature in moral theory', *Phronesis* 1, 1956, pp. 123-45.
G. Striker, 'The role of *oikeiôsis* in Stoic ethics', *Oxford Studies in Ancient Philosophy* 1, 1983, pp. 145-67.
H. Görgemanns, '*Oikeiôsis* in Arius Didymus', in W. Fortenbaugh, ed., *On Stoic and Peripatetic Ethics: The Work of Arius Didymus, Rutgers University Studies in Classical Humanities* 1, 1983, pp. 165-89.
Brad Inwood, 'Hierocles: theory and argument in the second century AD', *Oxford Studies in Ancient Philosophy* 2, 1984, pp. 151-84.

41. The idea of a world community in ancient thought
H.C. Baldry, *The Unity of Mankind in Greek Thought*, Cambridge, 1965.
W. Tarn, 'Alexander and the unity of mankind', *Proceedings of the British Academy* 19, 1933, pp. 123-66.
E. Badian, 'Alexander the Great and the unity of mankind', *Historia* 7, 1958, pp. 425-44.
Malcolm Schofield, *The Stoic Idea of the City*, Cambridge, 1991.
T. Cole, *Democritus and the Origins of Greek Anthropology*, Cleveland, 1967.

42. City of God
F.E. Cranz, 'De Civitate Dei XV 2 and Augustine's idea of a Christian Society', *Speculum* 25, 1950, pp. 215-25.
Gerhard B. Ladner, 'Homo Viator: medieval ideas on alienation and order', *Speculum* 42, 1967, pp. 233-59.
H.A. Deane, *The Political and Social Ideas of St Augustine*, N.Y., 1963.

43. Natural law and Stoicism
Gerard Watson, 'The natural law and Stoicism', in A.A. Long, *Problems in Stoicism*, London, 1971.
M. Colish, *The Stoic Tradition from Antiquity to the Early Middle Ages*, Leiden, 1985, pp. 356-64.
Paul Vander Waerdt, 'Philosophical influence on Roman jurisprudence? The case of Stoicism and natural law', *Aufstieg und Niedergang der römischen Welt* 2.36.6, 1992.
Paul Vander Waerdt, *The Theory of Natural Law in Antiquity*, Ithaca, N.Y., 1993, forthcoming.

44. The Stoics on what matters
Ian Kidd, 'Stoic intermediates and the end for man', in A.A. Long, ed., *Problems in Stoicism*, London, 1971.
A.A. Long, 'Carneades and the Stoic telos', *Phronesis* 12, 1967, pp. 59-90.
Gisela Striker, 'Following nature: a study in Stoic ethics', *Oxford Studies in Ancient Philosophy* 9, 1991, pp. 1-73.

45. Stoicism and slavery
Miriam Griffin, *Seneca, A Philosopher in Politics* 2, Oxford, 1992, ch. 8, and new appendix E.
Andrew Erskine, *The Hellenistic Stoa, Political Thought and Action*, London, 1990, ch. 2.
C.E. Manning, 'Stoicism and slavery in the Roman Empire', *Aufstieg und Niedergang der römischen Welt* 2.36.3, pp. 1518-1543.

46. Suicide
Miriam Griffin, *Seneca, A Philosopher in Politics* 2, Oxford, 1992, ch. 11.
John Cooper, 'Greek philosophers on euthanasia and suicide', in Baruch A. Brody, ed., *Suicide and Euthanasia*, Kluwer, 1989.
L.G. Westerink, *The Greek Commentaries on Plato's Phaedo*, vol. 1 *Olympiodorus*, Amsterdam, 1976, ad 1.8.
John Rist, *Stoic Philosophy*, Cambridge, 1969, ch. 13.

47. Epicurean theory of justice
Victor Goldschmidt, *La doctrine d'Épicure et le droit*, Paris, 1977.
Phillip Mitsis, *Epicurus' Ethical Theory*, Ithaca, N.Y., 1988.
Paul Vander Waerdt, 'The justice of the Epicurean wise man', *Classical Quarterly* 37, 1987, pp. 402-22.
Paul Vander Waerdt, 'Hermarchus and the Epicurean genealogy of morals', *Transactions of the American Philological Association* 118, 1988, pp. 87-106.
Dirk Obbink, 'Hermarchus *Against Empedocles*', *Classical Quarterly* 38, 1988, pp. 428-35.
For a modern example of contract theory applied to animals, *see* Jan Narveson, 'Animal rights', *Canadian Journal of Philosophy* 7, 1977, pp. 161-78.

48. Pets in antiquity
W.R. Halliday, 'Animal pets in ancient Greece', *Discovery* 3, 1922, pp. 151-4.
Jocelyn Toynbee, *Animals in Roman Life and Art*, London, 1973.

49. Warfare and hunting in antiquity
H.H. Scullard, *The Elephant in the Greek and Roman World*, London, 1974.
J. Anderson, *Ancient Greek Horsemanship*, Berkeley, Los Angeles, 1961.
J. Anderson, *Hunting in the Ancient World*, Berkeley, Los Angeles, 1985.
G. Bugh, *The Horsemen of Athens*, Princeton, 1988.

50. Zoos, shows, games
G. Jennison, *Animals for Show and Pleasure in Ancient Rome*, Manchester, 1937.
J. Balsdon, *Life and Leisure in Ancient Rome*, London, 1969, pp. 302-13, 'Wild animals'.
Ellen Rice, *The Grand Procession of Ptolemy Philadelphus*, Oxford, 1983, pp. 82-99.

51. Sacrifice and meat
W. Burkert, *Homo Necans*, Berlin 1972.
Marcel Detienne, *Les jardins d'Adonis*, Paris, 1972, with introduction by Jean-Pierre
    Vernant, which was later included in Jean-Pierre Vernant, *Myth and Society in Ancient
    Greece*, 'Between the beasts and the gods' translated in 1980 from the French of 1974.
Marcel Detienne and Jean-Pierre Vernant, eds., *The Cuisine of Sacrifice Among the
    Greeks*, translated in 1989 from the French of 1979.
Jean Louis Durand, *Sacrifice et labour en grèce ancienne*, Paris, 1986.
G. Zuntz, *Persephone*, Oxford, 1971.
Fondation Hardt, *Entretiens* 27, *Le sacrifice dans l'antiquité*, Geneva, 1981.
Frances M. Young, *The use of Sacrificial Ideas in Greek Christian Writers from the New
    Testament to John Chrysostom*, Cambridge, Mass., 1979.
Frances M. Young, 'The idea of sacrifice in Neoplatonic and Patristic texts', *Studia
    Patristica* XI, pp. 278-81.
Nancy Demand, 'Pindar's *Olympian* 2, Theron's faith and Empedocles' *Katharmoi*', *Greek,
    Roman and Byzantine Studies* 16, 1975.
H.D. Saffrey, 'Les livres 4 à 7 du *de Mysteriis* de Jamblique relus avec le lettre de Porphyre
    à Anébon, in H.J. Blumenthal et al., *Proceedings of the International Conference on
    Iamblichus* held at Liverpool, 24-26 September, 1990.
Dirk Obbink, 'The origin of Greek sacrifice: Theophrastus on religion and cultural history',
    in William Fortenbaugh and Robert Sharples, eds., *Theophrastean Studies, Rutgers
    University Studies in Classical Humanities* 3, 1988, ch. 14.
F.J. Simoons, *Food Avoidance in the Old World*, 1961.
See also J. Haussleiter under Ancient thought on animals and articles by M. Jameson and
    S. Hodkinson in C. Whittaker (see next section).

52. Animal husbandry
V. Hehn, *The Wandering of Plants and Animals From Their First Home*, tr. 1885 from the
    German editions of 1877 or 1883 (1st ed. 1870), new edition by James P. Mallory,
    Amsterdam, 1976, entitled *Cultivated Plants and Domesticated Animals*.
K.D. White, *Roman Farming*, London, 1970, ch. 10.
C. Whittaker, ed., *Pastoral Economies in Classical Antiquity*, Proceedings of the
    Cambridge Philological Society supp. vol. 14, 1988.
Robert Sallares, 'The uses of animals in antiquity', in preparation.

53. Transmigration of souls into animals in Neoplatonism
Andrew Smith, 'Did Porphyry reject the transmigration of souls into animals?' *Rheini-
    sches Museum* 127, 1984, pp. 277-84.

Heinrich Dörrie, 'Kontroversen um die Seelenwanderung im kaiserzeitlichen Platonismus', *Hermes* 85, 1957, pp. 165-92, repr. in his *Platonica Minora*, Munich, 1976.

Werner Deuse, *Untersuchungen zur mittelplatonischen und neuplatonischen Seelenlehre*, Akademie der Wissenschaft und Literatur zu Mainz, Abh. d. Geistes- und Sozialwiss. Kl., Wiesbaden, 1983, pp. 129-67.

Georges Vajda, 'La réfutation de la métensomatose d'après le théologien karaïte Yûsuf al-Basîr', in Robert B. Palmer and Robert Hamerton-Kelly, eds., *Philomathes, Studies and Essays in Memory of Philip Merlan*, The Hague, 1971, pp. 281-90.

General Index

Index Locorum

Numbers in bold type refer to the pages of this book. Where possible, abbreviations conform to Liddell and Scott's *Greek-English Lexicon* and to Lewis and Short's *Latin Dictionary*. Additional abbreviations include:

CAG = Commentaria in Aristotelem Graeca
DG = H. Diels, Doxographici Graeci
DK = H. Diels – W. Kranz, *Die Fragmente der Vorsokratiker*
EK = Edelstein and Kidd, *Posidonius*
PG = Patrologiae Cursus, series Graeca
SVF = von Arnim, *Stoicorum Veterum Fragmenta*

Aelian
  Nat. An. 2.2, **91**; 3.21, **46, 56, 91, 120**; 3.23, **121**; 4.8, **46, 56, 91, 120**; 4.10, **90**; 4.45, **46, 56, 91, 120**; 4.53, **91, 93**; 5.13, **91**; 6.50, **121, 165**; 6.59, **26**; 7.44, **90**; 10.16, **121**; 12.34, **215**; 15.11, 15.14, **91**
  Var. Hist. 1.15, **91**; 5.14, **215**; 14.40, **80**
Aeneas of Gaza
  Theophrastus (*PG* 85) 893A-B, **191, 192, 193**; 896B-897A, **190**
Aëtius
  4.5.12, **8**; 4.11.1-4 (*DG* 400; *SVF* 2.83), **21, 23, 32, 35, 40, 72, 113, 127**; 4.8.12 (*DG* 396,3-4, *SVF* 2.72), **41**; 4.12.1 (*DG* 401; *SVF* 2.54), **22**; 4.22.1 (= Empedocles A 74, DK), **100**; 5.15.1-5 (*DG* 425-6), **100**; 5.20 (*DG* 143a15ff), **80, 192**; 5.23.1 (*DG* 434-5, *SVF* 2.764), **127**; 5.26.3 (*DG* 438a15-20, *SVF* 2.708), **98, 99**
Albinus/Alcinous (?)
  Didaskalikos (Hermann) 155,27-30, **73**; 155,37-156,9, **48, 73**; 178,21-5, **29, 74**; 179,19.21-5, **201**
Alcmaeon
  DK fr. 1a (= Theophrastus *Sens.* 25), **9**
Alexander
  DA 67,16-20, **37**; 20-2, **20**; 159,16-22

(*SVF* 3.758), 160,20-31 (*SVF* 3.759), 168,1ff (*SVF* 3.764), **146**
  de Fato 183,21-184,5, **41, 42**; 186,3-12, **40**; 199,14-22 (*SVF* 3.658), **148**; 205,8-206,5, **110**; 205,28 (*SVF* 2.1002), **113**; 205,38, **53**
  Mant. 163,4 (*SVF* 3.192), **140**; 163,32, 164,7 (*SVF* 3.193), 164,32 (*SVF* 3.194), **141**
  in Metaph. 4,15, **34**
  Quaest. 3.13, 107,6-12, **41, 42**
Ammonius
  in Isag. 41,19-20; 42,10-21, **74**
  in Int. 30,23ff, **92**
Anaxagoras
  DK fr. 21 B (= Plutarch *de Fort.* 98F), **9, 91**
Anaximander
  DK fr. A 10 (*DG* 579), **91, 200**
ps.-Andronicus
  On Emotions 1 (*SVF* 3.391), **61**; 1.2-6 (*SVF* 3.391, 432), **114**; 19 (*SVF* 3.266), **142**
Anecdota Graeca (Cramer) vol. 1, p. 171 (*SVF* 3.214), **127**
Anonymus
  in Theaetetum (Diels-Schubert), 5.18-6.31, **124, 128**
  Life of Pythagoras (Photius) 439a24ff, **174**
Anonymus Iamblichi
  fr. 89 DK, **150**
Antiochus
  ap. Cicero, *Fin.* 5, **150**; 5.65, **123**
Antipater
  ap. Cicero, *Off.* 3.51-5, **138**
  ap. Plutarch, *CN* 1072E-F (*SVF* 3, Antip. 59), **139**
  ap. Stobaeus, 2.79.9-15 (*SVF* 3, Antip. 57), **139**

256